JOY

Poet, seeker and the woman
who captivated C. S. LEWIS

ABIGAIL
SANTAMARIA

First published in Great Britain in 2015 in hardback by special arrangement with Houghton Mifflin Harcourt Publishing Company, New York, USA

Paperback edition published 2016

Society for Promoting Christian Knowledge
36 Causton Street
London SW1P 4ST
www.spck.org.uk

British Library Cataloguing-in-Publication Data
A catalogue record for this book is available from the British Library

Hardback ISBN 978–0–281–07427–3
Paperback ISBN 978–0–281–07429–7
eBook ISBN 978–0–281–07428–0

Book design by Victoria Hartman

Manufacture managed by Jellyfish
First printed in Great Britain by CPI
Subsequently digitally printed in Great Britain

eBook by Graphicraft Limited, Hong Kong

Produced on paper from sustainable forests

'This brilliantly researched biography has changed me for good. Until I read this book, I could never take Joy Davidman to my heart; she now stands before me as real and believable as anyone I know. *Joy* offers a wonderful account of an unforgettable woman and her vibrant life; it is no wonder C. S. Lewis loved her so much.'

Walter Hooper, personal secretary to C. S. Lewis and editor of *The Collected Letters of C. S. Lewis*

'Superbly researched and stylishly written, Joy dissolves the soft-focus romanticism of *Shadowlands* and brings before us a real-life woman in all her complexity. Abigail Santamaria, in a fine first work, guides us expertly and fair-mindedly round the beautiful ruins of an extraordinary life.'

Michael Ward, University of Oxford, co-editor of *The Cambridge Companion to C. S. Lewis*

'This book gives Davidman her life back . . .' ***The Wall Street Journal***

'A tour de force. Plumbing the depths of unpublished documents, Santamaria reveals the vision and writing of a young woman whose coming of age in the turbulent 1930s is both distinctive and emblematic of her time.'

Susan Hertog, author of *Anne Morrow Lindbergh: Her Life*

'Joy Davidman was manipulative, endearing, brilliant, and obsessive – and C. S. Lewis, one of the most influential and beloved spiritual writers of the twentieth century, fell in love with all of it. A complicated woman for our time, Davidman's search for meaning and her final arrival at love will resonate deeply long after the reader has closed Santamaria's masterful biography.'

Kate Buford, author of *Native American Son: The Life and Sporting Legend of Jim Thorpe*

'*Joy* captures the toughness, the dreams, the hypocrisy, of a complex and controversial woman.' **BBC.com, One of Ten Books to Read in August**

'The narrative is crisp, and the subject matter is original and captivating. Santamaria examines Joy Davidman through a lens simultaneously critical and tender. Rather than presenting Lewis and his wife as saints, she depicts them as God's sinful patients. Out of the many books published on Lewis, his contemporaries and his writings in recent years, this one most thoroughly grabbed my attention.'

John G. Turner, Associate Professor, Religious Studies, George Mason University, *Christianity Today* 2016 Book Awards

'*Joy* is compelling even for the Lewis-indifferent, like me.'

Mark Oppenheimer, *New York Times Book Review*

'A relentlessly focused and detailed biography of Joy Davidman . . . This serious and substantial work takes the reader far beyond the familiar romance and play *Shadowlands*, and the brilliance of Lewis's meditation on Davidman's death, *A Grief Observed* . . . This groundbreaking study contributes not just to the established Lewis studies, but brings to the foreground the cost of being a talented woman in a patriarchal world. It makes a case for the possibility of Christian faith in a compromised world with elegance and skill.' ***Church Times***

'[A] biography as compelling as fiction.' ***Charlotte Observer***

'Santamaria's sympathetic and clear-eyed portrait of Joy Davidman might surprise people who assume that confirmed bachelor C. S. Lewis would fall only for an especially godly woman. Santamaria, relying heavily on Joy's own writings, paints a vivid portrait of the pre-Lewis Davidman. It's a fascinating portrait of Davidman's childhood in New York, her radical college years and membership in the Communist Party, her rocky marriage to Bill Gresham, and her long-distance infatuation with Lewis, whom she pursued with single-minded focus despite her marriage. Santamaria highlights Davidman's literary brilliance and shows her growing reliance on Christ.' ***World Magazine***

'A clear-eyed, insightful portrait of a fascinating woman, Santamaria's biography adds important depth and richness to the popular image of Joy Davidman.' ***Shelf Awareness***

'I now know that the life of Joy Davidman is a remarkable story, thanks to Abigail Santamaria's recently published *Joy* . . . [It] adds a full measure of humanity and tenderness . . . Out of the growing heap of books about Lewis's life and writings, *Joy* is an essential contribution.' ***Patheos***

'Humans are complex, and Santamaria has the guts to sacrifice simplicity and resolution to expose that truth. *Joy* is a story about longing and searching, hope and heartache. Every now and then, it's about seeing. More than anything else, then, Santamaria's portrait of Joy showed me the complexity of faith. It's a tough complexity, but a beautiful one nonetheless.'

The Gospel Coalition

For my parents,
Jaime and Sharon Santamaria

Contents

Introduction

Joy Davidman is best known today for her brief and tragic marriage to C. S. Lewis, a story immortalized in the Academy Award–winning film *Shadowlands* and the Broadway play of the same title. As ably portrayed by Debra Winger in her Oscar-nominated performance, Joy was a feisty Jewish divorced single mother from the Bronx. Lewis, seventeen years her senior, was a lifelong confirmed bachelor, contentedly uninterested in romance until Joy toppled his emotional ramparts and thrust her way into the heart of the Oxford don who was the author of *The Chronicles of Narnia* and arguably the greatest Christian thinker of the twentieth century. They exchanged vows at her hospital bedside after a devastating diagnosis of metastasized breast cancer. Joy spent her final days dying in the arms of her most unlikely husband.

Shadowlands was all I knew about Joy until, as a New Yorker rocked by the events of September 11, 2001, I found myself struggling to reconcile God and suffering. Having benefited from Lewis's spiritual wisdom in the past, I again turned to him for insight. I picked up *A Grief Observed*, his raw, deeply personal confession of anguish and crisis of faith in the weeks following his wife's death. Lewis's profound esteem for Joy intrigued me and moved me enormously. "Her mind was lithe and quick and muscular as a leopard," he writes in one particularly enchanting passage. "Passion, tenderness, and pain were all equally unable to disarm it. It scented the first whiff of cant or slush; then sprang, and knocked you over before you knew what was happening. How many bubbles of mine she pricked! I soon learned not to talk rot to her unless I did it for the sheer pleasure . . . of being exposed and laughed at. I was never less silly than as [Joy's] lover." She had filled every nook, said Lewis, of his heart, body, and mind.

What stunned me most, however, was his brokenness. I had recently read Lewis's *Mere Christianity* and *The Problem of Pain,* two nonfiction books in which he builds masterful cases for Christian tenets and dissects the purposes of pain without letting emotion muddle principle. Rife with logic and certainty, these texts speak to the parts of us that desire reason to override feelings. In contrast, the author of *A Grief Observed* is shattered, gripped by the power and primacy of emotion. I drew solace from the fact that this man whose faith I profoundly admired had responded to tragedy with the same reasonable questions: Where *was* God? And how *could* He? Like Lewis, I was skirting a danger more disturbing to me than ceasing to believe in God. "The conclusion I dread is not 'So there's no God after all,'" he explains, "but 'So this is what God's really like. Deceive yourself no longer.'" Without compromising his Christianity, Lewis laments like a modern psalmist, keening in prose, shaking his fist in outrage at God.

Who was this woman whose loss so ravaged the man whom I, and millions of others, admire for his rock-solid faith? What were the forces that shaped her intellect and personality, driving these two disparate characters together? A basic search made me hungrier to know more. I learned that Joy was born during the Great War and came of age during the Great Depression. She joined the Communist Party of the United States of America (CPUSA) during the turbulent 1930s and wrote her way into the red-hot spotlight of New York City's literary left. As the nation tumbled toward a second world war, she made a name for herself fighting fascism on the battlefield of the page, participating in rallies and symposiums alongside some of the most eminent voices of the century. I wanted to know more about her career, as well as about her troubled first marriage to the charismatic war veteran William Lindsay Gresham; about how she captivated the heart of C. S. Lewis; and about her influence on several of his finest books—*Surprised by Joy, Till We Have Faces, The Four Loves.* Contrary to what many people assume, Lewis's autobiography *Surprised by Joy* is not about the woman who edited its final draft and would become his wife two years after its publication. But it still has everything to do with what brought them together. Both Joy and Lewis longed, all their lives, for a spiritual realm that transcended both the beauty and the quotidian sting of earthly existence. I was intrigued by the spiritual journey that led this daughter of eastern European Jewish immigrants on a journey through Marxism and agnosticism, culminating in Christianity.

Everything I read about Joy left me wishing for a more thorough look at her pre-Lewis years, and a more balanced treatment of her story. Most accounts of her life seemed glazed with a kind of hero worship, perhaps meant to counterbalance disparaging characterizations by many of Lewis's Oxford friends. But Lewis, a Christian for whom humility was a way of life, would have eschewed the rose-colored-glasses approach. "[Joy] was a splendid thing," he writes in *A Grief Observed,* "a soul straight, bright, and tempered like a sword. But not a perfected saint. A sinful woman married to a sinful man; two of God's patients, not yet cured." I was intensely curious about the authentic human struggles behind the popular romanticization.

When I contacted Joy's son, Douglas Gresham, he put me in touch with a cousin, Susan Davidman Cleveland, Joy's niece and the daughter of Joy's only brother, Howard. Susan graciously invited me to Massachusetts to view and photocopy boxes of family papers, including a trove of Joy's childhood photos, and letters written to and from her, her parents, and her brother. No one outside the family had ever seen this material. It was a biographer's bliss. Susan connected me with her mother, Howard's first wife, Ruth. She had known Joy well, often spending weekends during the war with Joy and Bill Gresham while Howard was stationed overseas. When we first spoke, Ruth expressed hesitation about being interviewed. On the one hand, no one had ever interviewed her, and she was eager to "set the record straight" about a certain defining period of Joy's life. On the other hand, she was concerned that I wouldn't believe her.

The account Ruth disputed is presented consistently across Lewis biographies and *Shadowlands*. The salient segment goes like this: fleeing her abusive marriage to the philandering, alcoholic Bill Gresham, Joy moved her two small sons to England, where postwar living was cheaper. This version is consistent with what Joy herself told Lewis, his brother Warnie, and their friends Chad and Eva Walsh. But it's not exactly true, Ruth said.

Ruth wanted to know if I was another C. S. Lewis fan out to perpetuate the "myth." I assured her that my sole objective was to write a fair, accurate portrait of Joy based on reliable evidence; that I did not intend to idealize or demonize anyone; that I would be profoundly grateful to hear her memories; and that I would listen with an open mind. Ruth agreed to meet with me, and I began visiting regularly with my tape recorder and a few slices from the pizzeria around the corner.

Nevertheless, I was skeptical about Ruth's version. Certainly I couldn't accept the word of one person over a scholarly historical consensus. But as my research mounted, a pattern began to emerge: the majority of people I interviewed agreed with Ruth's account. Some of these people had been interviewed in the past, but the parts of their stories that didn't jibe with traditional accounts had not been reported. Over and over, I found myself repeating the promises I'd made to Ruth.

In the end it was Joy herself who cleared things up. One early December morning several years into my research, I was on my way out the door when the phone rang. On the other end was the now familiar baritone of Joy's son Douglas Gresham. "Are you sitting down?" he asked with urgency.

Douglas was in the Oxford home of Jean Wakeman, Joy's closest friend in England. Jean had spent many convivial evenings with Joy and Jack (as Lewis was known to friends) during Joy's last years. In the decades following Lewis's death in 1963, scholars had flocked to interview Jean. By the time I came around, Jean had decisively stopped speaking publicly, declining even Douglas's petition on my behalf. She was frail, her memory slipping, and she felt she'd said all there was to say.

One of the questions I wanted to ask had been posed to her for more years than I had been alive: Did she have any of Joy's papers? Documents, manuscript drafts, letters? The Marion E. Wade Center in Wheaton, Illinois, a research collection of materials by and about seven British authors including Lewis, held a few letters from Joy to friends, plus hundreds of letters between her and Bill Gresham, nearly all of which were written after their separation. Letters from the intense correspondence Joy initiated with Lewis three years before leaving Bill have never been found. My scouring of other archival repositories across the country unearthed many letters Joy wrote to friends and colleagues. But I hoped to find more. I desperately wanted not only additional information but also material that would guide me through Joy's internal world, especially the spiritual journey that defined her life.

Some speculated that Joy's papers had been consigned to a pyre that Lewis's brother built on their estate, the Kilns. Drunk and despondent in the wake of his brother's death, Warnie instructed the Kilns' caretaker, Fred Paxford, to burn manuscripts, diaries, and unknown other treasures. Lewis's secretary, Walter Hooper, managed to rescue enough to fill two suitcases just hours before they were to be destroyed, but Joy's things were not among them.

Reliable sources told me that Jean once claimed to have saved boxes of Joy's papers but had thrown them out after they got wet and moldy in a flood. I suspected she knew more than she let on, and I hoped someday to earn her trust. But in the months before Douglas's phone call, Jean's health rapidly declined. When it became clear that she would never live alone again, he took on the task of cleaning out her house—which is what he was doing when he rang me that December morning.

"I am now looking at a cardboard box filled to the brim with my mother's papers. Hundreds of poems, dozens of short stories, her oath of allegiance to the queen. A letter . . ." He began to read from one: "Dear Jack, here are some sonnets you may care to read."

Douglas told me that he would carry the papers back to his home in Malta, where I could see them. Three weeks later I was on a plane.

I spent most of my four days in Malta hovering over a copy machine in the cramped stockroom of an office supply shop, delicately peeling rusted paper clips off crumbling sheets and photocopying over 1,500 precious pages. No treasure trove of letters to or from Lewis emerged, but other materials were invaluable. There were college essays and unpublished short stories dating to 1927, when Joy was twelve; her marriage certificate to Lewis; her checkbook from her dying years, with "Wingfield Hospital" and the word "Help!" poignantly scrawled in a memo line.

The copying was so time-consuming that I didn't have a chance to pause and read. One night, though, I couldn't sleep. The heat had stopped working, and I shivered under my blankets, tossing and turning for hours. Eventually I got up, padded barefoot across the cold tiled floor, selected a bulging beige file folder from the cardboard box, and brought it back to bed. That file in particular had intrigued me; across its cover, in capital letters, Joy had written the word COURAGE. Inside were dozens of poems dating from the mid-1930s through 1956, four years before her death; some were drafts of published work I'd seen, but others were new to me—including passionate sonnets, fraught with infatuation and unrequited love. Many were dated during the final miserable years of her marriage to Bill, though he didn't seem to be the man she referred to in her verses as "Sir" and "my lord." My heart beat faster as I turned the pages. There was a reference to Oxford. Joy expressed heartbreak over rejection. And finally, the object of her desire became clear. "You have my heart, he has my bed," Joy typed in one poem; and in the margin, in her handwriting, "In a moment of insight, for CSL."

As I read on, I found further confirmation in an acrostic for Clive Staples Lewis, and mentions of "Jack." The dates and content of the poems made it clear that she had fallen in love with Lewis during her first marriage and went to England to pursue him. A new batch of letters between Joy and Bill confirmed that although Bill was no innocent victim, history has indeed judged him too harshly. Though Joy's feelings for Jack evolved into an indisputably mutual and profoundly rich love, her crusade to win his heart was clearly a more convoluted venture than has previously been acknowledged.

And then, huddled under my blankets, I came across a prediction Joy made: "I have wrenched sonnets out of my great pain . . . / For unknown followers to find . . . / Some woman who is cold / In bed may use my words to keep her warm / Some future night, and so recall my name." I was no longer freezing, but I shivered. I had not set out to unearth the particular realities I discovered behind the *Shadowlands* tale; they were imparted to me, first in the memories of those I interviewed, and finally in Joy's own words. She left them to be found: she was giving me her blessing.

· 1 ·

1892–1930

In a recurring dream throughout her childhood, Joy Davidman found herself walking down a road she called Daylight Street. In time, she rounded a corner and followed a crooked, grassy path into an unfamiliar world. Joy ambled through that world, lost but unafraid, until the trail opened onto "a strange, golden, immeasurable plane," as she described it, writing extensively about the dream in poetry and prose. Far in the distance rose the towers of Fairyland. Joy's heart swelled with longing as she beheld a perfect kingdom defined by love, devoid of sorrow, capable of consummating every good desire. "Hate and heartbreak / All were forgot there."

But before she could reach the castle gates, she woke up in the Bronx. Instead of a palace threshold, her round brown eyes saw only items in her bedroom: ballet slippers for the dreaded dance lessons her parents required, crisp dresses that made her into her mother's perfect doll, and books that were her waking sanctuary in what often felt like a foreign land. Among her favorites were Greek myths —she longed to visit the land of the gods—and "ghost stories and superscience stories" by Lord Dunsany and George MacDonald, the Victorian minister whose fantasies evoked the same visceral desire as her dream, suggesting that everything sad could become untrue.

Hope lingered in the morning hours. "If I remembered the way carefully, the dream told me, I should be able to find it when I woke up." For a fanciful child born during the Great War and raised in America's "New Era" of postwar prosperity, a Fairyland on earth—as rich with material resources as her dream kingdom was rich with the immaterial—seemed almost possible. In the distance, automobile motors roared above the clip-clop of horses' hooves on the Grand Concourse, the fashionable thoroughfare two blocks from 2707 Briggs Avenue in the genteel middle-class neighborhood where Joy lived with her parents, Joseph and Jeannette, and younger brother Howard, whom Joy came to call Howie. The rhythm of construction joined an orchestra of street sounds, heralding blocks of brand-new art deco apartment buildings with elegant sunken living rooms, electrical and waste disposal systems, refrigerators instead of iceboxes, elevators, and gracious lobbies adorned with marble inlay. "Every day, in every way, the world was getting more comfortable."

But not the world inside herself, and not the local landscape populated with peers and parents. Joy was a sickly, lonely girl, a social outcast at school and a disappointment at home to immigrant parents who governed according to the goals of assimilation and success. They, too, had been branded in childhood with the shame of otherness. "They showed their affection by almost incessant criticism," Joy told a newspaper reporter who profiled her life. They were "well-meaning but strict." Off the record, she was less subtle. "'Well-meaning but strict' . . . is certainly damning by faint praise," she wrote to a friend. "But since the truth would have called for loud damns, I don't know how I could have put it milder." She left the specifics to her reader's imagination.

It would be decades before Joy understood the meaning of her dreams, but for her, Fairyland was never the standard little girl's fantasy of opulence or romance. Joy would come to interpret the dream as a universal quest for eternal life, for a destination that could resolve her unconscious conviction that the perfect version of everything lay just ahead.

"There is a myth that has always haunted mankind, the legend of the Way Out," she would write many years later, "the door leading out of time and space into Somewhere Else. We all go out of that door eventually, calling it death. But the tale persists that for a few lucky ones the door has swung open *before* death, letting them through . . . or at least granting them a glimpse of the land on the other side. The symbol varies . . . [F]or some, the door itself is important; for others, the undiscovered country beyond it—the never-never land, Saint Brendan's Island, the Land of Heart's Desire . . . Whatever we call it, it is more our home than any earthly country." Joy called it Fairyland, a place she visited in her dreams and searched for in her waking hours.

C. S. Lewis, in his first published novel, *The Pilgrim's Regress,* calls it the Island. That book—an allegorical revision of John Bunyan's *Pilgrim's Progress* written shortly after Lewis's conversion from atheism to Christianity—would teach Joy the meaning of her childhood dreams. "By disguising fairyland as heaven," Joy wrote after becoming a Christian, "I was enabled to love heaven." Before this revelation and after, Joy's attempts to reach the castle would determine the course of her brief yet abundant life. In forty-five years she embraced more milestones and worldviews than most people experience in a lifetime twice as long. Her Daylight Street would detour into a romance with the Communist Party, whose propaganda would seduce her into mistaking the Soviet Union for her utopic Fairyland. The route would dead-end in a miserable first marriage to Bill Gresham, a troubled Spanish civil war veteran, Joy's partner in a misguided dance with Dianetics—another illusion. And the road would inevitably lead to C. S. Lewis, Joy's final embodiment of heaven on earth, and the man who would point her in the direction of the Fairyland that would finally satisfy her heart.

THE JOURNEY to Fairyland was a generational odyssey; Joy's grandparents in nineteenth-century tsarist eastern Europe had dreamed of it, too—a faraway land of peace, where the anti-Jewish regime of Alexander III could no longer threaten their lives and livelihoods with business boycotts, pogroms, and laws regulating the fundamentals of freedom. For Joy's father's parents, David and Tauba Davidman, living precariously along the northeast foothills of the Carpathian Mountains in the Galician city of Drohobycz, Joy's castle took the form of a literal, earthly country: America.

In the summer of 1892, David left his wife and three children —Joy's father, five year-old Yosef, and his two younger sisters, Frieda and Rosa—to join the crush of men establishing homes and jobs abroad before sending for their families. In Antwerp, David boarded the SS *Belgenland,* bound for the port of New York. On the ship's manifest, his "Calling or Occupation" was listed as "Merchant." He carried no baggage.

The *Belgenland* arrived in New York on August 1, 1892, delivering its steerage passengers to the brand-new Ellis Island immigration station. Other than the Chinese Exclusion Act, United States law included few restrictions on immigration. Joy's grandfather was among the nearly half-million individuals—including Irish, Italians, Germans, Swedes, Russians, and Canadians—to be processed during that inaugural year. Although the 1900 federal census would list David's occupation as, mysteriously, "Operator Cloaks," the story that was passed down indicates that he worked for a time as a presser in a sweatshop, packing burning coals into an iron until it weighed nearly twenty pounds, then smoothing cloth patches as they passed along the assembly line to produce pants, petticoats, blouses, dresses, and suits. Inhaling particles of cotton, hemp, and flax in poorly ventilated sweatshops may have led to, or exacerbated, the tuberculosis (dubbed "the Jewish disease" by well-to-do WASPs) that would kill him in 1910.

Some ten months after David arrived in America, Tauba and the children traveled to Hamburg, hauling two pieces of luggage among them, and boarded the double-masted SS *Dania.* At Ellis Island, Yosef became Joseph, Frieda became Frances, and Rosa became Rose. Over the next few years, four more siblings were born—Max, Leon, Nathan, and Ruth—and the family moved to a tenement at 100 Willett Street on the Lower East Side, where in 1900 they were joined by

David's brother Ben and his family of four, whom David also sponsored.

A few hundred feet from 100 Willett, just north of what would become the entrance to the Williamsburg Bridge—nicknamed the "Jewish Highway" for facilitating a mass exodus of immigrants from the Lower East Side to Brooklyn—lived Jacob Spivack, a jeweler; his wife, also named Tauba; and their children, Charles, Lena, and Jeannette, called Jen or Jenny. When Jeannette—originally named Yenta—was four years old, the family left their shtetl, Shpikov, outside Odessa. Jacob wanted his daughters to have the education denied them in Russia; he believed that no woman could be free unless she was able to earn a living.

America did not prove to be a perfect Fairyland. At the height of summer 1893, the year Joe and Jen (as they became known) arrived with their families, a reporter from the *New York Times* toured their Lower East Side neighborhood, collecting impressions for a story. An overwhelming stench spiked the hot air. Fruits and vegetables lay rotting in the gutters; the odor of decay mingled with the stink of raw sewage wafting from backyard toilets that served several families and drained nowhere. "Now the lowest scum of foreign countries has turned [the streets] into pestholes," the reporter declared. The "scum" consisted of men with "thin sharp features and black beards . . . dressed in filthy old clothes," women "even less tidy," and "dirty-faced children" playing in "stagnant pools of water." The reporter didn't mention that housing laws required no more than one outhouse—connected to city sewers "if possible"—for every twenty occupants. Landlords cut costs wherever they could, knowing that immigrants had little choice but to endure. Airshafts were clogged with trash because the city provided nowhere to dispose of it. Fire escapes functioned as storage for bedding cleared from floors after dawn to make room for work space. Two- or three-room apartments sometimes housed multiple families by night while serving as sweatshops by day. The article's headline read "Streets Where Once Fashionable People Lived Now Filled by an Undesirable Class;

Push-Cart Men and Street Peddlers Abound with Their Unwholesome Wares."

Joe and Jenny, Joy's parents, were among the "dirty-faced children." Marginalized by the greater society, they grew up believing that as Jews, they had to prove themselves through hard work and achievement. Education would be their way out of the Lower East Side. In 1903 Jen enrolled in the Normal College, the city's all-female teachers' training institute and the sister school to the City College of New York (CCNY), where Joe started classes that same year, following a Hebrew education and public school. Both colleges were tuition-free and catered largely to first- and second-generation Americans, particularly Jewish immigrants, who weren't overtly welcomed by Protestant-affiliated institutions.

Slight and lanky at five foot eight, Joe was a goal-oriented, civic-minded, driven young man who translated Yiddish poems into English for local papers and would spend the rest of his life trying to repay New York City for the gift of a free education. In his 1907 CCNY commencement address, Joe, serving as class speaker, exhorted his fellow graduates to "make a proper return to this city whose munificence has made it possible for us to be where we are tonight . . . Not by passively accepting present evils, not by sighing over the corruption of our civic institutions but by taking an active interest in politics, by supporting and by leading." His own goal was to become a district superintendent in the New York City public school system. "Joseph the Dreamer," as he called himself in an autobiographical short story, strove to be "at least as illustrious as Joseph the old in Egypt." He started low on the ladder, teaching kindergarten during the day, instructing immigrants in English at night. In years to come, Joy's father would be an active member of the New York City Principals Association, the New York Society of Experimental Study of Education, the National Education Association, and, among numerous Jewish organizations, the People's ORT Foundation, which had been founded in Russia in the late nineteenth century by a group of Jewish social philosophers "interested in the economic and social rehabilitation of their people" through the development of skills in agriculture, arts, and crafts. Joe took on leadership positions as a board member or president of numerous community organizations, including the Jewish Teachers Association, which ostensibly promoted religious, social, and moral welfare in schools, although in practice little attention was given to religion. The organization was primarily concerned with social justice, humanitarianism, championing the advancement of Jewish public school teachers, and promoting vigilance about anti-Semitism in the workplace. "Every real educator," said Dr. Davidman (as he insisted on being addressed after earning his Ph.D. from New York University in 1917, signing letters—even to his mother—"Dr. Jos. I. Davidman"), "should also be a social reformer in the true sense of the word, instead of a narrow, pedantic, iconoclastic visionary."

Joe's activities would never be as selflessly altruistic as they appeared on the surface; an intense self-righteousness pushed away even his siblings. "He was a pompous ass," according to one nephew. The greatest fault Joe himself admitted was awkwardness around women; he was fortunate to find one who saw through to his softer side.

Also a kindergarten teacher, Jenny Spivack was a lush, lovely woman, petite and moon-faced with thick dark hair in soft folds that twirled into a bun at the nape of her neck. The two could not have been more ideologically aligned. In high school and college, the racial and cultural significance of being Jews was more important to them than either religion or assimilation. Both largely discarded the faith of their fathers as if it were an outmoded heirloom but maintained remnants of their Jewish heritage, especially a shared enthusiasm for a Jewish nation. At City College, Joe became deeply involved in Zionist causes, serving first as treasurer, then president of the Student Zionist Society, and eventually becoming president of the New York City Collegiate Zionist League and editor of its newsletter. Jen was a member of the Collegiate Zionist League as well.

Joe and Jen were married by a justice of the peace on December 28, 1908, although the anniversary they would officially recognize was June 29, 1909, the date a rabbi conducted a traditional wedding in Brooklyn. The next day, the New York City Collegiate Zionist

League sent a handwritten blessing to its "esteemed chairman" Joseph I. Davidman and "beloved fellow-member" Jeannette Spivack Davidman: "Whereas it is one of the basic principles of the Zionist movement to counteract any tendency towards assimilation, but to encourage marriage among Jewish people . . . and Whereas two of our members have agreed to enter the state of connubial felicity . . . Be it resolved that the Collegiate Zionist League take the example set by these two members as encouragement for such future undertakings."

Although the Zionist League denounced assimilation, especially by way of intermarriage between Jews and Gentiles, the Davidmans became increasingly driven to achieve societal acceptance. Soon they were economically secure enough to join the ranks of vacationing city dwellers and summer upstate. They booked an extended excursion to Cairo, New York, "gateway to the Catskills." There the couple sat one summer for a strip of sepia-toned locket-size portraits. Jenny draped herself across Joe's lap, covering him with the billows of her skirt. Joe wrapped an arm around her narrow waist and rested a hand on the curve of her hip. Their eyes flashed with flirtation. They kissed for the camera.

Not every upstate tourist community welcomed "Hebrews"—it was not uncommon for hotels and boardinghouses to advertise "No Jews Allowed"—circumstances that compelled Jews to open their own restaurants and lodges. But Joe and Jen, like many young Jewish vacationers, were not interested in kosher menus; they didn't care how their beef was slaughtered, or if the kitchen staff used one set of pots and pans for meat and another for dairy. Rituals and faith conflicted with Joe's paradigm of logic and reason, and clashed with the mainstream Americanization the Davidmans increasingly craved. Above all else, Joe and Jen wanted to belong, to be accepted. Tourism and consumption signified an arrival. They were finally, fully beyond survival mode. A leisure trip to Cairo represented a journey that could not be measured in miles.

Joe and Jen had their own Fairyland in mind: the Bronx. Until late in the nineteenth century, the borough was a placid province of manor houses, cottages, and farms, with self-sustaining villages where locals worked as grocers, tailors, milkmen, carpenters, shoemakers, and piano designers. The subway, opened in 1904, dramatically redefined the landscape, merging urban development with mass migration. At five cents per ride, the transit system offered fast, affordable commutes to Manhattan for work, shopping, and visits with family. Farms, estates, private homes, and vacant lots were transformed into neighborhoods. The population grew by tens of thousands each year.

Finally middle class, the Davidmans moved to Boston Road, bordering the Bronx Zoo and Botanical Garden, where their neighbors were not sweatshop laborers but firemen, stenographers, carpenters, and bookkeepers. Their daughter would not live in some dark, airless tenement heaving with cholera and chaos. She would not wear threadbare rags, and her hair would not swarm with lice. She would be perfect.

HELEN JOY DAVIDMAN, always called Joy, was born on April 18, 1915, at St. Mark's Hospital, "the melting pot hospital" on Manhattan's Lower East Side, near the tenement slums her parents had abandoned. Why Joy's mother returned there to give birth is a mystery rife with symbolic consequence: Joy, who would never quite fit in anywhere, drew her first breath in a purgatory of a neighborhood where her parents had themselves been disgraced by the stigma of otherness.

But beginning with the hours Jen labored at St. Mark's Hospital, life with Joy was an unpredictable challenge. The delivery was complicated, the recovery slow, and there were "difficulties." Afterward, Jen was "sent away" to a dude ranch out west to recover, according to relatives. Were the "difficulties" physical, emotional, or both? Family whispers point to a history of mental illness, perhaps compounded by postpartum depression.

But Jen recovered, returned, and began enjoying her chubby baby girl, whose round face, dark hair, and huge wide eyes matched her own. Joy's early childhood was happy and comfortable. Her mother stopped working after she was born, and because her father had summers off, the family took extended vacations. Sometimes they stayed close to home and went to the Brighton Beach Hotel in Brooklyn, where visitors soaked up sun and entertainment—"Wild West" shows, vaudeville acts, horseracing, a carousel, a wild animal arena. The developer of the opulent hotel had dreamed of a Jew-free establishment, but the influx of Jews earned Brighton Beach the enduring nickname Little Odessa. Most summers, Joy's parents continued the tradition of vacationing in the Catskills and Adirondacks which they had begun early in their marriage. During the war, Joy toddled around the community War Gardens her father organized with his characteristic precision: "every row a masterpiece of surveying, every hill exactly four and one-quarter inches high yet, every ditch between rows precisely four and one-quarter inches deep." They sometimes took educational detours, like one to the gravesite of John Brown in North Elba, New York, when Joy was four—old enough so that his crusade for abolition made an indelible impact.

As educators, Joe and Jen recognized that their daughter had an exceptional mind. They taught her to read almost from infancy and were thrilled when reading became a favorite activity. From an early age, words, ideas, exotic realms, and fictional characters were her constant companions. *The Light Princess, The Princess and the Goblin,* and *At the Back of the North Wind* by George MacDonald were favorite books. Around the age of eight, Joy skimmed through H. G. Wells's *Outline of History: The Whole Story of Man,* some 1,300 pages that lured her with colorful illustrations of dinosaurs and convinced her that nothing existed beyond the material world. She announced to her father that she was an atheist.

Joy was five years old in 1920, when her father received his license to become principal of a public elementary school (in 1917 he had earned his Ph.D. in education from NYU), a position that generated prestige and a pay raise allowing the family to move to Briggs Avenue. During Joy's elementary school years at P.S. 21 in Woodlawn, New York City offered itself up as one great enchanted land of possibility. Yankee Stadium opened on her eighth birthday, April 18, 1923, with Babe Ruth hitting a three-run homer. Joy took piano lessons and ballet classes, and she roamed the nearby Botanical Garden, with its lavish acres of woods and streams and flowers, both wild and pristinely landscaped.

Her favorite playground, though, was the Bronx Zoo. One of her most cherished childhood memories was her first visit there. Walking through the zoo's main gate, Joy stepped into a storybook realm of magical creatures. First she passed the parrot house, vibrating with squawking cockatoos and macaws decked out in plumes of red, green, blue, and gold. Following the main paths, she came across Peter the Great, a two-ton hippopotamus who entertained visitors by stretching his heavy head over a fence and flashing his cavernous mouth in exchange for peanuts. In the nearby small mammal house, a flying fox ate grapes while suspended upside down from a branch. There were cages and tanks and dens. Joy was beguiled by the big cats, promoted as "the star animals of the zoo." It wasn't their star power that drew her, however, but their caged strength. Sometimes she reached a hand through the bars to pet them. "Friendship for animals is a form of sympathy for the underdog," she would say years later, reflecting on her childhood.

Growing up the daughter of Dr. Joseph I. Davidman was complicated and unpleasant. He had an uncompromising code of excellence, both at home and at P.S. 160, the junior high school he had attended, where he now served as principal. While not as destitute as in his day, the neighborhood served by the school remained characterized by poverty, disease, and language barriers. The city required morning health inspections to screen for contagious cases, and Joy's father went a step further by implementing daily afternoon assessments. Children with dental needs were sent to a dental clinic; those with poor eyesight went to a separate clinic to be fitted with free glasses. He made sure students also received free toothbrushes, toothpaste, and health literature, and drew on a social services fund to supply shoes and clothing to the poorest pupils. He prided himself on imposing "discipline without restraint." At P.S. 160, silence and decorum reigned.

His aims were admirable and his returns exemplary, but Dr. Davidman had a problem: he was such a tyrannical bully that in a single year, twenty-two members of his staff requested transfers, including his own former seventh-grade teacher. His standards of perfection were ridiculous and impossible to meet; woe to the teacher who did not maintain her window blinds evenly at Dr. Davidman's stipulated number of inches above the sill. "If you left a piece of paper on the floor he sent you a letter," remembered one substitute teacher. In one particularly gracious resignation notice, an employee wrote: "Tho I confess I had many sad days with you, days when I felt the world was a really miserable place, I most sincerely wish to thank you for what you did for me as a teacher. If I am a better teacher . . . I feel I owe it to your strict ways . . . Any success I anticipate in the 'system' I feel will in large measure be due to your iron discipline, which I confess I did not always enjoy."

None of this was lost on the board of examiners when Dr. Davidman applied for promotion to district superintendent. Not only was his application denied, but also the board accompanied its rejection with a scathing critique: "In the opinion of the members of the Examining Committee, Mr. Davidman seemed to be unable to detect many of the faults . . . observed by the visitors . . . The candidate seemed to be entirely lacking in the tact and perspective necessary in a District Superintendent."

"Absolutely false," he wrote in a seven-page "report," refuting the board's evaluation point by point, evidently blind to the irony of his response. "Some statements were apparently deliberately invented inasmuch as the alleged facts were either *untrue* or *impossible.*" While the board members credited him with being "an excellent student of education [with] fine ideas on many subjects," they felt that "there remained . . . in the minds of the examiners a question as to the candidate's ability to make these ideas effective." While this statement was accurate, the board, primarily consisting of individuals bearing Irish and Italian surnames, left a sinister impression of anti-Semitism, reinforced by the charge that Joy's father used "faulty English," an accusation at odds with his many letters and published editorials. Could it be, he asked in his report, that he and the eight other Jewish candidates—all rejected—were being unfairly criticized, not taken seriously?

Joy would always be vague about how her father's "iron discipline" manifested itself at home. Years later, Howard would tell stories of their father slapping Joy when she brought home a less than perfect grade. Because they were Jews, Joe stressed to his children, they must work harder to prove themselves. School, therefore, did not end with the closing bell. Supplementary homework occupied their evenings, math exams their summer vacations. He administered the intelligence quotient test, a faddish new measure of brilliance, and belittled Howard for registering a mere 147. Joy's off-the-chart score confirmed genius.

Joe and Jen believed that a child's "mental age," as opposed to the chronological age, should dictate grade placement, so at nine years old Joy was enrolled in P.S. 45, the junior high school headed by Angelo Patri, a slight Italian immigrant who wrote a syndicated newspaper column called "Our Children" and was nationally recognized as "America's greatest authority on children." Patri encouraged each child to develop "not in the spirit of passive obedience, but in one of mental emancipation." In theory Joy's parents agreed, but how Patri's avant-garde emphasis on individuality would shape their daughter had yet to be seen.

In her new school, Joy saw room after room full of desks, textbooks, and chalkboards, and studios where children "work away earnestly and happily at the things they do best," according to a journalist's profile of Patri. School days were structured around Patri's belief that what students are taught should flow from their individual interests, talents, and abilities. Children should be self-directed, and P.S. 45 provided opportunities for them to explore. The reporter set the scene:

> The printing shop was rehearsing its imminent pageant of printing. Potters' wheels were whirling as the clay rounded into form under knowing fingers, and young illustrators in one of the art rooms were blocking in gorgeous posters. Typewriters clicked in

> chorus from the business school. A luncheon was quite evidently being nicely cooked in the big kitchen. The swimming pool was brimful of boys. Machinery and carpenter's tools were plying fast, and in one of the science classrooms a radio outfit held a breathless audience. They all knew what they were about, these children, and they didn't bother over the principal's appearance in the least —he was just one of them.

When one boy was brought to Patri's attention for mouthing off, the principal perceived the child's ability to inject emotion into dialogue not as a deficit but as a gift gone awry. Patri enrolled the student in an oral English class and encouraged him to join the debate team and audition for school plays. That boy, later known as John Garfield, grew up to be an Academy Award–nominated actor.

"Every child has a potential inborn purpose in life," principal Patri said. "There is in him the essence of a desire to do some particular thing. It may be sculpture, or carpentry, or music or iron working, dramatics or machinery. But whatever it is he must be free to develop his purpose—the gift that is born in him." Under Patri's instruction, the teachers of P.S. 45 asked each student what she wanted to do with her life. For Joy, the answer was clear: to be a writer. "There was never really any alternative ambition."

Joy graduated from P.S. 45 on June 24, 1926, and enrolled in Evander Childs High School that fall. The next few years were fraught with chronic unpopularity, illness, and disintegrating relationships with her parents. As an eleven-year-old freshman, barely pubescent, Joy was instantly relegated to the shore alongside a sea of teenage girls who gossiped about boys and made rite-of-passage pilgrimages to corset shops. If they noticed Joy at all, it was with scornful sidelong glances. At least that was Joy's impression. She imagined the other girls found her "precious and dull."

Joy's mother was so focused on physical appearances that she neglected to foster other means of achieving social acceptance, such as nurturing friendships and socializing. "My parents were rather overprotective and kept me almost a prisoner," Joy said. "I'd never been allowed away from them or permitted to make friends. So I knew nothing of how to get along with other people."

Poor health made cultivating friendships even more of a challenge. A bout with scarlet fever kept Joy out of school for months. Anemia stole six more months of high school. Being housebound allowed for a self-paced course of academic study that suited Joy, but it also meant enduring her father's obsessive tutelage. Trapped in their apartment, unable to escape him, Joy found refuge on the printed page. She pressed and preserved herself like a flower between the pages of books, especially Greek mythology and the poetry of Keats and Shelley. And she wrote.

One of her earliest short stories, dated June 1927, opens with a sentence that is almost inconceivably cerebral for a child of twelve: "While perusing a venerable volume compiled by some learned though obscure scrivener of a long ago past age, I encountered a mournful anecdote concerning a man, a woman and a hat." A man in a shop models a hat for his wife. "How likest thou it thus?" he asks optimistically, fishing for approval. The woman likest it not, and the disagreement causes a rift that unfolds in sentences crammed with vocabulary like "mellifluous" and "auricular," all used correctly. The closing line is extravagantly verbose: "So may society and you be saved—so may your conjugal happiness prosper, and so, by the grace of God, may your days be long in the land which he has given you." Titled "The Influence of Headgear on the Happiness of Man," the story is a satire; whether intentionally or not, Joy targeted her mother for her petty materialism, and her father for his highbrow erudition.

To treat Joy's anemia, doctors prescribed a regimen of liver extract that increased her depleted iron levels but caused her to gain weight. At twelve years old, Joy was already as tall as she'd ever be at five feet, two inches, and weighed just under one hundred pounds. As she turned thirteen, her body became strikingly well proportioned, complimented by the in-vogue drop-waisted dress she wore in family pictures taken in July 1928. Sporting a bobbed hairdo and flapper shoes with chunky heels and gently rounded toes, Joy looks more like a trendy seventeen-year-old than a brainy, bookish girl who felt self-conscious and misunderstood.

The smart ensemble and chic hairstyle probably weren't Joy's idea; her attitude toward her appearance was the opposite of her mother's vanity. "Jen was very meticulous," Joy's cousin Renee remembered. "Very beautifully groomed, always. And Joy wasn't having any of that." While the intensity of Jen's pursuit of propriety did not match that of her husband's controlling perfectionism, decorum and appearances were nonetheless serious business. Her guidance in the ways of the world ranged from appropriately constructive to painfully denigrating. She coached another of Joy's cousins, Morton, in the gentlemanly practice of walking on the street side of a woman while strolling city sidewalks. She taught Renee about "the birds and the bees," and when Renee developed acne, Jen found a dermatologist and accompanied her niece on the train for a series of shots. "Aunt Jen was a sweet, sweet woman," Renee remembered. "She was perfect as a kindergarten teacher."

But for Joy, counsel was less sensitively dispensed. When Joy's weight continued to rise, Jen padlocked the refrigerator door, disgusted. "Why can't you be like Renee?" she nagged, frustrated by her daughter's disregard for stylish clothes and her general indifference to physical appearance.

The beauty that stirred Joy's spirit adorned a grander body; she was mesmerized by the sky, its celestial contours clothed in the sun, moon, and stars. Awe merged with melancholy, rousing feelings that she didn't understand but knew she needed to express. The first light of morning inspired her to pick up her pencil in January 1929. "What spur of gold is this that pricks the dawn," she began. "On the eager winds of morn / Comes blowing down the soul-devouring fire." The sky demanded no compliments, required nothing in return; it simply offered itself up as a muse.

She found a kindred spirit in a schoolmate named Nina Zimet. As Nina remembered: "We were . . . two oddball, overintellecual [*sic*], not very popular girls who expended [our] frenzied adolescent passion on poetry. [We] might have forsaken each other and the books for the athletic heroes who deeply appreciated the long-legged lovely giggling cheer leaders with upturned noses and glinging [*sic*] blonde tresses. But the option wasn't forthcoming, so I can only speak for myself." Nina had a little brother of her own, Julian, for whom Joy developed a big-sisterly fondness. "She took an interest in my reading," Julian recalled, "and gave me children's books, among them Booth Tarkington's *Penrod*, which I LOVED! and never forgot." Joy became closer to her own brother, too. Howard was an ally at home, a friend outdoors. They spent hours together reading in the library, visited the Botanical Garden, and developed an enduring passion for plant life, memorizing virtually all the Latin names of everything that grew there. They made regular sojourns to the zoo, a place where Joy continued to feel connected to other living creatures in a way she didn't with her peers. She had a knack with animals. She taught tricks to stray dogs and trained a little gray fox to snatch a piece of chocolate from between her teeth. Sometimes at night, she claimed, she would sneak past the Bronx Zoo gates to the lion cages, reach through the bars, and affectionately beckon to the cats.

In the summer of 1929, the summer before her senior year of high school, Joy was enchanted by the rapid transmogrification of the city she'd known since birth. The Museum of Modern Art opened that year at Fifth Avenue and Fifty-seventh Street. New Yorkers eagerly watched the Empire State Building compete for the title of world's tallest building. When Joy visited her relatives in Brooklyn and gazed westward over the East River beyond the Williamsburg Bridge, it was almost as if she were meeting New York for the first time. The city was growing taller, reaching toward the sun, moon, and stars. She described Manhattan in a poem: "Towers sky-climbing from the river-side / The river is a quiet flicker of gold . . . [a] sculptured statesman, watching, almost proud, / the splendid City that he helped to build." It was a "legacy," she wrote, "This City!"

But when the stock market crash of 1929 silenced the Jazz Age, the city lost its luster. Suicides supplied headlines for morning, afternoon, and evening editions of New York newspapers. Husbands shot their families and themselves, demoralized because they could no longer provide; others drank poison, leaped from rooftops, dove off the Brooklyn Bridge. America was no Fairyland after all. "Our schools and newspapers taught us to love [America] because she enriched us," Joy later wrote. "Our love of country, the upshot proved, was often no deeper than any other kind of cupboard love. In 1929 I believed in nothing but American prosperity; in 1930 I believed in nothing."

Financially, though, the Davidmans did better than most. After not having taught since Joy was born, Jen had fortuitously returned to the classroom just before the crash. She and Joe wanted to maintain their standard of living while saving for college tuition. They were exceedingly proud of the status they had achieved. Teachers' salaries had been rising for over a decade and would continue to increase for at least another year. Employment in the public school system meant job security. The Davidmans paid $125 a month for their apartment in the Bronx—they now lived at 2277 Andrews Avenue, just steps from Devoe Park—where the median monthly rent was $52 more than in the other boroughs. And they employed a live-in "servant," twenty-three-year-old Mary Murray, an Irish immigrant who even in these hard times was better fed and housed than Joe and Jen had been when they arrived in New York thirty-seven years earlier. The family continued to summer in cooler regions of upstate New York and New England, and sometimes took vacations to other parts of the country: the Grand Canyon, California, and Tacoma, Washington, where one of Joy's aunts lived.

Although daily life remained comfortable for Joy, a subconscious shift was under way. In November 1929, within weeks of the market crash, she wrote a short story about the last day in the life of a young widow, Mrs. Goldberg, and the three small children she struggled to feed. In the two years since "The Influence of Headgear on the Happiness of Man," Joy had learned that subtle details render deeper emotion than strings of polysyllabic words. The story opens with the dumbwaiter bell startling Mrs. Goldberg while she washes dishes. When the bell sounds, Mrs. Goldberg wipes her hands on the "torn and greasy towel" beside the sink, and "with an apathy born of utter ugly monotony she opened the dumbwaiter door." Every movement is laborious: "As she lifted her purchase painfully from the dumbwaiter a door banged above her, a flood of yellow light illuminated the half-plastered boards of the shaft, and a shrill voice yelled; 'Hey, hurry up, dope! I don' wanta wait all year!'" Mrs. Goldberg readies her older children, ages six and eight, for school, urges them to be safe on the street, then puts on her "shabby black coat," picks up her "battered umbrella" and her small baby, struggles out the door, and drops the child at "day-nursery," before rushing to her low-level job, fearful of getting fired for being late yet again.

While her characters are away at work and school, Joy lingers in their apartment. She looks around, absorbing the sadness, then describes an interior that could belong to any number of post-crash New York City apartments: "The cubby-hole kitchen remained without any life—except that of an occasional cockroach—to animate its horrible drab untidiness, until the children burst in breathlessly at noon, foraged in the icebox for food, and, bolting their cold potatoes and cabbage, dashed out again, leaving behind them a wake of sloppiness." Joy shows the progression of time by describing shadows moving ominously across the floor, portending imminent misfortune.

Mrs. Goldberg returns home and begins preparing dinner. There is a knock at the door. A doctor holds the dead body of her son Bernie, hit by a car. "There was a strange choking in her throat; and she must have been falling, for the young physician caught her and seated her gently in the nearest chair—it was, she noticed, the one with the broken rung." Joy takes her protagonist through a range of feelings, as the odor of burnt beef stew fills the room. Mrs. Goldberg thanks the doctor, tells him to leave, puts her other children to bed. "A numbing realization of the actuality of her grief swept over her. She clutched at the door-post with a hoarse inarticulate cry." She tries to make tea. The tap runs cold and the stove burner flickers. The gas meter requires another quarter, but Mrs. Goldberg has just twenty-five cents to her name, enough for carfare and lunch the next day. "Suddenly an idea struck her; she gasped, retreated to the furthest corner of the room, looking furtively about her." Mrs. Goldberg resolutely drops the quarter in the meter, then runs around the apartment shutting windows, having second thoughts. In the end, she sits down before the stove and quietly turns on its four unlighted jets.

JOY AND HER friend Nina shared "de Profundis melancholies," according to Nina, but Joy's age remained an obstacle to lasting friendships. By senior year, all the other girls talked about was finding a husband. Nina and her friends did have intellectual dialogues about subjects that intrigued Joy—"art for art or society's sake, free will vs. determinism, Freud's complexes"—but, Nina recalled, "no matter where our discussions began . . . we were always coming round as if on a Mobius strip to how long we would have to tarry before we could marry . . . Like Rosalind and Celia in *As You Like It,* no subject was so lofty that we couldn't drop into 'What think you of falling in love.'" Even their gym teacher played along. The girls were learning the fox-trot. "Follow your man," their coach instructed. "Don't think about where your feet are going." Joy didn't really care where her feet were going, but they were certainly not following a man.

The gaps between Joy's inner life, social life, and family life widened. "I was really two people," she said of her adolescent self. She began to develop a protective shield, a "persona," she called it, "a mask, a surface personality for dealing with the world." The mask was made of tough stuff: pride, intellectual superiority, and a self-sabotaging haughtiness that surpassed the bounds of youthful narcissism. Joy had "exhibited contempt for most of her classmates," she admitted years later, "but there had been a defensive element." She knew they considered her a child. And in many ways she was. Her IQ may have been above average, but her social skills were not. She felt increasingly awkward and alone.

In the winter of 1929–30, Joy looked up at the night sky and contemplated the myth of the moon goddess Selene and her mortal lover Endymion, whom Selene could visit only at night. Joy, too, longed for love from a power bright and beautiful; it was a yearning that her hero Keats understood well. He wrote his first epic poem from the perspective of Endymion, the human stranded on earth at the mercy of a divine being. Keats almost didn't publish *Endymion;* he believed that readers would perceive "great inexperience, immaturity, and every error denoting a feverish attempt, rather than a deed accomplished." Still, he couldn't bring himself to destroy the poem; neither could he bring himself to revise it. And so he published the work with a preface full of qualifiers, including one profound statement that gave Joy all the permission she needed to attempt her own version of the work: "The imagination of a boy is healthy, and the mature imagination of a man is healthy; but there is a space of life between, in which the soul is in a ferment, the character undecided, the way of life uncertain, the ambition thick-sighted; thence proceeds mawkishness." Writing from that same "space of life" between childhood and adulthood, Joy produced her most beautiful poem to date:

> I had prayed to the distant goddess all that while,
> With the mad wish that Deity would bend,
> Stoop to the level of a human love.
> And that clear distant silver would not heed
> Desire, imperious in its rule of me,
> But rode the night down with her pack of stars.
>
> And I knew that I dared the undefied,
> That this most magic of the mysteries
> Was not as fireflies to catch and crush,
> Nor even as the mocking light that lures
> A vain pursuit, but was beyond pursuit,
> A far-seen vision, throned upon a cloud.
>
> Then the moon answered and came down to me.
> Oh—I had lain for many nights and sighed
> Because she was no nearer, though I knew
> The moon was brighter for the distance. Now
> She has come down, the years' dream has come true.
> A silver shadow floating above my head,
> The cold white moon dissolving in the air,

And dripping liquid silver through the pines,
Till it surrounded me in silver dew,
All of the brightness soft within my arms.

Yet she was magic, high above the pines,
Being divine and unattainable,
And white-serene, while I looked up at her.

As a teenager, Joy had waking moments—mostly connected to nature and writing—when her dream Fairyland still seemed possible. Once, in the crisp dusk of a late Sunday afternoon during the winter of 1930, she went for a walk in the park and pondered her place in the universe. Snow glittered on the ground. The air was "clean, cold, luminous," she thought. This was a transitional season. She had graduated from Evander Childs in January at fourteen and would matriculate at Hunter College in the fall. The day was beautiful—a poem in itself. Joy observed its subtle features: "The trees tinkled with sleet; the city noises were muffled by the snow." Then, suddenly, everything seemed to surge, to come alive. The sky, the trees—all was bright, fiery, rich. "Winter sunset with a line of young maples sheathed in ice between me and the sun," she wrote. "As I looked up they burned unimaginably golden—burned and were not consumed." There was a fourth dimension to the material world, a metaphysical depth. "I heard the voice in the burning tree; the meaning of all things was revealed and the sacrament at the heart of all beauty lay bare; time and space fell away, and for a moment the world was only a door swinging ajar."

Joy had such episodes "fairly often"; she called them "prophetic moments." Beauty made her long for something she couldn't define. She thought about God and science. "It was only in my prophetic moments that I asked such questions," she recalled, big questions, like "Is life only a matter of satisfying one's appetite, or is there more?" Science had proven that matter was indestructible—she took that on faith—and she assumed that science also proved that God didn't exist. "A young poet like me could be seized and shaken by spiritual powers a dozen times a day, and still take for granted that there was no such thing as spirit," she wrote. "That was what beautiful things did to you." She guessed that such sensations were "only nerves" or "only glands."

Joy was stumbling toward the steep cliff of cynicism, but she wasn't there yet. "I suppose the very young carry a kind of insurance against atheist despair; though they believe in nothing else, they will believe firmly in the importance of their own emotions and desires." Faith in her own emotions and desires lived long enough for Joy to internalize these transcendental "aesthetic experiences," as she called them, experiences that penetrated her subconscious like needles injecting questions that would proliferate beneath her skin, accumulating undetected over time, asking until she answered.

Joy feared that these evanescent encounters would cease altogether, that such passion—whatever the source—was intrinsic to youth, something to outgrow. The natural assumption for a sheltered child is that all adults are like her parents. This was a dreadful proposition. "The world of school-teachers in which I grew up was an extraordinarily solemn and self-important world," she later wrote. As had become her habit, Joy expressed the force of her feelings in a poem, "A Moment of Ecstasy." Writing was primal, a hunt for something amorphous, an instinctive lyrical response to that "voice in the burning tree." The universal refrain of young adulthood reverberated through Joy's mind: Who am I? What do I believe? Where do I belong? "[I] was a girl with vague eyes who scribbled verses," she later wrote of her teenage self, "scribbled them in a blind fury, not knowing what she wrote or why, and read them afterward with wonder. We call that fury 'poetic inspiration.' We might be wiser to call it 'prophecy.'" But such moments always came to an end. In the park that winter's day, the radiance had blazed, then dimmed as usual. "The light faded," Joy said. "The cold stung my toes." She walked away.

· 2 ·

1930–1934

Everything about the monastic architecture of Hunter College's main building told Joy that she was entering academic holy ground. Commanding the Upper East Side block between Sixty-eighth and Sixty-ninth streets on Park Avenue, the brick-red neo-Gothic structure referenced prestigious British institutions like Cambridge and its American Ivy League descendants. There were four stories and two towers. Windows were tall, narrow, and pointed at the top, set beneath arches; they came in pairs, like candlesticks. Ivy graced the façade. This was not a finishing school where girls bided time until they could find husbands. Joy, a "subway student" commuting in from the Bronx, had arrived at the world's largest tuition-free, publicly funded women's liberal arts college. She was there for the education, and she was there to grow up.

The Park Avenue building was constructed when Hunter was still the Normal College—the teachers' training school for women from which Joy's mother had graduated in 1907. Back then, ladies arrived at Sixty-eighth and Park carrying books bound with straps, soldiered up twenty steps, and crossed a threshold crowned with a blooming quatrefoil and an arch that pointed toward the heavens. The long wooden-floored hallways were fifteen feet wide—built, it was said, to accommodate promenading women whose bustles doubled their size—and there were thirty classrooms. Therein trained the majority of New York City's female public school teachers. It wasn't until 1892 that the Normal College conferred its first B.A.; in the commencement address that year, the school's president, Thomas Hunter, a veteran of the Civil War, thanked God he'd lived to see the day.

On a September morning in 1930, Joy marched up those twenty steps, now worn smooth by the feet of three generations of educated women, including her mother. In Hunter's wide hallways, bustles had given way to straight calf-length skirts, but some things had not changed: Students were progressive, determined, and smart. Hunter College provided an education on par with Barnard and Vassar. Admission was competitive and meritocratic. Prospective students had to be capable of handling demanding course work. Applicants qualified if they lived in New York City, had successfully completed a secondary school curriculum, and passed a rigorous entrance exam. When Joy walked through that grand arching doorway, she joined a world in which she was no longer the best, brightest, or youngest.

Like Joy, most freshmen were young—only fifteen or sixteen. About half had won high school honors in the categories of academics, athletics, or public service. These girls were thoughtful visionaries. The upperclassmen welcomed each new freshman with a quixotic greeting on page one of the weekly student newspaper, the *Hunter Bulletin:* "She alone is free to embark upon limitless seas of fancy and to scale dizzy heights of achievement. What vast projects, what towering resolutions are revolving in the mind of many an entering freshman!" Adjacent columns announced an open lecture on Virgil and reported that Hunter's very own Thomas O. Mabbott—a leading Edgar Allan Poe scholar who was a popular English professor, soon to become especially popular with Joy—had just definitively authenticated three Poe sketches.

"I loved Hunter," said Belle Kaufman, who would become Joy's best friend. Belle was an attractive girl with a broad face, wavy hair, and a trace of a Russian accent. The granddaughter of famed Yiddish humorist Sholem Aleichem, she had come to America as a child and, like Joy, was an aspiring writer—the future author of the 1965 best-seller *Up the Down Staircase,* published under "Bel" Kaufman. "[Hunter] was free. It was safe. It was Manhattan, with all its riches. It was having rigorous courses, wonderful teachers and some marvelous electives." Students could study Latin, economics, philosophy; there were classes in charcoal drawing, early nineteenth-century poetry, Italian Renaissance painting. And included in Hunter's top-notch education was a dynamic undergraduate experience with quintessential New York trimmings. An anthropology class walked the mile west across Central Park to the American Museum of Natural History for quizzes on the species and era of sundry bones and fossils. The Grand Ballroom of the Ritz-Carlton hosted the senior hop; the Metropolitan Opera House provided a stage for the annual all-school singing competition, a decades-old tradition called "Sing!"; seniors received their diplomas at a ceremony in Carnegie Hall. Journalism classes took field trips to the offices of the *New York Times,* where students once pummeled an editor with provocative questions about prejudice against women reporters.

But Hunter College, despite its cosmopolitanism, refined architecture, and standards of scholarly excellence, was *not* Barnard or Vassar. It was a municipal college bearing a social stigma that segregated it from its Protestant-rooted private sisters. Most students could not afford, or were not particularly welcome at, the predominantly WASP women's colleges of the Northeast. The Hunter community was a heterogeneous hodgepodge of primarily eastern European Jews, Irish and Italian Catholics, and a few African Americans. One in five freshmen was, like Joy, of Russian descent. Jewish girls openly discussed the advantages of changing their names to appear less "Hebrew," lopping off "-son" or "-man" or "-stein." The Department of Speech and Dramatics offered voice and phonetics courses for ironing out accents. The staff of the college yearbook, *The Wistarion,* used their forum to sympathize with the particular plight of their peers while urging them to rise above it: "Here on the Atlantic seaboard, where peoples land and sit down with their old world dialects, [English] suffers from constant onslaught . . . Do your part to keep undefiled your heritage, whether native or adopted. Learn English syntax; build correct sentences. Master architectural laws by which the great writers have erected in words structures impalpable, imperishable."

For many immigrant parents, sending their daughters to college was an investment in the family's future. All of this was especially important during the struggle to survive the country's greatest economic crisis. Thus far the market crash had in general made a lighter impact on Jewish immigrants; unlike more established businessmen, many had invested relatively unsubstantial sums of income and savings. When Joy began college in the fall of 1930, most Hunter girls were fully supported by their families. About a third worked part-time as mother's helpers, seamstresses, typists, or clerks; a lucky handful were salesgirls at popular department stores like Gimbel's and Macy's, where Belle sold books from a basement book division. A few were completely self-sufficient.

The realities of the depression were sad, but not overwhelmingly so. Joy felt only what she called "a growing uneasiness in the region where my conscience should have been." As with so many of her classmates, her hierarchy of needs allowed for the perennial hallmarks of adolescence: narcissism, sexual exploration, and rebellion. Hunter girls were worldly-wise, but college was still something of a bubble, a community that included the typical haughty cliques, class beauties, and acts of subversion like pushing the boundaries of modesty and taunting the spinsterish Dean Hannah Egan, who warned that wearing organdy blouses might arouse the passions of men. Hunter may have looked like Cambridge, but for its students, at least, old-fashioned priggishness and British inhibitions didn't penetrate its façade.

This was a new phase of life. Joy could reinvent herself. Classmates didn't know her as sickly and unsophisticated. Not that she was trying hard to fit in. "I innocently went around in a blood-red hat and an aquamarine blouse," Joy wrote of her college days. "It just hadn't occurred to me that they didn't belong together." Her figure was dumpy, her complexion pasty.

Joe and Jen were strict about the typical things that parents were strict about. Movies, for instance. "Of all the problems posed by the machine age," reported the *New York Times,* "none perhaps perplexes parents more than that of persuading their children to a discriminating use of leisure." Radio, movies, and "other robot entertainers" must not be flatly forbidden, the article suggested, simply restricted; parents in New York City could offer their children numerous alternatives to "mechanized recreations." Joy did love museums, theater, and reading, but she was also developing a passion for film. Her parents allowed the occasional movie, but they prohibited her from going to a theater alone until she turned eighteen. In the meantime, Joy took Howard. One time she unleashed her pent-up rage on a woman wearing an obtrusive hat in the row ahead of them. The hat blocked Joy's view. Joy asked the woman to remove it, but she refused, so Joy snatched the hat from her head and flung it across the theater.

Other rules seemed excessive. Inexplicably, Joy's father insisted that she was not to participate in sleepovers. Living under her parents' thumb was becoming increasingly unbearable. Years later, Joy wrote an autobiographical short story about a tumultuous relationship between a teenager named Nella, "deep in adolescent transition," and her unsympathetic mother: "Nella recognized that a brand-new maturity was a difficult thing to keep up; the slightest strain and you collapsed into a little girl again. Therefore it was the duty of your mother never to yank your confidence from under you, but instead to strengthen it all she could. Wise parents did this." Joy vacillated between calling the story "Little Girl Lost" or "Little Girl Found."

Joy was writing more than ever—short stories and poems—at home and sometimes during class, a practice that was beginning to show in her grades. She found that writing short stories was a way of sorting out her thoughts, validating her feelings and experiences by transferring them onto a character. "My own emotions," she wrote in a college essay, "are of a sort to serve me excellently as material for short stories." She wanted to write about herself: "much the easiest topic I know," she said. "And the easiest way of handling it I consider to be writing about others; for thus I escape uncomfortable self-revelation, and have moreover a chance of showing how clever I am."

Hunter had a literary journal that could provide the perfect forum for her work. Aptly titled *Echo,* the journal was known as a conduit for reverberations of feelings and fantasies, an outlet that tended to embrace the melodramatic. The college's self-appointed sponsor of self-expression, it provided a forum for the exploration Joy was beginning to accomplish both on and off the page. "The poetry of youth is the beginning of . . . an adjustment to the life, an outcry of ecstasy or despair," wrote Harriet Monroe, founder of *Poetry* magazine, in *Echo*'s pages in November of Joy's freshman year. "It may be the beginning of a resolution to make the world over to a new pattern, to bring it nearer to the heart's desire. Perhaps it is the beginning of a love affair, or of a love of nature; of a dedication to some cause, or of an utter hatred of the incompetent human race." With pen in hand, Joy was there, on the brink.

Echo, however, was cliquish and not freshman-friendly. She joined the *Bulletin* staff instead, and on Monday, December 22, 1930, she saw her name in print for the first time—even if it was misspelled on the masthead as "Davidson." The *Bulletin* was thorough, covering everything from world politics to marriage announcements. The headline JUSTIFICATION OF EUROPEAN INDICTMENT OF AMERICAN CULTURE SUBJECT OF DEBATE; DEBATERS FAIL TO CONVINCE AUDIENCE appeared alongside plans for the senior hop. The impressive eight-page weekly reported on the mundane (SENIOR TEA HAS ATMOSPHERE OF REAL CHRISTMAS CHEER), the innovative ("Come to the auditorium . . . and see an excellent motion picture of the workings of the modern refrigerator"), the revolutionary ("Miss Antoinette Mancuso, an Hunter Alumna . . . just appointed as Italian Interpreter . . . at the City's Magistrate Court of the Borough of Manhattan"), the universal ("The Education Club . . . discussion centered about Realism and Idealism"), and the controversial ("Despite repeated requests to refrain from smoking in the College buildings, no appreciable abatement can be discerned").

Sometimes as Davidson, sometimes as Davidman, Joy's name

appeared on the masthead for several months alongside those of a dozen other "Reporting Staff." But unlike the more prestigious "Feature Writers," she never had her own byline. Perhaps owing to hurt pride, or perhaps because her second-semester grades were slipping toward C's and D's, the *Bulletin* dropped her name from the masthead shortly before her sixteenth birthday in April 1931.

By this time Joy was clearly not doing well academically. During her first semester at Hunter, she earned As in Composition and Greek and Roman Civilization, a B in General Mathematics, a C in American Government, and a D in Beginning German I—the language she'd declared as her minor alongside a major in French, the most popular major among freshmen. In the Davidman household, her grades were an abomination. Joy knew how her father would react when she brought home news of these marks. Writing and reading had proved adequate refuge from all kinds of pain, but even the printed page couldn't shield her against the physical and psychological sting of his cruel discipline. Being hit was degrading, a blow more damaging to her spirit than her body.

At Hunter she was exposed to girls whose lives and relationships with their parents were very different. In a story she titled "Spoiled Child," Joy's first-person narrator is jealous of her beautiful friend Angela, whose life seems ideal. Angela is "perfectly built," clever, and talented, but it is not these qualities that the narrator covets. "I envied Angela only because she had gotten the better of her parents," she confides.

> My own parents were on the strict side, and in that inevitable battle to become a person it seemed that I was never going to get anywhere. What I was or thought myself to be—the books I wanted to buy, the boys I wanted to go out with, the genteelly wild parties I wanted to attend, where ten girls sat on ten boys' laps fiercely chaperoning each other with their eyes while Poppa and Momma of the seventeen-year-old hostess fixed refreshments in the kitchen—all were taboo. They did not even exist. They were

only in the present, and my parents did not admit that anything counted except the future. Now was a preparation.

"But I'm living Now."

"You're only preparing for life. You'll be grateful to us when you're older."

The timeline of Joy's sixteenth year is ambiguous, and it's hard to tell which of several episodes was her first major act of rebellion, but a few things are certain. Between spring 1931 and spring 1932 her ethics crashed; her craving for paternal validation peaked; and her prose strengthened remarkably, becoming less "blind-fury" and more technique. Both on and off the page, Joy was finding her voice. As for the mystical "prophetic moments" that she explained away as "only nerves" or "only glands," she said: "As soon as I discovered Freud, it became 'only sex.'"

By the time she was sixteen, Joy had indeed discovered Freud. She began to infuse her stories with eroticism, and she learned—either by theory or by practice—that her sexuality could be a mechanism for gaining power over, and attention from, older men. "Joy had a vast oedipal complex," said one family acquaintance.

In the spring of 1931, Joy enrolled in the second of two freshman composition courses, some sections of which were taught by Thomas O. Mabbott—the beloved Poe scholar who had caught Joy's eye. Handsome, blond, blue-eyed, and married, Professor Mabbott was a novelty not only for being one of few male faculty members but also for conducting his classes with the kind of unorthodox irreverence that garnered adoration from feisty girls bucking the establishment. He sat cross-legged on his desk, let students smoke in class, and never bothered with a curriculum. His vast repertoire of literary knowledge was intoxicating—Chaucer, Shakespeare, Boccaccio, Donne, the Brontës, the ancient Greeks, and the moderns. "Students were ensorcelled by this singular and charming man who seemed to know so much about so many things," remembered one of his former students. Like Joy's father, Professor Mabbott placed high value on scholarship; otherwise, though, the two men were opposites in every possible way. Professor Mabbott was "good humored," unconventional, and nurturing. He listened to students and "considered it a privilege to be invited to join some of 'his girls' for coffee." All teenage girls yearn to be heard, to be known; Joy was not accustomed to having that need fulfilled by anyone, let alone an older man. Professor Mabbott was captivating, and she wanted him.

Joy's short stories clearly express her burgeoning sexuality. She wrote a sexy revision of the Greek myth of Coronis and Apollo, and a short story about a young woman who plots to sleep with a powerful married military man who already has a mistress. "I never held such things as a mistress or two against a man," Joy's narrator remarks. Indeed, the character she created views fidelity as a "vice." Joy named her protagonist Helen, after herself. Helen considers herself to be "above all romantic emotions. I had been too much alone during my adolescence to meet anyone who I could love," she admits, "and moreover my standards were high, and demigods at a premium." But Helen does find a demigod, and she wants him—in bed—if only for one night. The story is not about love; it's about conquest and power.

Joy bragged to Belle that she was sleeping with Professor Mabbott, and Belle didn't doubt her friend's claim. The "liaison," as she referred to the purported affair, made Joy seem "glamorous," and the story got around. Joy recounted the affair to Howard with less bravado. Her first sexual experience was with a married man who couldn't fully be hers.

Whether the sexual relationship was truth or fantasy, it was real enough in Joy's mind to be either the catalyst for or the consequence of her rebellion against her parents. An epic power shift was unfolding in the Davidman household. Joy's second-semester grades had been worse than her first—B's, C's, and a D in Beginning German II. When Joe raised his hand and slapped her face, the rage of years erupted. Joy flung herself forward and scratched his face with her nails. Joe never touched her again.

Lesser acts of defiance flowed from there. On a visit to an aunt in Brooklyn, a torrent of rain let loose. Joy did not want to schlep home in soaking weather. She used her aunt's phone to dial the operator and request her family's number, and when her father came on the line, she proposed spending the night in Brooklyn. "Come right home," Joe said abruptly. This order could not have been well received by a girl who was sleeping with a man old enough to be her father. Angry and bitter, Joy put on her coat and stepped into the downpour. "Outside the pavement was black and moving with rain," she remembered. This was absolutely ridiculous. She turned around, went back into her aunt's dry apartment, called her parents again, and told them she would not be coming home that night.

Family conversations at the dinner table became fraught. Joe and Jen promoted debate in theory as a stimulating exercise, but they weren't happy when their daughter began out-arguing them. Joy was developing into a cunning general of her own private army, with logic as her weapon for deflecting and dominating. A significant source of contention was that she no longer believed in standards of right and wrong—or, as she put it, "the ugly things called moral codes." Joy had internalized Angelo Patri's encouragement to develop "not in the spirit of passive obedience, but in one of mental emancipation."

"I've converted to hedonism," she told her parents. "Pleasure [is] the only goal in life." If her father was truly an atheist, she argued, this shouldn't be a problem. His moral code was based on "whim." For him, and most nonreligious people, she said, morality was only "habit and sentiment . . . coaxed into us by Mamma, knocked into us by Papa." She noticed that her father, like many Jews she knew, "got rid of the traditional forms of Judaism, but kept a vague and well-meaning belief in a vaguely well-meaning God." He prided himself on character: "justice, temperance, fortitude, and prudence." But as Joy saw it, that was just contaminated atheism—more like Unitarianism. Dialogues with her father began to look something like this:

JOY: How can you talk about ethics without religion?

JOE: Because it is fine, decent and right.

JOY: There is no materialistic basis for ethics. If there is no God, nothing is wrong.

JOE: Principles and character matter.

JOY *smiling at her parents condescendingly:* Can't you see that that's just circular reasoning?

They could not.

Joy redeemed herself somewhat by winning a New York State University Scholarship entitling her to receive $100 for each of her remaining three years of college to offset essentials including carfare, health care, and clothing. Scholarship eligibility was based on several factors, none of which had to do with grades—a lucky break.

Joy's Regent's exam scores show that her grades did not reflect her scholarly potential. "She was a brilliant young woman," remembered her high school friend Nina, "with an extraordinary, almost photographic memory." Rather those marks speak to her intolerance for work she found irrelevant. In the spring of her sophomore year, when she turned seventeen, she vented in an essay titled "Literary Adventure," her first formal work of criticism, which demonstrates her sharp wit and her nearly photographic memory. "I concern myself today," she wrote, "with the thoughts of Joy Davidman, which I have so often longed to express candidly in a variety of trying situations." The essay is a twelve-page exhalation, derivative of her father in tone. "Knowledge which the public-spirited college president condemns as unlikely to make money, which to the American is subversive and faintly obscene, and to the educator so much dead lumber to be eradicated from a curriculum designed to manufacture yet more Americans—stray exquisite knowledge which has, thank Heaven! no conceivable utility is my desire, and my delight, and I had rather read of the old Greek cave-temples than invent ever so much better a mousetrap."

The essay develops into an ostentatious tour de force of comparative literature. Joy states that she will write about herself through writing about her "loves," the great authors whose work has shaped her thoughts and actions. "To my thinking, Sappho is the only woman who was ever sufficiently unsexed to be a poet. I could never agree with Robert Browning about his wife, and concerning Edna

St. Vincent Millay I am always tactfully silent—it would seem then not in the nature of women to write poetry; a fact which has been remarked upon by others. I may, however, produce my own early attempts as additional confirmation." About the poetry of Catullus she writes: "He is delightfully free from the esoteric Christian conception of love. A reverend gentleman has reproached him for this, I believe, on the ground that to desire a woman's body is to insult the woman. I think I may be admitted to know something more of women than most reverend gentlemen, and I hereby take the opportunity of assuring this one that it is a very rare woman who would, in such circumstances, really think herself insulted." She discusses Horace: "To me the only test of poetry is the libertine ecstasy I get from reading it, and with Horace my ecstasy is unquenchable." She mocks the ignorant who dismiss his poetry because it is sterile of spirituality, and she says that Horace's work balances her own poetic intake because he is so "unlike Shelley," a literary hero of hers. She scoffs at the "rich and respectable bourgeois" who will have none of Villon, one of her favorite poets, declaring, "I would barter all my chances of success in this world and salvation in the doubtful next if I could write [like him]."

Joy mused on her own future; she was sure she would someday teach school like her parents—not because that was what she wanted, but because they were pushing and it seemed inevitable. Yet she longed to be a writer and was confident that her innate talent could evolve into something special: "I think that if I stay in of nights, and pay not too much attention to the art of Logic, and control my annoying tendency toward the use of French idioms, I may some day find new music in familiar words, some day become quite sure that I know how to write."

Joy did stay in and she did write, some poems more successful than others. Some of her work was youthfully sentimental, but her most successful poems spoke to the evolving world around her. The machine age that once seemed intoxicatingly futuristic now cast a menacing pall as Manhattan mutated into a metallic labyrinth that blocked Joy's view of the sky. She saw a religiosity in people's faith in and zeal for machines and their products, like the skyscrapers that littered the heavens when she gazed at the clouds. A skyscraper, she wrote, is a "silver sword" that cuts the sky, cuts sunlight away from her sight. "In the song of the machine there is a snarl." Machines equaled destruction. They were evil, seductive like the devil, claiming to be human beings' salvation. This is the message of the machine and the tower:

> I am the life,
> the resurrection.
> You have been troubled,
> I give you peace . . .
> I give you living.
> I have given beauty,
> will give you power.
> For your delight
> am I not fashioned?
> Let you be glad
> who have sworn me your lives.
> I give back the gladness
> that was in living
> before you were men!

Her response to this claim had become vehement: "Liar! / I say you have lied."

In Joy's sophomore year, *Echo* got a new charter requiring the editors to solicit contributions through posters, word of mouth, letters, and advertisements in the *Bulletin*. Included in the coming changes would be the selection of new members for a literary staff of eight. Students were offered the opportunity to "try out" by submitting three recent representative manuscripts in any genre. Joy chose three pieces and appended her name and locker number, dropped her submission into the *Echo* box in the Council Room, and then waited to find out if she'd made the cut. "I devote a single heart to literature," she had written in "Literary Adventure," and to consummate that devotion, in the fall of her junior year Joy changed her major to English and shifted French to a minor. External acknowledgment of her dedication came from her peers when she received word that she had been invited to join *Echo*'s ranks. She set her sights on becoming editor in chief.

On a March day in 1933, during the spring semester of her junior year, Joy stomped indignantly down the stairs into the creative heart of Hunter College, the basement where steam pipes sizzled and the sound of typewriters crackled through dim, dripping corridors. A resident mouse, affectionately named Eugene O'Neill, scampered to and fro, dividing his time among the offices of Hunter's student publications. Joy bypassed the *Bulletin* office, where her classmates struggled to cover conventional college stories alongside the most politically charged events of their time—the senior hop at the Ritz-Carlton, Hitler's appointment as chancellor of Germany, President Roosevelt's first one hundred days—and hurtled toward the *Echo* office, where sheaves of poetry feathered the bookshelves, piles of short stories awaited their fate, plants pushed upward from their pots despite the muted light, and matters of greater personal consequence than fascism and unemployment demanded confrontation.

The *Echo* staff sat behind desks and sprawled on a threadbare green couch. The girls looked up at Joy, five feet two inches of fury whose only nod to fashion was a sleek brown bob. "I demand a recount!" She was seething. Votes had just been tallied for the next year's editorial staff, and the election hadn't gone her way: Florence Howitt, Joy's archrival, had beaten her in the competition to become editor in chief. The staff begrudgingly consented to a recount. "You didn't say 'no' to Joy," they knew. A self-proclaimed "egoist," she disliked most people, and most people disliked her. The intuitive among her peers, though, recognized the complexity beneath Joy's haughty exterior. "She was brilliant, talented, and, at times, devastating," remarked one classmate. "Ironic, sardonic, but always with a kind of sadness behind those big brown doe eyes." It was the sadness of a poet, the curse of an artistic temperament fed by a lifetime of alienation.

The votes were tallied again, with the same result. Joy was named co-associate editor, a second-best, shared position. No one wanted to work under her management. Joy was more gifted than any of the others, and she knew it, and the defeat only drove her to make sure everyone else knew it, too.

Joy's vindication over Florence came in two stages. That spring, Joy was taking an elective in biography (a course developed by Professor Mabbott) and chose as her subject the Irish novelist George Moore, who united "phrases perfect to eye and ear, the perfect proportion of his tale, the delight he had in beautiful things, and the tenderness he had for human suffering—a tenderness which sentimentalists never see because it is always unspoken." Moore was unappreciated in his native land, in part because his rejection of Catholicism was unforgivable to Dubliners. Joy connected with his alienation and displacement. Feeling resentment on behalf of her hero, she regarded Dublin in perhaps the way she regarded Hunter, as "a vinegar city, in a world of champagne that has lost its bubbles." In his younger days, Joy commented, Moore was "too earnest not to be a little awkward." He "had the intemperate enthusiasm of youth." She wrote sympathetically of his escape to Paris, where he found comradeship with the likes of Degas, Cézanne, Mallarmé, and Verlaine. "He met everybody, he loved everybody, his accounts of those early years are heartbreaking to lonely students far away from Paris."

Moore attempted a career as a painter but succeeded only in being painted. He sat for Manet. Joy visited his portrait in the Metropolitan Museum of Art and was taken by his bohemian red beard. She lauded his lack of sexual inhibition. She identified with her subject, viewing his life in light of her own worldview, experiences, and emotional truths. She praised Moore's openness about "pleasant pagan lusts," agreed that "intellect and passion travel hand-in-hand," and admired his indifference to conventional ethics. The Moore essay bore a subtle undertone of arrogance, as if written by one who reveled in erudition, showing off her extraordinary repertoire of information on subjects ranging from world literature and visual arts to human sexuality. Conquering Professor Mabbott had stoked an already fiery ego, boosting her confidence and broadening the strong strokes of her pen.

The essay, "A Grecian Urn . . . of George Moore," was published in the spring 1933 edition of *Echo* to rave reviews in the *Bulletin:* "She has cast off the standardized 'history-of-literature-book' criticism which the average student accepts as readily as he does the Constitution or the Bible . . . Miss Davidman has a background that is more filled in with literary knowledge than that of most young writers." The reviewer criticized Joy for overwriting but ended the critique with praise: "Miss Davidman has, we believe, one of the most promising talents—nasty words, usually, to young writers who love to think they have arrived—of the writers in *Echo.*" Florence Howitt's work in that issue of *Echo* was panned.

Joy embraced her new responsibilities as a co-associate editor, which included broadcasting appeals like one that appeared on the front page of the *Bulletin* on October 3, 1933, during the fall of Joy's senior year: "From its secret headquarters in the basement—where the walls are newly painted and the floor was recently swept—*Echo* appeals to all true Huntresses to send in manuscripts." Next to it was a tiny notice—"Tag Day: Student Council and Dean Egan have endorsed a tag day for the relief of Hitlerism"—about a charity drive for unemployment relief initiated by Hunter students that involved selling buttons for ten cents that read *"I will share."*

By the fall of Joy's senior year, activism had spread like a fever. The *Bulletin* was running stories under headlines like U.S. ANTI-WAR CONGRESS DRAWS LARGE, ENTHUSIASTIC CROWDS and PEACE, YOUTH, FARMER, AND LABOR ORGANIZATIONS SEND DELEGATIONS. Hunter's president, Eugene A. Colligan, was not happy about the upsurge in student-led political symposiums, especially as city elections approached. If students wanted to discuss governmental problems and the responsibilities of citizens in relation to those problems, they should take courses in preparation for "intelligent participation in public life through a serious study of Political and Social Science," he wrote in an open letter to the student body. He listed courses in which students could learn, debate, and discuss, and he offered the option of student assemblies. But he strongly expressed his disapproval of what he called "the short cut of emotional appeal through brief speeches" at rallies which were igniting the enthusiasm of students who wanted to do something about the state of society. "Cultured and disciplined minds which bring real thinking and calm judgment to the consideration of problems understand that cold reason is of more worth than the emotion-provoking appeal of large group meetings which smack of the circus. Mere activity is not necessarily real progress."

President Colligan's disapproval did little to subdue the political activism that was sweeping through campuses across the United States. Written endorsements for the National Conference of Students in Politics, scheduled for December in Washington, D.C., urged young people to combat the rise of fascism through organized protests. And for the first time, Hunter girls held the staffs of their student publications accountable for signing contracts with union printers: the *Bulletin* and *Wistarion* had done so, but *Echo* had not.

If Joy and Florence could agree on one thing, it was that politics had little or no place in *Echo*'s pages. "I read about strikes and revolutions," Florence said, "but when I walk out into the night and see the sky above, I think: after all, are these things important to me? And I find that they are not." Like Florence, Joy was absorbed in matters of the heart. In *Echo*'s 1933 Christmas issue, released on December 19 of her senior year, Joy published "Sonnets," in which she found "a jeweled word for every wound."

> I hate you for your kind indifference,
> That tiptoes past the naked thing who cries
> A shocking lust; and, like a man of sense,
> Stares at my passion with a mild surprise . . .
> I meant to rouse you till your flesh divined
> Behind my eyes the hot and hostile Woman.

That spring, *Echo*'s unofficial position on publishing work that spoke to contemporary social issues shifted, or so Florence said, but the publication's selections suggest that the purported new position was adopted merely to placate student appeals for a magazine with content that reflected the events of the day. Florence told the *Bulletin* that "ECHO should be an organ of thought for College; it should reveal the reactions of students to the outside world, to significant events now taking place, to any phase of social, economic, or even academic life." Still, the pieces she included—or didn't include—in the spring issue left students asking, "Why doesn't Echo try to keep abreast of the times . . . Why not some social satire or something?" Florence's response was "We have that too—a charming little play."

On April 12, 1934, Joy was gazing out a window at Hunter College's Upper East Side campus and saw something unusual on the roof nearby. She had passed these same windows hundreds of times, and her eyes anticipated the familiar contours of Hunter's Gothic architecture—the tall, narrow windows capped with stone arches, the red clay façade graced with ivy. But why was a blond girl poised on the edge of the roof, with nothing but four stories of air between herself and a plot of grass on the hard earth below?

The scene, so unexpected, took a moment to register. Joy had always been the type to gaze contemplatively out of windows, and in these final weeks of her final semester there was plenty to contemplate. In a few days she would turn nineteen; in two months she would graduate in a grand ceremony at Carnegie Hall. Most of her classmates planned either to marry or to begin teaching in the New York City public school system, a career Joy desperately wished to escape. Her parents repeatedly insisted that teaching was the sensible career path. This was the height of the Great Depression; better to labor in a classroom than languish in a breadline. But Joy's desire to be a writer remained steadfast.

Meanwhile, she had a lot to wrap up. In addition to course work for seven classes, there were heaps of extracurricular responsibilities. She was the newly minted president of Hunter's English Club; "Recording Secretary" for Hunter's branch of the International English Honors Society, Sigma Tau Delta; a member of Phi Iota Sigma, the International Foreign Language Honors Society; and an editor of *Echo*. But among her chief preoccupations was a story called "Apostate" that she was writing for English 226, a class on the art of the short story, about a brash, sensual young Jewish woman named Chinya, who lived in the Russian shtetl of Tulchin, near where Joy's mother was born. With so many of Joy's classmates being of Russian descent, the country had become a popular setting for nostalgic stories submitted to *Echo*. Joy wasn't one to jump on bandwagons, but tales of the old country captivated her, and she wanted to write something different from a romantic take on family tales. She wove together bits of lore with projections of her own thoughts, feelings, and experiences, trying on the Old World like a child playing dress-up in her mother's cast-off clothes.

English 226 was taught by Blanche Colton Williams, head of the English department and loved by students. She treated English majors to tea at the Plaza hotel, furnished her office with a chaise longue, and often wore fresh orchids pinned to her blouse. Joy disdained ostentatious overtures. Showy extravagance was for superficial people like her mother and Florence Howitt, who pranced through the halls in fawn-colored riding breeches after private equestrian lessons. But Professor Williams loved Joy's writing, and accolades from her meant something. She had authored several books on the art of the short story and edited anthologies of Greek myths that Joy loved, including the tale of Psyche and Cupid. She had also helped create the prestigious O. Henry Award, and administered Hunter's own illustrious literary award, the Bernard Cohen Prize, given to a senior English major enrolled in English 226. But all of this was about to fly from Joy's mind.

The girl on the roof gazed up at the sky. She was Dorothy Scheer, a nineteen-year-old junior majoring in Romance languages. Her personal story was so commonplace that, had they been close, Joy might have guessed what was about to happen. A year and a half earlier, when Dorothy's mother died, her older sister Sadie dropped out of

Hunter and took a secretarial job with the government to help support Dorothy and the aunt with whom the girls now lived. But in late March, Sadie's position was terminated. Rumor had it that the relief check they depended on was late, and Dorothy had barely eaten in days. Joy watched, helpless and horrified, as her classmate leaped from the roof, blond hair trailing like the tail of a dying flare.

· 3 ·

1934–1938

The suicide haunted Joy as commencement day approached. She remembered Aesop's fable about the ant and the grasshopper. It had upset her when she heard it read aloud at age five, and now she understood why. The carefree grasshopper whiled away his days chirping in the field while the conscientious ant dutifully laid up corn for the winter. Months passed, the cold settled in, food became scarce, and the grasshopper was hungry. Dying of starvation, he watched as the thrifty ants feasted on a bounty of corn and grain. "No, I won't let it happen," she had cried. "He's got to give the grasshopper something!"

In 1934, at the height of the Great Depression, her interpretation of the fable was fraught with significance. The ant represented capitalists, while the grasshopper symbolized capitalist stereotypes of the hungry and unemployed. But what had Dorothy done—or not done—to deserve her fate? The answer, Joy knew, was nothing.

Commencement, held according to tradition at Carnegie Hall, would be defined by the tenor of the times. On the morning of June 13, as parents paraded into the opulent venue on West

Fifty-seventh Street, the Gilded Age seemed to laugh in the face of the depression.

An organist opened the ceremony with a processional from Wagner's *Tannhäuser*. Joy marched in her cap and purple gown, the school color. Her parents looked on, part of an audience of hundreds. The printed program for Hunter's sixty-fifth commencement announced that of the 621 graduates, 35 had finished with honors. Joy wasn't one of them, but she did receive two of several awards in English: the Randolph and Eliza Guggenheimer Memorial Prize for English Literature, an honor that garnered her a gold watch, and the Bernard Cohen Prize for English Composition, which awarded a $40 prize to the English 226 student who'd written the best short story. Joy won for "Apostate."

Joy and her classmates took their seats as the ceremony commenced. A clergyman offered the invocation, the Hunter College choir performed the prayer from Mascagni's opera *Cavalleria Rusticana,* and President Colligan conferred the degrees. Each woman symbolically switched her mortarboard tassel from the right to the left on receiving her diploma.

Now officially graduated, the members of the most politically outspoken class in the history of Hunter College settled into their chairs for the traditional series of speeches intended to launch them into the world with confidence and conviction. A year earlier, the class of 1933 had been cheated when the Board of Higher Education turned their commencement into a forum for denying accusations that the city's colleges had become nests for hatching young communists. The board itself had come under fire for allegedly using taxpayers' money to indirectly aid the Communist Party. Knowing that the press would cover Hunter's graduation, the board used the ceremony to broadcast a sharp denial, contending that of 75,000 students enrolled in New York's three public colleges—Hunter, City College, and Brooklyn College—a mere one hundred had been guilty of "improper acts" such as antiwar disturbances. Affronted by the public's criticism, the board condemned the accusations as "disloyal and unpatriotic." The class of '33 was warned at commencement against "disturbers who seek to further a theory—instead of cooperation, suggesting destruction; in place of honest thought, urging revolution." Newspapers ran headlines such as DENIES SCHOOLS ARE RED.

The burden of launching 1934's graduates into society fell heavily on Alexander Lyons, rabbi of Brooklyn's Eighth Avenue Temple, who was invited to give the baccalaureate address. Doubtless there were those who shifted uncomfortably in their seats as the rabbi delivered a talk—"Character and Culture"—tinged with the red hues of Marxism. "The world is in transition," he orated. "We must have a new economic order . . . Selfish competition must yield to social cooperation." These brand-new alumnae had unique opportunities to effect change in an era of progress. They had the energy and idealism of youth on their side, and a forward-thinking president who foresaw unprecedented prospects for women. Hadn't President Roosevelt recently appointed the first female U.S. cabinet member—Secretary of Labor Frances Perkins? Rabbi Lyons urged the class of '34 to look to strong women such as Perkins, Florence Nightingale, and especially Eleanor Roosevelt, the ultimate contemporary role model, a first lady who aligned herself more with working people than with high society. "We have too long had a man-made civilization," he said. "It must now be supplemented with a contribution of the world's women."

The next speaker, chairman of the Board of Education Mark Eisner, sounded a less partisan note but equally encouraged proactivity—without the undertones of passivity and meekness implied from the very same Carnegie Hall stage the previous June. This year, the chairman of the Board of Education encouraged a more balanced, open-minded approach. A female member of the Board of Higher Education, Ruth Lewinson, disappointingly gave the least intellectual, least feminist exhortation of all the speakers. "This is not a gloomy world," she told the graduates. "It is a thrilling one in which to live and make a contribution. New fields have been opened, new opportunities offer and there is always the prospect of a happy marriage and a full life as a wife and mother." The class of 1934 closed the ceremony by singing "Fame," and the entire auditorium joined in a rendition of "America."

JOY'S ENROLLMENT IN an Ivy League graduate program was, for a Jewish woman in 1934, an extraordinary achievement. In her father's day, Columbia routinely hinted that prospective Jewish applicants might be more comfortable at CCNY, where Joe received his degree. By the time Joy was born, the rising number of immigrant students prompted Columbia's dean to favor restricting Jewish enrollment to 20 percent. The student body itself was more tolerant than the dean, and Joy felt comfortable enough on campus.

Joy's M.A. would require thirty credits plus a thesis. Before attending classes, she presented herself at the registrar's office in 315 University Hall, where she filled out the requisite forms and paid her fees for the academic year. Her parents supported her, backing up the point they continued to push: Teaching was the safe, sensible career path for Joy. It was honorable and reliable work.

Between tuition, books, and a lunch plan for off-campus students, Joy's parents were looking at $545—a sum that, though prodigious, paid for a degree that no longer guaranteed future employment. Even the office that matched students and alumni with suitable short-term jobs—as clerks, tutors, stenographers, translators, salesmen—faced a well of work so dry that its administrators felt compelled to broadcast a warning in the annual *Columbia University Bulletin of Information, 1934–1935:* "At present . . . general economic conditions have so affected employment opportunities that very little work of any kind is available and no prospective student should come to Columbia expecting to depend largely upon the assistance of the Appointments Office, but should be prepared to meet practically all expenses."

Classes at Columbia began on September 27. Unlike Hunter, Columbia had a main campus, and when Joy walked through the wrought iron gates at 116th Street and Broadway, she entered a vast expanse of collegiality and intellectual stimulation. The buildings themselves proclaimed erudition. Beyond the gates, on Joy's right, stood the brand-new South Hall Library, with a granite base and fourteen Ionic columns beginning at the fourth floor and rising thirty-two feet to a frieze carved with the names of men Joy loved: Homer, Herodotus, Sophocles, Plato, Aristotle, Demosthenes, Cicero, Virgil, and on the west and east sides, Horace, Tacitus, Saint Augustine, Saint Thomas Aquinas, Dante, Cervantes, Shakespeare, Milton, Voltaire, Goethe. But just two blocks west, on Riverside Drive, the sun set over New York's Hooverville, a cluster of shacks built from the refuse of city life. Forty percent of New York City's workers were unemployed.

The juxtaposition was not lost on students. The collegiate atmosphere Joy encountered was relatively dispirited. "Only a few years ago the great events of undergraduate concern were the cane spree, the flag rush, the tug of war," lamented the dean of Columbia College, the university's undergraduate school, in an editorial in the *New York Times* that October. But just as strikes and peace committees had superseded Hunter College teas and singing competitions, Columbia's traditional tug-of-war was becoming displaced by global concerns. Leftist professors like critic Lionel Trilling and poet Mark Van Doren fanned the flames of students' antiwar passion. Yes, they wanted Hitler and Mussolini stopped, but they didn't want to see themselves, their peers, or their country go to Europe with guns drawn. In tweed coats and fedoras, Columbians on campus chanted, "No second front!" They gathered for intense dialogues about social and political concerns; the blind nationalism of their parents' generation had given way to questioning with eyes wide open. For some, Marxism provided an answer to the present and the future. The Soviet socialist "experiment" was the model society America should emulate. Some were joining the Communist Party and semi-secretively meeting in "units" or "cells," neighborhood groups of ten or twenty Party members. The dean was sympathetic, up to a point: "[Students] may talk unwisely, they may act rashly and impulsively, but back of it all is an urge that cannot be crushed by the rough hand of authority without understanding. After all, youth remain youth, and youth will continue to furnish the team which pushes things along . . . [T]hose of us whose function it is to serve as ballast must at least attempt to understand before we condemn."

If Joy had qualms about the Communist Party, it wasn't because she shared the average American's perception that communists were "fiery men with bombs up their sleeves." In the months after graduation, several of her former classmates had joined, and they were certainly not Benedict Arnolds, or Russian spies, or anti-American enemies of the Constitution. Most of them were just like her: Jewish, and either foreign born or first generation. Still, as a non–Party member, Joy understood only so much. What exactly *did* go on in those cell meetings?

There is no indication that Joy was one of the students who were "getting up steam," as the dean put it—not yet, anyway. For Joy, graduate school was about exploring her passions: reading great literature and writing. She focused on her heavy course load—four English classes and one in French—and on her poetry. One of her most significant poems written that fall was "This Woman": "Now do not put a ribbon in your hair; Abjure the spangled insult of design, / The filigree sterility, nor twine / A flower with your strength; go bare, go bare." She was articulating her own longing for independence and her tendency to reject the conventions of femininity.

Joy translated thirteen French poems and submitted them to *Literary World,* which agreed to publish them in January. Courage bolstered, she submitted a poem titled "Resurrection," written at Easter the previous year, to the prestigious magazine *Poetry*. Years later she would interpret the poem's preoccupation with the Christian cross as an attempt to answer "the desperate question: Is life really only a matter of satisfying one's appetites, or is there more?" Editor Morton Zabel turned down the poem, but his rejection letter wasn't wholly discouraging, and Joy felt strongly enough about "Resurrection" to resubmit it after an overhaul. "I slashed off three stanzas and rewrote nine lines," she told Zabel in a letter dated January 8, 1935. "This is all I can do to it, as the poem is a year and a half old, and I have gone other places since I thought it out. But I like it better as it is now, and perhaps you will." Along with her letter and the revised version of "Resurrection," Joy assembled a few other poems and, in a gesture of practicality and tempered hopes, enclosed a self-addressed stamped return envelope.

Within days of mailing her packet, she received a response from *Poetry*. Her poems had been accepted! Joy was elated. *Poetry* requested that she send an "autobiography." She hastily rolled a piece of paper into her typewriter and wrote up a breathless bio: "Born in New York City, 1915; educated in Hunter College, N.Y.C., B.A. June 1934. At present digging fantastic people out of the seventeenth century for a Columbia M.A. (English). Literary career incipient; prize story at Hunter, thirteen translations of modern French poems in the *Literary World* for January—expected to come out any day now, but you never can tell. Otherwise beautifully unpublished."

Then Joy's tone changed from whimsical to sober: "[I] will probably end up teaching English in the New York High Schools." She wanted to believe that a literary career was "incipient," but her dreams were battling reality, and reality was winning. Her options were limited. Marriage was unlikely, considering the dearth of promising suitors. She wanted to be a writer, but earning a living from poetry and prose is a time-honored non-tradition. Without her parents, Joy had no income. She couldn't very well move out on her own. Her parents informed her that if she wanted to write, she would have to do so in her free time; they would not provide room and board indefinitely for a child they had already put through college and graduate school.

But for Joy, not writing was not an option. There had to be a way. Her least gloomy course was to pad her résumé with publications; with some luck and an M.A., she might procure an undergraduate teaching position. "I should like to know, if possible, when you are thinking of using my poems," she added at the end of her letter to *Poetry*, "so that I can tell my friends—and my college, where I hope to get a job."

Meanwhile, Joy's primary task was to choose an unsung author as the subject for her M.A. thesis. She eagerly adapted the assignment into a rigorous personal challenge. She would write a sweeping epic biography of one of those "fantastic people" she'd dug up from the seventeenth century: Roger Boyle, the first Earl of Orrery, an Irish statesman who led revolts against the Irish rebels, served in the Parliamentary army, and wrote stories on the side. His life was "picturesque," of "unquestionable color," she wrote in her thesis's introduction, although the quality of his writing was at best debatable. Like a literary detective, Joy hunted material, filled out call slips, holed up in quiet nooks at South Hall Library, or spread out her work on long wooden tables in the main reading room at the New York Public Library. She wasn't interested in manufacturing an academic paper. She would take again the unconventional approach she attempted with George Moore at Hunter, telling Orrery's story "as amusingly as possible." Orrery was, she observed, a great admirer and imitator of "the pale porcelain confections of De Soudery and D'Urfé," authors of French romances, "perhaps the dullest form of popular literature ever hatched." But his personality and era captured her imagination. "He had a secret finger in many unsavory pies," she wrote in the introduction to her thesis. "[He] was a notable soldier under the Protector, an adroit politician at the Restoration court; was altogether a great man in his time." For reasons that made little sense to her, history remembered him "chiefly because when attacked by the gout he distracted his mind from the pain by writing tragedies in heroic verse." Having suffered long illnesses herself, Joy could identify.

Beginning that winter of 1935, Joy's attention was diverted to a different revolution. Her study of Orrery's revolts and battles coincided with a growing fascination with Soviet peasant uprisings. On January 12 a Soviet film called *Chapayev* premiered at Manhattan's Cameo Theatre and packed the house for ten weeks. The film was pure propaganda, and Joy was enthralled. From her seat in the dark theater one winter day, she watched as a Bolshevik guerrilla leader, Chapayev, rose to commander of the Red Army, rallying peasants to fight against the oppressive White Russians during a bloody revolt in 1919.

Audiences around the world embraced *Chapayev.* In Washington, D.C., when the historic Belasco Theatre reopened after heavy renovation, an orange neon sign spanning the façade announced that the inaugural film was CHAPAYEV! The film appealed especially to sensibilities that hungered for valor and heroism. Little Russian boys made up new games with names such as "Chapayev and his men," while teenage girls flocked to Moscow cinemas, hearts aflutter. When the film ended, young people lingered in the theaters and united their voices, chanting, "Chapayev! Chapayev!"

The film was hailed as a masterpiece of modern cinema. One reviewer said that *Chapayev* was among the few movies responsible for spoiling the American public's taste for "the amiable mediocrity which is the filmgoer's more usual ration." At Moscow's first annual Soviet Film Festival, the Leningrad studio that produced *Chapayev* was awarded first prize "for its affirmation of the realistic style of Soviet cinematography and combining with it depth of ideology, living truthfulness, simplicity and a high quality of directing, acting and camera work."

What Stalin called "living truthfulness" others called inflammatory red propaganda. Stalin was seductively deceptive. The dictator and his filmmakers did not hesitate to advertise their movies as enlightenment through entertainment, a way of educating "the people" about, among other things, Soviet advancements in science and technology, agricultural productivity, and maxims such as "the complete fusion of the human being with the mass does not mean that the individual has to disappear into the mass." To make those philosophies accessible to all, Stalin built thousands of theaters.

Joy was captivated by the concept of a classless civilization. Two recent Soviet art exhibits, one at the Pennsylvania Museum in Philadelphia, the other in Washington, D.C., had showcased idyllic living conditions, the antithesis of the breadlines, apple carts, and suicides that stalked the periphery of her life. The art was shipped to the United States by Russia's Society for Cultural Relations with Foreign Countries. Much of it featured strong men, buxom women, and ruddy-cheeked children glowing with health, all smiles and big blue eyes. They wore comfortable yet practical clothes, read books, and listened to the phonograph—rewards for conscientious toilers. Some Americans easily saw through it all, comparing Soviet art to American advertisements. But Joy bought Stalin's story, agreeing with reviews that claimed the art "represents the spirit of a people released: of a people free, at length, to warm itself at the hearth of human peace and comradeship." It was utopia. Here was hope. The Russian proletariat were thriving today, right now, while hungry citizens of New York City fainted in the streets. It was plenty versus poverty. Stalin had built a society incapable of degenerating into the kind of community where destitute orphans jump from buildings.

In 1929 Joy believed in "nothing but American prosperity," she said, and by 1930 she believed in "nothing at all." During her Hunter days, her trust was "firmly" embedded in her "own emotions and desires." Now her hope drifted toward Stalin, with art and literature acting as conduits for spreading his message of salvation. "Revolution" was becoming less an abstract theory, more a practical solution. "My visionary fairyland," Joy later wrote, "transferred from Somewhere-Out-of-Space to Somewhere-Ahead-in-Time, began to seem at last a possible, even a probable goal. The never-never land turned into the Comes-the-Revolution Country."

Had she not had more pressing commitments, Joy might have taken up with the Communist Party right then. For the moment, though, politics was little more than a distraction; the revolution she was committed to had taken place in Ireland two centuries before her birth. She spent the spring and summer synthesizing piles of notes and crafting a compelling narrative, fast-paced and witty. In the first few pages she more than achieved her goal of telling Orrery's story "as amusingly as possible." She takes her readers on a tour of the castle in which Orrery was born to Lord and Lady Cork. "Upstairs, my lady Countess bore a series of children in a great gilded bed that was covered in less troublous moments with quilts of Indian needlework. Velvet cushions were strewn about with a lavish hand . . . [Orrery] was eleventh of a set of fifteen," Joy wrote, "only three of whom died in childhood; which was a record for those days. After bearing her last daughter, however, Lady Cork did what might have been expected of her; she died."

Joy's photographic memory proved itself capable of retaining and organizing thousands of pages of decades-old documents and history books. Her list of footnotes grew to 1,326. Most of her classmates delivered papers 100 to 150 pages long. Joy's thesis included 269 pages of text, followed by multiple appendices: family trees; exegesis on the reliability of sources; a bibliography of Orrery's published letters, plays, poems and stories; and her own bibliography of over one hundred sources. By August 1 she had submitted her thesis for approval, which she easily received. Her degree was officially conferred in December 1935, a year and a half after she graduated from Hunter.

IN THE FALL of that year, Joy had reluctantly taken an entry-level teaching appointment as a "permanent substitute" at Walton High School for girls in the West Bronx. Parents from all over New York City eagerly sent their daughters to Walton for a premier public education that included extracurricular activities on a campus with its own tennis court and library. Outside of class, girls played basketball, learned how to dive, and whizzed around campus on roller skates.

Joy loathed teaching high school. Could this really be her destiny? Teaching day after day, decade after decade, like her parents? One of the few pluses was a captive audience for her new poems. But the Department of Education did nothing to win her allegiance. When Joy and her fellow teachers-in-training passed the exam to be licensed as regular teachers, the school board, under pressure to cut costs, kept them in what was called a "permanent substitute category." Permanent substitutes were typically saddled with floor scrubbing, mimeographing, and teaching the the toughest classes, but if they wanted to keep their jobs and someday move up the ranks, they were obliged to stick it out. With her teacher-in-training licence, Joy was not entitled to an annual salary. Instead, she earned around $24 per week. "The filthy permanent substitute trick," she called it.

Walton was only about a three-quarter-mile walk from the Davidman family apartment on Andrews Avenue, but Joy's journey seemed to stretch farther each week. As the school year wore on, lethargy intensified the force of gravity, pressing her down into the chair behind her desk in the classroom. Irritability increased with fatigue. Something was wrong—or perhaps the symptoms were a psychosomatic protest against a life she didn't really want. Joy dedicated her remaining energy not to teaching but to attending movies and plays, and to creative endeavors. She made a hobby of painting Japanese watercolors, a practice that lulled her into a serene mental space. And writing continued to be her reprieve.

In January 1936 Joy received much-needed validation and a glimmer of hope: *Poetry* finally printed "Resurrection" and "Amulet," pieces it had accepted exactly one year earlier. Then she learned of a poetry contest called the Yale Younger Poets Award Series, run by Yale University Press. Each spring the press invited unpublished poets under the age of thirty to submit book-length collections for consideration. The winner received $100, an appreciable award, but one that paled in comparison with the real prize: prestige and a first book to be published by Yale University Press. Joy selected her best poems, titled the collection "Ashes and Sparks," and mailed the manuscript.

As prospective books piled up in the Yale Press office, a preliminary round of readings weeded out less promising submissions, while fifty or so more auspicious manuscripts were forwarded to the final judge and editor, Stephen Vincent Benét, one of America's best-known poets. Benét frequently contributed fantasy stories and antifascist pieces to the *Saturday Evening Post* and *The New Yorker,* and had won the Pulitzer Prize for his 1929 epic *John Brown's Body,* a book of verse Joy had treasured since she first read it in high school. "His poetry," Joy would write years later in tribute after Benét's death, "was exactly that which a young poet dreams of writing, which young poets of this America would sell their souls to write."

Yale University Press hired Benét in 1933, hoping he would generate the publicity needed to attract fresh voices and transform the series into a prestigious launching pad for young poets. It was a privilege, he said, to shepherd talented aspiring writers toward success;

so deeply did he believe in this ideal that he made a noble financial sacrifice during a time when so many vigilantly watched their wallets. Before Benét's tenure, winners received no monetary award —they could earn at most $100 if they sold their entire print run of five hundred copies—while Yale Press paid Benét $250 for reading manuscripts and writing a foreword to each winning book. Benét suggested that $250 was disproportionate and requested that Yale Press cut his pay to $150 and award $100 to each winner; the press agreed.

One hundred dollars was a sum the Davidmans could use right about then. The second half of 1936 brought several major expenses. Howard would be attending the University of Virginia in the fall; the family moved from 2277 Andrews Avenue down the street to number 1950; and there was an unforeseen expenditure: medical bills. It had become clear that Joy was seriously ill. Her lethargy was overwhelming, and her eyes, always prominent, began to protrude with alarming intensity. A Dr. Solomon Ginszberg diagnosed a thyroid condition, Graves' disease. He prescribed plenty of rest and a course of treatment: for one twenty-four-hour period each week, Joy was to fasten around her neck a collar containing pockets filled with radium.

Convalescing at home, neck encircled in radium, Joy continued composing poems while awaiting the verdict from Yale. *Poetry* magazine accepted more of her work and requested a fresh bio, which Joy sent in July:

> I am twenty-one years old, majored in English at Hunter College, graduating in 1934 with a couple of prizes, took an M.A. in English at Columbia University in 1935, and have since taught school for a year; hated it, but wrote some of my favorite poetry in school. (By the way, my fourth-term highschool [*sic*] students were almost the only people who said they understood my poetry.) I was born in New York, cling to Broadway and the movies, and hate the country except in small doses. Hobbies: playing

the piano, making orchestrations, and painting slightly Japanese water-colors. Have no talent for anything except literary research, mathematics, and writing.

Writes more prose than poetry—expects to write historical novels all her life.

Thank you again for saying you'd like to discuss my poems; it made my whole family feel proud.

Yours very truly,
Miss Joy Davidman

And for the biography; I am unmarried, now and I trust forever.

In August, when the summer heat cooked the city concrete, the Davidmans escaped on another family vacation. Clean country air would do Joy some good. They had gotten in the habit of renting a log cabin on a lake in the Maine woods. Joy loved burrowing into that great expanse of nature. She rowed around the lake and found blissful peace away from her parents. When the family returned home, there in the mound of mail was a letter from Stephen Vincent Benét.

Joy's poems had made the cut and found their way into Benét's hands, but he'd decided to turn her down. Nevertheless, he thought highly enough of her work to write a personal letter of encouragement—something he took time to do only for applicants in whom he saw great promise. Press on, he urged. Hone your craft, persevere. Joy had the raw talent, but as with her take on Keats's "Endymion," the excellence in her work was derivative. Her collection lacked relevance and a certain freshness. "What I keep looking for is the live nerve, the live person speaking," Benét said of his selection criteria. His advice: "Write some more—always trying to expand your range, always trying to see and hear more clearly, to get the things on the paper closer to the thing in your mind." Finally, Benét suggested that Joy submit a new manuscript in the future.

Benét's favorable critique softened the blow, but losing was still bitter. On August 18 Joy responded to the poet's remarks, managing to contain her disappointment:

> I am very glad you thought highly of my work, and I should like to thank you for your encouragement. You mention the influences which have affected my poetry (among which your own is not lacking); I am somewhat uneasily conscious of them nowadays, yet I feel they are fading rapidly from my more ambitious work.
>
> If I am still unpublished in two years' time, I shall take advantage of your invitation to submit another manuscript for the Yale Series of Younger Poets, and I trust I shall then send a manuscript more worthy of your consideration. I'll not weary you with any more conclusion than to say again I am grateful.

What was that "thing" that Benét coached emerging writers to harness and articulate? That was the question Joy needed to consider. The Younger Poets series was important because it served as a kind of "clinical chart" tracking the viewpoints of young American poets. As a collection, Joy's work didn't speak uniquely to her generation; neither was it avant-garde. She had to find her way, had to decide who she was and what she believed, and then channel that viewpoint into her poems.

Joy had abundant time to contemplate her situation during the months that followed. Her illness came with one perk: she was not well enough to return to the classroom in the fall of 1936. Instead she spent the academic year resting and reading. Every day, city papers ran stories about members of the Communist Party marching hungry people into relief offices and demanding attention, or rallying groups for demonstrations in Union Square or outside City Hall, carrying picket signs that read "Rich Dine, We Starve"; "We Want Food and Milk for Our Baby"; "Bread or Revolution." They waved the American flag, and they waved the Soviet flag with its golden hammer and sickle blazoned on bright red cloth. Communists seemed to be the only ones working on behalf of the vast disenfranchised segment of society. They marched in solidarity, united.

Dorothy Scheer's suicide was a catalyst for Joy's interest in the Communist Party of the United States of America, Joy later suggested, and she wasn't the only one whose interest grew in tandem with the consequences of the depression. When Joy graduated from Hunter, Party membership was 25,000; now it was nearing 75,000. Joy needed to speak openly with someone she knew and trusted. A Hunter classmate who lived nearby in the Bronx was a Party member, Joy knew. She knocked on her door. The woman told Joy first to "read the literature" and mentioned some books and pamphlets. "Then we'll talk some more," she said.

Among the "literature" was *New Masses,* a Marxist weekly literary magazine closely tied to the CPUSA. *New Masses* was a mouthpiece for the League of American Writers, a group founded in 1935 by some sixty authors—including Richard Wright, Jack Conroy, Langston Hughes, and Theodore Dreiser—on the principle that literature should be infused with social consciousness, and that writers can change the world. Headquartered in New York, the league had branches in major cities across the country. Membership was open to writers published in any language who lived in the United States and whose work was printed beyond local venues. Some eight hundred American writers banded together to "fight against imperialist war and fascism, defend the Soviet Union against capitalist aggression; for the development and strengthening of the revolutionary labor movement; against white chauvinism (against all forms of Negro discrimination or persecution)." Both *New Masses* and the league denounced ivory tower "art for art's sake" attitudes. Writers had a responsibility, they asserted, to promote a "proletarian revolution" in a "united front," and to "personally help to accelerate the destruction of capitalism and the establishment of a workers' government." A new society was on the horizon.

Among the leading causes of the CPUSA, *New Masses,* and the League of American Writers was supporting Spain's loyalists during the civil war that began in the summer of 1936, when General Francisco Franco and his fascist cohort commenced their overthrow of the democratically elected government. Hitler and Mussolini would eventually offer military aid to Franco's Nationalists, while Stalin dispatched reinforcements to the ruling Spanish government, the Republican loyalists representing "the people"—farmers, laborers, and the middle class. The Hollywood branch of the league managed to close off four city blocks for a bazaar to raise money for the Abraham Lincoln Brigade, a company of largely untrained American volunteer soldiers who fought alongside an international group of revolutionaries battling fascism on behalf of the oppressed Republicans. In New York City, the league raised awareness and funds for the North American Committee to Aid Spanish Democracy by hosting a manuscript sale at Manhattan's Barbizon-Plaza Hotel, where dozens of prominent league members—including William Carlos Williams, Booth Tarkington, H. G. Wells, Edna Ferber, Archibald MacLeish, Albert Einstein, and Edna St. Vincent Millay—donated for auction loose pages, whole chapters, and even complete manuscript drafts bearing marks of editors' pencils. The event raised enough money to buy several ambulances in Spain.

Poetry had published four more of Joy's poems in March, but she wasn't having much luck elsewhere. Although she reveled in her sabbatical from teaching, by her birthday in April, Joy seems to have felt that she was simply taking up space. The radium treatment was apparently working, and she would be well enough to return to teaching in the fall. Her mother put in a good word for her with a friend who carried some weight at the newly founded Queens College. Joy looked back on her earlier poetry and fascination with fantasy stories and thought she "was getting a little old for the flitting-butterfly stuff." At twenty-two, Joy said, "a girl begins to want serious purpose."

That purpose came into sharper focus after April 26, when she learned that Nazi aviators had dropped explosives on the peaceful Basque town of Guernica, then machine-gunned men, women, and children as they ran screaming from their burning homes. Joy had been following the war, but to her it had been little more than just another news item. Before Guernica, she said, "I was conscious of no

interest beyond a faint wish that the aggressors would make a quick job of it and end the bloodshed." Afterward, the gruesome reports of brutality prompted an unshakable urge to somehow help the helpless.

Joy's teaching experience further pushed her toward the conviction that capitalism was an infectious disease for which the only antidote was a socialist revolution. By fall, no Queens College position had come through, and Joy went back to teaching high school—this time at Theodore Roosevelt High in the Bronx. Joy's new students had little in common with the relatively refined Walton girls. They came from poorer families, and there was ethnic conflict. Irish kids were known to harass Jewish classmates, and despite the fact that nearly half of all new teachers hired by the New York City Board of Education during the depression were Jewish, anti-Semitism lurked in faculty rooms as well.

Joy hated teaching, and she hated Theodore Roosevelt High. She abhorred the ever lower education standards, which she blamed on a "no-leave-back" rule that shoveled students from one grade to the next with little regard for academic achievement or integrity. That practice, combined with what she considered a shoddy curriculum, made for multitudes of illiterate New Yorkers. "Anybody who ever tried to teach 'Ivanhoe' to second term Italian-Americans, who hardly knew English because it wasn't spoken at home, will understand the problem," she said.

Joy now saw the Party as more than a valiant agency of collective action; the organization also offered a literary community and a sense of purpose. "We knew with absolute conviction," said one communist, "that we were part of a vanguard that was destined to lead an American working class to a socialist revolution. There was just simply no question at all in your mind [about] who you were and what you were and why you were. What was the meaning of life? You had that answered."

Joy understood, with a certainty she'd never experienced before, that the Party offered what she needed. Even the curved wings of gulls in her Japanese paintings aroused her allegiance to the Soviet flag. "How sweet the scythe / the blade, the wing," she wrote in a poem called "Japanese Print." Now Joy had a fire inside her which overcame the lethargy that lingered. She took Benét's advice and channeled this "live nerve," creating poems that were closer to "the thing in her mind." Verses poured out of her. She wrote all the time, "in offices full of clacking typewriters, in classrooms, at public dinners (during speeches) etc." In September she wrote a four-part poem called "Letter to a Comrade." In 225 lines, the poem's speaker guides a comrade on a cross-country journey, urging him to look closely at the realities of American life, from urban to suburban to rural. Joy expresses a growing sense of disheartenment owing to what she saw as "an end to regional peculiarities," as she later explained in an article, a casualty of Hollywood movies and "automobile roads." Writers were sentimentalizing unique traditions from Georgia dialects to Oklahoma hog-killing methods.

In December 1937 Joy wrote a poem called "Prayer Against Indifference," which expresses the strength of her conviction that her conscience would not allow her to stand silently by while fascists crushed the masses—especially in Spain. The final stanza, Joy said, "is the sentiment that took me in" to the Communist Party.

> Let me have eyes I need not shut;
> Let me have truth at my tongue's root;
> Let courage and the brain command
> The honest fingers of my hand;
> And when I wait to save my skin
> Break roof and let my death come in.

Early in 1938 Joy arranged a meeting with her Hunter friend. On a wintry day, the pair started out on a walk through the Bronx. Joy eagerly reported that she was ready to join the revolution. "I believe," she said, that "the only decent future for me lies in a socialist state." Her friend nodded. Joy was directed to a large branch meeting downtown on the West Side. The meeting was open—far from a subversive summit requiring secret handshakes, as some believed. When everyone was seated, the chairman surveyed the crowd. "Any new members, any outsiders?" he asked. Joy stood up. Half a dozen others joined her. They all raised their right hands and recited the oath of allegiance to the Party, pledging to dedicate their lives to fighting for the working class, battling against Jim Crowism, defending the Soviet Union, saving America from the devastation of capitalism, and loving their country with the same passion Lenin bore for Russia.

Joy began dutifully attending "cell" or "unit" meetings, neighborhood gatherings of comrades with whom she discussed the issues that occupied her mind. Comrades conferred about strike tactics. Unit leaders delivered assignments, such as who was to hand out what leaflets on which street corner. "It was in this subterranean activity that the romanticism of their youth finally got to express itself," said the son of a couple who hosted local cell meetings. "Here they lived outside the norms of other mortals, breathed the intoxicating air of a world revolution, and plotted their impossible dreams." Members took secret names in anticipation of the day when the Party would go underground and the revolution would begin—as they all believed it would.

Joy received her Party card that summer, along with a book in which to record monthly dues. She chose the name Nell Tulchin, aligning herself with the shtetl peasants of her Russian heritage. Tulchin, her mother's birthplace, was also the setting for a proletariat novel Joy was working on—an outgrowth of her award-winning short story "Apostate." Both of her parents had been helpful. Her mother, in particular, supplied authentic facts and folk stories Joy was incorporating to create a believable portrait of a sensual, rebellious young woman bucking a culture of religious rules and rituals.

Joe and Jen were beginning to accept, perhaps even admire, their daughter's proactive pursuit of a writing career, even if that meant giving up teaching—for after all, she was seeing some success. They could not, however, abide her membership in the Communist Party. They could tolerate her opinions, even her disdain for what she deemed their "bourgeois" lifestyle. But it was a big leap from private opinion to Party membership. More important, her actions could damage Joe's and Jen's status as public servants on the city payroll. Joy was not inconspicuous about her politics. When an obligation required her presence at Board of Education headquarters, she showed up with a copy of the *Daily Worker* tucked under her arm. She stood on street corners distributing leaflets, informing passersby about meetings and lectures. She spread the gospel of Marx with the fervor of a new convert.

During this time, Joy's father was serving as either chairman, board member, or president of numerous community organizations working for social justice. He was active in a Bronx branch of the Democratic Party and the American ORT, a Jewish labor organization, and was president of the Jewish Teachers Association, whose bulletin which he edited raised money to help German Jewish exiles. For Joy, those organizations didn't hold the appeal of the CPUSA, and not just because they were part of her father's world. The Party was more than a humanitarian organization; it was a way of life.

Once an exile on the social fringe, Joy now filled her evenings with branch meetings, lectures, and parties. Years later, she acknowledged that the chance to meet men increased her motivation to attend Party functions. Other than a fleeting romance with a classmate from postgraduate courses she took at CUNY after Columbia—a fellow substitute high school English teacher named Abraham—Joy had dated little. Sexual promiscuity, however, was an established reality inside the Party, Joy would later admit, and a not altogether unpleasant byproduct of Party experiences that tried to meet deeper needs. Monumental rallies at Madison Square Garden, unfolding like spectacular urban renditions of rural tent revivals, kept her from feeling alone. "You were part of something big," recalled one of Joy's comrades. "And that made you feel worthwhile because you knew that your own minuscule efforts weren't going to do any huge thing for the revolution, but combined with twenty thousand other people, you felt that you really were going to make a difference in the world." The rallies had all the trappings of religious services, except that the folksongs were not called hymns, the speeches were not called sermons, and the venue did not have stained glass or a steeple.

Perhaps the greatest of these gatherings, the opening of the tenth annual convention of the CPUSA, was scheduled for the evening of May 26, 1938. Joy and her comrades stormed through the main entrance at Eighth Avenue between Forty-ninth and Fiftieth streets. On the outside, Madison Square Garden was a nondescript brick building with jagged fire escapes zigzagging down its façade like lightning bolts. The Garden doors opened at six o'clock; attendees paid from forty cents to $1.10 for a ticket. Thousands surged into the arena. Joy could feel the crowd crackling with anticipation as the time ticked toward 7:30, when the extravaganza would begin. Red-white-and-blue banners decorated the arena, bearing words of welcome and slogans: "Communism Is 20th-Century Americanism!" There were steelworkers from Pittsburgh, sharecroppers from California, orange pickers from Florida, and seamen from both coasts. Fifteen hundred delegates from every state took up the arena's front section. Once all the seats were filled, the crowd jammed the aisles. People sat on steps; thousands were turned away for lack of space.

Scores of Americans tuned their radios to CBS and listened as a commentator's voice, surging over the airwaves, began narrating the scene. At 7:30, hundreds of members of the Young Communist League paraded in the "March of Flags." The children's uniforms were brightly patriotic—white shirts with red ties and dark trousers for the boys, and red kerchiefs and dark skirts for the girls—starkly contrasting with the khaki uniforms of one hundred members of the Abraham Lincoln Brigade who marched with them.

At eight o'clock, all rose and united their voices in a resounding rendition of "The Star-Spangled Banner," followed by the "Internationale." Then the Fur Workers Union celebrated a recent strike victory by adding sixteen flower baskets to the bouquets that lined the length of the stage, like offerings at an altar.

William Foster, president of the Party, and General Secretary Earl Browder took the stage alongside state delegates and speakers, including a metalworker and a Florida housewife identified as Mrs. Wiggins. With her honey-colored hair, blue-green eyes, and aura of serenity, she appeared too youthful to be the mother of grown children. Such was the effect of dedicating one's heart to the Communist Party, observed the *Daily Worker,* the Party's paper. Mrs. Wiggins praised the Party for all that was well with her soul. "I never really lived until I joined the Party last year," she testified. "Now every moment has meaning and life has purpose well worth while."

Joy raised her fist in solidarity. She understood. The Party and its politics were becoming the nucleus for her social life and career. Her new life was full of new people and energy. There were dances, picnics, dinners. "One could totally live one's whole life totally within that culture," one comrade recalled. "There was no dividing line between the personal and the political, between the private and the social. It was all intertwined and intermingled."

Browder's speech was the climax of the night. As he stepped to the podium, a massive map was lowered behind him—the United States outlined in blue, with red and white keywords radiating from it, summarizing the Party's vision for the nation: "Jobs," "Security," "Democracy," and "Peace." President Roosevelt had kindled "sparks of hope" with his "fighting words" and progressive proposals, Browder said. But flames of regeneration were dying, leaving citizens to grope in the darkness. Browder laced his talk with religious rhetoric, part of a campaign to draw believers who rejected atheism but might sympathize with other Marxist principles. "Christian brotherhood and charity," Browder said, were social virtues "that we of no religion appreciate." He orated like a preacher, his voice undulating, and raised his clenched fist, pounding the podium for emphasis. "The people are beginning to ask, whence comes the light? They turn toward it, they look for its origin. They find the light of understanding, burning clearer and clearer . . . They trace the light to the lamp held high by the Communist Party!"

The crowds leaped to their feet, clenching their fists and raising them high. Joy saw that light. "I and twenty thousand like me," she wrote. "There we felt ourselves linked by that surge of spiritual power which unites all meetings of genuine worshipers, whatever they worship. 'A feeling of solidarity!'"

A FRESH COLLECTION OF poems piled up next to Joy's typewriter during the winter and spring of 1938, singing a rallying cry for revolution. One of those she felt most passionately about, "Spartacus, 1938," was written in honor of Ernst Thaelmann. A German laborer turned trade union organizer, Thaelmann joined the Communist Party in 1920 and swiftly rose through the ranks to become leader of the Communist Party of Germany. Hitler ordered him arrested along with other Party officials, and he remained a prisoner, enduring torture and toiling in a labor camp. These were the horrors that Joy could expose with her pen. She had found her calling. She had tapped into that "thing" in her mind.

· 4 ·

1938–1939

Despite all that the Communist Party brought into her life—community, purpose, literary inspiration—ambivalence lurked beneath the surface of Joy's consciousness. In the spring of 1938, she later wrote, she was "an arrogant and uncertain creature," politically dogmatic but dubious about her future as a writer. Was she good enough? It had been a full year since she last saw her work in print in the March 1937 issue of *Poetry.* Confidence broke through occasionally, spurring her to send off poems to magazines and literary journals. But as the mailman made the rounds to 1950 Andrews Avenue, Joy received rejection letter after rejection letter.

Still, hope prevailed over self-doubt. The deadline for this year's Yale Series of Younger Poets contest was fast approaching, and she would make good on her word to Stephen Vincent Benét about submitting another manuscript. Joy had long been a fan of his poetry; now she understood him to be something of a kindred spirit politically as well. While she couldn't be sure if he belonged to or supported the Communist Party, Benét would certainly appreciate the antifascist message suffusing her new body of work. Perhaps he could give her some reassurance. She sent him a note and enclosed some poems.

From Benét she needed two things: encouragement, and a letter of recommendation for the prestigious MacDowell Colony in New Hampshire, a secluded haven where writers and artists worked free from routine responsibilities and distractions. The MacDowell Colony was the birthplace of many of America's greatest contemporary musical scores, poetry anthologies, novels, sculptures, and paintings. Its alumni included Willa Cather, Edward Arlington Robinson, Thornton Wilder, and Stephen Benét himself. Acceptance there would validate Joy's talent, give her an opportunity to rub shoulders with notable literary figures, and provide her with space and uninterrupted time to complete her novel. Joy knew that acceptance was a long shot. Talent was said to be the only criterion, but applicants' names and publication histories carried weight.

The response she received from Benét was more than she could have hoped for. Enormously impressed by Joy's new work, he wrote a personal letter of recommendation directly to Marian MacDowell, who had founded the colony thirty years earlier in honor of her late husband, the acclaimed composer Edward MacDowell. Joy felt deeply honored. On April 2 she sent Benét a heartfelt expression of gratitude: "I have to thank you, not only for your very kind letter of recommendation but also for something more subtle. When one is beset with rejection slips and tormented by distrust of one's work and ability, it is a comforting thing to receive encouragement from a man who knows. And so I am very grateful for your letter; it will justify the sunny moments in which I tell myself how good I am."

Full of hope, Joy addressed an envelope to Yale University Press and inserted the manuscript she dreamed would become her first book, *Letter to a Comrade*. "Dear Sir," she wrote in a cover letter, "I am enclosing a manuscript which I wish to enter in the Yale Series of Younger Poets competition. I am not quite twenty-three years old and have never published a volume of poetry." She indicated the pieces that had been published or were scheduled to be—five in all—and affixed a table of contents listing a total of forty-two poems. Several, including "Resurrection," dated back to her Hunter College years, but the vast majority had been written during the past twenty months, as her politics had aligned with the Party. Joy slipped the cover letter into the envelope and shipped off her manuscript. The waiting game began again.

Three days after sending her manuscript to Yale University Press, Joy saw her name in *New Masses* for the first time. On April 5 the magazine published her poem "Strength Through Joy"—the first of many Joy Davidman poems *New Masses* would run—in which she portrays Hitler as a grotesque sadist playing God:

> When any man is gnawed by the mouth of a cannon
> I grow new teeth. I am filled with iron,
> with fire and exhalations; I am magnificent . . .
> And when you die
> be sure to use my name upon your lips
> for your last word . . . your death shall be
> a suitable decoration of gold at my breast
> and I shall come bearing slaughter in the hand like bloodred
> berries
> seeded with poison; glory for me,
> glory, glory for me! and a bright crown of red berries.

When Joy opened the issue of *New Masses,* she saw pages filled with exposition echoing the thrust of *Letter to a Comrade*. The staff and readers of *New Masses* were angry. Angry at Hitler, angry at Mussolini for bombing Barcelona, and angry at Japan for tormenting China. They were incensed about the Scottsboro Boys. But they were angriest of all about complacent people who sit back and grumble about the state of the world yet take no action. Such people clearly didn't understand that isolation from outrages was "the surest way" to land America in "the most terrible war of all."

Shortly thereafter, Joy had a personal meeting with Marian MacDowell. A small woman, plainly dressed, wearing her gray hair in a high pompadour, Mrs. MacDowell had the look of a Victorian schoolmarm and the temperament of a competent governess—efficient, authoritative, and maternal. Joy initially felt "stiff and shy" in

Mrs. MacDowell's presence, despite Benét's support and her recent publication in *New Masses*. "I tried very hard to sound like a professional writer," Joy wrote to her later, but "you . . . put me at my ease very soon." Mrs. MacDowell was not the austere matron her appearance suggested. Indeed, part of her appeal was that she provided the validation for young artists and writers which so many parents did not. Joy's attitude was one of reverence and gratitude for this woman who took her seriously. Still, Joy didn't think she stood much chance of going to the colony. The decision to offer Joy a place was ultimately not Mrs. MacDowell's; her primary role by that point was to "superintend correspondence," while the admittance committee examined applications and made final selections. She thanked Benét for introducing Joy and assured him that his letter would go to the committee, which met in late April.

Later that spring, still awaiting word from Yale University Press, Joy received surprising news from the MacDowell Colony. Having reviewed her application, together with Benét's recommendation letter, the admissions panel had decided to offer her a spot. Having all but convinced herself she would not be accepted, Joy was elated. She arrived in Peterborough, New Hampshire, several weeks later. On July 2 she signed the registry at Colony Hall, the colonial-style house where meals were served and post-dinner socializing took place. She settled into her room in the women's residence, a Revolutionary period farmhouse situated a quarter mile from the men's stone lodge.

Joy had spent many family vacations in the woods and valleys of the northeastern states, but this was different. She had never been away from her parents or New York City for any appreciable length of time. This was liberation, a first real bid for freedom. The colony had few rules—the cardinal one being that visits to others' studios were by invitation only—but one of the guiding principles was "Nobody is expected to do anything he is not inclined to do."

The breakfast bell sounded early each morning. At 7:30 the dining hall offered a hearty meal before colonists scattered to their respective studios. By July the five-hundred-acre MacDowell property proclaimed the full earthy elegance of rural New England in summer.

Birds sang. Tiny wood creatures scampered about. Great boulders were cloaked in dense gray-green moss. The sun poured down in shafts of light amid the spruce, birch, and fir trees. Joy breathed in the pine-scented air. It was easy for her to believe she was in an enchanted Fairyland; the place was straight out of *Phantastes*, one of her favorite George MacDonald fairy tales.

Joy was assigned to Mansfield Studio. A pleasant walk through the forest from Colony Hall, Mansfield was a simple one-room clapboard cottage with a fireplace and modest furnishings—a cot for naps, a chair, and abundant desk space. A stack of wood outside the door would keep her warm during the occasional chilly New England summer day. Joy unpacked her typewriter, drafts, and sheaves of paper, and set to work on her novel and new poems. She had never experienced such profound, sustained quiet and solitude. Around noon each day, a boy drove up in a truck and quietly placed a basket on her doorstep, then left without a word. Inside the basket was her lunch: a thermos of hot tea or coffee, a sandwich, and often a special treat from the cook.

For most, the workday generally ended around five, when writers and artists closed up their studios and set out to exercise. Some played tennis on nearby courts, jogged along the bridle path, enjoyed croquet on the lawn, or hiked through the woods—one of Joy's favorite things to do. Dinners were delicious. At dusk, the pale birch trees looked like magical white beams of light against a backdrop of evergreen, but they vanished into darkness with the forest when the sun set.

There was an unspoken understanding that colonists were not to return to their studios after dinner. Open flames were the only source of light along the trails and in the cabins, and Mrs. MacDowell didn't want to risk a fire. On the whole, people respected Mrs. MacDowell; some even referred to her as a "fairy godmother." Each year she provided fifty to sixty artists and writers with the gift of time and space in which to create. Linens were supplied, rooms cleaned, meals prepared. Those accepted into the colony were asked to contribute $16 per week, if possible, but fellowships were always available for those who couldn't afford to pay. Mrs. MacDowell's house, Hillcrest, was set apart from Colony Hall and the men's and women's quarters, but she nevertheless had a hand in the goings-on, and while freedom was paramount, so was order. Colonists murmured that her prohibition of after-dark studio visits was her prudish way of discouraging hanky-panky.

Joy sought out kindred spirits and found plenty. When she wanted to escape from the crowd, she could lose herself in the library, with its full sets of lavishly bound classics and contemporary works, some inscribed by the authors themselves. But here at the colony, there was no urgency to lose herself. Joy felt part of something. She was accepted. The norm was that there was no norm. There was camaraderie, understanding. Nights at Colony Hall were filled with conversation, cowboy pool, chess, checkers, and poetry readings. This summer in particular, Mrs. MacDowell noted, there was "a rather exquisite binding together in a bridge of Colony unity." This unity pleased her. Sixty-two poets, fiction writers, playwrights, composers, painters, sculptors, and etchers came to the MacDowell Colony during 1938. Among those who overlapped with Joy were Stephen Benét's brother William Rose (Bill) Benét, writers Carl Carmer and James Still, composer Aaron Copland, painter Charlotte Blass, and Jean Starr Untermeyer, an older poet and active member of the League of American Writers, who became a beloved friend.

It wasn't long into her stay at the colony that Joy received a response from Yale University Press. This time she was not disappointed. Stephen Vincent Benét believed she was the voice of a generation. He had chosen her as recipient of the 1938 Yale Younger Poets Award. "Here," he said, "is what an intelligent, sensitive, and vivid mind thinks about itself and the things of the modern world." Throughout the second half of July, letters between Joy and Benét discussing editorial choices flew between New York City and Peterborough. He sensed limitations in the title *Letter to a Comrade*. Joy rethought it. She saw his point. Hoping to use the title of one of the poems as the book's title, she tried out several alternatives: "In Praise of Iron," "Survey Mankind," and "Waltzing Mouse." But those didn't sit right either. Benét ultimately came around to *Letter to a Comrade,* which pleased Joy: "I am glad you prefer the original title, for I find myself unable to think of the book by any other," she told him.

"I am sending you a revised table of contents and should like to give you a free hand in making any rearrangements or omissions you think necessary," Joy wrote Benét. She sent eight new poems she wished to be part of the book, including "Twentieth-Century Americanism," a version of an Earl Browder Party slogan that could be found on banners at Madison Square Garden rallies: "Communism Is 20th-Century Americanism." She told Benét that when she saw the table of contents, she would cut older work to make room. Benét responded with suggestions to omit five poems, including "Endymion" and "Resurrection."

"By all means leave them out," Joy replied. "They are all, I am glad to say, early work; Resurrection, for instance, was done when I was eighteen, and I suppose it was sentimental affection that prompted me to include it." She had written thirty new poems since submitting the manuscript. "I wish that I could find more of the old stuff that I don't like at all," she told Benét. They tossed around the idea of dividing the book into sections but decided against it. She asked if she would need permission from *Poetry* and *New Masses* to reprint pieces that had run in their pages. "I am sorry to give you so much trouble," she added, "but you know I am quite inexperienced in these things and need a good deal of assistance." There was one decision about which Joy was certain and firm. "The dedication of the book I should like to run as follows," she instructed. "To Ernst Thaelmann who will not know."

In late July, Benét sent her a copy of the preface he'd written for her book. "It will be obvious enough, to anyone who reads *Letter to a Comrade,* that the heroes of the Twenties are not Miss Davidman's heroes nor their demons her demons," he noted.

> Because of her power, her vividness, and her sharp expression of much that is felt and thought by many of her own generation, I hope that Miss Davidman's book will reach a rather larger audi-

> ence than that generally reserved for the first book of verse. For sometimes you may learn almost as much about a generation by reading its poetry as by making graphs and collecting voluminous statistics. This is a generation that knew the Depression in its 'teens, the War not at all. It is just now beginning to be articulate. And you will find plenty of indignation here, but not a willingness to accept frustration.
>
> Miss Davidman can see, with accuracy and freshness, the thing in front of her eyes.

After reading Benét's tribute, Joy ran around the colony showing it off in a burst of pride and then wrote him a letter of profuse gratitude: "Thank you very much for the preface, which, speechless with pride, I have been showing to my friends here. I do not think any more could be said for my poetry than you have done."

Benét took care not to scrub the book of flaws or elevate it to a masterpiece. Joy had "a very considerable command of technique," he said, but "there are echoes here, as there are in almost any first book, and there are a few practice pieces." Such is typical in a young poet stretching herself, exercising her craft. Benét felt that almost everything else about Joy's work was exceptional. "There is a richness of imagery here, a lively social consciousness, a varied command of forms and a bold power." Years later Joy would write Benét's obituary for *New Masses:* "The critical introductions he wrote [for Yale Younger Poets Award winners] seized upon our half-formed meanings and made passionate sense of them; seized our groping emotions, our uncertain technique, and showed us the way toward growth. There never was an editor at once so kind and so brilliant."

Joy asked Benét to send the proofs to her New York address. The date of her return to the Bronx was not set, but she would likely be home by early September. With the important editorial decisions out of the way, her first book was on schedule for fall publication. By late July her novel was almost finished. She felt confident about it, although she knew that one of her weaknesses was overusing adjectives and lush descriptions. "I'm apt to splash colors about like an impressionist painter," she confessed to fellow colonist and friend James Still, a poet from the South. She was growing as a writer in ways that would have been impossible outside the artistic fellowship the colony provided. Jim Still described to her the time-consuming labor he dedicated to each sentence; from him she learned "that admirable trick of understatement and quiet strength and precision of detail."

In August *New Masses* published "Prayer Against Indifference," and Joy's stay at the colony began winding down. She finished a play, though it would never be produced, wrote several poems, and developed an intense crush on Bill Benét. Nearly thirty years Joy's senior, he did not return her affection. In coming months, Joy would write a series of sonnets similar to those she wrote in college—impassioned, dark, obsessive. "She is ostentatious of her love," begins one sonnet.

> Running to everyone; see how I am hurt,
> Here is his name I continually repeat
> Like slow drops of water dribbling upon my head,
> Here is the unmistakable color of my blood;
> Here are the wounds upon my hands and feet.
> Examine my body, see it stripped upon the bed
> And admire the marks made by love and loneliness.

Another Bill Benét–inspired poem would be sillier: "I hate the thought of work, / When you are in Wisconsin / And I am in New York."

Nevertheless, for now Joy savored the last days of the summer that changed her life. "I had a high time improving my beer-drinking and sitting for my portrait," she wrote to Jim Still, who had departed earlier. "Charlotte Blass did it; and it came out very well—a sort of female Thinker brooding over beer."

Not only had she achieved professional success, but also her personality and personal life blossomed. The colony did for Joy what college does for most young adults. Years later Joy reflected on the summer of 1938 in a letter to Marian MacDowell: "I'd never been allowed away from [my parents] or permitted to make friends. So I knew nothing of how to get along with other people, and the Colony was really a new world to me. I got the most important part of my education there; it was almost like being born again." In Peterborough she felt accepted in a way she had never experienced before—not with peers, not in the Party, and certainly not at home. "It seems almost incredible, but at the Colony in 1938 I learned for the first time that grownups—real grown people of thirty and more, married and everything, could have *fun;* that they could relax and play and forget about dignity and make silly delightful jokes."

Joy left New Hampshire in late August feeling strong and healthy. "I praise my youth," she began a poem she called "Through Transitory." With the first print run of *Letter to a Comrade* soon to be churned out at the press, she was on the brink of a new life, about to be thrust into the red-hot spotlight of New York's literary left.

JOY'S RETURN TO the real world was bittersweet. "New York, much as I love it, doesn't keep me yet from missing the Colony," she wrote to Jim Still on September 1, shortly after her return. But although sad to be separated from the colony and all it represented, Joy was reminded that she was on the very cusp of her dreams. Yale University Press issued an official press release, and on September 4 the *New York Times* broadcast her triumph to the world: "Stephen Vincent Benét, editor of the Yale Series of Younger Poets, published by Yale University Press, has announced that the winner of this year's competition is Joy Davidman of New York. Her book of poems, 'Letter to a Comrade,' will be published in October."

The League of American Writers' fall bulletin listed *Letter to a Comrade* alongside books recently published by other members, including Ernest Hemingway, Granville Hicks, and Langston Hughes, whose essay "Writers and the World," on the issue's first page, expressed what Joy felt was the purpose of her new literary life and identity. Hughes wrote: "Words must now be used to make people believe and do. Writers who have the power to use words in terms of belief and action are responsible to that power not to make people believe in the wrong things. And the wrong things are (surely everyone will agree) death instead of life, suffering instead of joy, oppression instead of freedom—whether it be freedom of the body or of the mind . . . Such words can be of more value to humanity than food to the hungry or garments to the cold."

Joy paid a visit to the *New Masses* headquarters on Lexington Avenue and Twenty-seventh Street, where one of the magazine's editors, Norman Rosten, was assembling a group of young poets to sift the submission slush pile and solicit new pieces from established writers. The work was on a volunteer basis for the sake of the revolution, but Joy took it on, hoping she could eventually get a paying job out of it. A return to teaching was not off the table; she had to earn a living, and only time would tell what opportunities her literary success would bring her way. Having "Yale Younger Poets Award winner" attached to her name would surely open doors, but Joy tempered her expectations, bracing herself against the inevitable negative reviews that would threaten her self-confidence and possibly ground her career before it took off.

Norman, with whom she became fast friends, explained the criteria for eligible poems: selections must deal "with acute 'social' material as much as possible" and should be utilitarian, capable of immediate influence, accessible to blue-collar workers, and oriented toward the urban and industrial without a whiff of the bourgeois. In theory, the magazine's readership included dockhands and coal miners, whom the bourgeois presumed to prefer ball games over novels, or so Joy and her new colleagues believed. Communists contended that the ruling class used highbrow language to further alienate "the people." Critiquing the work of poet H. H. Lewis several years later, Joy explained: "As the political and social content of your poetry becomes more complex, the poems and their language tend to become obscure. You must remember that only a working class audience can create or respond to great poetry nowadays, and that working class audience will rightly reject involved, obscure, and fancy language in poetry. In fact, the best working rule for all poetry is 'Keep it simple.'"

The bourgeois and Communist Party positions were both condescending, each in its own way. As one of Joy's *New Masses* colleagues admitted in retrospect, "I think that we may have identified as radical values what were really intellectual values and assumed they were the same." Joy became dogmatic to the point of prioritizing content over quality, and Norman trusted her judgment. When a submission from John Malcolm Brinnin arrived, she told Norman she thought the poems exciting but too cerebral. Give him three years and he'll come of age, she predicted. Norman agreed, and followed their conversation with a rejection letter to Brinnin, explaining that he and Joy felt that Brinnin was too much a "poet's poet, a precious poet . . . The question of 'popular' understanding is very important for a revolutionary magazine." They would not compromise by publishing poems, no matter how superb, that didn't align with their ideology. "The revolution must go on—even with lousy poetry!"

Joy was thrilled by the pulse and passion of the *New Masses* editorial offices, teeming with newsroom staples like typewriters, cigarette smoke, and men. A poster of John Reed hung on one wall. Here was purpose. She took the initiative to solicit poetry reviews from acclaimed new colony connections, including Bill Benét, who ignored her. Norman, pleased with Joy's ambition and proud to welcome aboard a Yale Younger Poet whose Party-line poetry had won mainstream acclaim, offered Joy a position as his assistant and a modest salary. "*She's a great poet!*" he told Brinnin. "I believe Joy Davidman will outshine us all."

But doubt assailed Joy when she held her book for the first time. "I can no longer read the poems in it with any feeling they're mine," she wrote to friends from the colony. "I'm not writing quite the same way any more, and the lack of discipline in some of this stuff horrifies me." She felt all the more grateful for Benét's excisions. "I should have done worse if Stephen Benét hadn't (bless him) sternly taken the horrors out," she told another poet. Nevertheless, she was proud of the book and thrilled by its red cover. ("They would do me in red!")

The force with which Joy expressed her political convictions in her poetry earned both praise and criticism from reviewers. A NEW CITY-BORN POET read the headline in the *New York Herald Tribune* above a review by leftist poet and prominent League of American Writers member Ruth Lechlitner. She noted Joy's "masculine diction" and pegged her poetry as a reaction against the spiritual, while placing Joy in a grand tradition in American verse rife with "intense nationalism, sometimes blindly patriotic, sometimes devotedly critical."

All reviewers agreed that Joy showed great promise. The poet and critic R. P. Blackmur, writing in *Partisan Review,* noted the merits of her work: "She has respect for the language, for the traditions of poetry, and for her own intelligence; she is forthright and what is more important she is candid . . . she writes with authority." But he took issue with her political expression: "The spirit which conceives and the intellect which articulates the predominant element of protest in her poems are not entirely hers, not digested, not matured, but are a non-incorporated framework borrowed perhaps from the land of the *New Masses* where the best of these poems previously appeared . . . She has . . . permitted her sensibility to be violated by the ideas which have attracted her." The *Kenyon Review*'s critic felt that she had displayed no "integration of spirit and sensibility and method," but added that "the compulsive power of her feeling cannot but persuade one to foresee a quiet dignity of achievement, provided that she ignore the demands of popular communication which surely her social and economic interests and her recent extra-book publications impressively put upon her." The *Kenyon* write-up was one of many that employed the words "keen" and "sensitivity."

Joy took the criticism in stride, choosing to focus on the fact that nearly every review was more positive than negative. "[I] prepared myself heroically for attack, sealed myself into an armor of indifference—and then they patted me on the back." There was one, though, that got to her. *Poetry* magazine published the most harsh criticism of Joy's incorporation of politics into her work. The reviewer, poet Oscar Williams, agreed that Joy was deserving and showed promise, but he was disappointed by her "prosaic" perceptions of the world around her. "A poet's politics must come out of his poetry, and too much of Miss Davidman's poetry comes from her politics. Poets are leaders and not camp followers." The *New York Times*'s reviewer disagreed, declaring, "It is surprising, in view of much current verse, how little Miss Davidman's explicit political creed interferes with the imaginative dimensions of her work."

Joy vented to poet Kenneth Porter, an acquaintance, about the *Poetry* review: "The only thing that got me angry, was to have Oscar Williams (who is surely the world's worst poet) tell me he'd made his debut as a poetry reviewer by slamming me for Poetry and go on to say that if I followed his instructions I might some day learn to write. I had just rejected his awful masterpieces at the New Masses, but was too kind to tell him so. One of his latest lines, I think, beats anything yet: 'God lets the planets fall out of his hair.' Dandruff? bugs?"

By and large, though, reviewers were kind. With newfound acclaim, clout, and initiative, Joy began pitching reviews at *New Masses,* publishing her first at the end of December.

JOY RANG IN 1939 "with whiskey and headaches and remorse," she joked in a melodramatic letter to a MacDowell Colony friend. "Everybody here is sick and tormented by bad weather, especially me, lying gasping on my back . . . My family has just returned from the funeral of one of our least loved in-laws; the world is gray and rainy; the cat has scratched my hand; and my brother insists that I look at a scientific book of his filled with pictures of gorillas showing emotion." Joy's dreary depiction of the new year was little more than tongue-in-cheek hyperbole. In the same letter she portrayed a lifestyle that, one year earlier, she could not have imagined would be her own. Nineteen thirty-eight had given birth to a spectacular personal, political, and professional transformation. Literary parties, friendships with acclaimed writers, influence as both editor and critic —it was all so new and exciting. Joy couldn't resist dropping names and throwing her weight around: "I've had another monosyllabic letter from Jim Still the Vanishing American. Next time he sends me anything it will probably be a piece of birchbark inscribed 'How!' And I met Boris at a party; was too embarrassed to do anything but yodel 'Hello, how are you!' and seek the furthest corner. But my conscience bothered me so that I removed from the New Masses' next issue my review of his book, which contained some of my best dirty cracks. The book deserved them too. (Thus conscience doth make cowards, etc.)"

The new year promised greatness—for her, for the nation, and for New York City. Nearly every public space she passed was plastered with advertisements for the World's Fair, proclaiming the "Dawn of a New Day." Optimism sweetened the bitterly cold January air. The depression had not altogether lifted, but the pace of economic rehabilitation was quickening. After years of deprivation, Americans generally had little interest in becoming encumbered with Europe's troubles. New Yorkers diverted their attention to the World's Fair, set to open in Queens that April after years of anticipation. In 1935 a group of businessmen led by Grover Whalen had envisaged an elaborate bonanza showcasing social and technical developments that would enhance small-town American life, in turn enhancing universal harmony. The fair's official theme was "Building the World of Tomorrow." It would be "everyman's fair," the Board of Designers said. Hundreds of extravagant exhibits would display a future promising world peace and a dishwasher in every kitchen. "The plain American citizen will be able to see here what he could attain for his community and for himself by intelligent co-ordinated effort and will be made to realize the interdependence of every contributing form of life and work." Whalen's rhetoric was utopian. He and his business partners prided themselves on creating jobs and buoying the nation's spirit. For seventy-five cents, anyone could see the future.

All Joy saw was a ruse. The whole thing, she felt, was just another capitalist moneymaking scheme built on the backs of laborers who wouldn't get their due. Grover Whalen was a lot like Christopher Marlowe's Faustus, she suggested in a poem called "The Devil Will Come," where she riffs on the tale of Faustus—a German scholar who rejects logical means of prospering in society in favor of magic—and Mephistopheles, the devil to whom Faustus sells his soul.

Joy saw all of life through her Party-line worldview, and her literary career had fully merged with her commitment to communism. Norman gave her the power to select submissions autonomously while he focused on his own writing. Not everyone was as pleased by her performance. At *New Masses,* "the decisive factors influencing the publication of poetry and stories principally related to the kind of material submitted (which was already self-selected due to the frankly revolutionary and 'proletarian culture' orientation of the 'Third Period') and the tastes of the particular editor who appears to have had free rein," writes Alan Wald, a scholar of the mid-twentieth-century literary left who interviewed many of Joy's acquaintances in the 1980s and 1990s. That editor was Joy. One writer, Sender Garlin, dubbed her the "Poetry Czarina."

So much had changed. Now she was in the position of having to choose between literary parties and speaking engagements. She received an invitation from Willard Maas, who was becoming known for throwing bohemian soirees in his Brooklyn Heights loft and dinner parties on his rooftop terrace set against the glorious, glittering backdrop of Manhattan's skyline. Joy had to decline because she'd been asked to speak at the left-leaning Young Artist Association. In the meantime, she had a party of her own in the works—"a sort of musical-literary conglomeration," she called it, set for January 21—so she replied to Maas's invitation with an invitation of her own. Her social life was becoming as fast-paced as her career. Tickets for the Young Artist Association event were sold in advance, and Joy drew a good crowd despite snow and subfreezing temperatures. Hers was one of a series of talks, readings, and panels she would participate in that winter and spring—including a Poetry Society event scheduled for March, and various League of American Writers functions. The poet's life, she said in her lectures, must not be lived inside an ivory tower: "[Writers] must seize the media for widest expression." In the modern age, that meant writing screenplays and radio plays.

The Party smiled on members who went to Hollywood in order to reach the masses through film. Joy was considering going herself, if Metro-Goldwyn-Mayer would give her a shot. In an effort to import new talent, the studio had written to English department chairs at colleges around the country—particularly on the East Coast—soliciting recommendations for its junior screenwriting program. MGM was seeking promising young people who had earned recognition for literary excellence and who would be interested in coming on board for a six-month apprenticeship in script writing. Hunter College's English department chair, Blanche Colton Williams, submitted Joy's name, together with a copy of "Apostate" as a writing sample. Joy didn't know if she would receive an answer. She didn't fully understand what the junior screenwriting program entailed, except that it promised prestige and adventure, as well as a new platform: California was home to political kindred spirits and thriving branches of the Communist Party and the League of American Writers.

In the meantime, other professional opportunities presented themselves—so many that she had to turn some down. Selden Rodman, founder of the progressive journal *Common Sense,* wrote her to solicit poems. Joy hadn't been writing short poems lately because she was composing a long radio play. She told Rodman she had nothing suitable on hand but hoped to contribute in the future. For now there were events to organize and talks to give. "Capitalism divorced [poetry] from the people," she preached to crowds. "Our refinement and obscurity smack of degeneracy and snobbism." The duty of poets was to speak to and for the masses—to create "songs of the people." Joy objected to the argument that poetry should not teach. Indeed, it should not teach *didactically,* but it should incite indignation, courage, and hope through beauty, truth, and ideas.

Such opinions, combined with the fact that she was Jewish, communist, female, and twenty-three years old, made Joy a most unlikely recipient of a prize awarded by the conservative National Institute of Arts and Letters (now the American Academy of Arts and Letters). The National Institute, whose membership was by nomination only, was founded in 1898 by a group of political and literary figures including Mark Twain, Henry Adams, Theodore Roosevelt, William Dean Howells, Childe Hassam, and Edward MacDowell. Its goal was to nurture American art and literature, in part by honoring excellence through prestigious awards and prize money. But the decorous literature celebrated at the turn of the century was not the literature of the 1920s and 1930s. Older members argued that art should be about beauty; they feared "the impending degradation of the Institute from a conservative supporter of high literary standards, style, dignity, taste, sincerity, personal character, to a hot bed of radicalism." But Sinclair Lewis, who declined election in 1921, publicly condemning the institute for pressuring American writers "to become safe, polite, obedient and sterile," spoke for a younger generation when he vehemently contended that the institute "cuts itself off from so much of what is living and vigorous and original in American letters . . . It does not represent the America of today," he said. "It represents only Henry Wadsworth Longfellow."

That was precisely Joy's point when she told audiences that Whitman's work "exhale[d] a smell as ancient . . . as the catacombs." The institute barely acknowledged the depression, the New Deal, or international affairs, and when in 1933 one member suggested an anti-Hitler resolution, another member, Harrison Morris—the resident anti-Semite—asked, "Was it a Jew who uttered it?"

Now the old guard was clashing with younger members, including Stephen Vincent Benét, who commented that the institute was run by "incompetent old men" wearing monocles and favoring "mediocrities and suppressability." Benét was an officer of the institute and served on the Department of Literature Nomination Committee. In a clear demonstration that the younger generation was taking over, he and fellow officers voted at their annual meeting on January 18 to award Joy a prize of $1,000 from the Russell Loines Memorial Fund. The announcement was made that night at the annual dinner, where Robert Frost was accorded the institute's version of a lifetime achievement award. The next day's *New York Times* and *New York Herald Tribune* reported the news before Joy had even received official notification. A few days later, the institute's secretary, Grace Vanamee, sent Joy a letter together with the check, a receipt for her to sign and return, and the institute's "yearbook"—a small purple booklet bound with gold thread. Mrs. Vanamee suggested that Joy read page fifty, "that you may know something of the body which has paid you this high compliment, and also know something of the history of the Russell Loines Fund." Joy read with great interest that in 1931 the fund had given its first award to Frost. To be even remotely linked with Robert Frost—what an honor! Joy didn't know, however, that the Loines family had expressed outrage and dismay when the institute selected Frost, an accomplished poet. "The award was to be made, not to a poet who had arrived, but to one who gave great promise," the Loines family insisted. Now, eight years later, Benét put Joy forward as an ideal candidate.

His enthusiasm was not unanimous. Harrison Morris, for one, was indignant upon learning that the recipient's name was Joy Davidman. "There is an odor of Semitism in both cognomens," he remarked in a letter to Mrs. Vanamee. "Where we have fallen to!" Morris signed the letter "Yours rather woefully . . ." Vanamee responded sympathetically: "Miss Davidman is certainly a Jewess. She has not yet deigned to send me an acknowledgement of my special delivery letter containing the $1,000." In fact, Joy *had* responded to the secretary; their letters crossed in the mail. "I am extremely grateful to the Institute for recognizing my work in this way," Joy wrote sincerely. "Will you please convey my heartfelt thanks to the committee or other body which made the award?"

Joy was unaware of the hateful behind-the-scenes conversation, and the Russell Loines Award only added to the jubilance of her party. On January 21 snow lay sprinkled like confectioner's sugar over a sheet cake of ice as she made her way to 160 West Seventy-third Street, where the party in the Upper West Side studio of George Spiro, a comrade who operated under the pseudonym "George Marlin"—a surname derived from "Marx" and "Lenin." The party began at 8:30 P.M. A pianist played while Joy mingled, drink in hand, among a motley mix of family, college friends, and literary acquaintances. Belle Kaufman was there, along with an assortment of family schoolteacher friends, whose presence reminded Joy of the life she still desperately wanted to avoid. Just looking at them made her down one drink after another, until she had overdone it. "I was so drunk that I could hardly see, let alone think," she later wrote to Willard Maas, also in attendance, adding, "I wanted to talk to you about a lot of things Saturday night—especially my own book, naturally, being the egoist I am." When she stood up in front of the crowd to read a selection of her poetry, her vision was so blurred that she could hardly focus on the pages. "I shall never forget the horror," she said. "Fortunately, my memory was working—Scotch usually stimulates it, and I managed to keep from drifting off into Shelley." After groaning in bed all the next day, she joked that she didn't know if her hangover was due to the schoolteachers or the Scotch. Regardless, shortly thereafter Joy received another bit of welcome professional news: for reasons she didn't know or disclose, the Board of Examiners had denied her teacher's license application.

JOY BECAME INCREASINGLY involved in the League of American Writers, even volunteering to recruit others. "It's the logical organization for writers with left-wing sympathies," she wrote to Kenneth Porter. The league was the only literary organization taking strong "United Front action," she told him, using the slogan coined by the Comintern in the 1920s, referring to all unions, federations, societies, groups, and guilds that were proactive in pursuing the collective goals of the far left. "We've just published, for instance, a pamphlet listing anti-Semitic people and publications in this country with their inter-relations; a shocking list," she informed Porter.

That the Poetry Society was not such an organization became patently clear to Joy when she addressed the group at a meeting on March 30. "Good God, what an assemblage of pathetic hangers-on of the arts," she remarked afterward. "I mentioned politics and was nervously shushed . . . How the blazes do people expect to write poetry in a vacuum? I told 'em so, but I imagine each listener mentally excepted himself from my accusations." She had no respect for conventional types who stiffly omitted religion and politics from polite conversation, "pathetic old ladies who gather in societies and kneel before the altar of 'Poetry.'"

Joy volunteered to help organize a counter-event sponsored by the League of American Writers, a symposium chaired by poet Genevieve Taggard and featuring three progressive British poets: W. H. Auden, Louis MacNeice, and Christopher Isherwood. The event, titled "Modern Trends in English Poetry and Prose," was to be held at the Keynote Club at 201 West Fifty-second Street, at the northern edge of Times Square, on April 6 at 8:30 P.M., and was in part a fund-raiser to support Spanish refugees. The league's secretary, Franklin Folsom, touted the symposium as a prime example of the organization's efforts "on behalf of the professional work of writers."

The evening didn't start out as smoothly as Joy might have hoped. More than three hundred people arrived—including packs of liberal college students eager to save the world—but the three speakers did not. They had been directed to the wrong location, and the event had to be delayed by nearly two hours as writers were dispatched to fetch them. When the forum finally did begin, it was clear that the speakers had not been fully briefed on the program. "There was much speaking from behind the curtain," noted one league member, Millen Brand. "Joy Davidman of the large eyes [was] very much in evidence." At last, Genevieve Taggard, the appointed moderator, came to the front and introduced MacNeice, who then looked at Auden. Auden, poetically disheveled with a flop of blond hair and drooping socks, looked at MacNeice. And then both men signaled Taggard. Auden wanted to speak first. After an awkward moment, Taggard said, "I will now introduce Mr. Auden." After that bumbling beginning, Auden launched into what was supposed to be a talk that toed the Party line.

"Joy Davidman and Genevieve Taggard . . . were very serious, about art, about the revolution, about Spain & about their indivisibility," observed Selden Rodman, who was a good friend of all three panelists. "Wystan's first words were therefore a bombshell."

> "I don't want there to be any mistake about the responsibilities of a writer or the limitations of art," he said. "Two hundred years from now no-body will care much what our politics were. But if we were capable of being truly moved by the things that happened to us, they may read our poems. In his time Dante was a reactionary. It is also deplorable that Yeats' last poem called for war. But

> because Yeats was one of those most rare writers who continued to be moved by what happened to him right up until the day he died, his work has that authentic ring we recognize as poetry."

Auden walked around the room as he spoke. At one point he stopped at the window facing Broadway and said, with a wry wink, "I wonder . . . if that infernal noise could be stopped?" The crowd laughed. But Joy and some others were not amused by what came across as deficient faith in the revolutionary power of poetry as an instrument of social change. Auden had been invited because he was considered extremely left wing. "Everyone expected 'fighting words' from him," Joy later said. "We were all rather surprised at the conflict between his reputation and the things he has done, and the comparatively mild line he took."

LETTER TO A COMRADE was selling well enough for Yale University Press to consider another printing. "My mother claims it's all her work," Joy told Stephen Vincent Benét. "She walks into all the bookstores asking for it, and then looks terribly, terribly hurt when it isn't there." During Joy's past droughts of approbation, her ego operated as a protective shield. Now, as her colleagues, peers, and even her parents poured out validation, her ego produced a hybrid of hubris and entitlement.

New Masses invited Joy to write more book reviews, a form that swiftly became a venue for eviscerating fascism and evaluating effective means of spreading Marxism. Her job was to critique poems and novels on both literary and social levels. "A great poet can and should write prose, a) as a vehicle of ideas, b) [to] avoid aesthetic narrowness," Joy said in one of her talks. Reviewing *The Age of the Fish*, a novel about fascist school life by Ödön von Horváth, provided an opportunity to address what was happening in Germany. "For the present," Joy wrote, "Germany is living in the age of the fish, the cold time, the age of dull cold malevolence and the shark's tooth . . . The book [does not] neglect the economic implications of fascism; the pale children who sit all day in windows, painting dolls." And a review that spring of Benjamin Appel's *The Power-House* became Joy's vehicle for contrasting the World's Fair with the harsh realities of the day: "If the World's Fair visitor should tire of the glitter of the Ford exhibit or of the Broadway soft-drink stands, he might be inspired to wander westward along Forty-second Street, thus getting a taste of the New York we do not advertise. Beyond Eighth Avenue, where the ten-cent movie houses cease, this wide-eyed visitor will catch our city undressing with the shades up." Joy describes the "ancient grime of the rooming houses; the starved children hugging a starved cat on the front steps, and the decayed fruit peel in the gutter," and praises Appel for bringing "to the novelist's trade clear eyes and unfaltering honesty, a style capable of every beauty and the ultimate violence, a gift for idiomatic speech; he possesses, in addition, that profound scientific understanding of society without which no decent novel can be written; but greater than these are the understanding and compassion he has for human beings."

Appel's novel was one of very few that received Joy's high praise. "The cat in me comes out in reviewing," she told Kenneth Porter, a poet whose book *The High Plains* she had reviewed for the February 7 issue of *New Masses*. Overall she'd been kind to Porter, judging his work effectively strong on political fervor, if technically uneven. But "in an age when so much verse is verbally profuse and emotionally costive, technically dazzling and stale with the pedantry of an Ezra Pound, it is sometimes refreshing to come upon a book wherein purpose and passion somewhat outrun technique." Porter's poems, she wrote, "show a fiery sympathy with victims of the world's wrong." But content mattered as much as quality, if not more. Letting her own negativity toward religion impede any remnants of objectivity, she wrote that Porter's religious poems "rise to singular heights of silliness." Later, though, she recanted in a letter to Porter: "I was rather hasty in calling 'The Lord's Supper' silly, I'm afraid. Looking at it now, I see it was the whole sacramental idea which annoyed me. I'm inclined by nature to call anything sacramental sentimental, being an iron materialist."

In addition to reviews, Joy continued writing poetry, submitting new work to Selden Rodman as promised, and took up the study of Russian language. In a notebook, Joy copied out the Cyrillic alphabet and did grammar exercises. She started by learning sounds, pronunciation, the alphabet, and nouns, then graduated to complete sentences rife with idealizations: "I live in the Soviet Union and I work in a factory. There are other foreign workers. British and American. We study Russian. Some comrades know Russian well. Our factory has a kindergarten and playground for children. We have a room for resting and recreation. We have a dining room, a cafeteria, a library. There are sports grounds for volleyball and other games." It was an adult version of her childhood Fairyland, replete with community, belonging, love. In her fantasy Soviet Union, she lived with a group of comrades: Green, Atkins, Burnes, Davis, Phillips. In simple, terse Russian, Joy described the utopia: "This is a good house. Workers live here. They have all amenities. A dining room and laundry. Electricity, gas, central heating, bathrooms, showers. I also live here. I have a good room with a radio. In the Soviet Union we work and live in good conditions. New buildings are being built for workers in the Soviet Union. The rooms have balconies. The rooms have high ceilings, big windows and balcony doors are made of glass and there is a lot of light and fresh air."

By the end of the notebook, Joy had moved from nouns, conjunctions, and simple sentences to complex thoughts that conveyed Marxist philosophy: "Workers and toilers in the land are building a new society . . . In the Soviet Union there is a real brotherhood of people. Building socialism is our common cause."

Words like *bolshvinstvo* and *uslovye* whirled around her head. "God help me," she joked to John Gould Fletcher. "If only the Revolution had extended to the Cyrillic alphabet; they did drop two letters, but there are thirty-two left, all unexpected in sound and shape. After the five hissing consonants kill me I shall meet Archbishop Cyril's ghost and there will be a reckoning . . . No wonder [Russians] were gloomy—learning to read must have soured them for life." She began signing her letters "Dosvedanye tovarishch." Good-bye, Comrade.

• • •

JOY'S PLAN FOR the second half of 1939 was to spend the summer writing, possibly at the prestigious artists' colony Yaddo, in Saratoga Springs—if they accepted her—then continue working at *New Masses* while teaching at the league writers' school in the fall. Joy also taught poetry at the Jefferson School for Social Science, a Marxist adult education program whose core curriculum included *Das Kapital.* At its peak, the "Jeff School" would enroll some five thousand students. It offered courses on a range of subjects—Africa, philosophy, dance, art, music, short story writing. All were taught from a Marxist perspective, some more overtly than others. "Practically everyone" in any kind of CPUSA leadership position, or leadership in major leftist organizations, including *New Masses*, taught at least one course at some point.

THOUGHTS OF YADDO, and any other prospective summer plans, vanished from Joy's mind when she received surprising news: Metro-Goldwyn-Mayer had accepted her into its junior screenwriting program. Along with ten other young scribes, she was to report to the MGM studios on June 15. Joy was going to Hollywood.

·5·

June–December 1939

Joy boarded a California-bound train on June 10, 1939, commencing a symbolic journey that she had scripted nearly two years earlier with uncanny prescience in the title poem of *Letter to a Comrade:*

> Leaving New York, leaving the triple rivers
> netted in ships; turn again,
> wanderer, turn the eyes homeward. Remember the city
> settled in the eastward sky stiff with towers
> crested and curved in the tight circle of home
> cupped excellently in the sky. Possess understanding;
> see this is your heart, turn and perceive these towers.

As the "tight circle of home" faded with the puffs of steam behind her train, Joy hardly knew what to expect from Hollywood or her future. MGM offered her a six-month contract and an ample salary. "It pays for my food and drink, reasonably well, too," she wrote James Still. In December, if the studio liked her work, she might be hired onto the regular writing staff. But would she want that? In the bio Joy submitted to Yale University Press just a year earlier, she had emphatically declared that she couldn't imagine ever living anywhere but New York City.

But her move to Hollywood was for the sake of the revolution —vital work in the tradition of *Chapayev*. As Stalin himself had said after the film's release, "The cinema is an extraordinarily effective means toward the spiritual advancement of the masses toward raising their cultural level and toward rousing their political consciousness." If Stalin employed films to tout the beauty and bounty that socialism delivered to the Soviet masses, then the Party could employ the medium to unmask American capitalism and expose the realities of depression-era living. "If it weren't that I think I can be useful primarily as a writer," Joy told a friend, "I should give up writing entirely and turn organizer. I would, of course, have less fun. But I'll be damned if I want to live for fun anyhow." Just a week before her departure, the League of American Writers focused its Third American Writers Congress on "the question of how mass audiences can most effectively be reached by existing media, such as motion pictures, radio and television." The organization's president, Donald Ogden Stewart, himself a screenwriter, urged authors to wield their pens in defense of civil and cultural liberties, to create works in every genre that would plug the "million holes in the dyke of democracy." Joy was a missionary of sorts. "There was tremendous rejoicing whenever somebody would leave *New Masses* to go to Hollywood," remembered Annette Rubinstein, a colleague.

With black-and-white silent films having given way to "talkies" and Technicolor, Joy arrived in Hollywood during its golden age. Throughout the 1930s, while the depression darkened lives and industries, Americans escaped into adventures like *Tarzan* and *Treasure Island* and comforted themselves with the dependable humor of the Marx Brothers and the wholesomeness of Andy Hardy. Throughout 1939, approximately two thirds of the population visited America's movie theaters, which, at over fifteen thousand, outnumbered bank branches. "When the spirit of the people is lower than at any other time, during the Depression," President Roosevelt said, "it is a splendid thing that for just fifteen cents an American can go to a movie and look at the smiling face of [Shirley Temple]."

All of this meant hundreds of new jobs in Hollywood. (Those jobs Hollywood offered came at a price: the industry was so young that unions had yet to be formalized.) Advances in sound demanded stars who could perform vocally as well as physically, sultry voices to match beautiful faces, and funnymen who could merge wisecracks with slapstick. Studios needed sound crews, sound editors, and of course writers. Throughout the 1930s, journalists, novelists, poets, and playwrights journeyed west from the literary capital of New York City to the frontier of screenwriting. The writing staff at MGM more than doubled between 1934 and 1939, when the junior screenwriters program sputtered into what would prove to be a short-lived existence. Movie moguls promised gold, luring writers with contracts for stable jobs with steady paychecks and the opportunity to shape a new medium. Joy was following in the footsteps of Dorothy Parker, John Dos Passos, and William Faulkner.

Like fraternities at an elite university, the great studios of 1930s Hollywood each had its specific characteristics, and there was a hierarchy. Twentieth Century–Fox prided itself on technical refinement and Shirley Temple; Universal Pictures was known for horror films like *Dracula* and *The Bride of Frankenstein*; Paramount, with *Cleopatra* and Marlene Dietrich, had a reputation for opulence, sophistication, and sensuality. But the most glamorous of all was Metro-Goldwyn-Mayer. Founded in 1924 by Irving Thalberg and Louis B. Mayer, whose Jewish immigrant story paralleled Joy's parents', MGM was the fruit of the American dream, a financial powerhouse whose publicity slogan boasted of "More Stars Than There Are in Heaven." On the payroll were Spencer Tracy, Clark Gable, Greta Garbo, Joan Crawford, Robert Taylor, and Hedy Lamarr. Not only did MGM mean class and elegance, but also the studio prided itself on chaste, family-friendly pictures starring duos such as Nelson Eddy and Jeanette MacDonald, or Mickey Rooney and Judy Garland. Nineteen thirty-nine was the year when Rhett Butler told

Scarlett that he didn't give a damn and Dorothy followed the Yellow Brick Road to the Emerald City, where everything was possible.

When Mayer and Thalberg created the studio, they aimed to produce and release one full-length feature per week. In order to realize this goal, they needed all hands on deck, all the time. The factory town that was established to help fulfill this vision, Culver City, had its own school for child actors, as well as its own police force, hospital, and zoo. Altogether the city employed workers in over 150 different crafts and professions. There were directors, writers, carpenters, prop men, painters, set designers, wardrobe staff, makeup artists. Culver City employees ate together in the MGM commissary, famous for serving Mayer's mother's matzo ball soup. The commissary had the feel of a cliquey high school cafeteria, with an unspoken rule about keeping to one's own kind. The junior writers had their own table.

Joy arrived in Hollywood on June 15 and moved into an elegant Spanish-style house with two other young women in Beverly Hills, a few miles north of Culver City, at 221 South Arnaz Drive. A Juliet balcony adorned the space above the arched entrance, and palm trees dotted the lawn, waving in the hot breeze. When she arrived at Culver City, nine features and four shorts were in the works, including *Babes in Arms, The Women, Ninotchka,* and *At the Circus,* a Marx Brothers film that required as a set one of the largest circus tents in the world.

Joy reported to Kenneth McKenna, general supervisor of the junior writers. McKenna had formerly been a stage actor, director, and producer in New York City. He was older and liked by everyone, remembered one of Joy's fellow junior writers, Walter Doniger. McKenna was in charge, the one they went to with a problem or an idea. Richard Schayer was their immediate supervisor. He had written, edited, or contributed to over one hundred films. His job was to help them more closely with their writing. Joy was introduced to her cohort: three women and seven men, recent graduates of Vassar, Manhattanville, Yale, Harvard, Duke, Washington, the University of Southern California, and Grinnell. Although Joy had received her degree five years earlier, at twenty-four she wasn't much older than that June's graduates.

Ostensibly, Hollywood was in desperate need of new material. "Lack of Yarns Sending Studios to Remakes," announced the *Hollywood Reporter,* placing the blame on fewer new books, plots with "too many sex angles to meet with the demands of the Hays code," and writers turning political. Joy was assigned to take a crack at *Rage in Heaven,* based on the 1932 novel by James Hilton. Hilton's *Goodbye, Mr. Chips* was one of the most successful movies of 1939; this seemed like a good moment to produce another Hilton piece. A draft of the script was fished out of the vaults, where it had been collecting dust since July 1932. Joy worked on the project all summer and into the fall, submitting revised treatments and screenplays on July 3, July 12, August 2, and September 27. But the script would pass through several more hands, including Christopher Isherwood's, before being produced and released in early 1941. Recognition was generally given to the last writers who worked on the picture. Joy's name didn't appear in the credits.

F. Scott Fitzgerald explained the studio mindset this way: "We brought you here for your individuality, but while you're here we insist that you do everything to conceal it." According to Leo Rosten, "The Hollywood writer is not writing prose or producing literature. He is feeding an enormous machine that converts words, faces, sounds, and images into some nine thousand feet of celluloid. His material is thrown into the hopper of movie making, where other men and minds, other preferences and prejudices, grind it into pieces and champ it into a pattern." No fewer than seventeen writers worked on *Gone With the Wind.* Producers operated on the concept that there was a correlation between the quality of a screenplay and the number of writers who worked on it. MGM's motto, seen on the banner above its famous roaring lion, was "Art for Art's Sake," but the reality was more like "art for money's sake," or "art for fame and power's sake." Dos Passos called Hollywood "the world's great bullshit center."

Hollywood wasn't wholly at fault for its writers' unhappiness.

The problem had to do with expectations and a sense of entitlement. Joy hadn't realized that after entering the studio gates, she no longer was an autonomous agent but an employee—and her status as rising star on the New York literary left scene was nontransferable. She had been demoted from *New Masses* editor, with the power to reject or accept the work of her peers, to an underappreciated apprentice who was sometimes treated as little more than an errand girl. New York City writers—whether witty intellectuals of the elite Algonquin Round Table or bohemian poets from Greenwich Village—were celebrated and revered on their home turf, but in Hollywood the caste system was flipped. Producers and movie stars were at the top, writers on the bottom.

Internal support for the junior screenwriters program was minimal. "We discovered that, no matter how much we wrote," said a onetime junior writer, "nobody was reading anything we wrote. It wasn't taken seriously." It seemed to some that MGM was seeking cheap labor as much as fresh talent. Budd Schulberg, who ultimately earned enormous success as a screenwriter with credits for films such as *On the Waterfront,* also began as a junior writer. He grumbled, "The trouble is that when they hire you as a junior writer they rate you as a kind of excess baggage—you are supposed to sit around and mature and nobody fancies the idea of letting you work with them."

Disillusionment set in almost immediately. The previous summer at the colony, Joy's commute to work had involved ambling through a forest, and her office was a sweet, simple cabin. This summer, Joy took the bus to Culver City and worked from about 9:30 A.M. to 5 P.M. Much of the time was spent in her own office, a plain, uninspiring little room on the first floor of a building near the main structure where the regular writers worked. It contained a bookcase, window, desk, typewriter, and chair. Sometimes she and the other writers sat in on sets or the sound stage.

Joy had no creative power. She felt used and vastly undervalued. There was no seriousness of purpose. "The work here is not bad if you can take it as a sort of game, like anagrams; ingenious and utterly unimportant," she told Selden Rodman. Joy might have succeeded as a script writer, but without creative license she had little motivation. The skills she'd have needed were for playing games: sucking up to people, impressing people, and holding her tongue when she had to make a good impression—even if that meant suppressing her opinions, which was impossible for Joy.

She hated the superficiality and idle prattle that pervaded parties and conversations. Everyone was "dear" or "darling"; everything was "swell" and "terrific." Hollywood, with its Cadillacs, swimming pools, and mansions, was the epitome of extravagance and affluence. Actress Myrna Loy shielded her peach tree from the cold by swaddling it in her mink coat. Hollywood, said Fitzgerald, was "a hideous town, pointed up by the insulting gardens of its rich, full of the human spirit at a new low of debasement."

One time when Joy was getting out of a car, a middle-aged woman floated over and asked, "Have you seen a tortoise in your wanderings? We're looking for a tortoise. Oh, just a small tortoise." Joy recognized that Hollywood crazy was different from New York crazy—and she much preferred the latter, which was at least familiar. "I'm a New Yorker, used to crowds, strangers, loud noises and sudden explosions—but not to this," she complained to James Still. "All you have ever heard about Hollywood is true; not only are the people mad, dishonest, conscienceless, and money-grubbing, but they are all these things at the top of their voices. There is a continuous rapid-fire rattle of talk at a Hollywood party, louder than any machine gun. Perfect strangers rush over, wave their drinks in your face, tell you discreditable stories about their best friends (who are always famous stars), remark that Joan Crawford Is Slipping, and announce how much they paid for their clothes, manicures and cigarette holders." By June 27 she was begging for distractions from the outside world to take her mind off the formulaic fluff she was writing, which she gave the blanket title "Murder Prefers Blondes." MGM could have used the title for any number of its films.

Joy saw sellouts all around her, and she scorned them, those "who were once Marxists," she wrote in a letter to a friend, "and who have turned into collectors of swanky houses, expensive phonographs, beautiful automobiles, and who announce the price they paid for everything the minute you meet them. O I do not like this place." She added, "If Marxism needed any proving, for me, it would be proved ten times over by the cross-section of degenerate capitalism one sees in Hollywood." She later wrote in an article:

> There is a story told in Hollywood about a lion. Leo, poor beast, had grown old in the service of a certain film company. His duty was to appear on the screen at the beginning of each picture, open his mouth, and emit an impressive roar. For ten years he had never failed to roar perfectly.
>
> "You are one of our most valued employees," said the studio's Big Executive to Leo one day. "We would like to make you happy. What can we do for you, Leo, within reason?"
>
> "Well," the lion confessed shyly, "I always wanted to know what that Latin motto means. You know, the one that appears on the screen with me."
>
> "That?" said the Executive, betraying a pardonable embarrassment; "that, why, that, Leo, means Art for Art's Sake."
>
> Well, they finally had to retire poor Leo. It seems that ever afterward, when he appeared on the screen, the lion opened his mouth and emitted a horse laugh.

In fact, Joy said, the movie industry was guided by a different Latin motto: "Pecunia Non Olet, or freely translated, Money Smells Nice."

It quickly became clear to Joy that her lofty political ambitions were just another product of Hollywood illusion. Studio magnates, including L. B. Mayer, became livid when films with Marxist messages slipped through the cracks of management and found their way into theaters. He made an active effort to repudiate rumors of Hollywood being the Moscow-controlled American headquarters for the mass production of communist propaganda. In one of MGM's most widely marketed films of the year, *Ninotchka,* the character played by Greta Garbo mocks communists. It's a satire. "GARBO LAUGHS and the world will laugh with her in the comedy sensation of all time!" read the publicity for the picture. She consumes only enough calories to sustain life; she says that love is simply a chemical reaction. She feels nothing. When a bellboy tries to carry her bag, she says that it's a social injustice. (He says that depends on the tip.)

JOY AND ONE of her fellow junior writers—a "very nice boy of unexceptional G.O.P. antecedents"—were assigned to write a story involving animals, a subject she suspected was intended by her employers to limit opportunity for social commentary. "After all," she joked, "how political can you get with deer?" Joy borrowed Kipling's white deer theme and with her partner produced a script starring heroic fawns. The film was to be directed by Chester Franklin, of *Sequoia* fame, and filming was scheduled to begin in November. Fawns, however, proved difficult to come by in the fall, and the script was shelved.

Joy kept herself busy translating Catullus and writing outlandish scripts for her own amusement. She cast Nelson Eddy and Jeanette MacDonald as Tristan and Isolde in something she titled "Love at Sea." But her ridicule of Hollywood sensibilities was too obvious in another script she called "Man on the Moon," in which she invented a romance between "a girl scientist in a stratospheric balloon and a young pilot in a skywriting plane." A conference was scheduled. "Miss Davidman YOU ARE KIDDING MGM," Joy's superiors accused. "I knew then my days were numbered," she said.

"I am homesick for the peace and quiet of the subway in this horrible flat city of pink and green stucco and frowsy palms," Joy wrote to Jim Still on July 18. "Why on earth did they ever want me here anyhow?" she wondered. "I am a slave of the films now, degraded past all recognition. Every day at lunch I have to strain Robert Taylor out of my soup." But she didn't mind the actors as much as the writers, producers, and directors. "In six months the company can kick me out of here if it wants to," she wrote in July. "I am looking forward to it. God, I'm homesick."

• • •

JOY MADE SURE the other junior writers knew she was too accomplished to be accounted an equal. She had solid grounds for bragging, too. On July 5 the esteemed *New Republic* published her poem "Jews of No Man's Land." Joy didn't hesitate to spread the word, hoping her achievement would augment her reputation. "The boss, bless him, is sending it around to producers to show them what a wonderful writer they've snared in me." Reminders of her successful life in New York kept on coming. Joy received a letter from Charles Abbott, of the University of Buffalo, inviting her to contribute manuscripts to an archival collection of papers of prominent twentieth-century poets. (Joy's manuscripts were in New York, so she waited to respond.) Then her agent, Bernice Baumgarten, sold "Cookeh's Wife," the novel Joy had finished at the MacDowell Colony the previous summer. At the same time, she was being condescended to by MGM's hack staff writers. She resented being treated as anything less than a recognized talent. "I gloated over my writer-colleagues," she told Jim Still after her novel sold, "none of whom were capable of producing more than a ten-page screen story."

This attitude did not endear Joy to the other junior writers. Walter Doniger, a twenty-one-year-old from Duke who would go on to become a successful director and producer, remembered her as loud, unattractive, unlikable, and "bossy bossy bossy," he said. "She tried to run the group." Joy wasn't making friends at home, either. Her roommates annoyed her terribly by gabbing and leaving their undergarments lying about. She had no peace or privacy. In mid-August she found a more acceptable living situation in a house just down the street, at 203 South Arnaz Drive.

One of the saving graces of her stint at MGM was Leo Jr., a cuddly lion cub cast as the mascot for the short subjects department. At a studio party, for the amusement of all, their leading writer, Robert Benchley, fed Leo from a bottle. The little show wasn't entirely successful. The bottle's nipple slid off, spilling milk on Benchley's pants, and the chin strap on Leo's crown slipped into his mouth. There was much squealing from the spectators, but Joy took the cub into a corner and soothed it to sleep. They developed a friendship. "A lion is like a steel spring when you feel him, but he acts like a dog. When Leo became affectionate, I'd bat him down, and then look for damage. Invariably there would be another run in my stockings." As pets do, Leo became a blank slate for Joy's projections. He didn't like the starlets, she determined. They wore too much perfume and smelled awful. He was playful, almost like a neglected child starved for attention. "The nicest person I met [in Hollywood] was Leo the Lion," Joy later said.

In addition to Leo, hiking became a reprieve. Joy would tuck a knife into her belt "for protection" and "prowl through the mountains and canyons." She thought the mountains were beautiful, "although disfigured with film stars' Tudor mansions and French chateaux."

In December MGM would inform Joy that her contract would not be renewed. "The film business fired me with many compliments," she would recount to Jim Still. "The consensus of opinion was that I didn't take kindly to 'consultation.' Once, in a moment of emotion, I said No to a producer, so they were right. I'm too much of an egoist to listen to anyone tell me how to write; I wouldn't take it from Steinbeck, let alone some degenerate illiterate of a producer whose knowledge of America is gleaned from glimpses he gets from an airliner."

During her six months in Hollywood, letter writing became an intellectual lifeline for Joy, and she begged friends and acquaintances to send mail. A letter to Selden Rodman requesting news of poems she'd submitted led to a stimulating correspondence. In the absence of New York City intellectual society, she relished opportunities to flex her rhetorical muscles, and Rodman, the *Common Sense* editor who had solicited some of her poems earlier that year and was working on getting them published, was especially game for the challenge. After he had mildly criticized political organizing by writers, Joy responded on August 7:

> I understand your feelings . . . In any normal time I should consider it ridiculous. But in this damned mess of a time, when

> politics and economics are daily agonies instead of leisure-hour diversions, I can't help feeling that the fighter may be more needed than the writer. I don't mean actual physical fighting, of course; only that literature, somehow, ceases to mean much when people are getting shot. Many people have condemned the Nazis because they burned books; of course that's horrible, but it's an unimportant symptom of a serious disease. It's like sentencing a gangster for not paying his income tax. People are more important than books; that's a truism, but I might go further and say that writers who evade a fight as big as this one destroy their own importance. Something Auden said to me once is pretty relevant; he pointed out that it's general emotion—what I might call social anger. Our great writers are angry men—*The Grapes of Wrath* wasn't named by accident. What I'm getting at is this—do you think a writer can have genuine social emotion without doing something about it? Without fighting, and fighting in the most effective ways possible? There's where organization comes in. Any emotion that can be *completely* exorcised merely by writing a book about it isn't a very profound emotion—and it won't be a very profound book . . . Don't label me a literary heretic on the basis of what I've said. My passion for writing well is as great as anyone's. Only, to me literature is valuable as an expression of the human race—a decoration of life. It's life itself that matters.

Rodman enjoyed her letter and continued the exchange, openly and unapologetically expressing his own questions and beliefs in the custom of intellectual debate that Joy respected. He responded with an exposition on social love as a more constructive emotion than social anger. Pitting class against class, man against man, was a core problem of Marxism, he contended, generating more hate than love, undermining the feasibility of achieving its "noble objectives," including the classless society. As for *The Grapes of Wrath*, Steinbeck couldn't have produced such a fine work without infusing more compassion and love into this story than fury and anger. Rodman challenged Joy's assertion that a great writer must write to "exorcize" emotion. No, he said: "He writes because his emotion, whatever it is, expresses itself best in writing." Further, by presenting two sides of a struggle as completely white versus completely black, "the less you will see of the human, fallible beings involved, and the real issues for which both, with their particular coloring of idealism, are probably fighting . . . When, in addition, the writer 'organizes' (as a writer) he inevitably accepts opinions that he hasn't thought through for himself. Steffens' Autobiography is a good book because it is honest thinking-through of one man; when he became a Communist he accepted ideas on faith—and wrote drivel. Your old ladies 'kneeling before the altar of "Poetry"' are in the same category as the writer kneeling before a political doctrine."

The concept of accepting anything on faith was anathema to Joy. But what she considered hard evidence—Soviet films, Stalin's word—others increasingly understood to be propaganda, especially as the summer of 1939 came to a close.

On August 23, two months into Joy's Hollywood stint, the Communist Party was violently shaken by news that Stalin had aligned himself with Hitler in a nonaggression pact, agreeing that under no circumstances would the two countries oppose each other militarily or support hostile third powers, namely, Britain and France. As a result, Hitler could, and would, advance eastward to capture Poland without resistance from the Soviet Union, allowing the German army to concentrate its forces on Britain and France to the west.

Joy had never so much as entertained the possibility of Stalin siding with a fascist dictator. At the Munich Conference in 1938, the Soviets had attempted to establish a "collective-security" agreement with Britain and France, but the Western countries refused to support Stalin, leaving the Soviets unallied. American communists scoffed at subsequent rumors that Stalin might align with Hitler as a defense tactic. Earl Browder quipped publicly that "there is as much chance of agreement [between them] as of Earl Browder being elected president of the Chamber of Commerce." The immediate and long-term psychological implications of the Hitler-Stalin pact on the CPUSA and fellow travelers were devastating. The pact was a betrayal that cut to the core, giving rise to bewilderment, denial, and in many cases despondency. Panic ensued. Meetings were called.

Joy volunteered to conduct a discussion at the Los Angeles branch of the Party. She rounded up fifteen dazed comrades. They arrived late to the gathering. "As the mob of us marched down the center aisle to seats well up front," she recounted, "somebody got the idea that reinforcements were at hand and started a rolling cheer." Opinions were exchanged. Some condemned Stalin; the pact had ripped the blindfolds from their eyes. Others, including Joy, defended him. "I got up and said the pact seemed to be disconcerting the enemies of Russia. Therefore, it must be a good thing." She believed that Stalin had made a justifiable strategic defensive decision for the sake of self-preservation. But many found his actions inexcusable. In those days immediately after the pact, the 100,000 American communists were united as they would never be again, banding together for the common purpose of making sense of an event that had shaken their worldview. Those days of unity, however, were short-lived.

·6·

1939–1942

In December 1939, Joy returned to New York, where she belonged. "I rushed home howling with joy," she wrote to Jim Still that February, "and have been kissing skyscrapers and subway trains ever since." Her months in Hollywood faded out like a scene on the silver screen of her life. Being away from New York had renewed her appreciation for her hometown, her friends, and the burgeoning literary prestige that she felt Hollywood had so ignorantly disregarded. She immediately set about reuniting with friends, inviting a few of them to a New Year's Eve party at her parents' house. (The food she served was abundant and good, her friend Belle remembered, but the party itself was dull.) Even three bouts of "grippe" during the first two months of 1940 didn't subdue her elation. Awaking on February 15 to a festive foot of snow, Joy burst outdoors and played in the powder like a carefree child. "It's beautiful to be in a place with snow," she wrote to Still. "I go out and wallow in it. In Los Angeles, the only sign of winter is that the film stars appear in heavier furs."

Joy tried to pick up her career where she had left off. First, she caught up on neglected tasks. Charles Abbott's secretary at the University of Buffalo sent her a reminder about donating manuscripts to their new poetry collection. Joy found a notebook she'd used from September 1938 through June 1939 and wrote a cover letter apologizing for the delay ("I was serving a six-month sentence at Metro-Goldwyn-Mayer"), and describing the material: three pages of scribbled drafts of "Through Transitory" (along with a final typed copy), "Threat," and "Ex Voto" ("neither of which is any good"), plus "Yellow Girl," one of three poems that were part of a series called "Amateur Night in Harlem," and a draft of her review of Benjamin Appel's *The Power-House.* The notebook also contained one hundred pages of Russian grammar exercises, her "gallant attempt" to learn the language, admittedly "altogether quite a mess."

On January 25 she signed a contract with Macmillan for "Cookeh's Wife," slated for publication in August or September, then spent much of the remainder of the winter revising her manuscript and writing new poems. Selden Rodman still wanted poems from her, so she sent him a fresh batch on March 6. February turned out to be an unusually productive month. "I seem to be emerging from the Californian miasma," she told Rodman. "Any minute, now, my brain will begin to tick in acceptable prose."

The collection of poems she compiled in Hollywood and tentatively titled "Red Primer" was now in the hands of Yale University Press, and she eagerly awaited a response. Joy had judiciously renamed the collection "Rise and Shine," as the present political milieu didn't take kindly to anything that even blushed pink. She seemed to think "Rise and Shine" was all but a done deal, but Yale University Press turned it down. Deeply discouraged, Joy arranged a meeting with Stephen Vincent Benét, who invited her to his house. They had never met face-to-face. "I looked forward to meeting him with the sort of intemperate flutter of the nerves that one keeps for one's private gods," she later wrote. Norman Rosten accompanied her. Benét had rejected a manuscript Norman submitted for the 1939 Yale Younger Poets Award, giving the prize instead to Reuel Denney (Norman would win the following year), but saw great promise in the young poet and offered to help with revisions. Both Norman and Joy were thrilled by the opportunity to talk with their hero in person. In his late thirties, Benét was a slim man with a round balding head, small round glasses, and a remarkably humble nature. "We found a slight, quiet man with an extraordinary warmth of personality and glitter of wit," Joy later recalled. Benét was gracious as Joy chattered on about how much she'd hated Hollywood but enjoyed playing with Leo Jr. "It was characteristic of him that he put us at ease at once; he had none of the forbidding bardic affectations that often characterize lesser poets too conscious of their fame . . . [I]n five minutes I found myself rattling along about Hollywood and the musical glasses, as naturally as if he were my brother." Benét agreed to look at "Rise and Shine."

On May 20—the day Hitler invaded Holland, Luxembourg, Belgium, and France—Joy sent Benét a revised manuscript: "Here is my new book as it stands today, stripped of everything except what I really like; but a good deal may happen to it in the next few months . . . Do you think it's good enough to print as it stands, or ought I to wait a while?" It didn't take long for him to respond enthusiastically. Joy felt heartened and even emotional. "Thanks enormously for your letter," she wrote on June 3. "It came just when I was feeling that I'd never be any good as a poet so had better stick to prose, at which I'd never be any good either. I don't feel at all like that now." But "Rise and Shine" would never find a publisher.

In the same letter, Joy, on behalf of the League of American Writers, invited Benét to participate in an antiwar event on Thursday, June 18, at the Newspaper Guild. "We're going on record, while we can, against America's entering the war; and we should be grateful if you would consent to read some appropriate poems of your own (some of those in *Burning City,* for instance)." It was unlikely that he would accept. When Benét was invited to join the league, he had respectfully declined, expressing his thanks for the invitation but saying he'd prefer to protest as an individual rather than as part of an organization with which he might not agree on every point.

Joy's literary career had been inextricably entwined with the Communist Party, *New Masses,* and the League of American Writers, but the Hitler-Stalin pact changed everything. When she left New York for Hollywood in June 1939, the CPUSA was a thriving force. Membership peaked near 100,000. When she returned to the East Coast in December, her social, professional, and political community was in turmoil. Over the next year and a half, CPUSA membership would plummet to 44,000. At *New Masses* and the League of American Writers—the foundational forums for Joy's literary and intellectual life—irreparable cracks formed almost instantly. *New Masses* editor Granville Hicks abandoned the magazine and resigned from the Communist Party. In the spring and summer of 1940, one hundred members of the league officially withdrew from the organization; resignation letters were choked with emotions ranging from heartbreak to outrage. Auden blamed the passivity of liberal league members who didn't belong to the Party. "The American League of Writers was founded, I understand, as a Popular Front body," he said. "As in most such organizations, the Liberals were lazy, while the Communists did all the work and, in consequence, won the executive power they deserved. This did not matter much so long as the Popular Front was a reality: now it does." Suddenly, many league members saw the organization as a communist front—one in a horde of conglomerates of "useful idiots," as Lenin reportedly called them—whose members were naïve minions of the Party. There were scores of such organizations, with innocent nonpartisan titles such as the World Peace Counsel and the American Youth Congress. But their fundamental mission, whether they knew it or not, was "transposing the music of Moscow into the different registers of trade unionists, philosophers, pacifists, Christians, etc.," all the while under "the impression that what they play is not a transposition but an original work." Joy, for her part, was blinded to the fact that she was a mere puppet of the Comintern.

The league struggled to adopt a stance that would satisfy a majority of its eight hundred members, many of whom threatened to quit if the organization did not split from its communist contingent. A committee on policy was hastily cobbled together. The national board agreed on at least three things: "1.) the need for the League to do all it could to keep America from being involved in the present war; 2.) a campaign to preserve civil liberties, threatened now as never since the

League was formed; 3.) a campaign to give whatever financial and spiritual assistance we can to writers who are exiles from fascism and reaction or who are in any way war casualties."

That spring of 1940, the league drafted a statement, "In Defense of Peace." Joy signed it, along with three hundred other writers. A press release was issued on June 12. The league's official position on the war was that America should stay out. Peace and democracy should continue to reign as ruling principles of the American people. Joining the war wouldn't help Europe or America. "We insist, therefore, that the military defense program not be made an excuse for attack on social legislation or on the liberties of the people, for if that is done the defense program will be a concealed invasion of precisely the fascist type it proposes to guard us against."

But three days later, when Paris fell, joining Denmark, Norway, Belgium, and the Netherlands under German occupation, the United States took another giant leap toward entering the war. Congress set in motion legislation for imposing America's first mandatory peacetime draft, requiring all men between the ages of twenty-one and thirty-six to register with their local draft boards. In October the secretary of war would draw numbers from a glass bowl and hand them to President Roosevelt to read aloud over the radio. Everyone, it seemed, was eligible for the draft or had a brother, uncle, cousin, or husband who was. For Joy, that person was Howard.

Despite Joy's invitation to the antiwar meeting, Benét's name did not appear on the list of participants. Nevertheless, the meeting was a great success. By the time the event began at 8:30, the Newspaper Guild auditorium was packed. The work of more than two dozen poets—including Joy, her friend Jean Starr Untermeyer, and William Carlos Williams—was read aloud. The event lasted two hours. Afterward, Joy went out for beers with Belle and Howard.

Joy had kept in touch with her high school friend Nina, who, like many fellow travelers, now began distancing herself from card-carrying friends. Joy became intolerant of almost everyone who actively opposed the CPUSA. Friendships collapsed. "She was ardent," said Nina. "I was suspicious." They argued over the validity of New York's attempt to cleanse municipal colleges once and for all of "subversive activities." In a precursor to the McCarthy hearings, New York legislators formed the Rapp-Coudert committee; the teachers' union was scrutinized, the minutes of its meetings subpoenaed and dissected along with membership lists and financial records. Students, faculty, and staff were interrogated in private hearings stretching from September 1940 to December 1941. The committee demanded details of political activities and asked witnesses to name names. The New York City Board of Higher Education charged suspected communists with conduct unbecoming a teacher. Dozens of faculty were suspended and dismissed, their names plastered across the front pages of newspapers, their careers ruined. It was, as the league pronounced, a red-baiting attack on the teachers' union and on liberal opinion in the colleges in general. Such actions were indefensible in Joy's eyes, and she would not abide those who defended them. "Our quarrel was final and complete during the Rapp-Coudert investigations," Nina recalled, "when she demanded that I abandon friends who had 'turned' because of the Stalin-Hitler pact . . . Extreme positions were perhaps implicit in her nature."

Bill Benét had attended and applauded the Third American Writers Congress in June 1939, but in 1940 he told Joy: "I don't feel as cordial toward the League of American Writers as Comrade V. M. Molotoff feels toward Hitler. The League is dominated by Communists. I'm not at all respectable but I do not toe any party line." Just a year and a half earlier, he had praised the league's stance on "poetry in its relationship to the people, poetry as a vehicle for ideals, and what poetry might accomplish in the theater, over the radio, and in alliance with music." The pact had opened his eyes. He warned Joy to safeguard her talent: "Don't let the Red Propaganda boys and girls ruin your real gift." Joy respected Bill Benét, but she remained unswayed by his about-face.

Joy's "real gift" was reintroduced to the world when her novel was published on July 9. "Cookeh's Wife" had been retitled *Anya,* after its protagonist. The dust jacket was red, with a drawing of a dark, alluring Semitic-looking woman. Reviews were positive, and although few critics recognized the novel's autobiographical elements, their descriptions of *Anya* could have been about Joy. The book was chiefly a coming-of-age story, they said, about a girl who allowed her passions to overrule moral codes and convention. There was certainly an autobiographical quality to Anya's intense, wild spirit, Howard Davidman acknowledged years later.

Joy celebrated on July 20 over lunch with Belle in Times Square, proudly presenting her friend with a signed copy. Since her return from Hollywood, Joy had spent a lot of time with her old college pal. While her larger community—through the CPUSA, *New Masses,* and the league—collapsed around her, her friendship with Belle endured. Now a writer and high school teacher, Belle admired her friend's intensity of conviction and included her in intimate literary gatherings she hosted, where she served fried chicken, celery, and olives, while everyone played charades or gathered around the radio to listen to *Information Please.* Joy would go alone, or sometimes bring Norman. On November 23, Alfred Kazin, soon to be editor of the *New Republic,* and his wife joined the crowd.

"Scandal!" Belle recorded in her diary with characteristic hyperbole. "Fight between Joy and Kazin . . . about communism." Both had equally strong opinions. "The tragedy of today is simply this," Kazin asserted. "Never before has capitalism appeared so barbaric, so repulsively hypocritical, so formless, so irrational; never before has socialism in theory appeared so remote, or in practice—and I mean the Soviet Union, I mean the thinking and morals of most communists in this world, their complete inhumanity and sterility, their lack of culture, their muzhik [peasant] sense of life—appeared so unattractive." Kazin wrote these thoughts in his private journal and expressed them to the group at Belle's house. "They were *screaming!*" Belle remembered.

There was more to it than politics. Joy's and Kazin's worldviews were fundamentally at odds. Joy prided herself on being a devoted materialist, steadfastly believing in Marx and Engels's philosophy of dialectics: the material world has an objective truth perceptible through the senses. There is no such thing as spirit. "Men, I said, are only apes," Joy wrote years later. "Virtue is only custom. Life is only an electrochemical reaction. Mind is only a set of conditioned reflexes, and anyway most people aren't rational like ME. Love, art and altruism are only sex. The universe is only matter. Matter is only energy."

Kazin was contemptuous. "Middle-class philistinism is bad enough," he wrote in his diary a few weeks after the screaming fight at Belle's,

> but radicals—especially a certain type of Jewish, city Marxist, possess and impose a philistinism that is far more frightening than anything else. It is their knowingness, their complacent and puerile materialism, that total refusal to entertain even in hypostasis (not to say dialectically!) any possible alternative or controversion or to understand anything different . . . Tell a certain type of lumpen intelligentsia that religious significance—if only as an idea—and a more scrupulous, conscious sense of ethics are indispensable, and his face will grow blank. He will not disagree with you; he will merely not understand you.

Perhaps it was the fight with Kazin, or perhaps his denigration of the Soviet Union—the utopian society she still held dear—but Joy had her Fairyland dream again. This time, she wrote a poem about it.

Fairytale

At night, when we dreamed,
we went down a street
and turned a corner;
we went down the street
and turned the corner,
and there, it seemed,
there was the castle.

Always, if you knew,
if you knew how to go,
you could walk down a street

(the daylight street)
that twisted about
and ended in grass;
there it was
always, the castle.

Remote, unshadowed,
childish, immortal,
with two calm giants
guarding the portal,
stiff in the sunset,
strong to defend,
stood castle safety
at the world's end.

O castle safety,
Love without crying,
honey without cloying,
death without dying!
Hate and heartbreak
all were forgot there;
we always woke,
we never got there.

The mass exodus from the CPUSA left vacancies both at *New Masses,* whose masthead was dwindling, and at the league, whose officers turned over so rapidly that names could not be printed on its letterhead. New opportunities opened up for Joy at both places. "The League had nothing to offer members who remained loyal," said the organization's secretary, Franklin Folsom, "nothing except fellowship and a continuing chance to serve." For the next few years, Joy would teach poetry classes at the league's school for writers. For $10, students could enroll in "Theory and Technique of Poetry," which met every Wednesday night at 8:30 for twelve weeks. The class was "a workshop course in the technique of writing and marketing poetry," announced the league's course bulletin, "based on analysis of contemporary trends and of popular demand. Special attention will be given to new media such as radio, broadsheets. Ample time is provided for criticism of students' work." Much as Joy liked to complain about her regrettable six months in Hollywood, she added to her bio in the bulletin "Screenwriter for Metro-Goldwyn-Mayer, 1939." The experience was an asset.

Joy may have failed at writing for the pictures, but she excelled at critiquing them. On March 4, 1941, she made her debut as film critic at *New Masses* with her review of the Marx Brothers' movie *Go West.* Joy would arrive at the *New Masses* offices at 103 East Ninth Street and head up to the smoke-filled third floor, populated predominantly by men with cigarettes affixed to their lips. There she would sit down at her desk, roll a sheet of paper into her typewriter, and pound out polemics. "Truth and falsehood struggle for control over the film version of Hemingway's novel about Spain," she began a review of *For Whom the Bell Tolls.* By the end of the year she had reviewed no fewer than seventy-two films.

Writing movie reviews gave Joy the opportunity to get back at Hollywood. The best thing that came out of her MGM experience was a keen knowledge of what went into making a movie. When she wrote, "No one should ever give Hollywood a good idea to play with; the carnage is frightful," she spoke from experience. "There's a hole in the bottom of the sea," she wrote in a group review of *Washington Murderdrama, Power Dive,* and *Border Vigilantes.* "Far out in the beautiful blue ocean there is a five-mile depth you could drown the Alps in. It's too far down for the slithery octopus and the slimy giant squid, and no submarines have ever explored it. Into that black pit no sunlight ever comes. But if you could ever get to the floor of that abyss, dear reader, you would find eight Hollywood studios planted in the ooze, hard at work producing quickies. They like it there because it is the lowest they can get."

In 1941 the Pennsylvania state board of censors banned several Russian films deemed "Red propaganda," arguing: "The soviet system of government is an autocracy completely opposed to the American way of life. The people who have expressed an interest in the approval of these films are not interested in motion pictures as such, but in soviet propaganda as such." Joy couldn't see that she was one such person. In April, she swooned over *The New Teacher:*

> Coming from Hollywood films, you are hit in the face by this Russian comedy as by a blast of fresh air. You find the joy of life a little hard to understand. You are used to enameled wisecracks and painted faces brightly snarling at each other; you are used to a morbid straining for laughter. And suddenly you are shown a village full of ordinary people, not especially beautiful or elaborately adorned, going about the ordinary affairs of life—and enjoying themselves.
>
> The people who made this Soviet film, and the Soviet people it was made for, say that life is sweet, life has a future.

The film ends with a character, drunk on life, watching the moon set over a field, stretching up his arms and crying with ecstasy, "My life! My beautiful life!"

The propaganda had exactly the effect on Joy that Stalin was aiming for, reinforcing her enchantment even while the majority of communists were awaking from his spell. "Do the Soviets *have* to come out on top in everything?" she wrote in a review of *Volga Volga.* "They already have the best diplomats, the best kindergartens, the best economic system, the best life—but is that enough for them? No; they go and get the best musical comedies too. I turn green. I gnash my teeth with envy. It isn't fair."

Joy pilloried "reviewers on the commercial press, their heads full of mythical Soviet film censorship." Her only criticisms of Soviet films had to do with technical aspects of direction and editing; she begrudgingly admitted that Hollywood had an edge in those departments. She wasn't partial to the Soviet practice of sharply cutting from sequence to sequence: "Some day someone in Lenfilm

Studios is going to discover the lap-dissolve, and then Lord help Metro-Goldwyn-Mayer."

A frequent theme of Joy's reviews was Hollywood's demeaning depiction of women, who were placed into two categories: sex objects—"If Miss Veronica Lake ever puts on a brassiere, her acting ability will disappear"—and unmarried women, a topic that touched a nerve. In mid-March, Joy attended a screening of *Cheers for Miss Bishop* at Radio City Music Hall. "The most irritating thing in the film," she complained, "is its bland assumption that her school teaching is a mere second best; poor thing, she couldn't nail her men." Later in the year, reviewing *She Knew All the Answers,* Joy commented on the "offensive" and clichéd depiction "in the presentation of an office spinster of the old school, who lifts eyebrows constantly, simpers over her imaginary beauty, and faints at the mention of passion. If this lady ever really existed, she has gone to an unwept grave long ago. Cannot Hollywood give us a rest from the comic old maid?"

Joy wasn't shy about boasting of her own romantic trysts. She "talked of her many love affairs," Belle wrote in her diary after the two had lunch in Times Square in July 1940. When Joy returned from Hollywood, she told people she'd had an affair with Leo's lion tamer. Now she lusted after the actor Boris Karloff. She thought he had a "quiet silky sinister voice," she told friends. Beginning on January 10, 1941, his name blazed from the marquee at the Fulton Theatre on West Forty-sixth Street, where he was starring in *Arsenic and Old Lace*. Joy stalked him. She went to the stage door, her brother remembered. She found out which train Karloff rode home to Connecticut, and she went to Grand Central Station and took the same train. She paced back and forth in front of his house. "She always pursued with vigor what she wanted," said her brother, Howard, although she ultimately got nowhere with Karloff.

It is not clear exactly how or when Joy met the man who would become her first husband. Running in her circle of comrades was a charismatic Spanish civil war veteran named William Lindsay Gresham. The two may have met as early as 1938 or 1939, when Bill was teaching at the league writers' school. Six feet tall and lanky,

Bill had a trim mustache, a triangular face, and a mouth that seemed to wrap itself around his cheeks and touch his ears. His employment history included everything from the mundane to the mind-boggling, from selling insurance to performing in carnivals. After high school, he edited a house organ for Western Electric in Kearny, New Jersey, while saving money to attend Upsala College in East Orange. For a time he wrote book reviews for the *New York Evening Post,* but his true talent was storytelling. In person and on the page, Bill hooked people with his every word.

Joy and Bill shared a lifelong need to belong that stemmed from childhood loneliness and rejection, core factors that shaped their identities as writers, Marxists, and members of the CPUSA. A generational theme of alienation infiltrated their narratives. Joy's Jewish ancestors endured a forced transience; Bill was descended from "flotsam of the Old South," drifters wandering the Confederacy "with no guide save legends of a golden age when their ancestors had been slaveholders and gentlefolk." His "Grandy" was Presbyterian; through her faith "she saw the whole world." He wished she'd lived long enough to teach him to see the world too. His mother, Aline Lindsay, was a rebel against fundamentalism, "vaguely agnostic, vaguely Fabian socialist," and vaguely unstable. His father, Harry H. Gresham—arbitrarily called Steve, Hal, or Hank—crafted his own identity around being "a strong 'company man.'"

Born William Wilkins Gresham in Baltimore on August 20, 1909, Bill migrated north at the age of eight with his parents. The family settled in Brooklyn, where a brother was born and Bill's father found a job superintending a straw hat factory. Despite the prosperity of the 1920s, the Greshams floundered financially; they "accepted lower-middle-class life with bitterness but without hope." They didn't so much struggle as relent, and for most of his life, Bill would follow his parents' lead. "I had no confidence in possible future wealth to hold me up," he recalled. Dreams of success through traditional trades didn't visit Bill in the way they did his schoolmates. His peers, he said, "had a materialist creed in place of religion: they worshiped prosperity. It was called 'believing in America,' but it was not patriotism. America was a great slot machine; drop in your talents and out would come the good things of life—cars, beautiful women, suburban homes." The wealth Bill yearned for was more elusive than money. Like Joy, he was a lifetime outsider who understood that "man is not meant to be a solitary animal, and group participation is a necessity for healthy functioning. The thing is," he wrote, "to find the right group."

But Bill was impossibly shy, awkward, and self-conscious, even by the insecure standards of adolescence. Two traumas defined those formative years: his parents' divorce and the scourge of severe acne that followed, painful and prolonged, pockmarking his face and scarring his self-image. As a young man, Bill spent hours before a mirror conditioning himself not just to feel comfortable around people but to beguile them into fancying the splendid individual within—even if that splendid someone was merely a figment of projection. He coached himself in the art of conversation, rehearsing like an actor for a theatrical debut and transforming himself into a smooth-talking raconteur who could seduce any sucker into buying mind-reading acts.

Growing up, Bill had made a childhood playground of Coney Island and playmates of its magicians and knife-throwers, "freaks," and "geeks." Sideshows, séances—even simple card tricks—dazzled him with their capacity to awe, mesmerize, and ignite the imagination. Like a little girl who longs to be a ballerina, he was not content to watch from the audience. He yearned to join the spectacle, and eventually he did. Carny life accommodated a tension between autonomy and community. He surrounded himself with sideshow "freaks," whose deformities overshadowed the facial disfigurement he saw when he looked in the mirror. There was the Italian man with a vestigial twin dangling from his abdomen; a jovial Irishman called Sealo the "seal boy" because he had no arms and his hands sprouted from his shoulders; and "a sweet, intelligent little mite of a woman" born without arms or legs. "Perhaps," Bill later pondered, "we are all freaks, doing the best we can with the handicaps we carry through the world."

Eventually Bill drifted away from the drifters. There would be solo acts, but mostly he performed his one-man show on the stage of life. With his guitar and smooth bass vocals, he frequented the Dixie Hotel, "where the jazz blew hot in the Plantation Room and top performers on the vaudeville and carnival circuits swapped stories in the lobby." Life, he believed, was an enigma. He remained unsatisfied, unfulfilled. "[I] asked no definite questions because I was all question, ignorant that answers could be found." At the height of the depression, he decided to become a Unitarian minister. "I simply felt that a socially conscious preacher could do some good in the world," he said. But in 1933, unable to afford the requisite religious education, Bill answered the call to a different pulpit. He became a professional folksinger—a minstrel cousin of the Unitarian minister—practicing a genre that Joy heralded alongside poetry as an indispensable vehicle for communicating with and for the masses. If Bill couldn't preach social consciousness in a church, he would sing his sermons in the "cellar clubs" of Greenwich Village, locus of "revolt, poetry and romance." And here "at last," he wrote, "I found a world view—the first coherent philosophy that I had ever met." Marxism was "a doctrine of universal class war," an explanation of the universe.

On Election Day in 1936, Bill volunteered to be a poll watcher "for a legal party on the ballot." As he tells it, the police disputed the party's legitimacy. One cop even threatened him with a club. They tossed him out of the polling place three times. The next day he joined the CPUSA. Like Joy, he distributed leaflets, drew up petitions, lobbied Congress, and attended Party branch meetings. But his main reason for joining was the same as it was for Joy: "While a man is busy and can sink his identity in a feeling of 'mass solidarity,' it may give his life an illusion of meaning."

While Joy fought Franco on the terrain of the page, Bill took up arms in Spain itself. "We drew strength from three realities," he wrote; "the real misery brought by an industrial system, the real desire to help others, and a real cause: The Republic of Spain." In 1937, wearing silent rope-soled sandals, he hiked the Pyrenees alongside dozens of men from a dozen countries. In total, the Army of the Spanish Republic included about 2,800 American "Volunteers for Liberty," an arm of the International Brigade of volunteers. They called themselves the Abraham Lincoln Brigade, united in a worldwide brotherhood called to combat oppression of the proletariats who worked the land and built the cities. Bill never fired a shot. Demoralized by defeat, he reduced his role in the effort to transporting bandages. Witnessing bloodshed broke him. Bill was one of the last volunteers to leave Spain.

He returned with deep battle scars. "I came home to the bitterness of a lost war," he wrote, "a light attack of tuberculosis, and a long nightmare of neurotic conflict." In July and August 1939 he was treated at Beth Israel Hospital in New York for "pleurisy of tubercular origin." In December he was admitted to Hudson County Tuberculosis Hospital, where he remained until April 1940, when he left against medical advice. Doctors were concerned about his "anxiety and paranoic symptoms." His first marriage began to disintegrate. He drank to numb the pain.

After "two years of disintegration and despair," he was losing the will to bear up. One day, at the Abraham Lincoln Brigade veterans' organization in New York City, Bill met a social worker who recognized that he was an immediate danger to himself. She sent him straight to a psychoanalyst. For a while, therapy helped. Bill spent less time in bed and more time writing. He played music again. In the Village, in 1940, he made a lasting impression on a young Pete Seeger. "He had a nice bass voice," Seeger remembered. "Taught me some Spanish Loyalist songs. Played a little guitar."

"I snatched at love," Bill said, and "when my health improved, I snatched at writing . . . I tried to control my own mind by will power; diamond cut diamond." But "the big dragon," as Bill called his depression, the demon of his darkest days, returned. The cyclical bouts of insomnia, anxiety, paranoia, and impulsive behavior were given the all-purpose diagnosis of "neurosis" but today might qualify as bipolar disorder, triggered by posttraumatic stress. "Finally, since my mind was only a 'function of matter in motion,' and since it was filled with nightmare, I decided that this painful motion had gone on long enough." In January 1941, just a few months before the Fourth Congress, Bill nearly jumped from a window; later that year he crept into his closet, wrapped a leather belt around his neck, fastened it to a hook, and hanged himself. The world went black, but the hook didn't hold, and Bill tumbled to the floor. Newly aware of his need for professional help, he again sought out a psychiatrist and began Freudian analysis, which he credited with saving his life.

BEFORE THEIR WEDDING in August 1942, the only occasion when Bill and Joy can be placed in the same location at the same time is the weekend of June 6–8, 1941, when Manhattan's Commodore Hotel opened its doors to the League of American Writers for its Fourth Annual Congress. The conference was billed in the pages of *New Masses* as "The Outstanding Intellectual Event of 1941," with speakers including Richard Wright, Dashiell Hammett, and cartoonist Art Young. This would be "AN EXCITING DRAMATIZATION OF THE ROLE OF THE ARTS TODAY IN DEFENDING PEACE AND CIVIL LIBERTIES." The theme of the Congress was "In Defense of Culture," and the purpose was to discuss how writers could resist the drive toward reactionary war and assist persecuted writers around the world.

The conference opened with a business meeting, which included a report from the league's secretary, Franklin Folsom, a report from the league president, and elections to various committees. Joy was one of thirty-five elected to the national board. Her more prominent fellow board members included Clifford Odets, Ralph Ellison, and Christina Stead. Dashiell Hammett was now president, with vice presidents including George Seldes, Richard Wright, Donald Ogden Stewart, and poet Meridel Le Sueur.

At 8:30 P.M. Bill chaired a Young Writers Panel, with Joy as one of the panelists, attending the conference as a delegate from *New Masses* and an instructor at the writers' school. On the topic "How to break into print," she acknowledged that getting published was tough. "If you are honest, sincere, thoughtful; if you have something really worthwhile to say about the world, the chances are 999 out of

1000 against your getting anyone in the commercial press to print it." Joy encouraged contemporary poets to start off writing "songs of the people" in the tradition of the Almanac Singers.

Joy also got a chance to pay tribute to her late friend Alec Bergman, a young poet who had languished for years at Montefiore Hospital, a tuberculosis sanatorium. Bergman was a fighter even from his deathbed, where he helped hospital staff form a union. Joy admired that "[he] was never the mere mouther of slogans . . . never tried to substitute the bare bones of political argument for the living and breathing body of verse." In his hands, she said, intimate emotions resounded with social force. His poetry was intelligent, yet capable of evoking in her an emotional reaction that she didn't often express. "It may well make you cry," she said. Militancy and tenderness could coexist. At the Fourth Congress, she was proud to read three of his poems and announce the establishment of the Alexander Bergman Memorial Scholarship fund.

The congress only exacerbated the league's reputation as a communist front organization. One journalist who refused to attend condemned participants for paying more attention to politics than to literary pursuits. But it wasn't the imbalance that rankled him and other critics; it was the group's particular political disposition. "The word 'American' can mean various things," wrote the affronted reporter. "We think of the American Youth Congress, which eventually so unmasked itself as a fellow-traveling organization that a great part of its membership left it; of the American League for Peace and Democracy, ditto; of the American League Against War and Fascism, ditto . . . It is plainly not enough to estimate any organization's stand and character by the fact that it calls itself the American Something-or-other."

Such public dissension, published before and during the conference weekend, didn't detract from the earnestness and comradeship felt by Joy, Bill, and other participants, especially on the last day. The closing event was the "Poets, Song-Writers and Folk-Singers Panel," a three-hour event scheduled to begin with a reading of two poems by the Cuban poet Nicolás Guillén translated by Langston Hughes. Walter Lowenfeld sang the blues song "They Know," and Bill Gresham sang a "backwoods song" called "The Big Rock Candy Mountain." Burl Ives sang three "boogie woogie" tunes, and Earl Robinson sang too. A fifteen-minute intermission was followed by a debate titled "The People and the Poet," featuring Joy Davidman, Isidor Schneider, and Alfred Kreymborg. Kreymborg took the position of poets of the 1910s, Schneider the 1920s, and Joy the 1930s. The meeting minutes reflect a heated debate:

> Each accused the other two of having missed the important points in poetry in the other periods. Schneider defended his poets from the accusation by Davidman that they [the poets of the 1920s] were just as bourgeois as the people they condemned. They were merely seeking glory for self-justification and hence fitted right into the pattern they pretended to mock and look away from. Miss Davidman, after the debate which was brief (about 17 minutes), read several impressive poems of the recently honored and remembered young poet, Alexander Bergman, whose last days were described by Miss Davidman, as a bitter indictment in a society that is indifferent to true poets in their struggles.

The final number was "Joe Hill" by Alfred Hayes and Earl Robinson. The night continued with poetry readings from panelists and others, a discussion of folksongs as people's poetry, and ballad singing by groups and individuals including the Almanac Singers, Burl Ives, Woody Guthrie, and Bill Gresham.

BILL HAD FOR some time been separated from his wife, Beatrice McCollum, whom he married in 1933, although a legal divorce had never been finalized. After his return from Spain, he lived for a period with his girlfriend, the fiction writer Jean Karsavina, also a league member, at 27 Jane Street in Greenwich Village. That Bill was still technically married did not discourage Joy from commencing a relationship. Who pursued whom is not clear, but certainly Bill was not the type to be put off by an assertive woman. He liked Joy despite her reputation.

"She was aggressive, impertinent and intolerant," remembered Jerome Hoffman, a student in one of Joy's weekly poetry classes, which met in a building on Astor Place owned by the American Bible Society. Its students were two eighteen-year-olds and six adults in their forties and fifties. Each week every student would bring a new poem to class, read it aloud, and receive a critique. Joy was kind to the older students but "relatively merciless" to the teenagers. She was "extremely opinionated," said Hoffman. "I don't believe that she was a good teacher. The class lacked any structure, and she lacked the kind of warmth, enthusiasm, and interest in people (other than herself) that would kindle reciprocal interest in her students." As the semester wore on, the older folks dropped out one by one. Eventually, only the two young men were left. Joy would meet them at the classroom door and proceed to a nearby tavern, where they would drink ten-cent beers. "Ostensibly, we would discuss poetry, but we nearly always got into politics and philosophy and the nature of society and reshaping the world." The two men "were both radicals," Hoffman recalled, "but with the anarchy of the youthful rebel. We didn't have any system, but knew the world could be made better." He explained:

> [Joy] had a system which she professed complete belief and confidence in and tried to convert us to. It was the standard Communist party line of the early 1940's, with no original thought, variation or individual input by Joy. I had read the book of poetry which she had published and had listened to her in class and during our beer discussions. I had not agreed with her, but had thought she was an individualist who would retain her poetic individuality in her political philosophy. That was not the case. Her philosophy was rigid and admitted no thought of God, of religion, of anything outside dialectic naturalism. She was a New York Jewish girl

> (I am Jewish) who had rebelled against all religion and any manifestation of religion. In her sweater and tweed skirt, she was going to help remake the world in the image of the atheistic, worker's paradise, advocated by all true Marxists . . . [She] believe[d] and advocate[d] the true believers' line.

The boys also found Joy physically unattractive—"not particularly ugly or interesting, but rather dumpy and though obviously female, rather unfeminine." Hoffman and his friend experienced Joy much as Alfred Kazin had.

Bill Gresham felt differently. He admired Joy's tenacity and conviction and saw through the hard outer shell to her inner vulnerability. Joy's friend and league colleague the Australian novelist Christina Stead noted it too. "I see what she is now," Christina wrote to a friend in spring 1942. "We were deceived by her pompous airs, she is really a schoolgirl . . . Joy Davidman is a very clever girl ([intellectually] I mean), still with her family, still fighting her mother and father, who does not yet appreciate anything outside her particular training and the NM's [*New Masses'*] dreadful influence on the jargon of the young. She is a nice kid really, friendly." But she was ready for a change.

By this time, Joy was intent on marrying Bill Gresham. One of the by-products of the attack on Pearl Harbor on December 7, 1941, and President Roosevelt's subsequent declaration of war was a spike in the marriage rate. In the weeks that followed, around one thousand couples tied the knot each day. By January 1942 the marriage rate had risen by 20 percent. People were scared, and they clung to each other. Mayor La Guardia imposed a curfew. Bomb shelters were designated. Antiaircraft observation posts were assembled around the city. After dark, in Bryant Park, behind the New York Public Library, giant searchlights scanned the skies for enemy planes. "You cannot escape anxiety," said Eleanor Roosevelt in her weekly radio broadcast. "You cannot escape a clutch of fear at your heart and yet I hope that the certainty of what we have to meet will make you rise above these fears." Men were going to be leaving for the war, and they wanted wives to come home to.

Joy told Christina Stead about Bill. "Joy Davidman has a guy named Gresham," Christina wrote to a friend, "a Yankuh old as Washington's family and she is going to marry him, she hopes."

· 7 ·

1942–1944

Other than Joy's comments to Christina Stead, very few traces of her premarital relationship with Bill remain. Bill's wife, Beatrice, initiated divorce proceedings in early 1942, accusing him of committing adultery with an unnamed woman, presumably Jean Karsavina, at 27 Jane Street in Manhattan. The divorce still wasn't final in June 1942, when Joy was making plans to spend the later part of the summer at the MacDowell Colony, which had offered her several weeks in August. Bill wasn't a particularly jealous man, but he wasn't thrilled about her going to the colony alone. Joy was undeterred, her reasons perhaps outlined in the essay on Hollywood and women's emancipation that was her final contribution to *New Masses* before heading north to New Hampshire.

"Love is not a significant full-time occupation," she began, addressing both women and men. "Neither is having a baby." If the present war was about democracy, she asserted, then "the emancipation of women is part and parcel of the democracy we are fighting for." She went on:

> Increasingly, women succeed along lines once reserved for men; as in the Soviet Union and Britain, women replace men wherever

> possible in the war effort. Nor are their homes worse run, their children worse cared for. On the contrary; as any psychologist knows, women who have realized their potentialities as creative human beings make better mothers than frustrated women who must take all their ambitions out on their children. Thus the films are lagging behind the country. Their half unconscious war against the emancipation of women certainly gives unintended support to one of the tenets of fascism—the deliberate debasement of womanhood.

Joy skewered Hollywood for its gender discrimination: exploiting women's sexuality, portraying women as "dependent and inferior," "glorifying a morbidly passive and self-effacing female type," and depicting mothers as incapable of succeeding simultaneously in the home and in the workplace. In *Tom, Dick, and Harry,* for instance, the character played by Ginger Rogers summed up the prevailing attitude toward women with the overt message that "it's as natural for a girl to want to make a good marriage as for a man to want to get ahead in business!" Joy was disgusted. In the rare instances when a professional woman did grace the screen, she was punished. "Her career always separates her from her man or her child, and after spectacular suffering she comes to realize that she must abandon art for the home." Joy's critique was merciless:

> The cardinal point of women's emancipation—the admission that she can have a successful career and a successful marriage too —is almost never made. Then sometimes we have such movies as *Woman of the Year,* whose heroine is a pioneer in a profession—journalism—still considered by Hollywood to belong to the male. (The usual girl reporter of the films is only marking time till she can catch an editor.) The cards are therefore stacked against the heroine by making her not a sane journalist but an insane dynamo. In defense of this film it has been alleged that the heroine was not meant to retreat into the kitchen, being portrayed as capable of speaking twenty-seven languages simultaneously but as miserably

> incapable of making waffles. But this is just as male-chauvinist as the assumption that she belonged in the kitchen in the first place. Career women make very good waffles. So do career men.

"Women: Hollywood Style" ran on July 14. The piece ended with a rallying cry charging Americans to repudiate male chauvinism, especially as expressed in film. If that could be accomplished, Joy argued, "the movies will hastily follow suit."

She took her leave from *New Masses* and New York, journeying up to Peterborough for a fourth summer at the colony. In the sweet summer air of New Hampshire, Joy could breathe again; as always, she felt as if she'd come home. Uninterrupted weeks devoted to poetry and personal renewal were long overdue. She settled into the cozy Star Studio, a simple wood cabin built in 1911, complete with a screened porch. Ferns leaned toward the door like open palms, receiving her. Along pathways shaded by canopies of maple and pine, Joy took long therapeutic walks through the hemlock and the hollows, hunted wild mushrooms, and listened for the singing of thrushes.

She didn't write her best poems that summer, although she did draft a few promising pieces. Tucking them away for future consideration, Joy eagerly focused on news that took precedence: Bill's divorce would be finalized on August 20. Still at the colony, Joy approached Marian MacDowell with a proposition: How about a wedding at Hillcrest?

This was not the most suitable moment for such an event. With the war on, resources were strained across the home front; Mrs. MacDowell, as colony director, faced food and labor shortages that would complicate any such plan. Besides, she "couldn't feel quite right" about a Hillcrest wedding, she said. "It lacked a certain sincerity and warmth of a formal ceremony." Lightheartedly, however, she dismissed those notions as silly "mid-Victorian feelings" about convention. She would make it work, and gave Joy her blessing.

Mrs. MacDowell hosted five weddings in her lifetime. "There was always some reason why these five couples could not be married in church," she remembered. "In almost every case, there was a difference of race or religion. One a Jew, the other a Christian, or one of the bridal pair had been divorced and couldn't be married in church. In any event, one of them belonged to the Colony, either bride or groom." When Bill arrived, Joy happily showed him around. Mrs. MacDowell thought him delightful.

The wedding took place on August 24, and all the colonists were invited. Her parents and brother traveled up from New York. Peterborough's justice of the peace, Algie Holt, prepared "his own little solemn service which was really very beautiful," recalled Mrs. MacDowell. The day was lovely, bright and comfortably warm. Bill donned a light-colored suit, and Joy wore a white derby hat and white calf-length dress printed with strawberries, cinched at the waist with a thin black belt. Mrs. MacDowell opened a special bottle of champagne, and everyone toasted the newlyweds. Years later, she admitted in a letter to Joy that, even in the midst of that exceptionally taxing time, one thing always brought her great pleasure: "Marrying off my favorite colonists."

THE GRESHAMS (Joy changed her name legally but would continue to write under Davidman) briefly lived in Sunnyside, Queens, a neighborhood Bill referred to as "a human filing cabinet." From there they moved to a flat at 242 East Twenty-second Street, near the outer edge of Manhattan's Gramercy Park district. They had little money: Bill was a poor freelance writer and editor, and Joy's *New Masses* salary amounted to a paltry $25 per week. For now, though, finances didn't matter. They were two bohemians, young and in love. On September 20 the couple paid a late-afternoon visit to Belle. She was charmed by her friend's new husband; impressed by his humor and intrigued by his budding interest in yoga, she deemed him a "swell guy."

Although Bill was a materialist like Joy, he was interested in spirituality as a concept, and especially drawn to practices that promised healing and enlightenment. For a full year before his marriage to Joy, Bill underwent psychoanalysis with a Dr. Walter Briehl, who had to terminate treatment the August Joy and Bill married because he was called to serve abroad in the Medical Corps. By October of that year, the war wounds that Bill had been trying to mend since serving in Spain again tore open. He began having severe bouts of anxiety. Reading about yoga led him to attempt the practice, although as an atheist, he was careful to separate the mental from the physical discipline. "For a time," he later wrote,

> it actually brought me some peace and detachment. But as I grew more disciplined, another phase of reality, hitherto unsuspected, rose up to haunt me. It was this: Convinced, consciously at least, that mind was a "function of matter in motion," I had never dreamed of separating myself from my stream of thoughts. Yet the first mental exercise of Yoga is to sit still, eyes closed, and practice quieting the thoughts. Months of intense effort brought me to the point where I could actually do this, sometimes for a quarter of an hour; the mind would be free from thought-forms, yet alert, fully conscious—of what? I became aware of the mysterious watcher behind thought. The watcher does not change, does not move; it can be separated from thought, from emotion, from all save consciousness alone.

It was the concept of God, slowly creeping into his consciousness, and he didn't like it. Yoga was not a cure, but it helped.

When Bill was doing well, there was always laughter and music. The couple went to parties together at Belle's. Someone would bring a mandolin, and Bill sang bawdy ballads. Joy was completely smitten. "I seem, by blind instinct, to have found the almost mythical Perfect Husband," she wrote to her friend Jean Starr Untermeyer toward the end of her first year of marriage. "Oh, he gets purple with rage at a dropped collarbutton and all the normal things like that. But none of it comes my way! He's so gentle and civilized in the home that I wonder how a savage like me ever got him. Also he loves cats. Also he knows lots and lots of good funny stories."

Joy and Bill would later say they lost interest in Communist Party activities after their wedding, but even if Joy's attendance at gatherings waned, her political concern did not. The war was gaining strength. No longer was it an abstract news item for the average American, as the war in Spain had been. Its repercussions impacted daily life: sugar rationing had begun in May, and soon, coffee, red meat, and gasoline would be added to the list, while half of America's goods production went toward food and supplies for the military. Silk was used for parachutes and gunpowder sacks: no silk blouses. Nylon and rayon were used for military clothing: no stockings. Men were being called up, but Bill's history of tuberculosis, depression, anxiety, and suicide attempts earned him the classification of 4F—unfit for service—from his local draft board.

JOY STILL BELIEVED in the power of poetry, but the enthusiasm generated at the 1941 League of American Writers Congress was short-lived. The organization seemed on the precipice of destruction as league membership continued the decline that began with the Hitler-Stalin pact. Even so, Joy decided to spearhead a massive project, a poetry anthology, to be titled *War Poems of the United Nations,* which would include anti-Axis poems from contributors worldwide. Bill was fully supportive and wanted to contribute a poem of his own.

Dial Press—a book publisher spun off from a mid-nineteenth-century Transcendentalist literary magazine, *The Dial,* co-founded by Margaret Fuller and Ralph Waldo Emerson—agreed to publish the book. Dial drew up a contract naming Joy as editor of the collection, "to be not less than 70,000 words," and setting a delivery deadline of February 1, 1943. Joy's agent, Bernice Baumgarten, reviewed the clauses and was satisfied that the document was "safe" for the league to sign, but not for Joy. Bernice was wise to advise Joy not to become saddled with full contractual responsibility should the league die.

Dial provided Joy with company letterhead, and she wrote up a prospectus and form letter which she mailed to hundreds of poets, requesting a prompt reply. "The sooner this volume appears in print, the more valuable it will be as a morale builder," she told potential contributors.

Submissions poured in from poets across the nation, including

William Carlos Williams, Edna St. Vincent Millay, Langston Hughes, Bertolt Brecht, Carl Sandburg, Pablo Neruda, and her friends the three Benét siblings, Stephen, Bill, and Laura. Joy welcomed fresh talent into the forum as well. With this war came new voices. She wanted to include "young poets to whom the anti-Fascist struggle has been their first social inspiration," as it had been for her. The horrors of war "purified" young poets of "sterile self-contemplation," she believed, the classic navel-gazing, youthful "flitting butterfly stuff" that had admittedly characterized her own work in earlier years.

Joy's solicitation reached female members of a local poetry club. "There are 11 of us," wrote a representative. "We are each sending you a copy of a poem for your book." While the effort was sincere, Joy found the poems "unreadable." The letter, Joy intimated, came from a tea-sipping group of upper-middle-class aspiring poets—not the "masses" Joy particularly cared for. Other kinds of poems—the ones she craved—were unfortunately not so easy to come by. Joy queried the Soviet Writers Union, which did not respond until 1944. And by the end of December 1942, she was at her wits' end over the "appalling shortage of war poetry from England."

But Joy had bigger problems. The league designated a committee of poets to work with her on the project, but the group quickly disbanded. Joy's lack of social tact did not help her cause. League secretary Franklin Folsom remembered her as "a driving person who wanted to get the maximum attention for, and maximum income from, this collection of verse." Joy's desire for financial gain didn't detract from her genuine motivation, but the league was about to break apart. Folsom would write in his memoir that Joy's *War Poems* merely originated in the league. The organization's involvement appears not to have gone much further, leaving Joy in an unenviable position. Having heeded Bernice's advice not to sign the Dial Press contract herself but to let the league sign instead, Joy was under no legal obligation to carry the full, formidable workload. But withdrawing now, after pleading for cooperation from the most esteemed poets of her era, would make her look like a fool. Joy pressed on, looking outside the league for assistance. Over the next several months she selected, translated, and edited hundreds of poems from around the world. Various organizations heeded her call: a Library of Congress representative collected and translated Norwegian poetry; the Committee on Cultural Relations with Latin America did the same with the Spanish-language set; and individuals, too, backed the project in various ways. Belle, now married and pregnant, came through on the Russian front; her Russian-speaking mother helped select and translate. With the deadline approaching and a dearth of English submissions, Joy designated herself an honorary Brit. Under noms de plume Megan Coombs-Dawson and Hayden Weir, she contributed three poems to the relatively sparse compilation from the British Empire. In her introduction to that section she cleverly noted that "British poetry, somewhat precious before the war, is beginning to catch up with the British war effort." She had fun with the job. Joy wrote of "shires," "Sherwood forest," and "working chaps" riding home on the "Underground," and she took care with her spelling of words like "colour" and "valour." In perhaps her most drolly authentic touch, she crowned her alter ego's bio with heroism: "Hayden Weir was killed in action in 1942."

These weren't her only outright fabrications. The poems offered by the Russian American Institute were inadequate, she felt, leaving her little choice but to "supplement" that section as well. After the book was published, Joy saw a clipping from a Russian publication protesting her translation of a line by the Nobel Prize–winning poet Boris Pasternak. "The funny thing was," she said a few years later, "I had practically made up that whole poem except for the one line by Pasternak which had been in the middle of his poem and which I put at the end of mine . . . If anybody says this was dishonest, remember I was translating 20 poems a day . . . Where I could find anything decent to translate, I did translate accurately. In any event," she recounted with a sly smile, "it can now be told: anything resembling poetry in the Soviet section of that book owes a great deal to Joy Davidman. I also did a lot for the Poles."

In the end, *War Poems of the United Nations: The Songs and Battle Cries of a World at War* united an international brotherhood of 150 poets representing twenty countries. The three hundred collected poems provide an important social document. Joy, however, felt that the haste was all too apparent. "*That* was a rush job and shows it," she wrote to Kenneth Porter. "It was left on my shoulders . . . I did the whole thing—collection, translation, and what-not—in four months, and am not particularly proud of the result." Reviewers tended to agree. The *New York Times* published a dual review contrasting the volume with another new anthology of war poems. Joy's book received the more favorable critique, in part because, the reviewer said, it was devoid of "superficial patriotism" and was unified by a specific point of view. Contributors saw the current war as "not merely a military conflict but the climax of a profoundly rooted social struggle . . . What emerges most clearly is the folk ballad . . . It becomes evident that those who feel this war as a struggle to reassert the dignity of the common man, those who have suffered for a better life, have been able to create poetry out of their agony." The reviewer gave substantial attention to the translations, praising some but slamming others, including translations of two Brecht poems, one by Jean Starr Untermeyer ("captures nothing of Brecht's Biblical language and sonorous cadence"), and "the Davidman version of the ballad, 'What Did the Nazi Send His Wife?' [which] falls far short of the incisiveness of the original."

Yet "the weakest sections of all," said the reviewer, "are the English and American." He quoted Joy's assertion in the introduction to the American group that "in revealing various pretentious cultist poets as defeatist or worse, the war has freed young Americans from their hampering traditions of pedantry and obscurity, and a more honest poetry is beginning to emerge." The reviewer called that an oversimplification. "Miss Davidman's optimism is not borne out by her choice and the limitations of her taste are here most apparent. If burning convictions have given continental poetry new life, convictions alone can not produce art."

In addition to her work on *War Poems*, Joy continued participating in political events and working at *New Masses*. On May 10 she took part in an international commemoration, sponsored by Eleanor

Roosevelt and Albert Einstein, of the tenth anniversary of the Nazi book burning. At two separate events, one at the New York Public Library on Forty-second Street and the other at the Studio Theater on West Twelfth Street, poets including Bertolt Brecht, William Rose Benét, and José García Villa, as well as Joy, read their work aloud. There were radio broadcasts and dramatic and orchestral performances. A plea went out to the public requesting donations of books —especially those banned in Nazi Germany—to the "Service Man's Book Committee."

Joy's tasks as contributing editor at *New Masses* were prodigious. There were film screenings to attend and editorial meetings at the magazine's new offices at 104 East Ninth Street, a fifteen- or twenty-minute walk from the Greshams' Gramercy apartment. "This is job enough for two girls," Joy wrote on July 2 to her friend Jean Starr Untermeyer in Peterborough. "I write, each week, a regular long movie review; several editorials; a book review or two; a Between Ourselves page of a thousand words; sundry small pieces, heads, and subtitles. I frequently have some one else's not-too-expert story or article to rewrite completely. Total, about 10,000 words a week, which is an awful lot when most of it's close-reasoning analysis. Then there are films to see, meetings and the like to cover; and I've had quite a lot of outside work. Then, God help me, I'm doing a special piece on Poetry in Wartime, in my nonexistent spare moments—and it grows and grows."

The summer of 1943 was Joy's first spent entirely in New York since 1937. Except for her 1939 sojourn in Hollywood, she had in recent years spent part of each summer at the MacDowell Colony. Now, with her grinding workload at *New Masses,* she had little time for creative writing of her own. "So I've plenty of reasons to envy you your time at the Colony!" she told Jean, and sent love and kisses to "everybody there, especially the staff." But, she added, "when the alternative is spending time with Bill," she was happy. The couple planned a two-week vacation to Maine later in the summer at the place she had visited and fallen in love with in the past: "I'll be able to take Bill rowing and fishing in all my special corners of that enchanting lake."

But things did not go as planned. Shortly after writing to Jean, Joy learned she was pregnant, due in March. Her first trimester was beyond miserable. She vomited over and over. Bill could only watch, helpless. Dehydrated, weak, and losing weight by the day, Joy ended up in a hospital, where doctors filled her with sedatives and fluids. She had no choice but to resign temporarily from *New Masses*. "Love is not a significant full-time occupation," Joy had begun her article "Women in Hollywood" the previous summer. "Neither is having a baby." What would become of her career? In just this first trimester, her child had already eclipsed her life. Between July 27 and October 19, Joy did not contribute a single article to *New Masses;* during the remainder of 1943, she wrote only two book reviews.

Quitting her *New Masses* job meant relinquishing her salary, and small though it was, Joy and Bill were already barely scraping by. Bill had been working for *Daring Detective* magazine, writing blurbs, heads, and copy, but it folded under paper rationing. He got a new editorial job with *Click* magazine, and was reading up on "rackets" involving spiritualism for a dark novel he'd been working on that grew out of a conversation with a medic he knew in Spain who had once worked as a carnival hand on a "geek show." The star geek, said the medic, bit the heads off live chickens. "When I asked him where you get a geek," Bill recounted, "he said, 'You don't get a geek. You make one.'" You find an alcoholic so desperate for drink that he would agree to perform the gruesome stunt in exchange for a bottle. Bill talked over the idea with Joy. It was just a start for now. The book's plot would follow a swindling mind reader and, Bill decided, should be organized into twenty-two chapters, after the twenty-two major arcana cards in the tarot deck, a staple prop of sideshow psychics. Joy thought it had the makings of a riveting read.

She was feeling better by November, when the couple competed on a radio quiz show called *The Better Half,* which pitted husbands and wives against each other every weekday evening from 7:30 to

8:00 P.M. on WOR-Mutual. No recording of that particular episode exists, but the show's host wrote a paragraph for *Click* about Joy and Bill's broadcast escapade. "Smart, these CLICK folks!" reads the lead. "Bill Gresham of your editorial staff came over to WOR-Mutual with his wife the other night and carried off the cash and honors on 'The Better Half,' the quiz show I ride herd on. When the studio cameraman snapped our pictures my head was still in a whirl from hearing Bill beat out the answers. And his better half was right in there pitching too." *Click* ran a photograph of the couple in action, standing shoulder to shoulder in front of a microphone with a silvery slatted head the size of a giant fist. Bill towers over Joy, who looks exceptionally modish in an Empire-waist maternity dress that flatters her full bust. With her chin slightly tilted, her mouth open, poised to answer, and her hair settled in wide waves around her shoulders, she emanates an unconventional beauty.

Impending fatherhood and the stress of watching Joy endure her first-trimester anguish triggered in Bill new bouts of insomnia and anxiety. In October he resumed treatment with a psychoanalyst, a Miss Hurwitz, recommended by Dr. Briehl. And he drank—a lot. When, on February 9, 1944, he received a postcard from Local Board No. 16 stating that his 4F classification had been lifted and he was now eligible for service, Bill knew he would break in the trenches. He had already played the brave soldier in Spain and had paid dearly for it. The next day he filed an appeal on grounds of his history of tuberculosis. The draft board responded with a request for medical documentation, which he gathered from Beth Israel Hospital's records department. He also called Miss Hurwitz and requested documentation of his psychiatric troubles. She suggested he write to Dr. Briehl, now a major in the Neuropsychiatric Section of the Medical Corps, requesting a letter describing his mental health history. Bill wrote a fond note to his former psychiatrist that included an update on his condition: "By and large I have been feeling very well and the work with Miss H. seems to be progressing 'as well as could be expected' which is very well indeed. It is just as if I had slain the big dragon but that later a batch of dragon's eggs had hatched and now we are hard at it slaying the little dragons which will eventually clear the land." Dr. Briehl readily agreed to write a letter on Bill's behalf to the draft board:

> When Mr. Gresham came to me he had had a history of active tuberculosis with, I believe, a cavity. Further, there had been a history of alcoholism and episodes of depression with numerous attempts at suicide. Following his treatment he recovered sufficiently to work out some of his difficulties and to remain employed. It was my opinion, however, that he would have possible relapses of depression during which time he would require further periods of therapy whenever such episodes occurred. In my opinion and from the standards of mobilization regulations (MR-1-9) this man is unacceptable for any form of military duty because of his past physical and psychiatric history.

Local Board No. 16 agreed to restore Bill's 4F classification.

Bill's brother Lindsay and Joy's brother Howard had received no such exemptions; Lindsay was home on a brief leave, and Howard would be shipping out shortly. Joy and Bill decided to throw a party before they left, in part so Bill could fix Lindsay up with a nice girl he knew, a pretty young woman named Ruth Parsons. A ninth-generation descendant of William Bradford, who sailed to Plymouth on the *Mayflower,* Ruth was as WASP as they come. Petite, perky, and stylish, she was a former writer for *Glamour* magazine and now worked for *Screenguide,* a publication that shared Fifth Avenue office space with *Click*. Bill stopped by her desk one day and invited her to the party.

When she arrived at 242 East Twenty-second Street, Ruth found a shabby apartment with chairs lined up against the walls and not much other furniture. "Both of them were struggling artists," Ruth later recalled of Bill and Joy. "And they didn't have any money. And they were just barely making it, as it looked to me." Joy, she said, was "large with child—*very* large." Bill directed Ruth toward Lindsay, sitting off to the side, looking sullen. "He was weird" and depressive, she thought. She tried engaging him in conversation, but the two had nothing in common.

Howard Davidman arrived at the party wearing an old overcoat with pockets hanging out and buttons missing. He was chain-smoking and flicked ashes on the floor. Ruth took notice right away. "He was a mess," she remembered. Odd. Yet his quirks were sexy, perhaps because he seemed purposefully unorthodox, a quality he shared with his sister. Howard was now a handsome psychiatrist-in-training at Columbia University. Ruth was determined to marry a doctor. The two struck up a conversation and hit it off. Within weeks of the party, Howard brought Ruth up to the family apartment off the Grand Concourse to meet Dr. and Mrs. Davidman. Ruth recalled riding the elevator, a door opening, Mary the Irish maid, in uniform, and Joy's "gracious, gracious mother," Jeannette, with perfectly marcelled gray hair and a splendid purple dress. The maid served dinner, which they ate with expensive silverware that complemented the cut glassware. The couple married shortly thereafter.

Ruth was in awe of Joy, "terribly impressed" by her erudition and spirit. When Joy and a group of Jefferson School students went out to dinner after class one evening, Ruth joined them. They crowded into a Greenwich Village restaurant and were seated, with Joy at the head of the table. They had their menus open and "were in the midst of deciding what we were going to get," Ruth remembered, "when in walks a negro couple . . . The cashier was in full sight of all of us fourteen people, and I don't remember the conversation but I saw the cashier or the manager come up there and shake his head 'no.' And the couple turned around and walked out. Joy stood up and she said, 'Well, what are we waiting for!?' And fourteen of us stood up and walked out. That's Joy at her best." Joy was a woman of conviction and action, Ruth understood.

In her third trimester, Joy felt well and was even enjoying "the element of surprise" that came with a first pregnancy. Bill, too, eagerly anticipated parenthood. "We are both very happy about the whole business," he wrote to Dr. Briehl proudly. "Already the house is bulging with tiny garments and accessories." Despite their budget, the couple ate out often, and shopping was easy; in New York City, almost everything was right around the corner—groceries, laundry, friends, work.

"Young David or Miriam" was due around March 12, and although work had slowed considerably, Joy remained on the *New Masses* masthead as a contributing editor. She also contributed to a short anthology titled *Seven Poets in Search of an Answer,* which brought together the voices of Maxwell Bodenheim, Langston Hughes, Aaron Kramer, Alfred Kreymborg, Martha Millet, and Norman Rosten, in addition to Joy, "seven leading American poets of social change," according to the book's jacket. "Through the eyes of these poets . . . there is a message for America in the bombing of civilians in Spain and China, in the lynching of an innocent Negro in Mississippi, in the shooting of García Lorca, in the horror of a Nazi concentration camp." The collection featured seven of Joy's poems. In one, called "For the Nazis," she taunts Hitler's henchmen: "While you rave, / say, can you see now the depth of your grave?" Another, "Elegy for García Lorca," mourns the loss of the Spanish playwright; rumors about his death under Franco's regime suggested that he was murdered for being homosexual. "They killed him for the heart of man with which they can not come to terms," Joy wrote with compassion. Reviews were excellent. "Flaming words smoke and crackle in this brilliant symposium," declared the *San Francisco Chronicle.* "[The poets'] provocative protest is a ringing appeal for humane action—for democracy for all without reservations." The anthology was another successful publication for both Joy and her cause.

Joy's personal life was less triumphant. Her due date came and went. Bill cycled toward another spell of despair, unable to sleep without the aid of Nembutal. And Howard prepared for deployment. On March 24, President Roosevelt acknowledged to the American public a fact he had known for years: "In one of the blackest crimes of all history—begun by the Nazis in the day of peace and multiplied by them a hundred times in time of war—the wholesale, systematic murder of the Jews of Europe goes on unabated every hour." Joy offered sardonic parting words of advice to Howard to use in case, as a psychiatrist-in-training, he was assigned to confront Hitler's henchmen and probe their pathology: "Go easy with the Nazis, Howie. Strong as must be the temptation to prescribe strychnine, is better the psychologic approach. The arrogant and confident one who reads English is probably concealing a good deal of uncertainty." She recommended a regime of psychoanalysis and "laughing at them."

On March 27, more than two weeks past her due date, Joy gave birth to a son, David Lindsay Gresham. The baby was "an angel," large and healthy, with a full halo of hair. Joy chose to breast-feed—a disparaged practice at the time—in addition to formula-feeding, and observed the unconventional practice of satisfying the baby's appetite on demand. "Will take seven ounces at one feeding without turning a hair, the pig. Will probably be one of these disgustingly fat babies, but I haven't the heart to turn him down when he yells for a bottle after getting four ounces from the breast," she told Ruth and Howard. Joy found herself enjoying motherhood more than she expected. She loved watching Davy's smile develop. He flashed a brilliant grin whenever she cooed his name. Trips to the pediatrician replaced cultural events, but that wasn't so bad; her doctor was an art collector whose house was "practically wallpapered with Gauguins, Cézannes, Renoirs, El Grecos, etc.—originals!"

In the nineteen months since she had written "Women: Hollywood Style," the world had changed. Wartime shortages made the task of caring for a family far more arduous. Rubber was in short supply, and Joy had to craft diapers out of whatever cloth she could find. Fruit, meat, and other staples were scarce. Canned goods were rare, as most metal was sent to factories where women—primarily those whose husbands didn't need to be cooked and cleaned for because they were serving overseas—followed the example of Rosie the Riveter, welding plane parts and building fuselages for B-17 bombers. A U.S. Army poster presented women as soldiers without guns, depicting three beautiful women proudly doing their part on the home front: one with sleeves rolled up ready for manual labor, one with hair tied in a kerchief, one sitting at a typewriter. In 1943–44, the peak period of the war effort, one in every two women was employed.

Wartime shortages or no, Joy stood firm on her conviction that motherhood was "certainly not a full time business," but she admitted to Howard and Ruth that "it does tire me a little in combination with cooking, etc.," despite Bill's shouldering more of the load than many husbands did. She was nowhere near conceding to the prevailing notions of the day, but now was not the moment to ask Bill to contribute more time and energy to housework. With so many men abroad in valiant service to the country, the 4F designation was seen as a mark of shame, a blow to the ego. In addition, *Click* magazine was folding, putting Bill out of a job; its owners, he believed, wanted their share of paper to go toward another publication, *Seventeen.*

In the early weeks of Davy's life, Bill wrote a short horror story that Joy optimistically credited with exorcising his demons. His mood skyrocketed. Instantly, he quit taking the Nembutal, and by the time Davy was six weeks old, both father and son were sleeping soundly through the night. By May, Bill was feeling "better than ever in his life," and he was over the moon about the baby. "I guggle over [Davy] plenty myself," Joy told Howard and Ruth, "but you should see Bill. Expert with diapers, masterful with the carriage, will cuddle the baby for hours without tiring, hates to go out at night because he wants to rush home to look at the wonderful chile." When it comes to love and marriage, she advised her kid brother, having a baby "is more fun than anything before."

Like many young intellectual New Yorkers, Joy and Bill considered resettling in nearby Westchester County, raising a family where houses were charming and cheaper, the pace slower, and the commute manageable. Bill had found a full-time editorial job at *Theater Arts* magazine, but what he really wanted was to finish his novel. Joy wanted this for him too. In the two years since he began the book, psychiatric troubles, day jobs, the distractions of city living, and now the baby had limited his literary output to a mere six chapters. He saw only two options, he told Joy: either find a place where he could focus on the novel while not at the office or else postpone the project indefinitely. They decided to follow a minor migration of artists and writers to the Hudson River Valley and move to the town of Ossining, about twenty-five miles north of the city, with a quaint red-brick train station offering commuter rail service to and from Grand Central Station. With a move on the horizon, Bill had renewed energy and motivation and was "working like a demon on his novel," Joy wrote to Howard and Ruth on May 10.

The only major problem at present was Joy's mother, who had been driving Joy crazy since Davy's birth. Despite Jen's polish and poise, she was possessive and prone to hysteria that worsened with age. "I've got her in the habit of calling up our psychiatrist, who spares me the brunt," Joy wrote. "She was pretty good for a couple of weeks, then blam! she threw a hysterical scene for Dad's benefit, accusing me of loving Bill more than I love her (naturally!) and 'I'll see my grandchild in spite of you' etc. After that she was afraid to come near me for a while, and ran to the psychiatrist, who advised her to stay away. So did I, less politely."

Joy recalled this encounter when, months later, she wrote an article titled "Life with Mother," a review of Rosamond Lehmann's newly published novel, *The Ballad and the Source*. The book's leading lady, Sybil Jardine, was modeled after what Joy described as society's latest incarnation of the perfect matron, depicted in films and fiction as "sweet-voiced . . . well-dressed, well-lacquered, superlatively well-permanent-waved; devoted to worthy causes and bridge; a good housekeeper, with on the average two servants; a specialist in charm, understanding and motherly love; and a devourer of little children's bodies and hearts." Many mothers fit that modern formula, but Sybil was a narcissist who craved attention. Her natural wit, beauty, and charm were strategically used to win love and adoration. "Such a woman cannot afford to see anyone else receive love," Joy wrote. "She goes into paroxysms over her children's friends . . . and above all their mates." Joy laid down the law with Jen. "Now I've got her rationed," she told Howard and Ruth; "she can come for an hour or so once in two or three weeks. She's being very good again, but there are signs of strain. Boy, will I be tickled when we get up to Ossining, fairly well out of reach.

"Everything is very serene," she assured them, glowing with optimism that concealed any misgivings she may have had about moving to the relative isolation of the country with a new baby and an unstable husband. What could possibly go wrong?

· 8 ·

1944–1946

In the summer of 1944, the Gresham family moved into a three-room apartment in Ossining at number 173 North Highland Avenue, a house called Maple Lodge, situated on a wooded hillside high above the Hudson River. Joy and Bill plodded down a winding footpath through a meadow to bluffs overlooking the tidal "Muhhekunnetuk," an Algonquin name meaning "the river that flows both ways." There Joy could breathe the fragrant air—grassy, briny, and sweet—as she watched the flow of the same water that stroked Manhattan's West Side and caressed the Bronx, a back-and-forth rhythm that surged with symbolic possibilities. Would she be buoyed by her new routine or drown in the isolated simplicity of suburban stay-at-home motherhood?

Certainly the proximity to nature made country life more palatable. The lush land around the house inspired a hobby of identifying, gathering, and cooking edible wild plants and mushrooms—especially useful as wartime rationing heightened. Glancing out her window from where she sat at her typewriter composing a letter to Howard overseas, she surveyed the bounty. Within just twenty feet she could see mulberries, dandelion, sorrel, salsify, daylilies, lamb's quarters, milkweed, purslane, burdock, amaranth, ink cap mushrooms. "The Japanese have been eating all these things for generations, even in peacetime." With some ingenuity, she could make do with fruits, vegetables, and wild Westchester County rabbits.

Ossining's claim to fame, however, was not its scenic location or picturesque downtown. Before the Dutch settled much of the Hudson River Valley, the Sint Sinck Indians gave the land its original name, Sing Sing, which became the name of both the town and its state prison, opened in 1826. In 1901 a boycott of goods manufactured in Sing Sing, the prison, hurt local businesses that manufactured goods in Sing Sing, the village. Preferring an address unaffiliated with death row, residents changed the town's name to Ossining, but it remained best known for its penitentiary.

It seems appropriate that Joy was living in a town famous for its prison. Themes of captivity began seeping into her poems and letters. "Life up here is simpler and sweeter than in the city," she wrote to friends, "yet somehow, when a day is over, I do not burst into deathless prose." Between tending to Davy, washing diapers, managing meals, and cleaning house, she had little time or energy for writing. By summer's end, a haze of melancholy hovered over her; after just two years of marriage, she became conscious that passion with Bill was fading. She wrote a sonnet about the intensity she'd felt for an unrequited love five years earlier (most likely Bill Benét, though she didn't name him). Joy had been unable to see anything but him. He stood between her eyes and the light, eclipsing the sun. She'd written a poem for him back then, so intense, Joy admitted in a new sonnet, that it bore "the mark of madness." Joy was content in her marriage, but she missed a consuming passion. "Time brings a sad sobriety, I fear," she wrote in a poem that reads like a sigh of defeat; "And I'm a wife and mother all this year." A lot had happened in the year since she called Bill the "mythical Perfect Husband": her hospitalization, his drinking and depression, the threat of a 1A classification, the ebbing of her career, and parenthood. Now she thought of Bill as merely a "sufficient" husband.

Much as Joy wished success for her sufficient husband and financial stability for her family, it wasn't easy to watch Bill's career grow muscular while hers atrophied. In November, his agent, Carl Brandt, founder of the literary agency that represented Joy, sold his unfinished novel to Harcourt Brace. The publisher gave him a deadline of May 1, 1945, for the full manuscript. Meanwhile, Joy's entire published output for 1944 consisted of two poems and two book reviews for *New Masses*. Her name on the masthead had become little more than a formality.

Joy was accustomed to purging her powerful opinions in writing; she missed the time and platform for their expression. After reading an interview with Canada Lee, the stage and screen actor pioneering roles for African Americans, she found herself disapproving of his accepting the role of Caliban in a Broadway production of *The Tempest*. This fine "Negro" actor was not pushing Negro rights in the proper direction, Joy believed, by agreeing to the role of a mutant, outcast son of a witch impregnated by the devil. Joy secured Davy in his crib and stretched her fingers over the typewriter. The subject was *New Masses* material, but a paragraph in a letter to a friend was all she could manage. "I will be very glad to have some opportunity again to let loose my Sunday punch in print," she wrote later to Howard while snatching a few peaceful minutes before her "young man" began yelling for attention. Her best hope for career rejuvenation and a social life in the next few years, she said, was for Bill's book to become a best-seller.

As that transitional year ended, Joy realized with horror that she had succumbed to the life of a conventional housewife. Scrubbing the floor resentfully, she contemplated articles on "male chauvinism," but had only a few spare minutes to spew her polemics in letters. "Why, why, why is it always the Joys and Alices that stop writing to mind infants, and never the Bills and Jerrys?" she wrote to her friends Alice and Jerry Jerome. "Men is WORMS." But Joy didn't place blame only on husbands: "The real trouble is not with the men, but with the women." Look at the women's magazines, she pointed out. The *Ladies' Home Journal* alone published reams of articles by women arguing against their married sisters' joining the workforce. For one reason among many, they argued, if a wife earns success her husband can't match, "it hurts his male pride to have his woman winning, on her own, the business laurels he had hoped to lay at her feet . . . Whether he knows it or not, he has an age-old male resentment of the fact that his woman is out in the world about her business instead of staying safely in the cave he provides for her."

And yet Joy herself was becoming their accomplice, enabling and perpetuating the construct. What choice did she have? "I myself wouldn't dream of reversing the usual procedure and compelling Bill to stay home while I go out and work," she said.

> Staying at home would really make him suffer and feel inferior, whereas it only mildly incommodes me. What I'm mad about is the prevailing notion—even Bill falls into it at times—that, because I'm a woman, it's quite correct for me to be living this vegetable, parasitic life. I'm not suffering from overwork, but from a species of enforced mental and physical idleness; housework fills your time, but damn it, it doesn't make any really satisfactory demands either of your muscles or of your mind. You just get tired in a nasty, irritable sort of way. And you don't have the reward which gives productive work point, for when you have finished your housework there is nothing of any value to show for it and you start right over. In short, as Sherman did not say, socially unproductive labor is Hell. And I resent the contemptuous fashion in which the world demands no more of me—because I am female . . . Nobody ever tells [housewives] inertia is dishonorable; they're brought up to think homemaking (what a word) the crown of life, the greatest bliss, etc. Even in wartime, even in this America; take a look at the movies and the women's magazines. A gal who gets out and takes a war job is actually supposed to be making a sacrifice, instead of getting out of a prison. Now the real attraction of housework is that it is the most easy, irresponsible form of work in the world, but you don't catch any of the parasite-class of women admitting that. They do their damndest to escape from the real world into the dreamworld of housekeeping-with-soap-operas; not having been taught the truth that only productive work

> can ever fill an adult's life satisfactorily, they are then bored and miserable without knowing why.

Then there was the "housework-frustrated mamma" who "devour[s] the children's lives to make up for the one she hasn't got," or who unnecessarily complicates her housework. "She drapes her windows in fancy curtains to give her lotsa extra washing, she carefully selects furniture full of nooks and crannies hard to clean, she burrows into corners of the apartment that nobody knows are there . . . [E]ventually this insanely magnified task becomes so important to her that her family can't breathe or smoke or relax in a home which is no longer a home, but Momma's Substitute for Productive Work."

As ice floes formed on the Hudson, Joy felt increasingly trapped, burrowing into semi-hibernation along with the rest of Westchester County, limiting her human interaction to a drooling infant, a husband—who, when home from the office, furiously pounded away at his novel—and, for a brief time, "a forty year old adolescent upstairs who moved to Yonkers because Ossining had only one movie house . . . the sort of female . . . who will shrivel and die when separated from the movies and the juke joint for two weeks." Icicles hung like steel bars outside her window. "I can sit in a house looking out at the lovely icicles and be perfectly happy; but I can't stop writing and be perfectly happy, and I do like to see my friends." Other than a February visit to Belle in the city, Joy's life was almost as devoid of activity and companionship as in her lonely adolescence. As she'd done then, Joy sought solace in books. She began devoting free moments to studying psychological theory, specifically analyzing "the death-fear as primary human impulse, underlying libido and everything else." Death was on her mind. Over the summer her aunt Rose—Renee's mother—had received a wire from the War Department informing her that her son Bobby had been killed in action on July 13 in New Guinea. Joy knew Howard and Lindsay could be next.

Freud, Joy learned, conjectured that a fear of dying concealed various unconscious fears—of abandonment or castration, for example.

But Joy felt that he had not written enough on the topic. "Freud and his disciples" talked around death, she noted. "A dying class always denies or evades the death-fear, till it spreads out and swallows up their whole lives. I'm getting a Marxist theory of the unconscious into shape, slowly, with lots of references to Karen Horney"—a psychoanalyst who was blazing trails by building on Freud's theories and pioneering feminine psychology. Horney's books included *The Neurotic Personality of Our Time* and *Self-Analysis.* "No professional analyst will admit the death-fear as primary motive if he can help it, though; for of course the death-fear is the one thing analysis cannot remove; it's real."

In the disorienting milieu of war, isolation, and identity crisis, reading again served as a mechanism of self-preservation. Throughout 1945 and 1946, Joy lost herself in fantasy—*Astounding Science Fiction* magazine and books by a newly popular British author, C. S. Lewis: a trilogy of his adult novels (*Out of the Silent Planet, Perelandra,* and *That Hideous Strength*), *The Great Divorce,* and *The Screwtape Letters,* a Christian satire that had become a recent sensation on both sides of the Atlantic. An epistolary novel, it follows the diabolical Screwtape—undersecretary to "Our Father Below"—as he schools his devil-in-training nephew Wormwood in underhanded techniques to win back the soul of a young man who has joined the "Enemy" camp of Christianity. In the opening chapter, Screwtape relays an anecdote about one of his own "patients," a "sound atheist," possibly representing Karl Marx, who wrote *Das Kapital* in the British Museum. One morning in the library, he tells Wormwood, Screwtape noticed a train of thought running the wrong way through his patient's mind; God ("the Enemy") immediately attended to the man's mind, threatening to undo twenty years of the devil's work. Screwtape suggested that the man break for lunch; the Enemy urged the man to stay: this was more important than lunch. Screwtape slyly agreed. In fact, "much *too* important to tackle at the end of a morning." The patient perked up at the idea, relieved to shrug off the burden of strange contradictions to everything he stood for. "By the time I had added 'Much better come back after lunch and go into it with a fresh mind,' he was already half way to the door," Screwtape recounts. "Once he was in the street the battle was won . . . He knew he'd had a narrow escape and in later years was fond of talking about 'that inarticulate sense for actuality which is our ultimate safeguard against the aberrations of mere logic.' He is now safe in Our Father's house." Screwtape explains his strategy: "It's funny how mortals always picture us as putting things into their minds: in reality our best work is done by keeping things out." Reading this, Joy fleetingly wondered if she'd fallen for similar tricks.

Lewis's writing challenged Joy to think twice about her long-held convictions. "These books stirred an unused part of my brain to momentary sluggish life," she later wrote. "Of course, I thought, atheism was *true,* but I hadn't given quite enough attention to developing the proof of it. Someday, when the children were older, I'd work it out."

Children. Joy was pregnant again, due November 8. Her life was soon obliterated by morning, noon, and night sickness. Months away from being born, her second child was already cutting her off further from the world. When Joy received an invitation to tea from Charles D. Abbott, the man who had solicited her manuscripts in 1940 for the University of Buffalo's poetry collection, she had no choice but to decline, citing her "early, uneasy stage of pregnancy." Her thirtieth birthday that April could not have been much of a celebration; "uneasy stage of pregnancy" was formal parlance for, as she put it to Howard, "my next offspring . . . raising hell with my guts." Joy spent nearly two months in bed "fulla sedatives, with Bill going crazy tending to me and Davy." In addition to his editorial work, Bill had been supplementing their income by freelancing—writing detective stories for magazines like *Ellery Queen* and *American,* which paid anywhere from $100 to $350—while writing research-heavy features for *Theater Arts*. With most of his time at home that spring devoted to caring for Joy and the baby, delivering his novel to Harcourt Brace by May 1 was an impossibility.

Joy was relieved that she didn't have to spend time in a hospital, and she emerged from the worst of her pregnancy with her sense of humor still intact. "Suggested idea for Big Peacetime Research: Stop

Pregnancy Puking," she joked in a letter to Howard. "Most dames don't have it this bad—but why should any of us? Ought to be a simple and profitable research. I imagine it hadn't been done before because of old patterns of thinking about the curse of Eve, natural and correct suffering, etc. Grrr." In mid-May, Joy traveled into the city for an ob-gyn examination, and the doctor found everything "swell." By the end of the month, though still dizzy and weak, she was able to get around and look after Davy while Bill worked at a manic pace, "tearing through the last part of his novel in a lil cottage in the back yard which we've rented for a studio, MacDowell Colony fashion."

The cottage in the back became a sort of guesthouse, in addition to Bill's writing studio, with two furnished rooms, a bed, a stove, water, and electricity. Ruth slept there on her frequent weekend visits. She, Bill, and Joy would talk and laugh together, although Joy tended to weight the conversations with intellectualism. "Her erudition was overwhelming. No matter what small conversation we were having, her brilliance took over," Ruth recalled. While her sister-in-law wasn't dour, "she did not register as a happy person"—unlike Bill. "*He* did. He was happy all the time . . . singing Civil War songs, doing magic." Bill had resurrected the magic tricks of his carny days as a hobby. He had an overabundance of energy and was "grinding stories and his book out like sausages," Ruth observed. Joy provided editorial assistance as he completed his novel, titled *Nightmare Alley,* and on June 25, he went to the city to deliver the manuscript—"finished at last and first-rate I think," Joy pronounced.

Now that the war in Europe had ended, the little cottage out back, Joy told Howard, was "all ready for brother with wife to move into while getting breath and looking around, or whatever." She hoped that would be soon. The world had changed while Joy languished through the first trimester of her second pregnancy: "I suppose I ought to be grateful; it insulated me, at all events, from the political situation here." On April 12, President Roosevelt had died suddenly of a cerebral hemorrhage, just weeks before the Germans surrendered to the Allies. The United Nations Conference in San Francisco —a "circus," Joy scoffed—was in full swing, and Ezra Pound was arrested for treason by American troops in Italy. "Now watch our liberal literary pukes whine him off, on the ground that you must only expect social responsibility from an artist so long as there's money in it. Do I sound cynical? Put it down to my digestion."

After V-E Day, Joy entertained illusions of Howard savoring postwar Europe—sightseeing along the Rhine and lunching with Nazi generals, complying with what she felt was overly benevolent treatment of the Nazis on the part of the Allies. "Hell, I shoulda gone to war instead of becoming a wife and momma. Only I'm afraid my straightforward female nature would not mix with the beautiful military correctness your colleagues have been showing toward their captives. In plain civilian language, sooner I should shtick them a bayonet up the ass yet." Howard believed that some Germans had been coerced into becoming Nazis. This incensed Joy.

> Surely you realize by now that the average Fritz, like the average anybody else, doesn't make a fanatic and eager Nazi for more than five minutes at a time. He merely acquiesces in what is requested of him, because it's easier to acquiesce than to think or fight as an individual. But the acquiescent are as guilty as the active in these matters, and perhaps even more contemptible. Also, the law of history is that the acquiescent get it in the neck, and serve them right; if you had rather be a sheep than a man, you are entitled to a sheep's end, and any protection or encouragement of your sheephood merely delays the day when you realize you must be a man or die. There's been all sorts [of] jabber in our press by pseudopsychiatrists about the Germans being paranoic (with our psychoneurosis rejections we shouldn't throw stones) and by moralists about their being hopelessly wicked. Hooey. Their real offense is much greater. They were stupid . . .
>
> Anyone in Germany who had a genuine desire not to be a Nazi did something about it in spite of the danger—even if all he did was to run like hell out of there . . . I'm not saying you have to do anything mean to the simpler Fritzes, but I *would* like to see a certain confiscation of ill-gotten gains and ill-used factories. Noo?

In June, Joy felt well enough to climb the bluffs overlooking the Hudson once again, sometimes with Ruth when she visited. The two women were growing closer and made plans to go in late July to the lakeside log cabin the Davidmans rented each year in Maine, each of the women acting as a buffer state for the other, although Joy noted that her parents had recently been cowed by Davy. "I let Mother play with him to her heart's content one day not long ago. She came off with a damaged eye and a large tooth-wound on the cheek. What a child."

Ruth could tell that something was weighing on Joy's mind when they arrived at the cabin for what Joy jokingly dubbed "the Great Maine Expedition." During the first two days, she found Joy "very tense & not like herself." Being around her parents was never relaxing, and "seeing them through Ruth's eyes made them look worse," Joy told Howard. In scenes echoing moments from Joy's childhood with her cousin Renee, Joy's mother, "with a snarl of malice showing through the phony smile . . . praised [Ruth] for this and that, not for her own sake, but in order to imply how defective *I* was by contrast." Howard had warned his new wife about these games, and Ruth "saw through every little catty trick instantly," calling Jen's behavior "vicious."

As for Joy's father, he was "a confounded *bore,*" in Ruth's words—and a nuisance. He insisted on joining the two women in the rowboat to fish, insisted on rowing and baiting the lines, and, when he failed to land a catch, insisted that no one had caught fish in that lake the whole summer. One evening Joy and Ruth sneaked out on their own, rowed out into the lake, cast their lines, and floated about in peace. Suddenly they got a bite, and then another and another. It was after dusk when they finally rowed back to the dock, where Joy's father stood grimly. Grumbling, he secured the boat. The women didn't show him their bucket of fish; Ruth carried it straight into the house and plunked it down on the living room floor. Joy's mother and Mary, the Irish maid, "fluttered about and exclaimed over them." Joy's father came in, "peeked at them resentfully & said 'Why did you catch so many?'" The sisters-in-law exchanged sidelong, self-satisfied glances. "I hope you don't expect me to clean them," he barked. Joy and Ruth rolled up their sleeves "gleefully" and began to flay and gut their catch. "Well," Ruth recounted, "unable to see us so happy, he later came into the kitchen and took over. He looked at me. 'Ruth you said you hated fish—you'll have to eat these.'" Joy "accidentally" smacked him in the face with a fish.

Joy didn't divulge to Ruth the source of her tension, but it wasn't just her parents. Money was becoming an issue, though not the only one. The timeline isn't clear, but sometime after finishing his novel, Bill left his steady job at *Theater Arts*. The Greshams were now dependent on the pulp market, which Joy called merely "adequate," adding, "I wish we had another steady market so Bill wouldn't worry to excess as he has a way of doing." They had enough money for "reasonable comforts," although there were few to be found, owing to war shortages. As she told Howard:

> There just isn't any laundry, and all your household doodads break down and you can't get them fixed and the butcher denies you meat while sneaking a steak out of the back room for Mrs. Richbitch, and you are served in the restaurant, after an hour or so, by a droolmouthed moron who brings all the wrong orders and sneers if you protest . . . and your sheets wear out and you can't buy new ones . . . and no baby clothes or mending thread or needles . . . and the mask off the once-smiling face of Business, showing the real wolfleer . . . and no diaper deliveries . . . and my god nowhere to live, the lucky ones, like us, crammed into places too small for them and the unlucky offered, as a dream of hope, the prospect that New York may reopen some of its condemned cold-water slum flats for them.

Still, for the time being the Greshams' finances weren't too desperate.

There was something else—something surprising. Lewis's books had had more of an impact than Joy consciously realized. Three days into the vacation, Joy and Ruth went for a long walk in the woods. Joy started talking about suffering and sin. "She was beginning to talk about sin as a concept," Ruth remembered. In the gravest of tones, Joy told Ruth about a high school incident. "You know, I could do anything," she said. "I could get the best grades, I played the piano beautifully." There was a recital in the gymnasium. The performer before Joy walked to the piano and played Chopin. Joy knew the piece well. "When she sat down," Joy recounted, "it was my turn. What did I do? Played the same piece, only I played it ten times better. Ruth," Joy said, "that was sinful."

Joy's sudden acknowledgment of sin was very much an intellectual leap and made little difference to her behavior, especially toward her parents. In a letter to Howard, she referred to her mother as "the old bitch" and called her father "a bad-tempered, ill-mannered, pompous, domineering, petulant old jackass." But by the end of the week, Joy simply rolled her eyes at him, joking about his garden, "every row a masterpiece of surveying . . . every weed absent like Hitler from Berlin, every plant fairly bathed in manure. Po'lil plants. That much manure is like feeding a baby exclusively on chocolate marshmallow fudge sundaes, but I didn't even try to tell him so; what's the use. When we left all the plants—even the radishes, which normally take three weeks from seed to table—were exactly as when we came." Joy returned home to Maple Lodge and inspected her own "po'neglected unweeded patch of greens," heavily laden tomato plants, golden-yellow Bantam corn, Swiss chard, cucumbers, and more, "rows crooked or not even rows at all. Beans all snarled up with corn, etc. Manure practically absent all season," as she described it. "I shoulda been ashamed. I wasn't. I just got me a big pot and picked three pounds of wax beans." They lived for weeks on the yield. It was a good thing.

> The food shortage which all along has existed mainly in the minds of the spoilt, overfed, and lazy, has finally become a real problem, conjointly (strangely enough) with an intensive Congressional drive against price ceilings. Somewhere there must be alot [*sic*] of little lambs and steers and piggles frolicking, little knowing that their extended life will cease the moment that the OPA does. At any rate, there's been no discoverable meat or chicken in Os-

> sining for a month, barring stuff in cans and jars, and practically none in New York except in black-market butchers. Food queues are a commonplace, and the city reports considerable malnutrition; I've been dreaming about meat at night myself, though we do better than most . . . If you're in the habit of spending lots on food you can find some, but on closely-figured incomes it must be murder. Other shortages have been sugar, and even potatoes. Starvation, of course, is not in question; merely the ill effects of a starch diet, and housewife's neurosis—after all, how many different ways can you serve rice? . . . [S]o sorry would still like honorable piece beefsteak, to tell you the truth.

Surely life was better in Russia, Joy still believed. Although she had been steadily drifting away from the Communist Party, Joy continued to idealize Stalin: "It would seem the Russians are starting a program of reeducation, rebuilding, and feeding, with encouragement of trade unions and the like, whereas we have come out in favor of name-calling, semistarvation, and suppression of everything except big industrialists. Unerhört! Unmöglich!" *Outrageous! Impossible!* Meanwhile, the United States was a mess, as usual. "The State Department has just distinguished itself by arresting as spies and Red conspirators six journalists who were so ill-advised as to believe in freedom of the press, whereas everyone from Truman down is now patting Nazi agents on the head and saying Go in peace and sin no more."

JOY WAS GLAD to get home; she had missed Bill and Davy. Her son, nearly seventeen months old now, amused her daily with "new words, new teeth, new skills, new stunts, and new devilment," and his transformation into a personality: "He is developing a strong will (goody) and lots of independence and activity (hooray) and does not demand to be fussed over at all. *That's* training, of course. It has never occurred to him that you Gotta have momma around all the time or you will Die." He had developed a vocabulary, Joy said, of "seven or eight words, if you give him the benefit of every doubt." Bill relished nighttime check-ins after Davy was in bed; he glowed after glimpsing the round, dark eyes that peered back at him from beneath the covers.

The next child was developing on schedule as well, kicking "like a steer," Joy commented. "Ought to pass it in a file in a piece of pie so it can crush its way out." Overall, though, this pregnancy was a nuisance. "For one thing," Joy said, "the element of surprise is lacking, and it's just a routine and unexciting business. For another, last time I had practically nothing to do—no job, no baby, no cleaning, no shopping problems, and we ate out half the time." Being pregnant during the summer was "really painful," and Joy had given in to wearing a maternity girdle. "[I] feel as if I were cased in lead." Her biggest complaint, however, was boredom. Not long after she returned from Maine, Joy's energy dropped again, ending her hiking days for the season.

But what upset her most during this time, and for months to come, was not conditions during the war but the event that had ended it—the atomic bomb, the result of "the nullity of Truman as a leader" and America's "rush to get things finished, no matter how." Everyone wanted the war over—wanted their men home, meat on their tables, sugar in their coffee, gasoline in their tanks. But at this cost? The bomb—so enormous an event that, "relative to it, the war itself shrank to minor significance," declared *Time* magazine—polarized the nation and "created a bottomless wound in the living conscience of the race. [Humankind] had won the most Promethean of its conquests over nature, and had put into the hands of common man the fire and force of the sun itself. In an instant, without warning, the present had become the unthinkable future. Was there hope in that future, and if so, where did hope lie?" Horror, anxiety, fear, existential despair: all of it clamped itself onto Joy's psyche.

During her years with Bill, Joy had become an avid reader of the pulp magazines to which he now contributed, including *Astounding Stories,* which published "superscience" tales featuring, among other fantastical notions, atomic energy. When America destroyed Hiroshima and Nagasaki, fiction became reality. Joy, however, had long been a believer. "The last years of reading good old Astounding Stories, which being written by and for engineers has been talking atomic bombs quite plainly for some time now, have left me unsurprised but with at least enough knowledge of the damn thing to be somewhat upset." The harnessing of atomic energy "may be the beginning of the end of cities altogether . . . The next war finds me and kids hiding in a cave in the Great North Woods." She was only half-joking. The bomb had introduced the possibility "that civilization may be destroyed entirely, that all life may be destroyed. I am not an alarmist," she wrote to a friend. "This *can* be done." Joy went so far as to suggest to Howard the possibility of buying a yacht together and cruising the Southern Hemisphere with their families "in order to avoid the imminent catastrophe she felt was coming, and coming soon," he recounted.

Joy's identity as a poet had been cast from the mold of war, with its oppression, violence, insurrection, and death. Like young writers of every generation, she thought she could change the world with her words. She was beginning to contemplate futility. "I wanted to *do* something," she wrote. But what had she done? Had she saved lives? Righted wrongs? Empowered the masses? Joy couldn't know the range of impact she had on readers, but whatever her contributions toward the causes of peace and equality, the present state of the world made her feel defeated. In a poem titled "Tragic Muse," written in 1945, Joy expresses her helplessness and identifies with victims, seeming to feel almost as if she herself died their deaths—as if she were one of the four hundred Jewish women and children locked in a church and burned alive in the French village of Oradour-sur-Glane the previous year, or one of the Romanians hung on meat hooks and mutilated in mockery of kosher ritual slaughtering practices.

> Poor poet,
> they have killed you too often. The bird does not sing.
> They have buried you too often with the jagged bones of
> children

sprouting from the hasty trench. They have burned you in
    locked churches.
They have shut you in with the secret sigh of gas
too often, too often, too often, too often, too often.
You hung on meathooks in the Rumanian slaughterhouse.

And so the bird does not fly any more.

And then:

Do not ask her to sing any more.
She is tired.

Joy wrote of Spain, the battle of Teruel and schoolchildren murdered in the streets; of "the soldier whom it took twenty years to make / smashed willfully in a moment"; and of the baby whose last breath was poisoned air. "It does not matter" what one does, says, or writes. Maybe writing wasn't how she was going to change the world after all. Motherhood suddenly took on new meaning.

. . . Shed your tears,
Plant the sterile headstone over the grave
and make new children. Not in your time
perhaps, the whiteness, the singing and the peace,
and men will die whatever you can do;
but there is always the miracle, the child.

But Joy was bringing a second child into a world where "ashes that were babies / blew among the bamboo trees," as she wrote in another poem, implanting regret within the hope of new life.

SEPTEMBER BROUGHT NEW personal trials. Davy reached the terrible twos six months early. "In a week he's changed from a good little boy who clung to Momma's thumb and trotted along beside her to a young savage who runs down every alley, dashes into lovely ashpiles, bites Momma when she tries to hold him . . . Thank God for a kid who's into everything, afraid of nothing, and who considers Momma a handy appendage to be dragged along behind but not encouraged too much." Joy could no longer handle him and the housework by herself. "At present I am so damned unwieldy and ineffectual that the smallest job is a terror; I can't climb a hill, I can't breathe on hot days, and I HURT, damn it. Ouch." Bill took over, as he had done with her first pregnancy, but in addition to writing and caring for Davy, he became burdened by a nasty bout of hay fever that induced severe asthma attacks, leading to sleepless nights for both him and Joy. One night was so terrifying that a doctor had to be called to come and give him an injection. Meanwhile, diaper and laundry service ceased for reasons Joy didn't quite understand, and store shelves were curiously ill-stocked.

Bill had been writing enough detective tales to reassure Joy that their financial prospects were "good enough . . . as long as there are people willing to pay for stories about imaginary crimes, written so dully they sound as if they actually happened." She felt bad for Bill, having to tie down his soaring talent "to keep it uninteresting enough," but was grateful they had the money to afford modest comforts, even if comforts remained tough to come by. "I fear I have reached the point where a car, a maid, and a house big enough to hold us would be unutterable bliss. The life of a proletariat housewife, which is what I have been leading perforce lately, is perhaps even drearier than an enforced stay in Paris," she wrote Howard, teasing him for his complaints about being stuck there.

Bill was also trying his hand at making money from magic. Someone paid him $10 for mind reading, "our first income along these lines but something tells me not our last," Joy reported. Indeed, Bill began to be hired for gigs in the city, which often kept him away in the evenings. Ruth set one up at her childhood Methodist church in Yonkers and acted as his assistant. Joy and Bill "had a way of going their own way," Ruth recalled, the kind of couple who didn't need to be joined at the hip at all times. "They were probably a generation ahead of themselves in independence" within a marriage.

But while Joy gave the impression of being comfortable with Bill having a life outside of work and family, she herself was going stir-crazy. When Ruth told Joy that Howard couldn't wait to come home from Paris, make love to his wife, and start a family and a career, Joy spun into an irrational frenzy and wrote him a long chastising letter:

> Any other time, the chance to spend months in Paris during one of the most interesting crises of French history would have been meat and drink to you . . . I take it you are well fed, sleep on a proper bed, and have plenty to drink; have lots of time for sight-seeing; money enough for adequate pleasures; a chance to study psychiatry, etc. And all you can think of is getting back to the pleasures of reconversion and the diverting round of making a living in postwar America . . .
>
> Can't you imagine the future of all those homesick boys with you, once they do get back and make some shift at marrying, settling down and raising the kids, wringing some security and decency out of this crumbling world? Can't you see them turning up yearly at the Legion conventions, each year a little more sodden, a little more loud-mouthed, a little more defeated and corrupted and embittered, with a few more hatreds for convenient underdogs to make them forget they're underdogs themselves—can't you see them getting their only glory and glamour out of their soldiering memories, putting on silly caps and getting soused and pretending they're still the bright young army that conquered the world and screwed all the girls? Do you think they will find anything in peace better than what they find in war? Or isn't it, perhaps, an inner emptiness or corruption that makes them find nothing but emptiness in experiences for which I, frankly, would give what's left of my teeth? . . . Not that I blame them; they are as they have so carefully been made. Only I should hate to see you fall into their pattern, and toss away all the potential richness around you merely because you're in a hurry to screw your wife.

Joy was "a trifle uneasy" about sending the letter; she knew it was punishing. Howard responded by explaining the harsh reality of his living conditions: tents, cold chlorinated water, soldiers who had forgotten they were ever anything else. Joy felt terrible about her outburst. In what was for her almost an apology letter, she admitted that while she was aware of "the vast gulf these days between soldier-ignorance and civilian-ignorance," had she known the gritty details, she "shouldn't have said any of it." Her letter also had been written before Bill's brother spent five days with them after years in the army, returning from overseas with "no trade, no college degree, no friends, no attitude toward life except a gray despair, nowhere to live but that madhouse of cackling old people in Brooklyn, no money—and a serious character neurosis." Joy and Bill helped him seek psychiatric care.

Not that any of it mattered in the long run: "Over all of this, meanwhile, hangs the end." Joy contemplated the nation's problems: "Anti-Semitism . . . now respectable in the halls of Congress; a dock strike being blamed for the prolonged return of veterans; tax rebates for the rich through Congress, the new Dies (i.e. Rankin) Committee holding a red hunt, Congressional and state attacks on the union-labor rights so painfully won in the thirties . . . unemployment . . . inflation . . . unemployment." All of it was moot. "The atomic bomb, quite simply, makes our entire form of organization obsolete . . . Our cities are to all intents and purposes mere mausoleums already, peopled by the walking dead."

The combination of physical exhaustion, Bill's allergies, and Davy acting "like a runaway atom bomb" had become emotionally overwhelming, and as her November due date neared, Joy's dwindling energy nosedived. "I would love to be a strong heroic woman who could go on scrubbing floors and plowing fields right into labor pains," she told Howard, "but I'd better admit I am no such thing. I Get Tired. In fact, I feel too weak to stand up, and it bothers me." So Joy and Bill took a measure that demonstrated how far they'd strayed from their communist ethics: they hired a maid.

On November 9, Joy went into labor, and thus began a "rather unnecessarily drastic" two-week stay at the Bronx Hospital. She was given Demerol, which caused her to be violently sick with "paroxysms at both ends all day," she reported. "[I] screamed and threw myself about something pretty, beat with my fists on the wall, bit my arms, tore the skin off my thighs with my nails, and produced lots of new noises." A twenty-year-old woman in the earlier stages of labor with her first child looked on from her bed nearby, terrified. "Honey, it isn't as bad as it sounds!" Joy managed to shout between contractions. After twenty-four hours, she gave birth to Douglas Howard Gresham.

Labor and delivery were only the beginning of her troubles. With the nursing shortage due to the war, Joy wasn't exaggerating when she said that hospitals were determined to "overwork, starve, and underpay nurses just as long as they can get away with it." The first night after delivery, it took Joy hours just to get a glass of water. When it became clear that the nurses were taking out their bitterness on patients, Joy swung into action. "Your sister is now the Terror and Wonderment of the Bronx Hospital," she wrote to Howard. "She produces 9 lb. 6 oz. sons (first reaction of the average Grand Concourse elegant fimmale: My Gawd, didn't your doctor put you on a diet?) . . . she dares to ask the nurses for service (and doesn't get it); she criticizes the nursery's methods of handling babies (which stink); and she Nurses the child (referred to delicately as Feeding Him Yourself). Also she gets out of bed on the second day and proceeds to make life mizzable for evildoers."

Joy was fed up with some of her fellow patients, too. "These dames, whose expressed ideal in life is to be Just a Good Housewife with the Husband and Kiddies, don't even seem capable of bearing really good children." Preemies and "five and six pounders" populated the nursery alongside her own "gudgeous" child, who looked to Joy as if he'd been born a three-month-old. But Joy also showed a deep compassion for her disconsolate roommates. The hospital was disorganized and insensitive enough to put Joy in with a severely depressed patient who'd lost her baby at eight months after "a spectacular fall" that Joy sensed was not an accident. The woman had one child already and didn't really want another. "Sometime in life her self-confidence had been damaged to the point where she couldn't resist conventional social pressures forcing her into the housewife pattern," Joy said, without the least bit of irony. "I was frankly scared of the possible effect of psychological probing at a time like that . . . but was eventually forced to ask a couple of key questions." Her roommate opened up with "a great burst of rage against conventional housewifism; the gal suddenly realized that she loathed it and that other things were possible." Joy recommended that she take courses at the Jefferson School, gave her some books, and recited poetry about walking among Ossining beech woods.

While Joy was in the hospital, Bill stayed a week with Ruth and another week at home alone with Davy in Ossining. The second, he said, "was a killer"; remaining sober enough to care for a toddler on his own overwhelmed him. His drinking was getting out of control, and he didn't care. Bill gloated in a letter to Howard about a drunken night spent out dancing with the "babes" who lived upstairs, an episode hazy with flirtation and round after round of double Manhattans. Eventually, Bill recounted, he passed out. "I found myself home in bed but the bed spun around and shook me out on the floor and I made it to the can on hands and knees, in the traditional posture of the Greshams of Gresham Hall and shot the last four rounds of Manhattans down the krapper and got back to bed and that washow [*sic*] I celebrated the arrival of your nephew."

THE GRESHAM HOUSEHOLD at Maple Lodge now included six cats, two thousand books, and a pair of infants. Despite Bill's drinking and chronic sinus problems—for which he had regular "x-ray treatments" (radiation therapy)—exacerbated by the allergies, he brought in good money: $110 for a short monthly murder magazine column alone, which covered their rent. "My god how the money rolls in," Joy said. "This can't be us."

But things went downhill fast. As fall disintegrated into winter, the Hudson Valley landscape outside Maple Lodge resembled a skeletal version of its truer self. Nearby boulders now looked more like skulls amid the brittle bones and sinew of tree limbs and branches, a botanical graveyard on the cliffs rising above the frozen Hudson River. Atomic dread, postpartum depression, and an unstable husband converged to fill Joy with an inner world-weariness that made her feel darker than the dark Northeast winter days, which closed in tighter than the cramped quarters of their rooms at 173 North Highland Avenue. She was physically and mentally exhausted, apathetic, and unable to focus. Her misery dragged on like a low-grade fever. Worries about the bomb continued to plague her. "All the world had lost faith in gradual progress," she later reflected. "If now, in the day of the atomic bomb, I were to lose my trust in violent means of creating heaven on earth, what earthly hope was there?" She visited Belle in Manhattan one Friday in February; the two had an "eloquent talk about edible herbs, atomic war and decadence," Belle wrote in her diary, but Joy was otherwise isolated with her babies, her alcoholic husband, and her fears.

"I have two sons, two sons, two sons / And terror in my head," she wrote in an exquisite poem called "This Year of the Atom."

> this is nadir, the moment
> wet and black at the bottom of the world
> before the rotation lifts the ocean over the horizon
> bright, painted with brightness, wearing
> light, heartbreaking light.

Nadir. The moment. Heartbreaking light. Like so many poems written throughout her life, "This Year of the Atom" has a sibylline quality, as if Joy were touched with some divine gift of knowing. Something compelled her to close "This Year of the Atom" with hope for a miraculous new beginning.

> The light is quiet.
> The dry bones lift themselves out of the bottomless ditch,
> assemble into man and go to get their breakfast.
>
> sun, rise and shine.

It was the kind of resurrection Joy very much needed, but instead, things got worse. Inexplicably, on March 8, Harcourt Brace canceled Bill's contract for his novel *Nightmare Alley* before publication. Records offer no explanation. It had to have been a great blow. Bill's $1,000 advance would have to be repaid. He got a new job in the city, which kept him at work for long, late hours, but allowed him to refund the advance. Meanwhile, the book was resold to the publishing house Rinehart & Co.

Joy and Bill wore their troubles on their faces when they attended monthly meetings of a local leftist group that gathered "in a large, drafty old Victorian house off Ossining's Main Street," remembered Helen Puner, a fellow member. "The light inside was crepuscular; the heat in winter, non-existent. Joy and her husband would show up. They were *very nervous* people. Very high strung. I used to think that if I talked to her, she would run away in a fright. They didn't literally shake but they seemed to be shaking anyway. (Perhaps Gresham was a drinker?) . . . They looked to me as if they were living in a nightmare." Bill later agreed: "My days were filled with neurotic problems, writing problems, and the needs of my children."

THE "WEEKS HAVE gone so slowly and painfully here," Joy wrote on April 3, 1946, but spring soon revived her. Maple trees wore a haze of new leaves. The scraggly forsythia bushes, which bore a distant likeness to the ever-untidy bun of black hair Joy assembled at the nape of her neck, were now adorned with bright yellow blooms. The lawn had shed its pall of pale brown and sprouted a fresh northeastern blend of clover, fine fescue, and broad-bladed, deep-green Kentucky bluegrass. "There's violets and appil blossoms, and yesterday I dug me some wild oyster plant roots and they were delicious," Joy reported to Howard. She began planting her garden.

Joy's name was still on the masthead of *New Masses,* though in all of 1945 she contributed just two book reviews and one poem. The magazine was floundering. During the second week of April, she "escaped from prison and went to an *NM* meeting planned to improve the magazine." They wanted to go in a new direction with "a more open kind of poetry," according to poet Tom McGrath. Joy called the magazine "a dilution of the already milk-and-piss New Republic," suffocating under its incompetent current editors. "They didn't know there was such a thing as a technique of editing," she later wrote, "and [refused] to consider the possibility of learning it. They didn't know anything about their readers and did nothing to find out; their position was that reading *New Masses* was a moral duty, so it didn't have to be interesting. They existed only by begging money from soft-hearted Party groups and members." On April 16, Joy's name appeared on the masthead for the last time.

AT HOME, JOY felt "less chained down" as the woods sprouted violets and she regained the energy to walk among them. "Went out yesterday to get berry bushes for transplanting and fell inna swamp," she reported. "Pulled my leg out and left my shoe. Recaptured shoe and waded out half shoeless . . . More fun. Brought home a hunk of bloodroot and transplanted that; it takes very well and has already put out some new flowers. It used to grow near where Howie and I lived as kids, and we were very fond of it." Her beloved garden, imbued with a poetry of its own, flourished abundantly and with abandon, and she also had "lots of new writing cooking," if she ever got time to do it. Household duties didn't overwhelm her as they had before they hired a maid, and she enjoyed her firstborn more and more as his vocabulary increased. "Davy has sworn his first swear word," she recounted in late April. "Bill stuck umself on a safety pin and yelled Oh Christ! Small enthusiastic echo: Oh Ch'ist! He's been doing it ever since with great glee. I tried him on Jesus, but fortunately or unfortunately the best he can manage is Geegus, which doesn't sound very definite. He isn't bad on Goddam, though."

While she was feeling better, Bill was getting worse. His chronic psoriasis flared up, and he suffered a plague of "piles." "Po' Bill," she wrote. "His temper is rather uncertain, as you can imagine, but he does Yogic deep breathing or something and no longer explodes cakes." In April they received good news: Rinehart had ordered 25,600 copies for *Nightmare Alley*'s first printing, and the April issue of *Town & Country* marked the first anniversary of Hitler's suicide by featuring Bill's satirical piece "The Mask of Anarchy," which derided a grotesque prisoner resembling the dictator. More steady slick gigs like this, and the Greshams would be set. But there were not enough such opportunities. The market for the kind of stories that came easiest to Bill—hardboiled detective yarns in the tradition of contemporaries like Raymond Chandler and Dashiell Hammett—was neither profitable nor reliable enough to support a family of four. The strain was too much for Bill to endure. His drinking problem became more acute than ever. He started spending even more time at the office—"overworking," as Joy put it. His absence was, potentially, an all-too-familiar sign: the man she loved, the father of her children, her mate, was working himself down into the same old deep groove of despair.

One day the phone rang. It was Bill, calling from the office in a panic. "[I'm] having a nervous breakdown," he told her. His mind was going. He felt paralyzed. He couldn't stay where he was and he couldn't bring himself to come home.

Then he hung up.

Joy clutched the phone, making call after call—all in vain. Bill was nowhere to be found. She rejected the temptation to flee into Manhattan and search on foot; even if she could get someone to watch Davy and Douglas at the last minute, where would she go once she got to Grand Central? What if Bill called again and she wasn't home? What if the father of her children never returned?

Something else nagged at her. Perhaps it was all a ruse and Bill was with another woman. "She wasn't sure whether Bill was running around in New York with a rival she didn't care about or whether he was suicidal," recalled Howard, who claimed that Joy and Bill were progressive enough to make allowances for occasional extramarital dalliances. "I remember my sister boasting to me of her emancipated attitude about sex," Howard said, "and that Bill's occasional activities, according to her, had her approval. I don't necessarily believe this . . . but that's what she told me."

It was also possible that Bill was simply holed up in some bar, drunk. He later admitted that during this time, he "slogged along, tossing down the martinis at lunch until lunch stretched out and catching the 5:10 home became a problem. Eventually it was hard even to make the 11:55." One thing was certain, Howard said. "[Joy] was in acute distress."

"By nightfall," she would later write, "there was nothing left to do but wait and see if he turned up, alive or dead. I put the babies to sleep and waited." Joy was a self-assured woman accustomed to having all the answers—or at least believing she did. But, she said, "for the first time my pride was forced to admit that I was not, after all, 'the master of my fate' and 'the captain of my soul.'" In 1943 she had written a review for *New Masses* of her friend Norman Rosten's second book, *The Fourth Decade,* highlighting his praise of men who fought fascism. "There is only one final beauty, to be on your feet, and only one ultimate ugliness, to fall to your knees," she wrote. But alone in her room, "there was nothing left to do but wait." Her philosophy had always been "rigid and admitted no thought of God, of religion, of anything outside of dialectic materialism." In the scope of a jarring, unanticipated half minute, all that would change. "All my defenses—the walls of arrogance and cocksureness and self-love behind which I had hid from God—went down momentarily. And God came in." Joy somehow knew that what she was feeling was "the direct perception of God . . . infinite and unique."

> There was a Person with me in the room, directly present to my consciousness—a Person so real that all my previous life was by comparison mere shadow play. And I myself was more alive than I had ever been; it was like waking from sleep. So intense a life cannot be endured for long by flesh and blood; we must ordinarily take our life watered down, diluted as it were, by time and space and matter. My perception of God lasted perhaps half a minute.
>
> In that time, however, many things happened. I forgave some of my enemies. I understood that God had always been there, and that since childhood, I had been pouring half my energy into the task of keeping him out . . .

> When it was over I found myself on my knees, praying. I think I must have been the world's most astonished atheist. My surprise was so great that for a moment it distracted me from my fear; only for a moment, however. My awareness of God was no comforting illusion, conjured up to reassure me about my husband's safety. I was just as worried afterward as before. No; it was terror and ecstasy, repentance and rebirth.

Joy could think of nothing she had done to elicit such a reprieve. It could only be described as a moment of grace.

Bill did return. Where he was and what he did during those missing hours is a mystery; if he told Joy what happened, the secret stayed between them. The crisis became incidental to Joy's encounter. "When my husband came home," she recounted, "he accepted my experience without question; he was himself on the way to something of the kind. Together, in spite of illness and anxiety, we set about remaking our minds. For obviously they needed it. If my knowledge of God was true, the thinking of my whole life had been false."

· 9 ·

1946–1950

Joy felt blindsided. All her life she had taken atheism for granted, believing every material mystery would someday be explained by scientific advances. She suddenly realized she had believed in science the way religious people believe in God. "I assumed that science had disproved God, just as I assumed that science had proved that matter was indestructible." Then came the bomb. The event left her vulnerable, laying a foundation for her supernatural experience. Now she saw Marxism in a different light, as "just another of man's hopeless attempts to foresee and control the future, and a crystal ball would have done nearly as well. It's always the unforeseen that happens, as it happened with a bang at Hiroshima." So it was for Bill, too, who observed, "It suddenly seemed illogical and, even worse, naive, to believe that the wonders of the atom had evolved blindly out of chaos."

Joy now felt shockingly certain that there was a God. "Revelation: Once experienced, how could it be questioned?" she reflected years later. "Revelation became the point of departure from which Reason must begin to work." In less intense ways, the revelation kept happening, as it always had, but by a different name. When she reflected on those "aesthetic experiences" that assailed her in adolescence, the ones she had explained away as "some visceral or glandular experience that hadn't been fully explored by science just yet," she now saw in them something spiritual. Still, Joy wanted to understand; she didn't want to repeat with religion the mistake she'd made with atheism, passively accepting the creed without examining its logical implications. "My previous reasoning was at fault," she wrote, "and I must somehow find the error . . . I had learned my lesson, and this time I looked before I leaped; I *studied* religions."

In 1946, alongside Bill, Joy commenced a quest that would consume her for the next three years, what Bill called "an unsystematic but intense course of study and debate—history, philosophy, formal logic, the scriptures of half a dozen nations, the Bible itself and its modern interpretation." Joy's initial impulse was "to become a good Jew, of the comfortable 'Reformed' persuasion." As Bill explained, Joy was "drawn to the Judaism of her grandparents, as was natural. The beauty of the Seder, the Passover supper, with its rich symbolism of the release from bondage, struck a powerful answering chord in the heart of a girl who was both a poet and a Communist." But Joy's return to her heritage did not last long. The adherence to the letter of the law did not align with her experience of receiving some sort of reprieve via grace.

Another consequence was a revived interest in the Communist Party. When Joy was in the city one day, she stopped at the *New Masses* office, where she spotted a recently published book called *The Christian Significance of Karl Marx*. Its publisher, Macmillan, had sent a copy for review. Joy picked up the volume and asked some of the editors if she could review it. "What do you want to bother with that for!" they responded. Their attitude was familiar.

"What we comrades were doing," Joy explained to a friend, "was hating the Church instead of constructing a philosophy which could dispose of the Church by going beyond it." She ditched Marx's atheist philosophy while retaining his principles of economics and social justice. "Logical enough," she later reflected, "for though materialism had proved false, I still thought Marxist economic theory was sound. While I remained an atheist, Party work had been a matter of inclination, but once I recognized God I recognized moral responsibility, and it seemed I had a duty to do Party work . . . If I had found, as I thought, a mistake in Marxist philosophy, my job was to show that the Party didn't need atheism—couldn't socialism be built upon the Golden Rule?" The answer she received from comrades was a resounding *no*. Joy submitted a review of the book, but it was rejected on grounds that such reasoning contradicted everything communism stood for. "Hmm," Joy said. "If it were the *Jewish* significance of Marx you'd be fighting for it." She concluded that communism and faith could coexist.

In the fall of 1946, America received its first substantive introduction to C. S. Lewis in an *Atlantic Monthly* profile titled "C. S. Lewis: Apostle to the Skeptics," by Beloit College English professor Chad Walsh. Until now, Joy's knowledge of the British author had come mainly from the dust jackets of his books. The first American edition of *Screwtape,* published by Macmillan in 1943, provided just one line of biographical background: "Fellow of Magdalen College, Oxford." Walsh's article told her that Clive Staples Lewis had been born in Belfast and served with the Somerset Light Infantry during the Great War. A lifelong bachelor, Lewis was "famous for his lectures on Chaucer and fond of gardening, amuses himself tramping about the countryside with three or four old friends, putting up at small pubs, and enjoying the pleasure of a pipe while talking 'nonsense, poetry, theology, metaphysics' until an advanced hour." The author photo on the jacket of *The Great Divorce* showed a man who appeared to have been caught awkwardly unawares by the camera, as if the photographer told him to smile on the count of three but snapped the picture on one. Lewis was balding and had thick lips, thick eyebrows, and thick circles under wide-set eyes, looking rather like a basset hound; his tie was remarkably askew, his jacket rumpled.

Walsh's *Atlantic Monthly* piece examined an angle that critics tended to talk around, "the fact that Lewis is systematically waging a private war against the religious skepticism of the English-reading world." *The Screwtape Letters* had been acclaimed as a work of "keen social satire" and "brilliant irony," but the book's didactic purposes—among them, to debunk philosophical materialism—

were largely ignored, along with the breadth of Christian themes and theology in his other works. There were more than a dozen books, including essays, the science-fiction trilogy, and *The Case for Christianity,* a collection of wartime BBC addresses that captivated a half-million listeners per broadcast and made C. S. Lewis a household name across Britain. What distinguished Lewis from most religious writers was his mainstream appeal and his ability to reach intellectuals, like Joy, who tended to dismiss overtly evangelical literature for two main reasons: because it was overtly evangelical, and because, in most cases, it wasn't intelligent or well written. Christian writing was often either dry and erudite or pious and laced with churchy jargon. Joy admired Lewis as a dazzling storyteller whose books were not only richly imaginative and entertaining but also smart without being rhetorically elitist.

Joy had no intention of becoming a Christian. For one thing, the idea of it was excessively uncomfortable, given her heritage. "The Jew who enters Christianity is always haunted by ghosts," she would write years later. "Voices out of his past assure him that he is making a fool of himself, betraying his traditions and his ancestry; he must keep arguing constantly, defending the truth of his new faith against the jeering shadows in his own mind." Yet Lewis earned her trust, and she wanted to learn from his theist perspective. She and Bill began to use his books as "constant reference points," said Bill. "Lewis's clear and vivid statement of Christian principles served as a standard by which to measure the other religions we studied."

As JOY GRAPPLED with the implications of her Road to Damascus experience, another miracle transpired. *Nightmare Alley,* published on September 9, had begun generating press as early as July 7, with the *Washington Post* promising a "sinister and compelling piece of fiction" that would "shock some readers but send the public clamoring to the bookstores." And it did. The novel, a work of brilliance, would become a noir classic with a cult following for decades to come. But first, a bigger payoff presented itself: Twentieth Century–Fox bought the film rights for $50,000. And the studio invited Bill to Hollywood for the first two months of 1947 to collaborate with writer Jules Furthman on adapting the novel for the screen. In January, Bill took a train west. The picture, starring Tyrone Power and Joan Blondell, would be produced at lightning speed for a New York City premiere at the Mayfair Theater on October 7, 1947.

The windfall was more money than Bill or Joy had ever seen, and they knew exactly how they wanted to spend it. "We looked around for the biggest house we could find," Bill said. After two years of living and writing in a cramped three-room apartment with one, and then two babies, the Greshams wanted a home with land where Davy and Douglas could grow "husky and brown and tough and mischievous. That is all one can ask." And they "had to have a woodlot," Joy insisted. "We wanted the feeling of walking in our own woods." Ample workspace was also a priority, private studies in which to think and write. Both of them had new projects in the works. Bill had signed contracts for Canadian and Danish editions of *Nightmare Alley* and was beginning a Marxist novel about Spain while freelancing stories to slicks including *Esquire* and *Collier's*. Joy had on hand a partial manuscript for a novel she'd begun at the MacDowell Colony years earlier and was selecting poems for a new collection. The future once again promised great things. Now they could settle down. Now everything would be fine.

The Greshams bought an Oldsmobile and began searching for their ideal Hudson Valley country estate. They found what they were looking for on Endekill Road off Route 9G, eleven miles north of downtown Poughkeepsie, nestled in the crease of land bordering Pleasant Plains to the east and, to the west, Hyde Park, where New Yorkers of the Gilded Age once held elaborate summer soirees overlooking a vast swath of the Hudson River. The white clapboard farmhouse several miles inland came with sharp green shutters, a porch lined with columns, a barn, and twenty-two acres of pastures, woods, and apple orchards. Joy and Bill were smitten. Inside were rooms upon rooms, fourteen of them, including a proper playroom off the kitchen for the boys, and gorgeous wood floors where in coming years Davy would saunter about carrying armloads of books while

Douglas clomped around in his father's cowboy boots. When the long Hudson Valley winters buried the Gresham family under feet of snow, their coal furnace would keep them cozy, burning all day and night. The official address was Staatsburg, a hamlet of Hyde Park, where Franklin and Eleanor Roosevelt had lived in a riverfront estate named Crum Elbow, just south of the same Crum Elbow Creek that flowed through the Greshams' own twenty-two acres. Joy could drop a stick in the water and it might bob past a Vanderbilt mansion neighboring the late president's home and on into the Hudson. "[My] southern plantation," Bill called it. On March 21, 1947, the Dutchess County Clerk's office recorded a deed in the name of Helen J. Gresham. "They were very, very, very proud of that house," remembered Mary Stevenson, a neighbor who had two little boys, Jim and Mitchell, about the ages of David and Douglas.

Joy painted a coat of blue over wallpaper printed with cabbage-sized roses and chose furniture with about as much care as she selected clothes. Dutchess County abounded with antique shops selling Victorian furniture and old Dutch pieces, often at bargain prices, but she went for the utilitarian. "Upper-level Salvation Army" is how Mary described the décor. One of Joy's prized possessions was a grand piano in the otherwise sparsely appointed living room.

The house was so large that it would have cost a fortune to furnish properly—and Joy and Bill no longer had a fortune. Their money went out as swiftly as it came in. They had rebounded from rock bottom to sky-high, failing to recognize middle-ground responsibilities. Not only did they not save, but they didn't even pay income tax. For now, *Nightmare Alley* remained their golden goose; in May, Bill received a royalty check for $9,660.25. Brandt & Brandt sold the foreign-language rights (Portuguese, German, Japanese, Korean) and a few of Bill's short stories to *Esquire,* the *Atlantic Monthly,* and *Collier's*. Bill transformed the half-finished attic into a sprawling study, while Joy set up her workspace in a second-floor room lined with bookshelves, overlooking the barn and Crum Elbow Creek.

Spring settled in: "Everything [is] coming to life," she remarked to a friend, "hepaticas and anemones and columbines and apple-blossoms, scarlet tanagers and orioles and gold-finches, and ducks among the marsh-marigolds in our brook." She planted a new garden, collected a new crop of cats, and furiously made up for years of lost writing time. More than anything else, Joy continued studying religion and philosophy.

She wasn't alone in her search for the sacred. Postwar atomic age America was experiencing something of a spiritual renaissance. "We are crying out to be rescued from the deadly terrors of the world we have made," Joy wrote. Many people were becoming more concerned with eternal afterlife than earthly prosperity. More books were being written on religion and theology than on business and economics. And C. S. Lewis continued to be smack in the middle of the religious resurgence.

On September 8, 1947, *Time* magazine made Lewis the subject of its cover story, "Don v. Devil," naming him "one of the most influential spokesmen for Christianity in the English-speaking world." The article opened by describing a stocky, ruddy-cheeked man in horn-rimmed spectacles, a tweed jacket, and gray flannel trousers standing on a platform, lecturing to a packed audience of students who hung on his every word. When he finished speaking, the forty-nine-year-old Lewis hustled away, arms full of books and papers, avoiding the crush of students sure to monopolize his time if he lingered. Not only was Lewis declared to be "the most popular lecturer in the University," but also his books of literary criticism—including *A Preface to Paradise Lost* and *The Allegory of Love,* on medieval allegory and courtly love—were hailed as works of genius.

As a Christian, Lewis defied convention and categories, both in his life and in his "strictly unorthodox presentation of strict orthodoxy." Fundamentalist evangelicals considered his use of alcohol and tobacco an abomination. Academic colleagues scoffed at him for being a "popularizer." Still, they read him, as did millions of others whose Christian tenets sprawled between extremes. "With erudition, good humor and skill, Lewis is writing about religion for a generation of religion-hungry readers brought up on a diet of 'scientific' jargon and Freudian clichés," proclaimed the *Time* article, which called him one of Britain's "literary evangelists" and placed him alongside T. S. Eliot, Graham Greene, W. H. Auden, and the detective writer Dorothy L. Sayers, who herself interpreted the recent renewal of interest in Christianity as "spontaneous . . . and not a sort of 'Let's-get-together-and-pep-up-Christianity' stunt by excited missioners, than which nothing could be more detestable." No; between the war, the bomb, and fascism, she explained, "people have discovered by bitter experience that when man starts out on his own to build a society by his own power and knowledge, he succeeds in building something uncommonly like Hell; and they have seriously begun to ask why." Sayers's description certainly resonated with Joy's journey.

The *Time* article was occasioned by the publication of Lewis's book *Miracles*. From it, Joy culled two more foundational axioms proving the existence of God: in her words, "1) That the material universe is a single interlocking system governed by relentless causation. 2) That man has within certain narrow limits a degree of free will (he can choose a or b; he can't fly down from a tall building, but he can take the elevator or the stairs)."

Lewis had convincing arguments not only for the existence of God but for the divinity of Christ as well. In *The Case for Christianity,* he made a profound impact on Joy with his "lunatic, liar, or Lord" trilemma. It is downright nonsensical, Lewis asserted, to say, "'I'm ready to accept Jesus as a great moral teacher, but I don't accept His claim to be God.' . . . A man who was merely man and said the sort of things Jesus said wouldn't be a great moral teacher. He'd either be a lunatic—on a level with the man who says he's a poached egg—or else he'd be the Devil of Hell. Either this man was, and is, the Son of God: or else a madman or something worse." This rang true for Joy. "History is full of self-appointed Messiahs," she wrote to a friend, "and they all sound the same, mad with pride. The humor and commonsense of Jesus never came from a disturbed mind."

Joy had read the Bible in the past and appreciated it as a great work of fiction, but now she read the New Testament through the lens of a specific question: Could this be a report of fact? She was struck by biblical incongruities, but to her, and to Bill, who read along with her, those incongruities proved rather than disproved the veracity of scripture. "What convinced us was our sense of the difference between fiction and life. Fiction is always congruous, life usually incongruous. In fiction there is a unity of effect, of style; the people all say exactly what they should say to be in character and in the mood. And all the effects are heightened, arranged. If there *is* an incongruous reaction, that too is obviously arranged—either for humor or for some plot reason." The Apostles' attitudes were prime examples. "If [they] had been romancing, they would never have told so many stories which made them look silly. Nor would their immediate followers. They would have said, '*We* knew Him when, *we* were the extra-special faithful who understood Him perfectly, *we* were the ones appointed to govern the rest of you!' If they had lied, they would have been lying for their own advantage, surely? Instead of which—continual rebukes, and 'He that would be first among you, let him be last.'" As she read on, example after example supported that theory.

And there was her personal experience, beginning with her encounter during Bill's disappearance. "Some [religions] had wisdom up to a point," she wrote in an account of her journey to Christianity; "some of them had flashes of spiritual insight; but only one of them had complete understanding of the grace and repentance and charity that had come to me from God." She continued:

> And the Redeemer who had made himself known, whose personality I would have recognized among ten thousand—well, when I read the New Testament, I recognized him. He was Jesus.
>
> The rest was fairly simple. I could not doubt the divinity of Jesus, and, step by step, orthodox Christian theology followed logically from it. My modernist objections to the miraculous proved to be mere superstition, unsupported by logic. I am a writer of fiction; I have made up stories myself, and I think I can tell a made-up story from a true one. The men who told of the resurrection told of something they had *seen.* Not Shakespeare himself could have invented the Synoptic Gospels. My beliefs took shape.

As Jesus seemed to Joy a strong proponent of socialism, she found ways to remain distantly involved in leftist causes throughout 1947. *New Masses* was dissolving, giving way to a publication called *Mainstream: A New Literary Quarterly,* "a forum for the most significant American writing today." *Mainstream* promised to feature in forthcoming issues Joy Davidman, Arthur Miller, Langston Hughes, and Dalton Trumbo, among others. Despite Joy's having faded into the periphery of the literary left, her name was also used to attract a crowd at Camp Unity in Wingdale, a place that prided itself on being one of the early interracial resorts in New York State. It had a labor education program intended to convert non–union members to union status. The *Daily Worker* advertised that Joy was to give a poetry lecture there on July 29, 1947.

Yet Joy had become disillusioned with the Party. She realized that her idealization of Stalin's Soviet Russia was, like her allegiance to atheism, not based on proof: "I reminded myself of the wonderful achievements of Soviet Russia—and realized that I had taken them all on faith; I had no idea *what* went on in Russia. Gradually my Communism shriveled up and blew away like a withered tumbleweed; I cannot tell exactly when it went, but I looked and found it gone." Determined to understand where and how she had got it wrong, Joy became consumed with studying Marxist theory. As Lewis directs in his introduction to *The Great Divorce,* "A sum can be put right: but only by going back till you find the error and working it afresh from that point, never by simply *going on.*" Between 1948 and 1950 she would pound out dozens of pages in letters that, taken together, read like a doctoral dissertation.

"It was a difficult and painful study," she later said. When she read Lenin's *Materialism and Empirio-Criticism* through fresh eyes, she was appalled. "The book is pathetic," she wrote to Jerry and Alice Jerome in January 1948. "Merely from the standpoint of construction it is rambling, repetitious to idiocy, irrelevant; its language, probably further corrupted by the translator, is of almost hysterical violence and bad manners. Even the jokes ain't funny, they're just insults. As for its logic, it is unbelievable; the premises are wrong, the conclusions are wrong, and they're all non sequiturs anyway." As she put it more succinctly to Bill, "Why *this* is *bull*shit!" Joy was ashamed at her younger self for not attending to the grunt work of studying the convictions that she allowed to rule her life.

In October, Joy's old MacDowell acquaintance and crush, William Rose Benét, wrote a piece called "To a Communist" for the *Saturday Review of Literature,* where he presided over a column called "The Phoenix Nest." He condemned communism on "the *real* ground," as Joy now understood it: "that it is false." Yet he took a balanced approach, acknowledging communists as well intended. Joy contemplated writing a letter to the editor about her own experiences but sent it to Benét instead. She thanked him for his informed, fair analysis in the face of press and politicians who, she commented, "resort so freely to abuse, bullying, and plain lying that it almost seems they fear in their hearts that Communism may be true!" She and her circle had been oblivious to spy plots; their primary offense was ignorance of Marxist theory. Now she knew better. "I had to have a direct and shattering experience of God, and then plow my way through Lenin's *Materialism,* surely the world's most unreadable book (not to mention side excursions into light literature like the *Critique of Pure Reason,* God help me)—in order to find out that Marxism was philosophically nonsensical, logically unsound, historically arbitrary, and scientifically half false from the start and the other half overthrown by Einstein's first work." She was also coming to terms with the idea that she didn't know what actually went on in Soviet Russia. "Whatever they've got there, it doesn't seem to be the New Jerusalem."

Joy told Benét that she had debated sending her letter to the editor.

> I don't mind confessing in public that I've made a damn fool of myself, and besides I can hardly pass as a Marxist writer in future; my literary reputation is almost non-existent, but what there is of it I don't want to enjoy under false colors. All the same; I knew the comrades and worked with them, and for all their unreasoning fanaticism they were good people in most ways; very good people,

> if you compare them to the advertising man, the Hollywood executive, the machine politician—all our Pharisees. I didn't leave them in order to run to safety, and I don't like kicking them when they're down . . . If you think this letter would have any point in print, pass it on. If not, burn it.

Benét asked to use anonymous excerpts in another piece for "The Phoenix Nest," and Joy readily agreed. Excerpts from her letter would appear in the *Saturday Review of Literature* on January 29, 1949.

In early 1948 Joy toyed with the idea of writing a book of philosophy, but her top priority was finishing her novel, *Weeping Bay,* about life dominated by poverty and strict Catholicism in a poor fishing village along the Canadian Gaspé Peninsula. In February 1949 she had ten chapters ready for her agent to sell. Macmillan picked up the book but offered a paltry advance of $250, plus another $250 on publication—almost an insult, but Joy took it. Bill's work was progressing, too. On April 27 he signed a contract with Rinehart for a second novel, *Limbo Tower,* a fictionalized account of his time in a tuberculosis ward, to be published the following spring.

JOY WAS DISCOVERING that her new faith aligned most closely with Protestantism. Bill agreed. They looked around for the nearest Christian house of worship, which turned out to be Pleasant Plains Presbyterian Church, one mile east, at the junction of bucolic Hollow Road and Fiddlers Bridge. Founded in 1837, the church had 116 members. The outside of the clapboard building was painted a crisp white; the inside was shabby but cozy. On Saturday nights the furnace would be stoked to warm the building for Sunday services. Fewer than half of the church's members regularly arrived in their Sunday best to take part in the traditional Protestant service: hymns, communion, scripture recitation, the Lord's Prayer, and the sermon—the central focus.

By spring of 1948, Joy and Bill were regular attendees; soon, Joy and the boys were baptized there. (Bill had been baptized as a baby.) At a congregational meeting on January 10, 1948, Joy was elected a deaconess and Bill an elder. Church became a social outlet. A core of eight or ten young to middle-aged couples with children ran a "supper club," casual monthly social gatherings, sometimes a potluck or a square dance. Always there was food; usually there was music. Joy and Bill occasionally attended.

"Bill had social skills to spare," remembered their neighbor Mary Stevenson, who was also a member of Pleasant Plains Presbyterian and spearheaded the supper club. But Joy was the opposite. "She'd look at you intensely and ask an inappropriately intimate question out of the blue. For example: 'Which brand of girdle do you wear. Why do you wear them?'" Bill was playful, outgoing, pleasant to be with, an entertainer. To new acquaintances, he and Joy seemed mismatched. He was suave; she was frumpy. Her wardrobe staples included long skirts and shawls. At thirty-three, Joy could easily have been taken for a matron of fifty. Every morning she wadded her hair into a disheveled bun at the nape of her neck. "She dressed like someone who didn't have a lot of clothes and kept what they did have on their back in case they had to leave quickly," said Mary. In social gatherings the Greshams didn't interact much with each other. Bill would be in the rowdy crowd, laughing, backslapping, singing. It was clear to everyone that he drank too much—his current beverage of choice was cheap Chianti by the gallon, downed straight from the jug. But alcohol only accentuated the qualities that made him so much fun, turning him into a storyteller, an entertainer. He was a happy drunk. "He would pass out with a smile on his face," Mary recalled.

Joy had fallen in love with that entertainer. Now she seemed to crave something deeper, richer, more substantive. She appeared "impatient when people were comfortable and having fun," and she often tried to change the subject to something serious. Although the atomic age jolted many people with fear, others felt more relaxed than they had in years; there was an air of postwar jubilance. At parties, while Bill danced around, Joy, shrouded in her shawls and long dowdy skirts, would corner someone and strike up a conversation about doctrine.

Their minister, Dwight Beller, a former military chaplain, indulged her. After services ended, Pastor Beller always stood at the church door greeting congregants as they filed out. They shook his hand, thanked him, reported family events, requested prayer, asked questions about the sermon. Joy had no qualms about holding up the line. One time she invited Howard to attend a service. Doing so was not the way he would typically choose to spend a Sunday morning, but he went out of curiosity. He thought Joy's behavior at the church door to be "self-centered, arrogant, show-offish." Her brother interpreted her zeal as little more than a new cause. "My sister got converted with the same enthusiasm with which she embraced the Communist Party," he said, "and there's similar psychological attitudes, in my opinion."

BETWEEN THEM, JOY and Bill weren't earning enough from their writing to maintain the lifestyle to which they aspired. In the spring they had to let the maid go. In September, Joy took out a mortgage on the house. They explained the state of their financial affairs to the *Poughkeepsie Sunday New Yorker,* which featured them in a June 6 column called "Neighbors Who Write": "'We're broke,' Mr. Gresham said cheerfully. 'Free lancers do that. Go broke.'"

The article focused on the couple's literary careers but veered into their newfound spirituality. Asked by the interviewer why most writers become writers, Bill suggested childhood loneliness, the quest for adventure, and boredom. "Don't forget the didactic function of writing," Joy added. "Consciously or unconsciously writing is teaching, a gentle push to impress your way, even if it is only your way of seeing a sunset, on other people." She continued: "I'm so amused when people get into those violent discussions, 'Should art teach?' How are you going to prevent it from teaching? The question is, what should it teach?" For many years, Joy's answer to that question had been the Party line. Now her answer reflected her new ideological reality. Bill was of the same mind. "Joy and I agree that no story is worthwhile for its own sake," he continued. "I mean, it isn't worthwhile unless it stresses some ethical or religious principle. So long as you start with the theory that man is essentially good, the Rousseau idea . . . the world assumes the nature of a horror, a nightmare alley. If you take the position that man is essentially sinful, everything good you discover is just so much gravy."

As FINANCIAL TROUBLES continued to escalate, so did Bill's drinking. For many years now, Bill had turned to alcohol in good times and bad, but following the success of *Nightmare Alley,* this bad time involved failure on a grander scale, and it drew him into another abyss. "One of the most destructive experiences a writer can have is to sell a novel to the movies after years of grinding, hand-to-mouth existence," Bill wrote years later. "Like a deep-sea fish, accustomed to the pressure of the deep, when brought to the surface suddenly by a net, he often explodes when the pressure is removed." His mental health again took a dangerous turn. He realized that he wasn't the happy drunk he used to be. "Drinking was no longer fun; it was a bitter necessity. And my personality was being poisoned by it. I had always been a genial, expansive drunk; now I was getting pugnacious and irrational." His guitar, so closely associated with boozy parties, became an enabler. One night, in a fit of frustration, Bill smashed it to pieces on the back of a chair. "By the spring of 1948," he said, "my drinking had begun to frighten me. Then something happened which is, I think, more important to the Christian than his own search for God. God sought me."

He and Joy were coming to a Calvinistic view that free will and predestination were inscrutably intertwined. When Joy reread "The Hound of Heaven," a 182-line Christian poem by Francis Thompson —a book she'd once ridiculed as "phoney rhetoric"—she started to cry: "Understanding it suddenly," she said, "[I] burst into tears . . . (Also a new thing; I had seldom previously cried except with rage.)" When she looked back at her aesthetic moments in adolescence, her dream of Fairyland, and the seeds of atheist doubt planted in her mind when she read *Screwtape,* she saw that God had been relentlessly pursuing her, "stalking" her like a cat. "He crept nearer so silently that I never knew he was there. Then, all at once, he sprang."

Similarly, Bill felt that God was propelling him to pray as he never had before. "I said, 'God—if you are really out there and you help people, as they claim, show me what to do next week for I have tried everything and I am really licked.'" In June, the answer came from his conscience, imbued by God with common sense, Bill believed: "Look up A.A., you're ready for it." Bill knew that he was supposed to follow this directive, but he brushed it off and binged on booze one more time. "I woke up in the afternoon next day, having missed a vital business appointment. I kept having spells of amnesia during which I did not recognize familiar streets and didn't know where I was going or what I was doing." When his head cleared for a "lucid moment," Bill did look up Alcoholics Anonymous and called a cab to take him to the nearest meeting. This trip marked the beginning of four years of sobriety, with occasional "slips." Bill began regularly attending Alcoholics Anonymous meetings. For him, "sobriety was a daily miracle." He became secretary of the Poughkeepsie group, "which means the guy who makes the coffee," he joked. Of the things he learned at A.A., Bill was most relieved to hear a friend tell him that alcoholism wasn't a symptom of neurosis but a disease. "It was like a millstone cut away from around my neck."

Joining Alcoholics Anonymous marked a major turning point for Bill. Soon his social life was dominated by A.A. activities. And a major spiritual shift happened. He felt that his past interests in tarot cards and yoga were his "first attempts to find a spiritual answer" for needs that he drowned in alcohol. Now he was clear-headed. "I no longer doubted the divinity of Christ—the Helper who had come to me was unmistakable. At this point I felt that a task had been assigned to me: the building of a rational Christian faith." He studied with renewed vigor.

But Bill's sobriety didn't solve their practical problems; neither did his faith make him immune to regrets and frustration. "When *Nightmare Alley* sold to Fox," he wrote a friend in July, "I took the money and bought this place with it, still owing the government all the income tax. This was a foolish thing to do, since the interest on the tax mounts up higher and higher but I was not thinking very clearly at the time and we were desperate, with two kids in three rooms down in Ossining going crazy. If I had been able then to think as clearly as I do now," he said, "when we got the movie money I would have simply gone down to the internal revenue dept. and given them half of it, bought a trailer with the other half and moved out to Venice, Laguna Beach, Long Beach or San Diego."

But there wasn't time to wallow in regret; they needed income. For long hours, Joy and Bill holed up in the attic together, pounding at their typewriters and reading aloud from works in progress. They worked in a frenzy, writing less what compelled them than what they thought magazines would buy. Joy wrote fluffy short stories and sent them to Bernice to sell to women's magazines. One, called "Theater Party," sold to *Bluebook* in December for $125, but mostly they just piled up in the offices of Brandt & Brandt. Fiction was not her forte. Bill's lifelong fascination with carny life served as fodder for dozens of stories—pieces with titles like "Dr. Dorton: Tar-Heel Genius of the County Fairs," "The Art of Knife Throwing," and "Fortune Tellers Never Starve." Later that year, *Life* magazine bought an article called "The World of Mirth" for $1,200. But for every $1,000 story sold to the *Saturday Evening Post,* there were half a dozen rejects. "A free-lance has a strange view of writing," Bill wrote to friends in August 1949. "When we're young it is the Impossible Dream. A little older and it is the Great Adventure (when we first publish stuff). Then it becomes our Career as a Writer. And last, it's just a way of scratching out a living." Bill and Joy were scratching hard.

They couldn't hide the strain of their financial struggles when Franklin Folsom, former secretary of the League of American Writers, and his wife, Mary, who had bought a home in the area, paid a visit. Folsom was appalled by what he found when he walked in the door. "The house Joy lived in was a grim place," he recalled. "The living room was sparsely—almost Spartanly—furnished, and the mood of its occupants was unsmiling and tense," Franklin said, adding, "During the visit I kept recalling Charles Addams' cartoons," referring to the macabre sketches that appeared regularly in the pages of *The New Yorker*. Addams's satirical cartoons featured a cast of characters that included Morticia, the mirthless matriarch, Gomez, whose genial personality masked a general fiendishness, and their Victorian mansion. Ghoulish and decaying, the house was a character itself, furnished with chandeliers, settees, medieval torture devices, cobwebs, and a broken mirror above the fireplace. The interior of the Gresham household seemed similarly morbid, though without comical eccentricity.

IN EARLY 1949, Joy went to New York to hear a lecture by Father Victor White, a Catholic priest who wrote extensively about Jungian psychology and religion. After the talk, Joy spoke with Father White, whom she knew to be an acquaintance of C. S. Lewis. As he recalled: "[She] told me that she was fascinated by him, and wanted to hear all I could tell her about him. She asked how difficult it would be to meet him. I told her pretty difficult. I suggested she might write. It was said that he answered all letters that seemed to come from people who needed help or advice."

Joy learned more when she read the newly published first biography of Lewis, *C. S. Lewis: Apostle to the Skeptics,* by Chad Walsh, the Beloit College professor whose profile of Lewis had run under the same title in the *Atlantic Monthly* in 1946. Walsh had struck up a correspondence with Lewis while researching the magazine piece. When he decided to write a book, he sailed to England to meet, interview, and observe his subject in his natural habitat.

Joy eagerly read Walsh's first-person account of his voyage to meet Lewis. Walsh explained the reason behind his fervor for the English scholar. During the war, a friend had given him *Perelandra,* which led him to read everything Lewis had written—which in turn led to his writing a fan letter. Lewis responded. "I *felt* I knew him from his books, and from his many letters," Walsh confessed. "But a writer can easily wear a literary mask when he holds pen in hand. I wanted to know him, person to person, and to check that impression against those I had gained from his books." Interested in Lewis as philosopher, theologian, and creative writer, he traveled by ship across the ocean, hoping to reconcile the jacket photo of Lewis with the man who'd written the books. "The books had wit and grace," said Walsh. "The picture was sad-eyed, world-weary." But when Walsh arrived in Oxford, he met a spirited man whose ruddy face was full of light and life. He was at once urbane and blunt, even about sex—a topic that was, much to Lewis's annoyance, generally cloaked in euphemisms. In a conversation with "psychology-minded friends," he'd exposed the absurdity of phrases such as "release of tensions." Reflecting on his friends' dialogue, Lewis remarked with gusto: "If a visitor from Mars had overheard them, he would never have suspected that sex has any connection with pleasure! They made you think of skeletons copulating. Sometimes you want to teach such people vice so that they can know what virtue means." Unself-conscious and unpretentious, Lewis was oblivious to his popularity in America. Like Joy, he had an eidetic memory and could quote vast amounts of text; he did so without airs, purely delighting in language and literature. He wasn't one for casual conversation or erudition at highbrow affairs; he preferred intimate exchanges with friends in pubs over pints.

Apostle to the Skeptics made Lewis seem real and approachable. Joy learned about his daily routine. At least part of every morning was devoted to reading and responding to heaps of fan mail. Lewis replied to nearly every letter, "no matter how asinine its contents," Walsh wrote. Lewis and his friends met every Tuesday at an Oxford pub that Walsh promised not to name. The members of the group, who called themselves the Inklings, had been meeting weekly since the war. Charles Williams, an essayist and novelist, was one of the core members. J. R. R. Tolkien, a fellow Oxford don, was a fixture. Lewis was also a member of the Socratic Club, which began as a forum for dialogue between Christians and atheists, with each side given an opportunity to defend itself on alternating weeks, but evolved into an exploration of Christianity and comparative religion. "We discovered there was an undersupply of atheists willing to speak without pay," Lewis commented wryly. He was disappointed; he enjoyed eviscerating atheists' papers. He loved debating in general, formally and informally, and he was brilliant at it.

Joy and Bill wrote Lewis a joint first letter in May or early June

1949. Around the same time, she began to correspond with Chad Walsh. On June 21, in an aside at the end of a long letter, she wrote, "By the way, your remark that Lewis answered even asinine letters gave us courage to write him—so we sent the unfortunate man five single-spaced pages of personal history and what not." Not until January 1950 would Lewis, who received heaps of confessional missives daily, take note of Joy as a standout. That was many eventful months away.

CHAD WALSH, HIMSELF a poet and novelist, was more bohemian than academic. He and his wife, Eva, loved hosting writers and intellectuals at their home in Wisconsin and at their summer cottage on Lake Iroquois in Vermont. They invited the Greshams to Beloit for a visit, but with two little boys, it was too far afield. So Joy responded with an invitation of her own: "We more than share your feelings for Lewis . . . [and] would love to talk about [his] work." Chad and Eva, with their four young daughters, stopped in Staatsburg on the way either to or from Vermont that summer. To them, Joy and Bill's marriage seemed "idyllic."

But as finances stretched thinner and thinner, so did love. Although Joy mentioned in a letter to Chad that she no longer considered herself a poet ("I'm afraid my inspiration gave out when I discovered that people would *pay* for prose"), she again began expressing her deepest feelings in private verse. And in 1949, those feelings concerned a man other than Bill. She referred to this individual in a sonnet as the "terrible third" in her marriage, and she fantasized about him when she and Bill made love.

> Having loved my love tonight with you between,
> My lord, I pray you of your courtesy
> That I may give as much as he gives me;
> Lie mouth to mouth, skin upon naked skin,
>
> Joy upon joy. Love, it would not be love
> If the disposing of it were not yours;

Give me away then wholly, let him have
A splendor uncorrupted by these tears.

Because you have my heart, he has my bed,
And let him have it then conditionless
With all my heart; nor ever let him guess
How I, staring above his quiet head,

Knew, in the lonely midnight afterward,
The terrible third between us like a sword.

Late that July, Joy wrote a letter about the Communist Party to the *Saturday Review of Literature,* this time signing her name. In a separate note to Bill Benét she wrote, "[I] thought it was about time I went on record against *both* the idea that the CP is a band of efficient archangels and the idea that it's a band of efficient devils, since in my own experience it was never anything but a collection of confused and quite inefficient human beings." She named no names, but when the *Daily News*—with a circulation many times greater than *Saturday Review*'s—quoted her in an editorial, her outward bravado briefly lapsed: "I'm feeling rather shaken . . . I can't quite decide whether to laugh or to hide under the bed." Anticommunism was on the rise; America was building up to McCarthyism. Within weeks an opportunity to take full control of her story presented itself. The *New York Post*—virtuoso of sensational headlines and champion of American liberalism—approached her with a proposition. The paper wanted to give its readers a look at life inside the Communist Party. Would she tell her story? A top reporter would do the writing, a photographer would be dispatched, and the profile would run in twelve parts under the title "Girl Communist."

It was a risky proposition. Outing herself in the mainstream press as a former communist could have consequences for her family; no one fully understood the potential legal repercussions. At the very least, reputations could be ruined. Joy's parents were still employed by the New York City Board of Education. Howard was embarked on a promising career as a Manhattan psychiatrist. Joy told him about the *Post*'s request. "As your brother," he said gravely, "I ask you not to." She talked it over with Bill. He, too, did not think it a good idea but told her to do whatever felt right. Joy agreed to the story. She wrote out her reasoning. "My conscience wouldn't let me refuse!" she said.

> For a long time I shuddered at the very thought of criticizing the Party in public. But some of my Christian friends (who are no reactionaries) made me see that I was considering my comfort instead of my duty . . . [I]n my Party days . . . I had orated, I had poetized, I had played on people's emotions; I had concealed Party failings, explained away Party mistakes, denied my own convictions on my own subject when the Party told me to; I had satirized and slandered and sneered. And all for a cause which I believed was true, which I believed justified any means—although, like you, I had accepted it in a burst of emotion without ever checking its underlying philosophy.
>
> Now I had found that my cause was false as hell. Could I honestly get out of apologizing to those I had tried to deceive?
>
> The New York Post's readers are as near my old audience as I could get—the liberal, middle-class, half-educated Jews of New York. (For these, with their rejection of Christian charity as a means to the good world, are after all the main strength of the Party.) I could not reach them with theoretical analysis—they wouldn't pause to read. I must submit to the Post's version of human interest.

But there were other motivations. She was also taking stock of her life. "I tell my memories over like beads," she wrote that September in a poem that wistfully reminisces about a passionate romance gone cold. Joy had been out of the spotlight for years. The *Post* series was a chance to be noticed again. She broadcast not just her former Party affiliation but a detailed portrait of her formative years, including her difficult home life and sexual liberation. Her parents and Howard were mortified. Joy's decision caused an irreparable family rift. Howard never spoke to her again, although a correspondence would resume years later when he learned she was dying.

The *Post* photographer arrived in Staatsburg just as the bittersweet splendor of fall was spreading over Dutchess County. Fields erupted with fat orange pumpkins, ruddy-cheeked children bounced on hay bales in horse-drawn carts, and leaves wore their seasonal regalia of gold, saffron, and russet. Joy's apple orchard was laden with fruit; she picked potfuls for pies and cider. Thus, when the *Post*'s staff photographer asked to observe emblematic moments of Joy's daily life—moments portraying her as a wholesome, dedicated housewife who flawlessly balanced marriage, motherhood, a writing career, and her responsibilities as a deaconess at the local Presbyterian church ("It shouldn't happen to a good Jewish girl," Joy joked), she led him to the orchard. Wearing a frumpy wool coat to keep out the fall chill and a flowered babushka on her head (her mother would be appalled), Joy reached up for a ripe apple, touched it with her fingertips, and held the pose. The photographer snapped a portrait in profile, capturing the right side of her face and body. He would take other pictures of her—scrolling a page through her Underwood typewriter, pulling a book from one of her many shelves, playing her piano while her older son, six-year-old Davy, sits atop it gazing at her admiringly. But it is the portrait in the orchard, an echo of Eve in the Garden, that hints at a story more compelling than the superficial version she fed to the newspaper. Joy had taken off her thick horn-rimmed glasses, and her eye revealed a haunting otherness that made readers look twice. Seduction, soul, mischief, mystery.

In "Girl Communist," Joy portrayed a life finally, fully realized. In a private poem she told a different story, one of dissatisfaction and love gone cold:

> You would not think it now, but we were young
> one time, went wandering in the sweet white clover

and watched the bees make honey. That was all
we needed then for love, a clover field
and honey and the sun.

Now the honey was eaten, the bees dead, the clover cut. Wheat replaced the clover in a spot where, one harvest time, they made love under the bright autumn moon, "a moon you could get drunk on . . . we lived on moon." That was all in the past. "I loved him once, and it was long ago," she wrote.

And yet
there should be somewhere I shall find again
the wheat, the clover, honey, sun, and love.

The *Daily Worker* blasted "Girl Communist" from every angle: "With Miss Davidman's cooperation in one of the more fantastic pieces of exhibitionism that we've seen in a long time, the new editors of the Post are trying to prove to the advertisers that sex plus anti-Communist is the liberal way to circulation . . . The lady has obviously been living in a world of mirrors. Oscar Wilde once said that people who think well of themselves are in for a life-long romance. The lady in question just saw herself in everything and everybody around her, and naturally she found everything inadequate." The *Daily Worker*'s critique was spot-on. Joy's account of her life read like a desperate cry for attention from a washed-up writer.

Other consequences of "Girl Communist" included the loss of friends and the acquisition of an FBI file. "Helen Joy Davidman, aka Mrs. William Lindsay Gresham" was classified under "Security Matter–C." A month after the *New York Post* series concluded, the FBI opened a dossier with a detailed memo summarizing the articles. The memo concluded that "no information of real value to the Bureau appears" and "it is apparent that Joy Davidman was never a leader in the Communist movement." Then the FBI cross-referenced her and discovered her involvement with the League of American Writers, which increased suspicion. An internal memo dated May 5, 1953, reads, "It is noted the subject was expected to be a witness at HCUA hearings in New York City and was not called." There is no record of Joy's having been aware of the potential questioning, and she never testified.

By the new year, 1950, an intellectually intimate correspondence with C. S. Lewis was beginning to deepen. None of the letters have survived, including the long introductory missive that Joy told Chad Walsh she and Bill sent in June 1949; many years later, however, Lewis's brother and bachelor housemate, Warnie, noted in his diary the date when Joy's correspondence made a lasting impression: "Until 10th January 1950 neither of us had ever heard of her; then she appeared in the mail as just another American fan, Mrs. W. L. Gresham from the neighborhood of New York. With however the difference that she stood out from the ruck by her amusing and well-written letters, and soon J"—meaning Jack, as Lewis was known to intimates—"and she had become 'pen-friends.'" On January 27 Joy told Chad that she had just received a letter from Lewis:

> I think I told you I'd raised an argument or two on some points? Lord, he knocked my props out from under me unerringly; one shot to a pigeon. I haven't a scrap of my case left. And, what's more, I've seldom enjoyed anything more. Being disposed of so neatly by a master of debate, all fair and square—it seems to be one of the great pleasures of life, though I'd never have suspected it in my arrogant youth. I suppose it's *unfair* tricks of argument that leave wounds. But after the sort of thing that Lewis does, what I feel is a craftsman's joy at the sight of a superior performance.

Joy had not met an intellectual equal; she had met a superior, and she liked it.

"Girl Communist" also kicked off a successful few months for both Joy and Bill. Despite a streptococcus infection, Joy launched herself into preparations for the publication of *Weeping Bay*, her first book since *Anya* had come out a full decade earlier. With Davy, almost seven, in school and Douglas old enough at age five to amuse himself, the couple had more time for writing. Joy's life buzzed with the kind of energy from which she had felt estranged since the boys were born. Publicity shots had to be taken. Joy sat for the esteemed photographer Lotte Jacobi and was stunned when she received the photos. "You've not only made me look handsome," Joy wrote to Jacobi on February 12, "but you've made my hair look tidy, which is harder; and, harder still, you've made me look as if I have a nice character. And all this without prettying me up and making me unrecognizable; it's unmistakably me. You must have a genius for bringing out the good in people." Macmillan shared her enthusiasm, proposing to devote the entire back cover to a single image. In a phone conference they discussed which image to use. One of the photos made Joy look beautiful but not remarkably intelligent, her publishers thought, while another favorite made her look intelligent but not remarkably beautiful. "Which should we use?" they asked. "Use the beautiful one, of course," Joy told them on the phone. "Any fool can look intelligent." The photo was published in papers across the country, including the *New York Times* and the *New York Post,* and was more successful than the book itself. Joy got plenty of compliments; she joked to Jacobi, "It'll sell more books than the reviews will!"

In fact, the book did not do well, and any hope Joy may have had for *Weeping Bay* to revive her career proved a pipe dream. Reviews were mostly negative, especially from Catholics, who thought it blasphemous. Macmillan of Canada refused to publish the novel and released the Canadian rights, washing its hands of the matter. Joy was convinced that a U.S. editor curtailed marketing efforts for similar reasons. But the *Los Angeles Times* provided a different kind of lament: one novel in ten years from Joy Davidman was far from enough. The reviewer praised her skill and sensitivity, her "insight" into the human condition, and her "courage" in addressing the question of birth control in a devoutly Catholic community that produced more mouths to feed than food to feed them.

Meanwhile, another photographer was sent to Staatsburg, this time by *Presbyterian Life* magazine, to photograph Bill and the whole family for images to accompany Bill's essay "From Communist to Christian," which would be published in three installments beginning February 18. Bill posed at his Underwood typewriter, sitting on a patio chair, wearing a light leather jacket, dark sweater vest, shirt, and tie all askew; the whole Gresham family were photographed in front of Pleasant Plains Presbyterian Church. *Newsweek* was intrigued enough by Bill's story to write a brief profile, including a photo of the family sitting on the steps of the church, and plugged Bill's forthcoming publication: "How Gresham freed himself from Communist ideals, neuroticism, suicidal tendencies, and finally alcoholism and found peace in the Presbyterian Church is told in a series of articles beginning this week in *Presbyterian Life.*" Chad Walsh wrote a beautiful introductory bio for the series. "Looking at his face, you sense that he has lived as many lives as the proverbial cat; there are the indelible marks of enough strain and suffering to have killed anyone not made of tough stuff. But the main thing you remember is the gentleness, wit, and simple friendliness of the man."

Bill told his story, beginning with the misty November night in 1937 when he scaled the Pyrenees. He testified to the impact Lewis had made on his and Joy's lives: "No story of our spiritual growth would be complete without a tribute to C. S. Lewis. His books exposed the shallowness of our atheist prejudices; his vision illumined the Mystery which lay behind the appearance of daily life." With deep conviction, Bill stated that his long search for truth had come to an end.

The three-part "From Communist to Christian" series was condensed into a single piece for the anthology *These Found the Way: Thirteen Converts to Protestant Christianity,* published in 1951. Joy was one of the thirteen; in an essay called "The Longest Way Round," she chronicles how her upbringing and times shaped an ideological journey that culminated in Christianity. She began by recounting the transcendent moment in the park when she was fourteen—a moment, like so many others, that she had explained away as "some visceral or glandular reaction" to beauty, owing to her atheist perspective on what she now understood to be supernatural encounters. "Aesthetic experiences," she called them. Lewis would later use the same words in his autobiography to describe similar episodes in his own life. The experience in the park, she explained, and so many others like it, were about God revealing Himself through nature, imbuing in her a sense that there was more to existence than the material world. She detailed her childhood in the prosperous 1920s, her compulsion to write, her adherence to atheism—which she now firmly saw as a kind of religion that required faith—and how her search for meaning had taken her into and out of the CPUSA.

And she wrote about Fairyland. It was Lewis's first book of prose, *A Pilgrim's Regress,* published in 1933, that taught her the meaning of her childhood dream. The book's protagonist, John, sets out on a pilgrimage to satisfy a deep longing that seizes him when he sees an alluring island. "Most of his struggles thereafter arise because he is pursuing some false means of fulfilling the desire aroused in him by that sight," writes one Lewis critic. "Moral and intellectual errors alike arise from misunderstandings of this desire and of how to respond to it." This, Joy knew, was her experience, too.

"It's strange," Joy wrote, "how completely I failed to see where my emotions and desires were leading. For what I read, eagerly and untiringly, was fantasy . . . I believed the three-dimensional material world was the only thing that existed, but in literature it bored me. I didn't believe in the supernatural, but it interested me above all else. Only it had to be written as fiction; the supernatural presented as fact outraged my convictions. By disguising heaven as fairyland I was enabled to love heaven." She continued:

> There is a myth that has always haunted mankind, the legend of the Way Out. "A stone, a leaf, an unfound door," wrote Thomas Wolfe—the door leading out of time and space into Somewhere Else. We all go out of that door eventually, calling it death. But the tale persists that for a few lucky ones the door has swung open *before* death, letting them through, perhaps for the week of fairy time which is seven long years on earth; or at least granting them

> a glimpse of the land on the other side. The symbol varies with different men; for some, the door itself is important; for others, the undiscovered country beyond it—the never-never land, Saint Brendan's Island, the Land of Heart's Desire. C. S. Lewis, whose *Pilgrim's Regress* taught me its meaning, calls it simply the Island. Whatever we call it, it is more our home than any earthly country.

Without Lewis's works, she wrote in tribute, "I wonder if I and many others might not still be infants 'crying in the night.'"

In both their essays, Joy and Bill looked on the day of Bill's breakdown as the turning point in what they now saw as their lifelong journey inevitably leading to faith in Christ, facilitated by the Holy Spirit's gentle guidance, which she confessed she needed:

> My present hope is twofold. I want to go deeper into the mystical knowledge of God, and I want that knowledge to govern my daily life. I had a good deal of pride and anger to overcome, and at times my progress is heartbreakingly slow—yet I think that I am going somewhere, by God's grace, according to plan. My present tasks are to look after my children and my husband and my garden and my house—and, perhaps, to serve God in books and letters as best I can. And my reward is a happiness such as I never dreamed possible. In His will is our peace.

· 10 ·

1950–1952

As if cued by Wormwood himself, an insidious subverter infiltrated Joy's life. She'd first encountered the name L. Ron Hubbard through the penny-a-word pulps that published Hubbard's stories. Now Hubbard claimed to have uncovered "the hidden source of all psychosomatic ills and human aberrations" and the skills to cure ailments ranging from arthritis to coronary disease and from allergies to schizophrenia. He called this breakthrough panacea Dianetics.

Hubbard debuted Dianetics in the May 1950 issue of *Astounding Science Fiction*—the magazine where Joy had read tall tales about atomic energy before the bomb proved them true. Like atomic energy, wrote the magazine's editor, John Campbell, the power of Dianetics was "almost unbelievable"—but "not a hoax." That power could be harnessed and implemented at home by any "intelligent layman." Those with sick bodies and troubled minds could avoid doctor visits, expensive medical tests, and exorbitant psychoanalyst bills. Seekers needed only to purchase Hubbard's 452-page manual *Dianetics: The Modern Science of Mental Health,* for the low price of $4.

Joy and Bill bought it, and so did tens of thousands of others—suckers and intelligentsia alike. Appealing to the educated, Hubbard tipped his hat to a dozen innovators including Voltaire, Isaac

Newton, Plato, Descartes, Thomas Paine, Thomas Jefferson, Francis Bacon, and Sigmund Freud—"without whose speculations and observations the creation and construction of Dianetics would not have been possible." He garnered credibility from the likes of Walter Winchell, influential syndicated columnist at the *New York Daily Mirror,* who legitimized Dianetics by proclaiming to the American public that "from all indications, it will prove to be as revolutionary for humanity as the first caveman's discovery and utilization of fire." The *Washington Post* added *Dianetics* to its list of recommended summer reading, alongside Churchill's *Grand Alliance.* Within two months of publication, *Dianetics* was a best-seller. Hubbard took his show on the road in a lecture tour that packed auditoriums across the nation. By the end of 1950, his book had sold half a million copies.

Perhaps Hubbard had stumbled onto something, Joy thought. His premise was that every mind consists of two parts. First there was the *analytical mind,* comparable to Freud's conscious mind; then came the *reactive mind,* similar to the subconscious. The former is a "computing machine" that processes information and events—remembering, receiving, and perceiving. The latter does not reason; it records, imprinting physically and emotionally painful events on the very protoplasm of cells. These records are called *engrams,* "complete recording[s], down to the last accurate detail, of every perception present in a moment of . . . 'unconsciousness.'" Engrams can begin immediately after conception; thus, anything that happens inside or near the mother has potentially devastating consequences. In fact, Hubbard claimed, many basic engrams occur during *attempted abortions,* or "AAs." Multiple sclerosis might be the result of a mother using a "corrosive douche" to try to kill the baby, instead scalding the surface layer of cells. Assessing another case—of a woman who felt sharp pains whenever she heard the sound of running water or a chair overturning—Hubbard concluded that at some point in her history she had been knocked unconscious by a man who subsequently overturned a chair and kicked her while the faucet had been left running.

To eliminate engrams, Hubbard prescribed that patients undergo a process called "auditing," a kind of hybrid of hypnosis and psychoanalysis guided by an auditor—any family member, friend, or stranger who has studied Hubbard's manual. The auditor gently leads the patient to recall and relive traumas, a process that moves engrams from the reactive to the analytical mind, where they can be consciously "blown." One woman experiencing persistent headaches in which the pain manifested on either side of her head was led back, memory by memory, across what Hubbard called a "time track," or a sequence of events, until she curled up in a fetal position with her head between her knees and recalled the grip of forceps during her own birth. Once a person's every engram is located and blown, she becomes a "Clear."

If Dianetics was indeed a medical advance capable of resolving every physiological and psychological affliction, not only would it be one of the greatest discoveries in the history of humankind, but also it could transform Joy and Bill into truly happy, healthy, productive individuals. Hubbard promised that practitioners of Dianetics could "achieve at least one-third more than present capacity for work and happiness." Joy was taking thyroid pills, as well as antihistamines for allergies. She found a lump in one breast—though a doctor dismissed it as nothing to worry about. Bill had hay fever, weeping eczema, a tormentingly itchy scalp, nightmares that jolted him awake, a phobia about eating poultry (developed during traumatic nights in Spain when the only food source was raw rodents), and "bursts of irrational rage" that frightened the children.

And there was something else. One hot summer day in Staatsburg, Bill suffered what can only be described as a psychotic break. "I was cutting back to the house through the corn stalks," he recounted years later to a friend,

> when I came upon a corn smut big and burst-open, showing the inner mass of black hair. My nerves have always been hyper-sensitive to the sight of a squirming mass of ants, etc., [and] when I saw the hideous corn smut I felt that my nerves had all caught fire

> and that instead of burning they were itching—all through my body. I began to claw at my eyebrows (one focus of the itching) and then the thought struck me: "This is unbearable as it is. Learn from it what can be learned!" Like Blake's tyger, "did He who made the lamb make thee?" And the corn smut became a child of God along with intestinal parasitic worms, deadly viruses, Adolf Hitler, Joe McCarthy . . . I fell to my knees between the rows of corn overcome by tears, always a sign that I have come closer to the Everlasting Mercy. Like Moody and Sankey's favorite hymn ". . . she just touched the hem of his garment."

The break marked a terrifying progression in Bill's extensive history of mental health problems. For him, Christianity hadn't proved a comprehensive cure—but neither did it claim to be. In Christian theology, disease results from the fall and is one aspect of recurring challenges inherent in the human condition, life in this broken world. Dianetics, by contrast, was introduced as a "science," not overtly subverting either religious or anti-religious tenets, thus alienating no one.

ALTHOUGH JOY AND BILL found the concept of prenatal engrams far-fetched, they were eager to test this new "technology." Employing Hubbard's "code," Bill lay down on the couch. Nearby, Joy led him through the time track to a moment when he was five and his mother said, "Don't suck your thumb, baby, it will get all sore." The eczema on his thumb disappeared. Before long, the couple were believers, even in the prenatal theories. Although they made "no attempt . . . to force out uterine engrams," Bill told a friend, they "did come to expect a basic engram in the pre-natal area, through experience."

That experience included auditing others, sometimes for profit. Hubbard opened the Hubbard Dianetics Research Foundation in Elizabeth, New Jersey, where applicants could pay $500 for a four-week course to become a professional auditor, permitting them to charge $25 per session. Joy and Bill didn't have the $500 for Hubbard's certification course, so they taught themselves. *Dianetics* includes a glossary with hundreds of "Words, Terms and Phrases" that Hubbard created or adapted, a language in which Joy and Bill became increasingly proficient. About one of her "pre-clears," Joy wrote: "I've given her three runs, assisting quite a lot where necessary, and am quite sure I've got an AA case—nasty blow to the head probably in the 2d month, containing probably 'I can't see anything!' and a memory denier. She's a visio shut-off and has a lot of 'can't remember' in therapy, also believes herself to have a bad memory though she evidences a good one. The engram contains terrific deniers but I think it's about to pop. Lock chains cannot be run off the ordinary way because of conscious memory-shutoff, but examiner runs 'em and blows terrific grief charges."

Howard, who was still not speaking to Joy, was alarmed by family reports about his sister's dabbling in what he and the medical community at large considered a "pseudo-psychiatric cult." If sick people chose auditing over professional care, the results could be catastrophic. Repercussions could be similarly devastating for healthy people predisposed to emotional disturbances; "the encouragement of intrauterine fantasies may aggravate already dangerous tendencies and cause insanity," said a doctor from the Psychoanalytic Society and Association. Newspaper editorial pages became battlegrounds for skirmishes between those who swore by Dianetics and those who swore against it. Hubbard was widely denounced as a snake oil salesman peddling a cure-all potion for personal profit, preying on the sick and desperate. In September, after a subset of psychologists adopted Hubbard's techniques, the American Psychological Association announced a resolution urging its eight thousand members not to implement Dianetics methods in the absence of empirical evidence. They warned practitioners and the public alike: this was not an innocent fad. Dianetics was dangerous.

IN THE FALL of 1950, in their drafty old farmhouse on Endekill Road, Joy and Bill audited each other twice a week. Bill's conditions appeared to improve—his scalp itching was reduced, his mood stabilized—and when they unfurled the winter wool blankets, he didn't wheeze and sniffle. In November, when a friend came to stay for the better part of two months, they audited her, too. The friend, Phyllis Haring, lived in South Africa and was visiting the United States from November to January before moving to England permanently with her small redheaded son, Robin. A thirty-one-year-old single mother, she had long been a depressive. Her despondency stemmed in part from what she believed to be a deviant sexual attraction to women; she was fighting a losing battle against it. Neither Joy nor Bill ever expressed moral trepidations when they spoke of homosexuality—not before their conversion to Christianity and not after. They, like many progressive contemporaries, considered the behavior a form of acting out, a symptom of an emotional disorder, and they wanted to help their friend. Bill's heart was heavy with compassion for Phyl's struggle; during his Greenwich Village years he'd "had a long and scarifying love affair with a girl who had a similar problem."

Before Phyl sailed from South Africa, Joy had written to her about Dianetics. Hubbard claimed that his technology could cure homosexuality. He had discovered the scenario that created the engram for this aberration. "You see, chances are Mamma has been playing around," explained the editor of *Astounding Science Fiction*, who became a spokesman for Hubbard. "Papa knows it, gives Mamma a punch in the stomach. This knocks the kid unconscious. Mamma cries and screams, swears the baby is his, but he gives her another punch in the stomach and says 'It better be mine. It better be exactly like me, or by God, I'll wring its neck.' Then the kid turns out to be a girl and what happens? She goes through life trying to be just like Papa and ends up a lesbian."

But Dianetics did not alter Phyl's lesbianism. Neither did it cure Bill and the boys that winter when they came down with mumps and bronchitis. It failed to dissolve the lump in Joy's breast or heal a painful kidney infection that sent her to the hospital early in the new year. Instead, it drove Bill to deep melancholy, pushed Phyl into an abyss of suicidal despair, and flung Joy into paranoiac rage. As Bill guided her further and further back on the time track, she began reliving disturbing traumas. "She accused my mother of having tried to abort her before she was born," Howard said. "She also thought she remembered my father having sexually abused her." Howard was skeptical of these accusations. The latter has at least some grounding in circumstantial evidence: her early sexualization, her excessive hatred toward her father, her penchant for much older, married academics. Nevertheless, no other mentions of such a weighty allegation have emerged from Joy's letters or interviews with those who knew her well.

JOY WAS NOT fully recovered from her kidney infection by the time Phyl and Robin prepared to leave in January 1951, so she stayed with a friend while Bill drove them to Pier 88 in Manhattan. He felt powerless watching Phyl being devoured by that "dragon" of despair he knew all too well. "I don't think any outsider could understand how I felt toward you," he later wrote her, "but it was really a feeling of understanding love for a sensitive person going through an emotional storm which I could understand . . . I felt so helpless in the face of your misery."

At Pier 88, Bill stood on the dock while Phyl boarded her ship, sailing toward a suicide attempt of her own. Then he started off toward Poughkeepsie to pick up Joy. Somewhere north of Manhattan, the car began to sputter. Rather than chance getting stranded on a roadside, Bill decided to spend the night at the Hotel Woodstock. He called Joy and said he would be a day late.

Joy didn't buy Bill's story. She accused him of staying in New York to seduce Phyl. She knew Phyl's departure date but was overcome with paranoia—perhaps not wholly unfounded. During a chat with Chad Walsh, Bill alluded to indulging in extramarital sex. "One of the things he was convinced of," Chad recounted, "was that every man needs to recharge his batteries once in a while."

Joy screamed at Bill over the phone. He in turn "cussed her out proper" and slammed down the receiver. "It was really the finish," Bill wrote to Phyl years later. "She never forgave me. She was firmly convinced that I had spent the time in New York trying to seduce you!"

Joy's conviction about Bill's infidelity did indeed create an indelible break in their marriage. "My love for him died very suddenly and completely," she later confided to Chad. Neither Joy nor Bill, however, indicated a desire for a separation, and she downplayed those horrid months. "It's been an unpleasant winter," she told friends in late March 1951 with considerable understatement, recounting the family's collective illnesses and mentioning that their houseguest "also needed a good bit of nursing."

THERE WAS ANOTHER reason why she and Bill were drifting apart: their hard work at the typewriter wasn't paying off. Both of them generated piles of stories, plots, and proposals, but Bill enjoyed few sales, and Joy's attempts at marketable fiction—short stories targeting women's magazines—went nowhere. She didn't publish poetry anymore, explaining to a friend: "Bill and I, being freelance writers with two kids, have become severely professional. We write for money, damn it." But they couldn't dig out of debt and had to borrow from Joy's parents. Money was "all they were good for anyway," she once told Howard.

The financial crisis had traumatic consequences for the boys as well. One day Mary Stevenson stopped by the Gresham house to ask if Davy and Douglas could come over to play with her sons. Mary kept goats, chickens, and horses, and the boys loved to visit. When she pulled into the driveway and got out of the car, she heard the boys "crying and hollering." They were locked in the playroom. Mary called out, but there was no sign of Bill or Joy. She was able to get in through the front door. The boys had soiled themselves. Searching the house, Mary discovered Joy and Bill in the attic, writing furiously. She confronted them. "They didn't want the boys to get hurt or in trouble playing outside on their own, without supervision," Mary recounted. But to Mary, this was a case of neglect. It upset her that Joy had the time to throw herself into philosophical conversations and a literary career but not to mother her children adequately. "I had no patience for that sort of thing," she said. From then on she distanced herself from the Gresham family. For his part, Douglas would remember his mother as alternately "big and warm and cuddly" and "quite ready to hand out the 'lickings' with a leather belt, the slaps for misdemeanors. Once, she locked me into a cupboard, in the dark."

Further chafing the marriage, Bill's dedication to Christianity began to wane while Joy's continued to solidify. In early 1950 he read *An Introduction to Zen Buddhism,* by D. T. Suzuki, and "began to have an inkling of a supernormal consciousness." He started studying Buddhism seriously as a supplement to Christianity. "Do you know anything about a weird and wonderful world-view called 'Zen'?" he wrote to Chad. "Started in China (called *Ch'an*), from Buddhism, developed in Japan. Fascinating stuff . . . Will tell more later if you are interested. And I want to write to Lewis about it. It may have something we can use." If Bill did write to Lewis about Zen, that letter has never surfaced. But Lewis would have responded with the unwavering position he maintained in his books and adhered to in his life: Christianity doesn't require or allow for additives. Bill would later point to 1950 as the year when he began drifting away from Christianity. He had tried it on for size, he told a friend, but it didn't fit.

At the same time, Joy feasted on a spiritually invigorating correspondence with Lewis, who fed an intellectual appetite for theology and a conceptual understanding—if not an application—of Christian living. She referred to him as "my teacher," a guru of sorts, both role model and adviser. On defining her type of Christianity, she agreed foremost with his views on fundamentalism's literal interpretation of scripture. "If fundamentalism means accepting as a point of faith at the outset the proposition 'Every statement in the Bible is completely true in the literal, historical sense,'" Lewis wrote to an acquaintance, "that wd. break down at once on the parables . . . Of course I believe the composition, presentation, & selection for inclusion in the Bible, of all the books to be guided by the Holy Ghost. But

I think He meant us to have sacred myth & sacred fiction as well as sacred history."

Likewise, Joy told her old pen friend Kenneth Porter: "I don't believe for a moment that the Old Testament is anything but an excellent compendium of a nation's literature, with amazing flashes of prophecy and insight and divine inspiration shooting through it now and then like lightning! I do, however, believe unshakably in the incarnation, the Atonement, and the Resurrection." Additionally, American fundamentalists' rigid rules against drinking, smoking, and dancing seemed to Joy to be arbitrary, irrelevant, and disproportionately emphasized. "Essentially [fundamentalists] are, I think, more responsible for the spread of atheism than any *directly* atheist teaching could ever be." Ultimately, it didn't matter how she classified herself. "Since I am one of C. S. Lewis' converts," Joy wrote, "I tend to follow him fairly closely, and nobody has yet been able to define *him!*"

Joy was not alone in speaking of Lewis almost as disciples spoke of Jesus—a symptom of hero worship that Lewis shunned. "I am shocked to hear that your friends think of following me," he wrote to a correspondent. "I wanted them to follow Christ." But, tangible and modern, Lewis became an unwitting casualty in the battle between the human axiom that seeing is believing, and the biblical definition of faith as "the substance of things hoped for, the evidence of things not seen."

Although she followed him, Joy remained a freethinker; they had a "running argument" on birth control, for example ("I'm not quite as traditional as my teacher"), and she sensed that he enjoyed their correspondence all the more for the rhetorical challenge. Their "pen-friendship" could not have thrived had Joy blindly agreed with him; neither would it have grown muscular without her noticing subtle inconsistencies in his arguments. She was willing to push back, and Lewis loved that. He was, he said, "hungry for rational opposition." Especially when it came to literature and doctrine, "to find an opponent is almost to find a friend."

As their camaraderie grew, Lewis invited Joy to call him by his nickname, Jack. Joy became increasingly preoccupied with thoughts of him, as she had been with Professor Mabbott at Hunter and Bill Benét at the MacDowell Colony—men whose erudition matched their imagination, who challenged her intellectually, men who were accomplished and widely admired. Jack's reputation continued to swell. *Vogue* magazine called him "one of the most powerful forces in Oxford today," a lecturer who "draws huge audiences, no less for the weight of his matter than for the clarity of his exposition . . . the doyen of the Socratic Club, which indeed has the air of a band of disciples sitting around the feet of their Master, as at their meetings they discuss questions of philosophy and theology, and set themselves with heartiness and intellectual muscularity to confute agnosticism. As with those other Christian litterateurs, Chesterton and Belloc, neither his Christianity nor his literary taste has destroyed the healthy, earthy, gusto of his pleasure in walking, talking, eating, argument and beer."

IN EARLY AUGUST, Joy, Bill, Davy, and Douglas fled to the cool comfort of New England, leaving behind oppressive heat and "the handsomest thunderstorms you ever saw," as Joy described them to a friend. "People are saying it's all the fault of the atom bomb, and here and there I catch dark mutters that the end of the world is at hand." The Walshes had invited them for several days to their cabin, "Rock Haven," on Lake Iroquois in Vermont—a Fairyland-like realm where the beginning of the world felt at hand, with fresh evenings and woodsy walks among wild berries, ferns, and moss evoking the quiet freedom of Joy's MacDowell Colony days. It was a much-needed respite.

Every day for hours, Davy, Douglas, and the Walsh girls would splash in the shallows while the adults indulged in highbrow conversations about God, poetry, theology, and even Dianetics—which Joy and Bill continued practicing despite firsthand evidence that it damaged more than it repaired. The centerpiece of their conversations, of course, was Lewis. Previously Joy had discussed Lewis primarily "in literary terms," Chad recalled, and "in religious terms." But he took note of a tonal shift in Joy's words about this man whom they both adored; the new affection in her voice was not lost on him. "A more personal politic began to come into her remarks about [Lewis]," he observed.

INDEED, JOY HAD begun to fantasize about Jack. She had few friends to confide in about her newest love. Although her bond with Belle endured, distance and children precluded the intimacy they'd once shared. Joy looked again to verse as a repository for emotional burdens. As with her earlier obsessions, Mabbott and Benét, she began writing sonnets, poems from a deep, desperate place, privately confessing her love but acknowledging its impossibility. C. S. Lewis, her teacher, was now her "lord" and "love."

The same disconnection from reality that allowed for her continued involvement with Dianetics and her conviction about Bill's infidelity led Joy to read "distinctly sexual undertones" in Jack's words. Only two letters from Jack to Joy—and just one from her to him—are known to have survived. Lewis was in the habit of destroying all letters after responding; he didn't have the space to keep them, and he didn't want future biographers to exploit those who had entrusted him with their troubles. Thousands of correspondents, however—including hundreds of women—saved his letters; they reveal nothing sexually suggestive (although mild flirtation surfaces in Lewis's long-term correspondence with the poet Ruth Pitter, an unmarried Englishwoman who was attracted to him). It is not difficult, though, to understand why the bachelor received care packages from female admirers—especially from those in America, where he was receiving the most press. He filled a void many husbands left empty. He listened and responded respectfully without placating or patronizing. He promised prayers for comfort, healing, reconciliation. And, like Joy, he was uninhibited about discussing sensitive subjects, ranging from marital issues to masturbation.

In years to come, Joy would compile her sonnets in a manila folder; she would write COURAGE on the front, and on the back two lines in German from a poem by Heinrich Heine: "Aus meinen großen Schmerzen / Mach' ich die kleinen Liede" (From my great pain / do

I make little songs). One of her sonnets reads: "Begin again, must I begin again / Who have begun so many loves in fire / And ended them in dirty ash?" She was deeply ambivalent about loving him; she did not want to lose or abuse his friendship.

Honoured sir, I am
Somewhat your friend;
as far as courtesy
Requires, your servant . . .
I love you far too well to give you love.

She would include in the collection the poem, written several years earlier, in which she expresses the sense of a "terrible third" in bed while she and Bill made love. In the margin of the draft she would write, "1948 or 1949," and "In a moment of insight, for CSL." She would gather the sonnets into a series, later grouping the first four together as "America, 1951," but she would never seek to publish them.

Joy was not the only woman whose feelings for Lewis evolved from friendship to flirtation to, ultimately, infatuation. There was a one-legged nurse named Margaret Radcliffe who wrote him reams of letters. "It was her ambition to live at the Kilns," Lewis's estate, "and look after him, and he had constantly to tell her that he did not need her help," said Walter Hooper, who would become Jack's secretary during the last months of his life. Lewis didn't discourage Radcliffe; rather, he asked his editor to send her a complete set of the Narnia stories. He was less accommodating when a psychotic antique dealer, Kitty Martin, arranged a wedding date and placed a marriage announcement in the newspaper. She, too, wrote Lewis incessantly, beginning in the early 1940s with "quite sensible" letters requesting religious advice; over time, her letters became "unintelligible," and Lewis stopped replying. The letters ceased coming for a while, but she resumed writing to him again around the time he and Joy first began corresponding. When "a delusion of marriage appeared," he started throwing away her letters unopened.

"When he stopped replying," Kitty told a newspaper reporter who interviewed her about the alleged romance, "it seemed obvious that he was really answering the letters in his books. For instance, I once asked him for a jewel. He never sent one, but later in one of his books mentioned a jewel, and to me that was his reply . . . I am in love with him. All his best books are based on our correspondence."

For her part, Joy tried to accept the fact that a relationship with him would never happen; nevertheless, a fantasy flourished, as she became increasingly infatuated and increasingly tormented.

> Let me not lie about it; there are worse pains.
> There is seeing your children shot before your face.
> There is being buried alive in the shallow graves
> Where afterward the torn sods heaved in vain.
> There is gripping the bars and staring out at the rain
> With fear cutting your belly like a knife.
> There are many deaths and several sorts of life
> That are much worse than what I feel for you;
> And yet this loss is loss, this love hurts too—
>
> A pinprick surely, fit to make a song of?
> A nuisance like a cinder in the eye,
> A fleabite; I would not do you the wrong of
> Pretending that I sicken and must die.
> Believe me, I am sound—
> Why, no; I lie.

Joy began actively plotting some way to get to England. Bernice suggested the Fulbright program—it supported whole families in Europe—but nothing came of the proposition. An idea for a story about Charles II had been brewing for a while; Joy could use research as an excuse to make the trip.

As the urgency of her desire gained momentum, an unexpected opportunity presented itself. By the beginning of 1952, Joy's cousin Renee was in trouble. She had been living in Mobile, Alabama, with her two small children and her husband, Claude Pierce, an abusive alcoholic who was becoming increasingly violent. Fearing for her life and the safety of her children, Renee made plans to leave despite Claude's threat to kill her if she tried. Renee wrote to her mother, Joy's aunt Rose, begging her to stage a ruse by sending word that she was seriously ill and needed her daughter in New York at once. Rose complied, sending a dramatic telegram. Claude agreed to let Renee and the children go for a visit. Once safe in New York, Renee mustered the courage to call Claude. She told him she was never going home. Enraged, Claude roared that he would kill anyone who stood between him and his children. Renee was terrified. It was only a matter of time before Claude would show up, banging on Rose's door. The family conferred and suggested that Renee and the children hide out in Staatsburg with the Greshams. Joy and Bill welcomed the proposal; Renee could help with household chores, giving Joy more hours to write.

Joy had recently become consumed with writing a pair of Lewis-inspired theological articles for *Presbyterian Life* magazine—one on the commandment "Thou shalt have no other gods before me," and the other on Matthew 22:37–40, "Jesus said unto him, Thou shalt love the Lord thy God with all thy heart, and with all thy soul, and with all thy mind. This is the first and great commandment. And the second is like unto it, Thou shalt love thy neighbor as thyself. On these two commandments hang all the law and the prophets." The first, Joy said, was "the greatest discovery ever made . . . The belief in One God slew a host of horrors: malign storm-demons, evil djinns of sickness, blighters of the harvest, unholy tyrants over life and death; the belief in God destroyed the fetishes, the totems, the beast-headed bullies of old time. It laid the ax to sacred trees watered by the blood of virgins; it smashed the child-eating furnaces of Moloch and toppled the gem-encrusted statues of the peevish divinities half-heartedly served by Greece and Rome." The knowledge of God followed: "An almost unimaginable thing; a single being, creator of heaven and earth, not to be bribed with golden images or children burned alive; loving only righteousness. A being who demanded your whole heart." Then came "the moral law of the Decalogue—a shining rainbow bridge stretching between earth and heaven." For moderns, though, all that was old news, taken for granted, and most nominal self-identified deists were really just self-deceived atheists, Joy posited. Leading contemporary false gods, she said, included "Sex, the State, Science, and Society," with the "self" being the greatest of all. In the current post-atomic "Age of Fear," she wrote, "an age of lost faith and lost hope and empty hearts . . . 'Thou shalt have no other gods before me' must include 'Thou shalt have me.'" The thesis of the second article was that "the real test of belief is action."

Writing theology did not come easily, Joy admitted. The essays, which would not be published until the spring of 1953, try to cover too much territory—the Jews of Christ's day, the current Marxist climate, virtue as "an excuse for self-righteousness," and the "small bright glow" that spread deep inside her when Joy sacrificed a day to cheer up an imposing "neighborhood nuisance." She needed more space, and so the articles led her to begin a book about the Ten Commandments, to be titled *Smoke on the Mountain.* "What should a Jewish Christian write on if not the Law?" Jack would say of the work. Joy had been drawn to the subject since her hedonistic Hunter years, when she consciously abandoned "the ugly things called moral codes." But perhaps part of the reason why Joy struggled had to do with the vast divide that was about to appear between what she preached and what she practiced. "The beast in the heart is always the self," she wrote in the essay she titled "God Comes First." If we hold to the commandment "Thou shalt have no other gods before me," she writes, "the beast in the heart has no power. The present loses its confusions, the future its terrors, and death itself is but the opening of the door . . . That is the law of life and happiness. Whatever we desire, whatever we love, whatever we find worth suffering for will be Dead Sea fruit in our mouths unless God comes first." In a private sonnet to Jack, though, she would confess, "I have loved you better than I loved my God." And in the margin notes of her copy of Jack's book *The Problem of Pain,* she asked: "What if the medium of your salvation becomes the medium of your torment? I am more hurt now through my love of God than I should have been if you had not taught me to love him; for then I could at least have avoided my pains, now I must bear them. If there is no heaven, then are we Christians of all men most miserable!"

THE AMOUNT OF time Joy devoted to her articles and Decalogue book idea became an escalating source of contention with Bill. While he thought she needed the confidence boost of a good sale and publication, he still expected Joy to carry the bulk of homemaking responsibilities. It was clear to him that they couldn't both be full-time writers. "It has been said that there are two things a man must have to be a writer," he told a friend, "a wife and a typewriter and both must work." Joy was not working for him.

Renee—the cousin to whom Joy's mother had pointed as a model of femininity in their youth—had grown up to be stunningly beautiful. With her father's Latin complexion, her voluptuous figure, and lustrous dark hair gathered elegantly at the nape of her neck, she could have been a flamenco dancer. On a cold winter day, Bill met her and her two children, Rosemary and Bobby, at Grand Central Station and escorted them to Staatsburg. It was dark and snowy when they pulled up to the house on Endekill Road. Joy ushered them inside, fed them, and helped them settle in.

Renee was surprised by Joy's dowdy figure, sloppy clothes, and socks that drooped under the heels of her Mary Janes. When the three adults went out to a restaurant one night, Joy put on a coat with a missing button, replaced with a safety pin. Renee cringed.

At first, things went smoothly. Renee found a job at a factory in Poughkeepsie so she would be able to contribute to household expenses and afford necessities for Rosemary and Bobby. The two women developed a sisterly rapport, sharing kitchen chores and alternating morning shifts of feeding the four children and seeing them off to school. Joy had more time to write. In the evenings they played Chinese checkers together, and Joy and Bill took turns auditing Renee. Joy now believed she'd had occasional experiences of Hubbard's "ESPER"—foretelling an event in the near future. But while they remained devoted to the techniques of Dianetics, they became increasingly suspicious of Hubbard's claim of producing Clears. They had never seen one; no one had.

Enjoying the freedom of time to write, Joy began transferring more of her domestic duties onto Renee. Soon Renee was cooking most of the meals and washing all the dishes. "[Joy] was an opportunist," a neighbor said. "She presumed on a slight acquaintance that you would be there for her if she wanted something." Besides that, Joy and Renee had different approaches to parenting. Renee was hands-on. Joy let her boys help themselves to cold cereal and milk before school, but Renee set out a heartier "proper breakfast." At night, she laid out her children's clothes and made sure their shoes were polished. Joy had no qualms about letting Douglas go to school with the back of his shoe broken and one overall strap swinging loose because of a missing button. Tension built. Joy told Renee she was too domestic. Renee viewed Joy as lazy and neither a proper mother nor wife.

Joy was overwhelmed with dissatisfaction about her life. She drank a lot—too much, Renee thought. Bill attended A.A. regularly, and Joy often accompanied him to open meetings, but she kept hard liquor in the house, which Renee thought insensitive. "We'd sit at the dinner table and [Joy] was constantly making remarks to Bill, and he'd sit there just letting it roll off . . . Denigrating remarks . . . cutting and biting remarks." Renee wondered if there was an element of professional jealousy. Her perceptions, though, recollected decades later, came from the perspective of a woman who was beginning to fall in love with Bill. She was right, all the same. The years of living with Bill's mood swings and drunkenness had left Joy with little respect for her husband. Her resentment toward him grew in tandem with her infatuation with Jack.

On April 21 Joy received a disbursement voucher from *Presbyterian Life* for $400 and began actively planning a trip to England, buying new clothes and applying for a passport. She would leave in August. Joy urged Renee to quit the factory job so she could stay home, keep house, and care for the kids and Bill. Renee resented this.

Work gave her a sense of independence, and she didn't want to feel like an indentured servant. But she felt beholden to Joy for taking her in when she was in trouble.

Soon, Joy made a shocking admission to Renee. "Every evening practically we played Chinese checkers," Renee remembered. "She'd have a bottle of Myers rum beside her . . . and after a couple of drinks, she'd tell me that she was going to England to get to bed with C. S. Lewis. This was planned . . . [S]he didn't say it just once. Several times she repeated it. Which made me think later on that part of her reason of taking me in . . . was so she'd have somebody to take over while she went pursuing C. S. Lewis."

Renee was not alone in that conclusion. Later, Douglas Gresham would write in his memoir, "I must ask myself if in fact Mother saw Renee's arrival in our household as an opportunity not to be missed and left for England, not only aware of the likelihood of [Renee and Bill] falling in love, but also hoping that they would, thus giving her the chance of escaping from a marriage which was fast disintegrating." Howard, learning about the trip secondhand from the family, was convinced that Joy had one specific goal in mind: "My sister always knew what she was doing. [She was] fearless in a sense. When she left to go to England to meet C. S. Lewis, she left Renee, who was running away from her husband, and Renee's two children with her own two children and Bill Gresham in one big mansion. And Renee was taking care of the house. My sister was no fool. My sister knew damn well she'd have grounds for divorce when she came back. And I think she expected to marry Lewis . . . In fact I knew it."

When and how Joy made her intentions known to Bill is unclear. Initially he was supportive of the trip. He could see that "Joy was in a very unsettled state of mind" in the months leading up to her departure. She spent money they didn't have. The following year, she would write off $925 in her tax return as "research" expenses incurred for this trip, as its ostensible purpose was to investigate the life of Charles II and seek Lewis's guidance for her *Presbyterian Life* articles and Decalogue book.

Eventually Joy was fully open with Bill about her intentions. Years later, when she and Jack were together and Bill was trying to get custody of the boys, he would tell Jack: "As the time for her sailing drew nearer she began telling people that she was not coming back. This was usually said after she had had a few beers. I tried to be calm and reassuring, telling her over and over, 'No need to make any vital decisions now, just wait.' She often told me, when she was upset, that she felt she was dying and had to get to England to see you. She said many times that she was in love with you . . . although at the time she had no hope of ever marrying you."

Before she left, Bill pointed out to Joy that Lewis had certain convictions, that he seemed content in bachelorhood, that the image he projected showed him to be "not the marrying sort of chap at all." Joy conceded the logic, yet her drive to meet Jack was overpowering, rendering her beyond self-control and reason. Bill saw no future there but felt that Joy needed to get this obsession out of her system. "I was all for it, if we could swing it [financially]," he told Lewis. They could not swing it. His nonchalance about Joy's quest to "seduce" Lewis suggests that either their marriage was an open one or he felt this was a way for him to make up for his own infidelities. Or perhaps Joy's resolve left him no viable alternative, but he felt he didn't need one because he didn't think it would go anywhere.

· 11 ·

August 1952–January 1953

In the second week of August 1952, Joy boarded the SS *United States,* bound for the port of Southampton. The brand-new sleek black steamship had recently become the fastest passenger ocean liner ever constructed in America, breaking the *Queen Mary*'s transatlantic speed record when it crossed the sea in just three and a half days—all of which aligned with Joy's urgency to reach the shores of England. As her ship pulled out of Manhattan's Hudson River piers and sailed through New York Harbor, whisking her away from America for the first time, she had glorious views of the Statue of Liberty and the city's skyline, but her heart's gaze remained firmly fixed eastward.

Yet she felt pangs of guilt. Adult responsibilities, maternal obligations, and Christian principles: Joy was compromising them all. She had said good-bye to Bill and Renee, Rosemary, Bobby, and her boys. Davy, now eight, felt abandoned, and six-year-old Douglas was simply confused; they knew only that Mommy had left on a very long trip and couldn't say when she would be back. She had no return ticket, few solid plans, and a few hundred dollars in cash. Phyl Haring had agreed to put her up for a while. Bill said he would send money when some came in. And Macmillan promised Joy a royalty check in November. If both followed through, her finances would just work out, Joy trusted.

Disembarking at Southampton on August 13, Joy boarded a train for London and made her way to Phyl's flat at 11 Elsworthy Road. Phyl, having now embraced her lesbianism, greeted Joy with new poise and a new lover, Selma. Joy liked "Sel" immediately; in fact, they turned out to be distant cousins—a coincidence that became an excuse to offer up to those who clucked their tongues at Joy's unorthodox escapade. "So," Joy wrote to Bill, "you can say I'm staying with relatives in London, if anyone asks!" And people would ask.

LONDON SEDUCED JOY like an exotic foreign lover, and she threw herself at it with abandon. She walked for hours along the Thames, around Piccadilly, inside the "enormous stone jewel" of Westminster Abbey, and through the open-air markets of Camden Town, which reminded her of the East Bronx, only with stalls heaped with rabbit and fowl—chickens, ducks, pigeons—plus mounds of fruit and vegetables, and slabs stacked with giant crabs, lobsters, plaice, turbot, sole, and more. She bought pints of prawns and brown ale for supper.

In long dispatches to Renee and Bill, Joy gushed about the superlative quality of everything English. Her idealization of the country and its people was so extravagant that it's hard to believe she wasn't being tongue-in-cheek. Brits, Joy said, were "an incredible law-abiding people. They've lots of passion and sex and murders—but afterward the murderer always toddles off to the police station and says, like one this week; You'd better arrest me, I done something to my young lady that I shouldn't. Sometimes a criminal does try to get away, but they usually get him inside of two days—and mostly even the criminals cooperate with the police!"

The English were purely angelic, she thought. People rushed to assist her whenever she looked lost, and bus conductors "practically mother you." On one bus ride, when Joy was told that the driver couldn't make change for a £1 note, she commented woefully that she had no other way to pay her fare. Joy had a hunch that the conductor would give her a free ride ("they're like that"), but before he could say anything, a fellow passenger insisted on springing "thruppeny" to cover the cost. When Sel and Phyl gave Joy coupons for a run to the grocer and butcher, Joy was informed at the store that the coupons were no good. She apologized and smiled demurely, "and they showered me with bacon and cheese and steak and butter!" she recounted, chalking it up to her effect on men.

Even the weather was always perfect. "London sunlight is never glaring white, always pale gold and just a little mysterious—the air's miraculously clear but with a softness that is like haze but isn't . . . It must be the wonderful light which makes the English so mad about their country—though Heaven knows trees and grass and flowers are miraculous too. *And,* in spite of all these open parks, no bugs, no flies! There isn't a screen in all of London, or a need for one." On a stroll with Sel on Hampstead Heath, Joy felt she'd found utopia: "Londoners basking, couples lying on the grass clasping in each other's arms and no one paying any mind."

English food was extraordinary and cheap. "God help my figure," Joy groaned in satisfaction after lunching at a Spanish restaurant off Trafalgar Square with Phyl, Sel, and a friend. "I'm eating three times as much as at home," she wrote to Bill, "not to mention a cuppa (short for a nice hot cup of tea) about every half hour." Joy marveled at the cost of a meal for four: beer, sherry, grilled sole, turbot, chicken with rice, french fries ("they call 'em chips"), and coffee, all for the equivalent of about $5.80, total.

One of England's most notable distinctions—what Joy commented on most frequently and emphatically—was the low cost of everything she wanted, needed, or didn't need but bought anyway. Despite the financial disaster at home, Joy spent recklessly; and because of the financial disaster at home, she vigorously defended every dollar, trying to convince herself as much as Bill that each purchase was justified. "Got a luscious Jaeger wool-Jersey dress for 5 guineas. That's $14.70 and you can ask Renee or the New Yorker ads what it would be in New York." At an open-air art exhibit on Hampstead Heath she bought three paintings, cheap for their remarkable quality, she said. And she splurged on house seats for a play. She went window-shopping on Regent Street. "You know what?" she wrote to Renee. "You can take Bonwit Teller and stick it up your mama's tochus. Clothes here are wonderful, much better made than ours and far better style, no doodads or frills, just beautiful simple lines—and a really *good* dress (except for the feelthy rich) runs about six guineas, i.e. $17.50 . . . If Bill sends more money I'll buy like mad."

But Bill could not send more money, he told Joy in late August. The little he could spare after food and necessities went toward bills. By then, two weeks into her trip, Joy had so completely detached herself that she no longer considered this a joint problem. "Sorry . . . you're still busted," she responded, "but it was a good idea to pay the taxes and milk, and I've plenty of money to hold *me* for a while yet."

DURING HER FIRST week, Joy went to a local Dianetics society meeting. Instead of kindred spirits, she found a cult-like group that regarded L. Ron Hubbard as a messiah. The mantel in the meeting room displayed a life-sized bust of him. Joy didn't know whether to laugh or gasp. "I shocked 'em by referring to marmosets," she recounted to Bill. Nevertheless, she was an American, from the land of their leader, and when Joy said she had visited the foundation, they treated her as a special emissary dispatched by Hubbard himself. Amused, Joy didn't demur. When she described the results she'd got auditing people at home, the group responded with murmurs of awe. Could she teach them her methods? They asked her to audit one of their own, and someone suggested she help write a documentary film script.

While Joy continued to have faith in engrams and auditing, the London assemblage somewhat discredited Hubbard in her eyes. It wasn't only the blind adoration. "Hubbard has now gone completely over the edge," she reported to Bill. "He has dropped the original Dianetics as beneath his notice, since it's only concerned with curing mortal bodies . . . Says there are *two* kinds of beings inhabiting a human body, besides its own somatic mind—genetic entities, a sort of spirit-of-evolution, and decaying theta beings who slip into a nice comfortable body in their old age and thus give it a personality." Joy learned more about Hubbard's reputation when she attended an informal weekly gathering of science-fiction writers and fans that met on Thursday nights at the White Horse tavern on Fetter Lane off Fleet Street. The group, which called itself the London Circle, first met in 1937, lost its way during the war years, then revived as a vibrant open forum for discussing literature, metaphysics, and politics over pints at the otherwise quiet pub. A core number attended faithfully, and occasionally a celebrated sci-fi writer joined them. Despite its allegiance to Hubbard's genre, the London Circle regarded him "with deep dark distrust," Joy reported to Bill, "and no wonder, judging by the locals." Regardless, she felt no compunctions about discussing Dianetics, and she made at least one friend.

John Christopher, a writer, sci-fi enthusiast, and regular at the London Circle, enjoyed Joy's forthrightness and spirited conversations about metaphysics and theology, and they bonded over discussions about C. S. Lewis. Christopher told Joy that he had read *Perelandra* —the same book that had led Chad Walsh to Lewis—during the last winter of World War II. He wrote an admittedly "callow" letter to Lewis taking issue with his depiction of the scientist, Weston, as categorically evil. Christopher saw the story as a generalization of all scientists. Lewis, Christopher said, responded with the following:

> Dear Sir,
> There may be something in what you say.
>
> Yours sincerely,
> C. S. Lewis

Joy found the anecdote amusing. "That's a stock reply," she told Christopher. Lewis tended to be dismissive of male critics but indulgent with females, she said.

Joy made another friend. Michal Williams, the widow of Lewis's writer friend Charles Williams, lived nearby. Joy walked over and knocked on her door. She wasn't home, so Joy left a message, to which Mrs. Williams replied with an invitation to tea on August 31. Michal Williams was tall and elegant, a good conversationalist who shared Joy's appreciation of Lewis. She was also exceptionally intuitive. Joy reported to Bill: "Mrs. Williams suggested (out of a quite clear sky) that I wear something pretty when I go to see Jack; says the dons may lead a cloistered life, but they take notice—and feel flattered! Ulp?" Unbeknown to Joy, Michal Williams wrote to Jack expressing great affection for her new American acquaintance, to which Jack responded on September 12: "Joy Gresham is an old & valued pen-friend of mine: I'm so glad you like her. Prod her to say *when* she is coming to us."

Once some dental work was complete (Joy took advantage of England's health care, even as a visitor), Joy left London for Oxford, arriving at last on September 15. She had arranged to stay with a friend of a friend for ten days, during which time she hoped to see as much of Jack as possible. The chronology of those first meetings remains uncertain, but a promising friendship was progressing by the seventeenth, when he presented her with a first edition of *Mere Christianity*. Joy invited Jack to lunch at the Eastgate Hotel, a comfortable Oxford establishment adjacent to Magdalen College, mentioned in both *Time* magazine and Chad's book as one of Lewis's favorite haunts. Jack invited Joy to lunch in his private rooms, along with Phyl and his dear friend George Sayer.

Joy arrived at the lunch neatly dressed and discreetly made up, Sayer recalled. But that was the extent of her discretion. When the customary glass of sherry was served before the meal, Joy broke the refined ambiance by declaring: "I call this civilized. In the States they give you so much hard stuff that you start the meal drunk and end with a hang-over." Salmon mousse followed the sherry, and Joy continued to amuse the group with a "flow of sharp, almost outrageous comments." Jack "laughed uproariously." Sayer asked about her first impressions of England, and she responded glowingly. "Everything she saw in England seemed to her far better than what she left behind." She scoffed at modern technology, skyscrapers, and the inhumanity of urban living, especially in New York City. Small farm life suited her, she said, speaking passionately about her gardens and "the green earth." Jack interjected that his father's family descended from farming stock. "I felt that," Joy said. "Where else could you get the vitality?"

After lots of food and lots of wine, Joy asked for a tour of Magdalen. Jack led the party downstairs and through the medieval cloisters. Joy was dazzled. "What's that place there . . . is it one of the dungeons?" she teased. "What happens behind that door?" Jack "produced equally amusing replies," recalled Sayer. "Her enthusiasm, interest, and many impudent questions made us roar with laughter." The foursome split into pairs, with Joy and Jack moving into their own private realm. In the flesh, the man was everything she had known he would be—wise and brilliant like his books, as luminous as his letters. She felt euphoric in his presence. She later reminisced in a sonnet:

> When I first loved you,
> Daylight sang and blazed
> With angels; the incarnate miracle
> Rang in my heart like ocean in a shell,
> The sky was loud with God.

Jack did nothing to discourage Joy's flirtation; he enjoyed her company too much. So much, in fact, that he invited her to come back to Oxford as his guest before returning to America. "Jack asked me to stay behind for a minute after his other guests had gone," Sayer recounted. "He had asked Joy to stay at the Kilns, and he wanted my advice." Should he and his brother, Warnie, follow their natural routines of taking walks and eating basic plowman's lunches, or should they adapt a routine more suitable to the company of a lady? He was concerned about bathroom arrangements as well. While the Kilns had a perfectly competent hot water system, the scarcity of coal precluded baths. Jack and Warnie took advantage of the facilities at the college, which were off limits to women. Thus Joy would have to make do with jugs of hot water. "Live your normal life!" Sayer said emphatically. "She obviously enjoys your company and conversation and will be happier if you do things that are natural to you."

Sayer was shocked by Jack's invitation to Joy, a younger, married American woman. It seemed out of character, and he didn't know what to make of it. Had Joy invited herself, or baited Jack with the suggestion of a stay? One thing was certain: Jack was obviously feeling freer than he'd felt in decades, having recently been unchained from a long, strange relationship with the mother of his old military friend Paddy Moore.

Paddy's mother, Janie Moore, had monopolized Jack's finances and freedom for decades. They met in Oxford in 1917, when Paddy invited some friends, including Jack, to visit his mother's home. Jack, who had no family nearby and no mother anywhere, eagerly accepted her invitations to return for meals. Soon he began spending nights there without Paddy. Scholars have long suspected that the relationship turned sexual. At the very least, Jack swiftly became enamored with her as the nurturer he had mourned and yearned for since his own mother died when he was a little boy, an event that devastated him. Mrs. Moore, more than twenty-five years his senior, took care of him when he was ill, putting him to bed as a mother would. In fact, he began calling her "Mother."

In 1917, as he and Paddy went abroad to fight in the war, they promised each other that if one of them didn't make it, the other would look after his dead friend's surviving parent. When Paddy was killed in action, Jack shackled himself to Mrs. Moore for three decades. "Mother" grew progressively dependent on him for comfort and money. They lunched and spent most afternoons together. Jack helped pay her rent and eventually moved in. He led a quiet life, teaching at Oxford and gardening among his peas and beans. Later, though, she took to treating him like a personal assistant. Jack's father was concerned from the start. "I confess I do not know what to do or say about Jack's affair," he wrote to Warnie. "It worries and depresses me greatly. All I know about the lady is that she is old enough to be his mother—that she is separated from her husband and that she is in poor circumstances. I also know that Jacks [as his family called him] has frequently drawn cheques in her favour." Warnie was appalled when he moved in with them after retiring from the army in 1932. "I don't think I ever saw J[ack] work more than half an hour" without Mrs. Moore calling for him, he recorded in his diary. "COMING, Dear!" Then "down would go the pen, and he would be away perhaps five minutes, perhaps half an hour." It was under these conditions that *Screwtape Letters* was written. Warnie recalled Mrs. Moore telling visitors that Jack was "as good as an extra maid in the house" and accused her of perpetrating "the rape of J's life."

Had it not been for Mrs. Moore, perhaps Jack would have married. She limited his social life and, no doubt, his romantic life. As he explained when declining an invitation to a confirmation in 1949, "For most men Saturday afternoon is a free time, but I have an invalid old lady to look after and the weekend is the time when I have no freedom at all, and have to try to be Nurse, Kennel-Maid, Wood-cutter, Butler, Housemaid, and Secretary all in one." He was miserably unhappy but felt duty bound to care for her; he would not go back on his word to Paddy. Mrs. Moore died in 1951, a year into Jack and Joy's vigorous correspondence, and a year and a half before their first meeting.

Joy saw Jack several more times during her stay in Oxford after their lunch with Sayer. He brought her to the "Bird and Baby," code for the Eagle and Child, the pub where he communed with the Inklings. Over pork pies and cider, conversation ambled from triviality to philosophy, from forays into curing home-grown tobacco to logic versus faith. "One evening with him I got a little sozzled," she wrote to Bill, "and debated reason vs. the Inner Light till I was completely muddled." Their beer-hazed conversations were intense, erudite, and mutually gratifying.

Joy observed how Lewis's ethics permitted indiscretions: "I notice Jack's principles don't forbid things like black-market eggs etc, which everybody here grabs when they can." What else did Jack's principles not forbid? He was either oblivious to or dismissive of her flirting. She was his friend, she was married, and she was a Christian. None of these things precluded her from entertaining romantic feelings or advances, yet he treated Joy more like one of his male friends. He didn't care for "either the ultra masculine or the ultra feminine," he once told his good friend Dorothy Sayers. "I prefer *people.*"

While Jack clearly enjoyed her company, Joy did not sense from him any romantic or sexual interest. Downcast, she set off to do the Charles II research that was her ostensible reason for being in England, first visiting the Powick Bridge battlefield, then Edinburgh, where Charles had paid a memorable visit. Joy adored Edinburgh, with its wide streets, its shops and homes arranged neatly around the foot of Castle Rock, as if in deference. The city could have come straight out of one of Jack's fairy tales, she thought.

She visited the library to read up on Charles's visit, but research that should have energized her only drained her further. Perhaps a visit to the Highlands would hearten her. She inquired about companies offering organized tours, but all were closed for the season. Not that she could have afforded the trip; money was running low. Bill was not keeping her in cash, and in her despair Joy lost patience. "I'm enjoying myself, although no money to spend," she wrote from Edinburgh. "Bill, I do hope you will have some to spare before November; or I can hardly pay for a passage . . . though I know how hard you are trying." Something else was troubling her. In addition to his grousing about taxes and bills, Bill's letters seemed distant. He barely acknowledged her adventures and requests. Since her first week in England, she had asked him and Renee to send canned fruit (peaches, apricots, and sliced pineapple), eggs (the ration in England was one per person per week), gift copies of *Weeping Bay* and *These Found the Way,* American science-fiction anthologies for Jack, thyroid pills, "and, above all, sliced bacon." Renee hadn't responded to her letters at all. Was something happening in Staatsburg that she wasn't being told about?

Overwhelmed with exhaustion and defeat, Joy bought a ticket to London, returned to her Edinburgh hotel for the night, and collapsed into bed. Nausea set in, and her chest tightened. Joy pulled the covers over her head. She was having an anxiety attack, she thought. If only Bill were there to audit her and "run it off." The next morning, Joy boarded the train for the twelve-hour trip back to London along England's eastern seaboard—coal country, much of it, Joy thought, speckled with mounds of slag and shabby houses, reprieved by the occasional emerald field populated by sheep and cattle. When she arrived on Phyl's stoop around 11 P.M., the doors were locked. No one was home. Bags in tow, she stumbled around the streets, found a hotel, and once again buried herself in bed.

But worse was yet to come. Two letters from Bill bore bad news. The first contained more of the same, plus a list of ailments. Joy lashed out in exasperation: "Lawsy, what a tale of woe to find waiting in London! 'Davy has poison ivy, Renee's got the curse, I've got the crud, our agent is going blooey, there's no money in the house and little prospect of more; do have a nice time!'" Things were not all sunshine and lollipops on her side of the pond, either, she responded: her anxiety attack and fatigue, the aborted Highlands tour, and Bill's continuing failure to fill her orders, a constant vexation. "I can imagine the pressure you're working under," she told him, "but please do acknowledge my requests and do something about them." She did at least have sufficient funds to hold her for a while and thought she could "pick up some spare change doing dianetics runs on people" and churning out fiction, despite her history of inadequate earnings in that genre. "Also if the worst comes to the worst I *could* always borrow money from Jack—though I'd rather cut off my right arm." Suggesting to her husband that his failure to provide might drive her to borrow from another man was surely a punishing ego blow. Hinting at her suspicions, Joy commented on the negativity of Bill's letter: "Ah, well, it's better than getting the sort of bland assurances that all's well which make every woman wonder what's being hid from her. At least I can always feel sure that you'll tell me the worst."

She was right. In his next dispatch, Bill implored her to take seriously the severity of their financial troubles. His primary concerns were taxes and groceries. One thing kept him going: Renee. They had fallen in love.

Joy responded on October 6 without skipping a beat or showing any emotion, barely even acknowledging his admission. "Golly, I had no idea things would get as tough . . . Feel like a heel, being out from under at a time like this, but will do my best to help from this end. How about the freak idea for True?" she suggested, referring to one of her and Bill's heaps of story plots and partial manuscripts. "Try Rinehart on Frankie; they *might* come across with an advance . . . Is there a story in the Pierce kindred? . . . Chad Walsh wanted you to do something for Episcopal whatsits, might be a quick few bucks." How about placing an ad for paying Dianetics patients? Political campaigning? Could Renee's father pitch in some dough? "As for me I will work like a demon from here on," she promised, and requested that he check her desk for partial manuscripts and typed lists of story ideas and send them along. "Also if absolutely desperate *could* probably borrow from banks." Interspersed throughout the letter were breezy descriptions of autumnal London, the view of England's east coast by train, Jack's inscription for the boys in a copy of his latest Narnia book, and a peculiar congratulatory aside: "Glad of the one bright spot, anyhow. Wish you both all the luck in the world. As to where I fit in, I shall postpone any decision until the financial matters are straightened out, also I want to get some advice."

Joy sealed and sent the letter. For two nights she hardly slept. This was not how things were meant to work out: Jack sexually indifferent to her; Bill interested in Renee. She could end up with no one. Alone. And the boys—if Bill really *was* having trouble feeding the household, should she pack up and go home? No. Hurt though she was, Joy decided to savor the rest of her trip. The Thursday night White Horse crowd accepted her as a fixture. There were more sights to see, friends to be made. And there was Jack. She wrote to Bill and Renee that she was "panic-stricken . . . feeling guilty" for being on holiday "instead of home helping." But, she said, she could contribute more by staying in England: "I can live far more cheaply here . . . and work better." The truth was, freedom from family and responsibilities had given rise to an intellectual and social renaissance. Joy had built a temporary life that she wasn't done living.

WHEN JOY ARRIVED in Oxford, she met Jack at Magdalen for lunch with several friends and Warnie. "I was some little time in making up my mind about her," Jack's brother wrote in his diary. "She proved to be a Jewess, or rather a Christian convert of Jewish race, medium height, good figure, horn rimmed specs, quite extraordinarily uninhibited. Our first meeting was at a lunch in Magdalen, where she turned to me in the presence of three or four men, and asked in the most natural tone in the world, 'Is there anywhere in this monastic establishment where a lady can relieve herself?'"

But she delighted Warnie with a shared passion for seventeenth-century literary life and royalty. He was just finishing a book about Louis XIV, the Sun King, who ruled France at the same time that Joy's Lord Orrery sat in the House of Commons. Their conversations grew rich. "A rapid friendship developed," he wrote in his diary. "She liked walking, and she liked beer, and we had many merry days together." The brothers "treated her just as if she were a man," he said. They frequented pubs, drank ample pints of beer, and walked all over. "[Lewis] had not met anyone like her before," George Sayer said. "She had high spiritual and intellectual qualities. She had a brilliant mind. She could argue and discuss with him as well as anyone he knew. And I'm sure she loved him."

Joy told Jack she was doing Dianetics treatments for extra cash, and even persuaded him to let her audit him. "[I] returned Jack to a pleasure moment in childhood, just for demonstration," she wrote to Bill. "Lawsy, what recalls . . . [L]ovely to hit a really healthy mind, after all the 'I dunno!' and 'Oo, how I suffer!' cases." She asked Jack if she could interview him for an article (he said yes), suggested to Jack that they "cook up something together—anything to earn an honest dollar" (he seemed amenable), and told Bill she was considering "a quality sale for [a] Lewis piece; might do two, one for Pres. Life, and one on Jack as children's writer *or* as scholar."

Joy returned to London as her time with Jack receded into the past, October proved a horror of a month. Sel left the second week to look after a friend's child, and Phyl became progressively inhospitable. When Joy did the dishes, they were never clean enough. When Joy was cold, Phyl refused to light the fire. It had been two months since Joy's arrival; she had outstayed her welcome, and she wasn't taking the hint. At first, Joy dismissed Phyl's behavior, mindful that she was "a poor loony." But by the eighteenth, Joy could bear it no longer. She spent the morning searching for a hotel, then had tea with a new friend, Clare Gay, whom she'd met at a recent party. "I did an ESPER and realized Clare Gay was going to ask me to stay with her," Joy told Bill. Joy helped the matter along by telling her how badly she wanted to leave Phyl's place, but couldn't do so until she secured new accommodations. "And the rest arranged itself!"

They made a deal: Joy would perform Dianetics runs on Clare in exchange for room and board. This went well at first. Joy determined Clare to be an attempted abortion case who had experienced a damaging blow to the head, probably in the second month of gestation, resulting in excruciating headaches. Joy thought the case was much like her own. Clare had "rage" and was a "memory denier," often responding to Joy's questions with "can't remember!" Air-raid engrams—almost a given for anyone who'd lived in wartime London—needed to be run off as well.

Joy brought Clare to the local Dianetics group but was horrified by the deterioration since her visit in August. "Hubbard is now taking their spirits out of their bodies—he says," she wrote to Bill,

> and enabling them to perform telekinesis, communicate with Mars, etc. They can't be bothered with such trivia as curing ailments, they're going to run the world and end war . . . The latest gimmick is "illusion therapy." As I argued the leading Hubbardite to a stand still (took off the gloves a bit, I was aiming at the waverers in the group and did a lot of good) and he was a violently aggressive Cockney lad, he naturally picked me to demonstrate on. The idea is, the auditor tells you to imagine doing all sorts of horrible things; if you don't like the image, this means that you actually *have* done the thing in a previous life. He told me to imagine rolling my eyes around inside my head, taking out the left eye and moving it about in front of me: "What do you see?" To which I, inspired by Charles Lamb: "My eye, sir, rolling rapidly!" Alas, nobody got it—how I missed you!

England was bursting with people who needed real treatment. "Chillun crying for bread," Joy wrote to Bill. "If you're ever gonna be an auditor *this* is the country to be it in." Within a week, Clare was feeling much better, was "singing among the soup pots," and even gave Joy an E-run. "I scanned off some more locks On Being Scared Bill Would Kill Himself," she wrote to Bill, marveling at the grip of that old trauma. By the end of the month, Joy had other paying cases and was rushing around London on the Tube and on foot, auditing people while squeezing in visits to the British Museum and a two-day tour of Avon. She was also working hard on short stories that would never sell, and on her *Presbyterian Life* articles and her Decalogue book.

But when Joy resisted Clare's request for continued daily audits, Clare became "demanding and bossy." Her migraines returned, and no matter how hard Joy tried to convince her that they resulted from an attempted abortion, Clare believed there must be an alternative psychological explanation.

> She must have something *compelling* independence, she insists on running on examiner alone and resists questioning. Has had a lot of love affairs with dependent and inferior men whom she first dominated then drove away. Golly, you should hear London women talk about their sex life! *I've* been shocked. A natural result I suppose where men are scarce and women accustomed to making their own living, but they do seem to take promiscuity and an aggressive role for the woman completely for granted. And it makes them miserable, naturally; and they don't know why, and keep yelling for auditors, occultists, evangelists, swamis, hypnotists, and what have you . . . 'Tain't what they need. I always knew the Career Woman's life wasn't very rewarding, but I'd no idea it was as bad as this; I'm learning a lot.

Other things about staying with Clare became intolerable. Her house was inconveniently located nine miles from London's center. She was an unimaginative vegetarian, and, like Phyl, scrimped on coal and gas. Joy shivered relentlessly. She needed to find a new place.

Joy Davidman at two years old, 1917

Joy with her parents, Jeannette and Joseph Davidman, on one of their many summer family excursions to the country, 1918

ABOVE: Joy, age five, on Briggs Avenue in the Bronx, September 1920. She stands with her mother and an unidentified boy in front of a baby carriage ten months after the birth of her brother, Howard.

LEFT: Thirteen-year-old Joy with her father and brother Howard, July 1928

Dr. Joseph Isaac Davidman prided himself on being an authoritative academician, circa 1940.

Joy and Howard at Devoe Park, the Bronx, July 1931

The Catskills were a favorite vacation destination for New York City's Jewish families, including the Davidmans. Here, Joy stands in Lake Florence, in Roscoe, New York, in August 1931, shortly before starting her sophomore year at Hunter College.

Joy (front row, second from left) posed for a yearbook photo with the staff of *Echo,* including editor in chief Florence Wolfson (front row, right).

Right: After meeting as students at Hunter College, Belle became Joy's closest lifelong friend. *Below:* Joy's senior portrait, 1934.

All photos are from the Hunter College Yearbook, Wisterion.

KAUFMAN, BELLE
Major — English; ΦΒΚ; ΣΤΔ; Make-Up Box, 7, 8; Journalism, 7, 8; Secy., Eng. Club, 8; Shakespeare Society, 4.

DAVIDMAN, HELEN JOY
Major—English; Σ Τ Δ; ΦΙΣ; Bulletin, 1; Echo, 5, [illegible] Editor, Echo, 7, 8; Exec. Secy., ΣΤΔ; Pres., Eng. Club, 8.

Joy Davidman at the MacDowell Colony, Summer 1938

Joy, circa 1940

Joy and Bill Gresham on their wedding day at the MacDowell Colony. Joy is holding a leash for the cat in Bill's arms. August 24, 1942.

Howard Davidman in his World War II military uniform, circa 1943

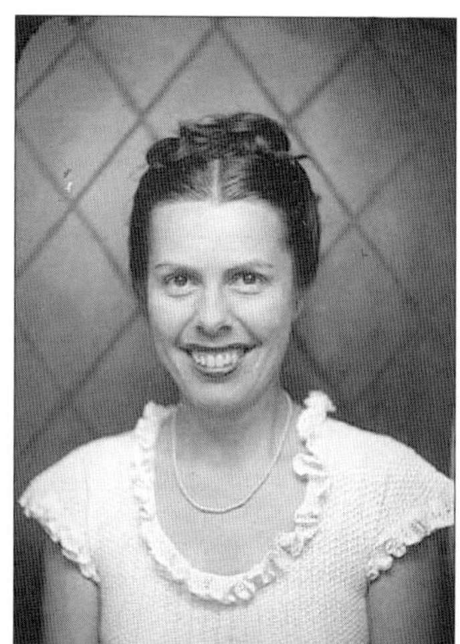

Ruth Davidman, circa 1943

The Gresham family's fourteen-room Hudson Valley dream home, in Staatsburg, New York

Bill Gresham smoking on the porch of the house on Endekill Road, Staatsburg, circa 1949

Douglas and David Gresham with one of many family pets, Topsy, circa 1949. Joy had nursed the dog back to health after discovering her, wounded and abandoned, in the middle of a road.

Girl Communist

An Intimate Story Of 8 Years in the Party

NEW YORK POST HOME NEWS, MONDAY, OCTOBER 31, 1949

The legal issues involved in the operations of U.S. Communists are on their way to higher courts. Much of the current controversy, however, has obscured the real questions facing a democracy. Why do some Americans become Communists? What lure does the Communist Party retain for any young American, in view of its long record of servitude to Russian foreign policy? How do Communists live, labor and love? What happens to them after they have been recruited? How do people behave inside this strange, underground, political realm? What kind of people are the native commissars? What do they demand of their followers? In this series Oliver Pilat tells the story of an American girl who was attracted to Communism in 1937 and remained a member of the Party for eight years. No story is completely typical, but neither is this one unique. Joy Davidman's experiences throw new and revealing light on the attraction—and ultimate weakness—of the American Communist Party.

By OLIVER PILAT

The Woodlawn section of The Bronx is all built up now, but when Joy Davidman knew it as a little girl it possessed the quality of a bit of forgotten country in the city. You could still find rabbit tracks in the snow, and there was an old-fashioned orchard with blue creeping myrtle under the trees.

Joy Davidman wonders now whether things would have been any different if her parents had remained in Woodlawn. She believes a great deal of inarticulate rebelliousness which finds expression in Communism stems from resentment against city life. Perhaps not for her; she was never very inarticulate.

"Being raised in a room where you can't sit, stand or lie down," she says. "That's what city life means to many kids. No use saying a healthy human being must adjust to our society, if the conditions of society are crazy."

Anyway, her parents didn't stay long in Woodlawn. They moved down to the Grand Concourse, a middle-class neighborhood which gave them a comfortable feeling. They were immigrants, the father from

straight brown hair, which her mother insisted for years on putting in painful leather curlers every night. Joy had a minor twist of the spine which was not noticed for some years. As she grew older, spells of illness caused her parents concern and led to a certain amount of coddling. Perhaps she was overcoddled.

In those early years of growth, Joy felt strongly about people and things. She didn't want anybody to be hurt. When

JOY DAVIDMAN

The first article in a twelve-part profile of Joy published in the *New York Post,* October 31–November 12, 1949

Joy, David, Bill, and Douglas in 1950 on the porch of Pleasant Plains Presbyterian Church, where she and the boys were baptized. Joy served as a deaconess and Bill as an elder.

Dust jacket photograph for Joy's novel *Weeping Bay,* 1950. When her publisher asked whether they should use a photo that made her look beautiful or one that made her look intelligent, Joy replied, "Use the beautiful one, of course; any fool can look intelligent."

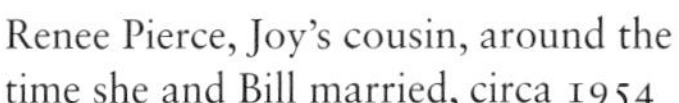

Renee Pierce, Joy's cousin, around the time she and Bill married, circa 1954

Renee and Bill in Florida with her children, Bobby and Rosemary, circa 1954

C. S. Lewis in his rooms at Magdalen College, Oxford, 1946

The Kilns, Lewis's home in Headington Quarry, Oxford, June 1958

C. S. Lewis and his brother Warren (Warnie) in Annagassan, on their annual summer holiday to Ireland, circa 1952

David, Joy, and Douglas in a passport photo taken before the three moved to England in November 1953

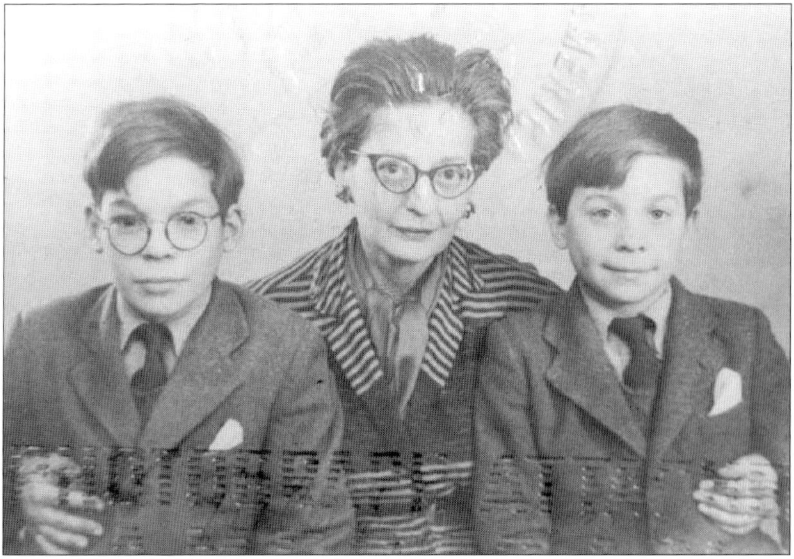

Registration Certificate No. A607299.
Issued at A.R.O. Metro.
on 10.2.54.
Name (Surname first in Roman Capitals)
~~GRESHAM~~ Helen Joy
LEWIS,

Left Thumb Print (if unable to sign name in English Characters).
PHOTOGRAPH

Signature of Holder) Helen Joy Gresham

Nationality U.S.C.
Born on 18.4.15 in New York.
Previous Nationality (if any) —
Profession or Occupation No occupation (Writer).
~~Single or~~ Married
Address of Residence 14, Belsize Park, N.W.3
Arrival in United Kingdom on 13.8.52.
Address of last Residence outside U.K. Staatsburg New York, U.S.A.
Government Service
Passport or other papers as to Nationality and Identity.
U.S. Ppt. 661090.
Washington 29.5.52

A "certificate of registration" was issued to Helen Joy Gresham as an alien resident of England in February 1954. It is not known who crossed out "Gresham" and substituted "Lewis."

The newlyweds spent many intimate hours in the garden of the Kilns after Joy's terminal cancer diagnosis, circa 1957.

Crocheting colorful afghans became a therapeutic hobby while Joy convalesced, circa 1957.

September 1957. Jack was determined to keep David (left) and Douglas in his custody after Joy's death, despite Bill's wish to raise them in America.

Joy and Jack talking in the Kilns garden when her cancer was in remission, 1958

"Mrs. Lewis" fired a shotgun into the air to chase trespassing neighborhood children from the Kilns property, circa 1959.

Jack and Joy paused to rest at Kamiros, in Rhodes, Greece, in April 1960, three months before her death.

Then the flu hit. Joy collapsed into bed, deeply depressed. Her friendship with Jack had continued to grow but remained platonic. She could hardly bear it. "I felt I was really going to die," she wrote to Bill shortly afterward, in early November. He must take her back. He would, she decided. He needed to know how much she suddenly wanted to be with him, that things would be different when she returned. "[I] went through another sort of spiritual experience," she continued,

> got my emotions to rights. They needed it! I am sick to death of love-languishing; no man in the world, not even the greatest, is worth dying for, and I am BORED with the whole fruitless business. I really was clinging to suffering and self-pity, wasn't I? what a dreary time I must have given you, and no wonder you were so glad to pack me off! Well, I realized (like the dames in magazine stories) that I was doing it to myself and didn't *have* to; so I stopped. As for That Man, he is certainly fond of me and rather attracted by me, but not enough to disturb his peace of mind (thank goodness); and if it were ten times as strong a feeling, his belief would still be stronger. Funny; I've never before been with a man who looked at me and talked to me like that and then did *not* make a pass—and, do you know, I half like it! I'll be a Christian yet.

She was homesick for Bill and the boys, she admitted, and vowed to get the most out of her remaining days in England, return home, and do her job as a wife and mother with a smile. "And *you* will be happy too, if I can do anything about it! Though I seem to have done some of it already, with Dianetics' assistance."

Michal Williams noted Joy's distress and wrote to Chad Walsh that something seemed amiss. She, Jack, Warnie, and Joy had had drinks together at the Mitre lounge. "The inhabitants," she reported, "forgot their drinks & nakedly & unashamedly listened to the great man cascading brilliance . . . I like Joy so much. She is most unusual. I think she may be going through some sort of crisis . . . She comes here quite a lot and we talk of mice & men & cabbages and kings . . . & somehow I think she is a forlorn child & very brave & rather hurt by life."

JOY HADN'T HEARD from Bill in a while, and that worried her. On November 4 she wrote another desperate letter: "I think you'll find me quite a nice girl when I come back! But I am curiously uneasy over not hearing from you this week; probably just one of those premonitions that never mean much." Taking her mind off the future, Joy had dinner at Michal Williams's house, debated theology with the White Horse "boys," took in a vaudeville show, and searched for a hotel. She didn't hear from Bill until November 8, by which time she had moved to Nottingham Place, a quiet street near enough to the center of things. The room was drab, a fourth-floor walk-up, but she spruced it up with bundles of red and gold chrysanthemums, a pot of white heather, glazed chintz, an Indian-print bedspread, and the three paintings she'd bought in Hampstead back in August.

She "had a brain wave" and "espered there was a letter at Clare's" that hadn't been forwarded. A phone call to Clare confirmed the ESPER, so Joy ran over to find not just a letter but a letter bearing a check. "London is mine to run mad in!" she wrote to Bill. Again, utterly disregarding her family's drastic financial straits, Joy shopped recklessly: three silk Liberty scarves, belts, shoes, and a dress from one of Regent Street's swanky shops—perhaps per Michal Williams's suggestion that dons take notice. "I've been having a spending spree on that blessed seventy quid you sent me (don't I sound idiomatic)," she wrote to Bill. "Such a relief—one hates to be Spartan on a trip like this one!" She made plans for a trip to Devon and Cornwall, and placed a deposit on a return passage on the SS *Franconia,* departing from Liverpool on January 3.

In the letters that have survived, Bill did not address her return home, nor did he comment on her spending, her trips, her hotel, Clare, or Phyl—or anything else Joy mentioned. Family life in Staatsburg had hit its stride, he told Joy. Writing was going well. He was more inspired than ever; Renee created ideal working conditions. Incidentally, she looked "very lovely" in her oversized Mexican earrings, he said, layering his accounts with hints of his continued affection for his wife's cousin. A little money had come in ("the old Alley just paid off a couple hundred skins"), and he was putting together a collection of his carny articles. The kids had a grand time at a Halloween party hosted at the Staatsburg firehouse. Renee had sewn fantastic costumes: Will Scarlet for Bobby, Maid Marian for Rosemary, Robin Hood and Nero for Douglas and Davy, respectively. Davy, it turned out, was severely nearsighted and badly in need of glasses. Plans were under way for Douglas's seventh birthday party: the neighborhood kids were invited, and Bill would perform magic tricks. "Also we have had to let Dianetics slide for a while but both of us are in good spirits and I have never in all my life been so busting with ideas and been able to work so well." The boys missed her, he added, but were otherwise happy.

Bill's sustained distance deepened her concern, and the fact that family life was blooming in her absence was disconcerting. On November 10, Douglas's birthday, Joy attended a children's presentation Jack gave at a public library. Watching the boys and girls "spellbound" by Lewis's stories, "hypnotized" as he encouraged them to "always read what they liked and never mind about the grown-ups, who are usually silly," Joy wished her own boys could be there. In the two and a half months since leaving Staatsburg, she had written to Davy and Douglas only a couple of times and rarely mentioned them in her other letters. Their contentedness in a new family situation added another dimension to her concerns about losing Bill. The following week, while waiting at Victoria Coach Station to board an Oxford-bound bus, Joy dashed off a candid letter to Bill, this time admitting her own contribution to the deterioration of their ten-year marriage and adding that, however things played out between them, the boys would remain with her:

> I wonder why I find your letters so chilly? They're cheerful and friendly enough; but, well . . . hardly affectionate. You were always good at wounding by omission; such a nice method, can be

> used with a clear conscience. But what, after all, can I expect? I must have wounded *you* pretty deeply, and *not* by omission. I am not sure I ever hurt your heart, but I know damn well I damaged your ego. And egos don't forgive, though hearts may. Well, not much use worrying about it now. Things have got to go differently in the future, one way or another, and I shall do my best . . . I find myself missing the boys quite badly . . . One thing this trip has made quite clear to me is that the boys *do* come first with me and that no power on earth will ever separate me from them again.

In Oxford, Joy attended a lecture Jack gave on Richard Hooker to the Fellowship of St. Alban and St. Sergius, designed to reconcile Anglicans and Greek Orthodox, held in a lecture hall at Christ Church College. She chose a dress designed to catch Jack's eye, admitting as much to Bill—"Lingering vestiges of sin . . . , in spite of all my good intentions," she told her husband, perhaps hoping to elicit jealousy. Joy went to the event with two friends and found seats in the back, "behind a forest of Russian beards." When Jack arrived, Joy watched him glance around, nodding distractedly to acquaintances. Then he spotted her in the crowd. "I didn't realize he was looking for me until he saw me," she told Bill, "gave me a delightful sunburst of a smile, and sat down content." Was Joy simply seeing what she wanted to see? Or did Jack's equanimity indeed rely on her presence?

Watching him in front of a crowd was both thrilling and enlightening. He managed to bring down the house with laughter, even while lecturing on "Hooker's Laws of Ecclesiastical Polity, and the rising Calvinism of Elizabethan times." Afterward, he found her in the crowd. Joy was so moved by his attention to her that something unexpected happened: "My Feelings of Rejection curled up and died at that moment." Either Jack's friendship and respect finally felt like enough, or Joy was experiencing renewed hope that he might return her affection.

Simultaneously, she was gaining more insight into her marital troubles. She wrote Bill:

> I find that whenever I did not satisfy you as a wife (no matter why) I [would] try doubly hard, fail anyhow, *then* go into a rage against the person who asks too much. And I did not see that it was usually myself, not you. Actually you're very easygoing about most matters and demand far less than most husbands. It's true that I blamed myself a bit for failing to make you happy when your neurosis was bad, that hooks up with lotsa stuff about "*You're* responsible for my unhappiness!" But the only thing you really did on that chain wasn't you, but your engrams. You unconsciously expected of me the almost superhuman strength, patience, devotion, calm, and understanding which you remembered in your grandmother. And I at first would try to produce them; thus, when I *did* fail and relapse into mere wifeliness, your disappointment was all the keener, since I'd led you to believe I could deliver the goods. What happened was that I tried to be a superwoman, fell flat on my face, and blamed my discomfort on you.

If Joy believed that expressing and resolving these issues would mend their marriage, she was undeceived by the blow Bill dealt next. In late November she received a letter that no longer required reading between the lines, no longer allowed for self-deception or subtextual appeals to make another go of their relationship. Bill had decided it was time to be firm and clear. In a heartbreaking missive, he told Joy in no uncertain terms that their marriage was over:

> You have written several times that you can't understand the cool tone of my letters . . . I didn't think the letters were cool but if I understand you right, you have wanted me to say definitely what was going to happen when you come home. I wanted to get things clear in my own mind . . . Also I didn't want to cloud your holiday with things which would upset you.
>
> Renee and I are in love and have been since about the middle of August. If it had not been for our love I could not have come through this summer with as little anguish as I have for things have been rugged financially. I hate making a poor mouth and

> didn't want to darken your trip with too much complaining about finances but the main problem we have had over here has been seeing that we all had enough to eat. I wanted you to have your England trip and just before you left I tried to do everything I could to expedite it. But this left us with lots of unpaid bills and most of them are still unpaid . . . So far we have always eaten and most miraculous of all I have plowed away, working like blazes right through it, with Renee's love and care to help me. I couldn't have done it without her . . .
>
> I can understand, I believe, what resolutions you have made about coming home and trying to make a go of our marriage. But I feel that all such decisions are sacrifices of human life on the altar of Will Power. I have never yet know[n] will power and determination to "make a go of marriage," to take the place of love in its complete sense. I have tremendous affection for you and have certainly missed you, although I was glad you were having fun and adventures and seeing all the things you wanted to see. But affection and intellectual camaraderie are not marriage.

Bill added that it was unrealistic to expect Joy ever to be anything other than a writer, and unrealistic to expect him to earn enough money to hire a staff of servants to clean, cook, and watch the children so they could both enjoy careers. Renee, by contrast, understood his needs and tended to them. "Her only interest is in taking care of her husband and children and making a home for them." And then there was the physical chemistry, which, he told Joy, had been missing from their marriage for years—a fact that Joy had readily admitted in her heart and in her poems: "What Renee and I have found together came as an earth-shaking surprise for both of us. We never knew any such happiness nor knew there was such a thing." He proposed that after the divorce, Joy marry "some really swell guy" and both couples settle in close proximity so the boys could have their mother and father at hand. Davy and Douglas missed her, he said, more than they tended to admit.

Joy wept in pain and anger. Then she walked. She walked for

days: across Westminster Bridge at blue twilight, around Big Ben, over London Bridge, into the "Gothic forest" of Westminster Abbey, where "the arches and roof seem to bend over and *listen.*" It was the last day the abbey would be fully open until after Queen Elizabeth's coronation. Joy attended the evening service, then walked to St. Paul's cathedral. She climbed to the Whispering Gallery, through the Stone Gallery overlooking all of London—"beautiful, glinting, misty and melancholy with the great bombed-out spaces and the fragile towers that are all that's left of ruined churches." Wandering through the library and trophy room, Joy happened across a verger who suggested she climb the belfry and listen to the great bell toll. Others were there, but when the ringing began, they couldn't bear the noise. Joy stood there, her feelings echoed in the thunderous toll. "I was sorry when it stopped."

JOY CONTINUED TO pine after Jack. Her visit to the Kilns would begin on December 15. She would try again to win him over; this time she would confess her feelings. She remembered her first visit, nearly three months earlier, and the defeated hope. On December 10, she added a new sonnet to her collection:

> My lord and love, the yellow leaves were sailing
> Confusing sorrowful air and earth together
> Between two rivers, in the wistful weather,
> Sky changing, tree undressing, summer failing;
>
> September. And the waterbirds were calling,
> Heartbroken, harsh, under their reedy cover;
> That was no golden season for lover and lover
> But for dying light and bright things falling.
>
> Even the bells in Magdalen tower were ringing
> Death to the drooping afternoon, and never
> A merry note to comfort him, for neither
> Angels nor larks had any heart for singing;

And yet, not too forlorn a memory:
Oxford, autumn leaves, and you, and me.

Joy was on Jack's mind, too. He mentioned her in an aside in a letter to a friend in the context of an anticipated influx of American visitors owing to the coronation:

> Talking of Americans, we have just had a "pen friend" of long standing from New York (state not city) stopping with us; she belongs to the small income group, and is delightful—a rolling stone, authoress, journalist, housewife and mother, and has been "doing" England in a way which few Americans must have done before. Last time I heard from her, she had been at a Cockney wedding in the East End of London, where the guests slept on the kitchen floor after the festivities! She comes back to us next week before sailing for America, and we look forward to hearing her experiences. She ran out of money a little while ago, but has apparently supported herself quite comfortably by giving treatment in "dianetics" (whatever that may be).

Joy arrived at the Kilns in the midst of bitter chill—snow, ice, biting wind. She and Jack immediately picked up where they had left off, bantering over beers and enjoying Oxford Christmas traditions. He and Warnie brought Joy to a Christmas pantomime, where they all roared with laughter even at the oldest jokes and joined in the choruses of familiar songs. Joy gave Jack a copy of Ray Bradbury's novel *The Illustrated Man,* inscribed with a mildly altered quote from G. K. Chesterton's epic poem "The Ballad of the White Horse": "and men grow weary of green wine and sick of crimson seas." Lewis, in turn, inscribed her copy of *The Great Divorce,* "There are three images in my mind which I must continually forsake and replace by better ones: The false image of god, the false image of my neighbors, and the false image of myself."

Joy and Jack spent long hours discussing their respective works in progress. He let her read part of a new book on prayer, and proofs of his *English Literature in the Sixteenth Century* for the Oxford History of English Literature series, which he gave the tongue-in-cheek abbreviation "OHEL," as in "O Hell!" Joy asked him to read her Decalogue manuscript and provide feedback, which he did. Two years later Lewis would write a foreword to the British edition, focusing on the importance of an examination of the Ten Commandments from the perspective of a Jewish convert to Christianity:

> In a sense the converted Jew is the only normal human being in the world. To him, in the first instance, the promises were made, and he has availed himself of them. He calls Abraham his father by hereditary right as well as by divine courtesy. He has taken the whole syllabus in order, as it was set; eaten the dinner according to the menu . . . To us Christians the unconverted Jew (I mean no offence) must appear as a Christian *manqué;* someone very carefully prepared for a certain destiny and then missing it. And we ourselves, we christened gentiles, are after all the graft, the wild vine, possessing "joys not promised to our birth"; though perhaps we do not think of this so often as we might. And when the Jew does come in, he brings with him into the fold dispositions different from, and complementary of, ours.

In Joy's writing Lewis saw that "the Jewish fierceness, being here also modern and feminine, can be very quiet; the paw looked as if it were velveted, till we felt the scratch."

But Joy's companionship soon became a burden to Jack, by his own account. This was meant to be a working vacation; he was trying to finish his book on prayer, correct the OHEL proofs, set exam papers, and complete his seventh Narnia book. Joy monopolized his time and, if her sonnets are to be read literally, came on strong. She talked incessantly and complained about the Kilns' inadequate heating system. A typically gracious and forbearing host, he began to feel overwhelmed by her. "I am completely 'circumvented' by a guest," Jack wrote to his godson Laurence Harwood, "asked for one week but staying for three, who talks from morning till night. I hope you'll all have a nicer Christmas than I. I can't write (write? I can hardly think or breathe. I can't believe it's all real)." To George Sayer he vented: "The whole vac. is in in fact a shambles. Perpetual conversation is a most exhausting thing." He signed the letter "(what is left of) Jack." A few years later, when Lewis wrote in *The Four Loves* "What is offered as Friendship on one side may be mistaken for Eros on the other, with painful and embarrassing results," he certainly could have been reflecting on the Christmas of 1952.

In early January, Joy took her scheduled leave. Saying good-bye to Jack, she felt spurned; his displeasure was apparent enough to make her feel deeply rejected. After the *Franconia* sailed from Liverpool and the Atlantic began to fill the gulf between her and the man she loved, she wrote a new poem for her collection, titling this one "Sonnet of Misunderstanding":

> I brought my love obedience; cupped my hand
> And held submission to his thirsty mouth,
> A cooling water in a burning land;
> And he, being hot and desperate with drouth,
>
> Deigned to bend his head and drink it up.
> Love was the water, loneliness the thirst,
> And my poor earthen soul could serve for cup
> To offer comfort. He was glad at first,
>
> Until the taste of water grew a bore
> And a small coin of thanks too much to pay;
> Whereat he led me to an open door
> And sent me and my empty soul away;
>
> Saying I must not love him any more;
> But now at last I learn to disobey.

· 12 ·

January–November 1953

When Joy walked into the house on Endekill Road, the peaceful family circle Bill's letters had described became distorted into an ugly love triangle. She hollered about his cheating; he howled about her missing Christmas with the boys while she worked on what Bill referred to as her "project" of seducing Jack. Livid, she insisted she was moving to England and taking the boys with her; Bill insisted otherwise. Neither of them had the money to go anywhere or even pay for a divorce. Renee, also broke, was caught in the middle but afraid to move into her mother's Bronx apartment, where Claude might track her down. No one knew where to go, so no one went anywhere. Deep in the dark winter woods of upstate New York, Renee shut herself in a room and cried. Bill, in the bare back bedroom, "gnawed [his] knuckles in frustration and bitterness." Rosemary, Bobby, Davy, and Douglas tiptoed around, bewildered. And Joy wrote letters to Jack.

The tale she told him would take on a life of its own, a myth made of half truths, exaggerations, omissions, and self-pity—facts and fictions cast into a land of shadows. "Clever spiderwebs I weave in my head / To catch you with," she wrote in a sonnet for Jack. In letters to both Jack and Chad Walsh, Joy painted an increasingly unflattering portrait of Bill, punishing him for his infidelity, illnesses, and flaws, making him the whipping boy for Jack's rejection. Not only was he an adulterer, she lamented, but also he was a physically abusive, lazy, neurotic alcoholic who drank up their cash and left trails of unpaid bills in his wake. "He earned almost no money while I was away and there's a mountain of debt," she wrote to Chad, leaving out her own reckless spending in England and the fact that they couldn't afford the trip in the first place. "[He] has always insisted on blowing all his money on his own impulse," she complained. "He did his best to keep me penniless and helpless." And the lethal blow: on her return from England, she wrote, "Bill greeted me by knocking me about a bit . . . [He] half choked me."

By Bill's own admission, he had a temper: he'd been known to yell, to smash a guitar to smithereens. "The worst part about Dad's rages was his roaring and swearing around the house," remembered Douglas. "He was actually quite terrifying." On one occasion, when some guests had overstayed their welcome, Bill grabbed his old Springfield rifle off the wall and angrily brandished it about. "Forgetting that it was loaded," Douglas recalled, "he blasted a hole straight through the ceiling and through the floor of the room above!" But no one who knew Bill well—including Howard, Ruth, Renee, Rosemary, David, and Douglas—ever saw him become physically violent toward another person, then or in years to come. Today Douglas questions the details of an often cited story of his father breaking a bottle over his head, an incident that Joy told Jack had happened when he was a small boy. Nevertheless, Joy's accounts of home life upon her return convinced Jack and Warnie that Bill was, as Warnie wrote in his diary, a "drunken wastrel of a husband" who physically attacked her. It was "a propaganda campaign," David said decades later. "It is also a fact that my mother told innumerable lies about my father." In the end, though, the full truth about what happened between Joy and Bill behind closed doors remains a mystery.

Meanwhile, Jack responded to Joy's report of physical abuse by strongly encouraging her to leave. Chad and Eva agreed. They had sensed strains, but her accusation was a shock; they hadn't imagined

Bill capable of such brutality. Joy told them she had tried in vain to keep the marriage together, but she now knew that divorce was the right decision. "My conscience wouldn't let me quit," she wrote Chad a month after returning from abroad. "I had hoped that my vacation in England would soothe my shattered nerves and give me strength to go on . . . [I] felt I ought to put up with anything I could bear for the children's sake." Jack's approval, though, confirmed her belief that she was doing the right thing. "So now I'm rid of the feeling that it's my duty to go on!"

Only to Belle did Joy confide the true source of her misery. On January 30 she took an early train to Manhattan to spend the afternoon with her old friend before attending a MacDowell Colony dinner at the Columbia Club. Joy was "very upset and in a panic," Belle recorded in her diary. "Marriage with Bill breaking up. He in love with her cousin. She in love with C. S. Lewis."

Ironically, things changed for the better when Claude learned that Renee and the kids were hiding in Staatsburg. It had been over a year since she'd left him; he wanted to see Rosemary and Bobby. Renee, feeling protected by Bill, consented to Claude's visit but did not tell him about the affair. She was terrified that Joy might reveal something. When Claude arrived, he announced that he wanted his family back. Bill threatened to knife him if he laid a finger on Renee. Joy stayed silent. Claude didn't put up a fight.

Between finding herself in the hellish love triangle and Claude knowing her whereabouts, Renee could no longer stay in Staatsburg. Bill, though, wasn't prepared to accompany her; he loved Renee but couldn't leave the boys. A close friend living in Miami invited Renee to move in until she found a job and a place to live. Divorce laws were more relaxed in Florida. "Look, it's up to you," Renee told Bill. "I'm going to Miami. If you decide to come down there, I'll welcome you with open arms. But I'm not going to stick around." Afraid to leave Rosemary and Bobby where Claude could find them, she asked Bill to put them in a boarding school until she could establish residency in Florida, then she boarded a plane to Miami.

The cousins parted amicably. Both wanted divorces from their husbands—Renee so she could marry Bill, and Joy so she could be free of Bill and available to Jack. Still, even if Jack were to fall in love with her, he believed remarriage to be contrary to the Bible. Joy hinted at the remarriage issue in a letter to Chad, leaving out any mention of Jack as the prospect she had in mind. Her friend responded that "there is actually nothing in Christianity to prevent a divorce per se. The complications and theological deep waters come with the question of remarriage—but that's a bridge you must cross, when and if." Joy and Renee, wife and mistress, became allies in prodding Bill to action. "I keep at it, gently, and make slight but visible progress," Joy wrote to Renee. She persuaded him to consult an attorney, but Bill dragged his feet, terrified of losing the boys overseas and unable to afford separate housing.

Joy was resolute. "I hope to take the children to England and bring them up there," she told Chad a month after returning to Staatsburg, "not so much because I'm completely in love with England, though that's part of it, as because living is so much cheaper there and I'll be able to live decently on what Bill can pay. Knowing him, I'm very doubtful whether he will pay for long; but perhaps I can sell enough stuff myself through my American agent to keep me going no matter what." In reality, Joy couldn't even earn grocery money. That winter she wrote one abysmal short story after another. In March, though, her confidence was buoyed when she finished revising her two *Presbyterian Life* articles, which ran successively in April and May, and she and Chad corresponded about publishers for her Decalogue book.

As weeks passed, Joy became increasingly repulsed by Bill. The contrast between the man she loved and the man she had married was devastating. Bill had just finished his nonfiction book, titled *Monster Midway,* about life in the carny world. Ever the amateur magician, he began developing a fire-eating act and chattered incessantly about techniques and costuming. "I feel as if I'm looking at a kid of fourteen planning what he'll do when he grows up," she wrote to Renee. Joy remembered Oxford, Jack's Hooker lecture, drinks at the Bird and Baby, deep intellectual conversations—moments that were "so much alive," she wrote in a sonnet, but growing elusive with the passage of time. She was becoming resigned to never knowing that happiness again.

> I have forgot
> Innumerable joys, that dreaming of
> Might have made night less dreadful all the years
> I am to bear without you. Even tears Fade and leave blank
> eyelids; only not,
> O love, this bitter endless pain, my love.

Joy continued to bite her tongue and bide her time. She couldn't tell Jack how terribly she missed him, how miserably she ached from his rejection. "I said it did not hurt. My lord, I lied; / Painted my face into a smiling shape . . . I jested even while I died."

Joy assured Renee that she was still pushing Bill for a divorce. "Don't worry, cookie," she told her cousin. "I haven't forgotten my promise. And promise or no, I wouldn't have him back for a million bucks. He gives me the creeps." The disgust Joy felt for Bill was mutual as they continued to bring out the worst in each other. Her unrelenting bitterness kindled his neuroses; his neuroses fed her resentment. Although "most of the time he is quite nice and reasonable," Joy told Renee, he became heavily addicted to sleeping pills, which fogged his mind and made writing impossible. In April he found a traveling job as a press agent with George A. Hamid & Son, producer of grandstand musical reviews. "Living in the same house with Joy had become too much of a strain," Bill wrote to a friend, "what with her mental condition and my own. I could not seem to pull myself together to write anything anymore and I did want to become an active part of show business."

Bill hit the road but returned most weekends to visit the boys. The informal separation gave way to a legal agreement instigated by Joy in June, requiring Bill to pay alimony of $120 per month, plus an additional $60 per month per child. But the time away from Davy and

Douglas caused Bill to waver; he missed them. In early July he asked Joy to take him back. Joy refused to entertain the proposal. Bill, undeterred, continued to press. "I begged her to stay at home and told her that I would do anything she wanted as long as she kept the boys in this country where I could visit them but she refused." The children "needed and wanted" him, he pleaded. No, Joy said, they did not. He argued that she was turning them against him. "It is not that they have turned against you," Joy wrote him, "but rather that there has never been anything positive to turn *to* . . . They find your temper just as wearing as I do . . . I cannot lie to the boys about facts . . . What I *can* do, and have done, is to soften the intolerant judgments of childhood and remind them constantly of all the good and kind things you have done for them. Perhaps with separation their resentments, which after all are not based on physical pain, will dissipate easily enough."

Joy had her attorney call his attorney to request that Bill discontinue his weekly visits. When he refused, she disappeared with the boys during his scheduled visitations. "I cannot bear his presence," she told Renee. She felt all the more justified when, for the first time in some years, Bill began abusing alcohol again.

Renee was devastated when she learned that Bill had asked Joy to take him back. Joy wrote to her in consolation:

> One of the things about being the victim of such a man is the self-contempt it brings—the woman despises herself for being a fool and a sucker. And I know you tend to undervalue yourself anyway. So remember this; I'm a fairly bright girl, and yet I was so much under Bill's influence that I had to run away from him physically and consult one of the clearest thinkers of our time for help, before I could see clearly what he was! So don't call yourself a stupid fool. People with honest emotions are always more or less at the mercy of the clever, conscienceless, heartless scoundrel with a talent for acting . . . Part of the truth about him is that he *likes* to hurt people, likes the sadistic use of power, and is always

> subtly undermining one's self-confidence . . . [H]e likes his women helpless.

As "fellow victims," they could support each other, Joy told her cousin. She had a request, though. Joy was hesitant to take Bill to court without solid evidence of adultery, as required by New York State law. Would Renee write a letter "specifically admitting adultery?" Renee resisted, saying she didn't think it wise to do so until her own divorce went through. Joy responded sympathetically but warned Renee that she could be worse off if Bill tried to fight the divorce: "Considering that he is pretty well known as a writer, this might lead to newspaper publicity." Renee apologetically declined, and Joy respected her wish to keep her name out of the proceedings.

There were moments when the wreckage of Joy's life seemed to be falling in on her. She put the house on the market—the home that had once symbolized a secure future, that had promised stability for Joy's young family. Now the entire proceeds were to be turned over to the Treasury Department. By the beginning of August, prospective buyers wandered in daily, swooning over Crum Elbow Creek, peering into the barn, touring the orchard, inspecting the fourteen rooms—upstairs, downstairs, and straight through the heart of Joy's ruined dreams. She was selling off furniture, including her Steinway piano, which she'd treasured since she was a teenager. She barely played anymore, but she wept when it was taken away—another piece of her life dismantled. The house sold, and Joy moved the boys to a boardinghouse by the shore in New Rochelle, where she shared a kitchen with several other women.

She projected all her pain onto Bill. Playing the innocent victim, Joy told Jack that her resolve to leave Bill was weakening. Was she really doing the right thing? Jack responded by "saying what I thought myself," she told Chad, "that I must disregard my own feelings and base my decision on what is best for the boys. The boys, Davy particularly, beg me *not* to take Bill back—they say he makes them nervous and jumpy, and Lord knows I've seen it happen! Worse yet, I think, is what they learn from him—I've known both of them to try tantrums just like his on me. If only *his* mother had used the paddle as I do, how much better off he'd be!"

Jack was wonderful, she told Renee. "[He] continues to build up my morale and help me think things out." Joy resolved that when she returned to England, she would make herself into a cheerful companion rather than a needy burden: "I shall come lightly as a flower or leaf / Dancing on April wind—and bring you, Jack, / Something a little sweeter than my grief." Then everything would be all right. Jack had become a kind of savior in her mind, a new Fairyland.

One night as she was preparing dinner, Joy told Douglas a story. She had been alone, lost in a dark fog along the English moors on the brink of nightfall. "Stumbling among the tussocky, coarse grass and slipping on the mud she became more and more lost and more despairing. At last, off in the distance she saw through the mists a dim barely perceivable light and immediately turned her steps in that direction. The light seemed to be further away than she had realised, and she approached it only slowly as she clambered and struggled across the moorland." The house she described was straight out of *The Silver Chair,* one of Jack's Narnia books, made of sticks, tepee-style, with a single glowing window. "A little apprehensively, she knocked at the door, and it opened at once to reveal a warm, cozy room, well furnished—all around its walls were bookcases full of books. The door was held open by a kindly and wise-looking man, not handsome exactly, but interesting-looking, who invited her in and told her to warm herself by the lively fire while he prepared something to eat." Joy picked up a pot to narrate, adding water, chopping wild onions, adding dried vegetables and lentils. "He was a shepherd," she said, "living out in this wild country to find and take care of lost and sick or injured sheep and return them to the flock."

"Was that Jack?" Douglas interjected.

"Yes," she answered. "That was Jack."

In october, increasingly anxious to leave for England, Joy agreed not to pursue an official divorce for a while, hoping that evidence might become available (such as Renee's eventual admission or witnesses testifying to Bill's infidelity), but under one condition: that she could take the boys with her to England. Bill would, however, have full visiting privileges.

Bill was devastated; it was clear that Joy would not back down. She bought three passages on the SS *Britannic* in early November and told Bill to come and say good-bye. Bill, gentle with the boys, was affable toward her despite his anguish over losing his sons. Seeing Bill gave her pause. "You were so sweet," she wrote him a few weeks later. "I found myself beginning to trust you again." But she pushed aside lingering doubts as she boarded the *Britannic,* once again setting sail for England with little cash, no long-term plans—and this time, two boys in tow.

· 13 ·

November 1953–April 1954

The *Britannic* docked in Liverpool on November 13 under a wan, weepy sky. Joy, Davy, and Douglas stood on deck surveying the port city, a gray industrial swath obscured by a pall of fog. Just ten months earlier, Joy had boarded the *Franconia* and watched the same docks disappear with the setting sun while the ship carried her westward toward disaster. As England had faded behind her, so had the realities of daily living: the cold houses, the lonely nights and penniless days, Jack's rejection. But with time and distance, her fantasies flourished. Life would be grand in England. Jack would love her. "O may the rooks caw to the rising sun," she exulted in another sonnet, "For joy, when I come back to Headington."

England challenged her fantasies even before she set foot on its shores. "I do not like England, Mommy," Davy murmured into the mist. It looked nothing like the magical kingdom that had cast a spell on his mother. Douglas was slightly less dubious. This was where Jack lived—the man who created Narnia, the man whose name his mother invoked almost as often as God's, and with similar reverence. He envisioned a man "dressed in a knight's armor," as "heroes were supposed to be."

Time, distance, and Joy's reports of Bill's behavior had softened

Jack toward her in the months since her Christmas visit. Their return to letter writing smoothed the frayed edges of their friendship. Communication had grown comfortable again; familiar and gratifying for them both, correspondence was what had drawn Jack to Joy in the first place. Besides that, her insightful input on his OHEL manuscript had proved useful, and he wrote a kind appreciation of her in the book's acknowledgments. Joy's move to England signaled to him a fresh start, and the opportunity to show kindness to the boys, who had lost a parent—an experience with which Jack, whose mother died when he was around their age, deeply identified—no doubt appealed to his compassionate sensibilities. Joy had no problem securing an invitation to the Kilns for several days in mid-December.

Meanwhile, there was much to do. She had little cash, no job, no work papers, no home, and two small boys to care for. The sole advance plan she had made before leaving New York was a reservation at Avoca House, an inn in Belsize Park, the residential neighborhood where Phyl had recently moved with her son Robin and Sel. Avoca House proved clean and comfortable, especially after many days in a small cabin on the *Britannic,* but its rates were higher than Joy could afford; she would need to find long-term accommodations as soon as possible. First, though, she needed money. Bill had agreed to send child support payments care of Phyl until Joy established permanent housing. She expected a check to be waiting upon arrival.

Joy hustled to Phyl and Sel's the next morning. The streets were lined with centuries-old townhouses and trees, bare-branched in the November chill. When she reached 65 Belsize Park Gardens, her friends greeted her, but a check did not. Joy returned to Avoca House and banged out a furious letter to Bill. He was nearly a month behind on child-support payments. "You know I can't possibly support the children by myself here," she chided. "I can't even get a job at first." Under the Aliens Order of 1920—an amendment to the 1919 Aliens Restriction Act ratified in reaction to widespread postwar unemployment—Joy was required to register with the police as a foreign national, and her employment options were severely limited.

While awaiting a response, she took the boys sightseeing. They toured Westminster Abbey and St. James's Park. Pigeons sat on their heads in Trafalgar Square. At the iron gates of Buckingham Palace, they watched with wide eyes as guards marched like toy soldiers, clicking their heels on the turns. But as much as Davy and Douglas enjoyed exploring London, homesickness had already set in. Their mother had moved them across the ocean from their house, their friends, their school, their father, and all things culturally familiar. They complained about the unrelenting fog. They could no longer gallop outside and catch bugs or splash in Crum Elbow Creek.

Joy wasn't sure they would take to city life; neither was she sure she would take to city life with them underfoot. London had become synonymous in her mind with liberation from the "prison" of motherhood. As a sole caregiver unable to afford hired help, she couldn't possibly re-create the freedom of her first trip—Thursdays with the London Circle, spontaneous weekend excursions, pub crawls, nights at the theater. Joy could see only one solution: boarding school. It was, after all, the English way, and she wanted the boys to become Anglicized. She floated the idea with Davy and Douglas. No, they told her; they did not want to be sent away. But within days of arriving in England, she had made her decision. "The boys are clamoring for a boarding school in the country rather than a London day school," she told Bill, and began asking around about schools and fees.

But Joy's meager cash reserve was fast eroding, and housing options proved limited. Owners of furnished flats rarely considered tenants with small children. Joy mentioned her plight to the innkeeper of Avoca House, who empathized; she, too, had once been poor and on her own with young children. Sympathetic, she offered Joy two large rooms in a lofty townhouse annex for twelve guineas ($36). The cost exceeded Joy's budget, but she took a look. The moment Joy entered the flat, a film of idealism glazed her eyes. Each room seemed to her as large as the living room in Staatsburg but "even *better* proportioned." Built-in mirrors and molded plaster detail on soaring ceilings prompted fantasies of an eighteenth-century lady's drawing room. A grand piano beckoned from the corner. The place was modernized with gas heat, an indulgence after years of burning coal in Staatsburg. Interior doors opened onto a private garden where the boys could play. When the fog burned off, she imagined, sunlight would burst through the windows. The only drawback was the bathroom, a share in an upstairs hall. But other amenities more than compensated: daily housekeeping, utilities, linens, laundry, breakfast, and dinner. Joy accepted the innkeeper's offer. "The Lord really *is* my shepherd, by gum!"

The arrangement wasn't financially sustainable, Joy admitted, but she felt too tired to search for something permanent—unusually tired, in fact. She attributed the exhaustion to sharing a room with the children, first on the *Britannic,* then at Avoca House. She would take time off before writing again. On November 18 Bill wired $60—nowhere near what he owed in mounting back payments, but it was something—and the threesome moved into their semi-permanent quarters.

Housing arrangements settled, Joy embarked on a search for a boarding school that would restore her freedom and transform her sons into proper English gentlemen. "What I want most for the boys," she told Bill, "is the coherent view of life which makes England tick—the tradition we recognize, for instance, in Burke's conservatism. I believe a great deal of the mental disturbance in America, and certainly the aimlessness and restlessness, comes from our lack of it." Joy was scrupulous about her choice, making lists, examining cleanliness of facilities and academic qualifications of instructors as well as their personalities and the emotional health of the students. She visited four schools. One was unkempt and cold, though somewhat redemptively headmastered by Robert Graves's "vague dreamy" brother. Another was lovely but too regimented, operated by a German Jew and his partner, an elderly widow lacking academic qualifications. "The boys seemed drilled to a Prussian perfection of discipline," Joy reported. "*He* said he didn't go in for games much and believed in hard work . . . Ulp." A third, newer school seemed undeveloped. The one she liked best was Dane Court, in Surrey, about twenty miles southwest of London. It was the most expensive, "gracious, well-established, comfortable without being luxurious and modern without being faddist," having adopted a progressive policy of not "whack[ing] the children." The school's references included P. L. Travers, author of the Mary Poppins books, whom Joy consulted over tea. Mrs. Travers's high praise confirmed Joy's impressions, and the decision was made. Beginning in January, the start of the next term, Davy and Douglas would move to Dane Court for training in subjects and skills ranging from Latin to the long jump.

Regardless of Joy's motivations, boarding school was one of the few sound decisions she made on the boys' behalf. "You and I had no stability to give the boys," she wrote to Bill, "and they were beginning to suffer from its absence, but Dane Court people have it, all right . . . I do really feel that giving them the right education, particularly the right moral and social education, ought to be the chief aim of both our lives, and that it's worth any sacrifice." She added: "As I grow older and untangle my own emotional tizzies, I get a good deal more conservative about all these things; no doubt you do, too. We had no right to live so much in the present that we made no provision for the boys' future."

While Joy imagined herself untangling her tizzies, she was in fact weaving a tightening noose of self-deception. She still could barely afford her daily living expenses, let alone a costly boarding school—even if Bill sent every payment in full and on time, which she rightly suspected would never happen. She counted on royalty checks that might or might not appear. She counted on peddling frivolous short stories to women's magazines, yet when Bill talked about freelancing himself, she reminded him of "the roller-coaster ride of the last few years . . . Even if one *can* make a go of it, the wear and tear on one's nerves and temper is too great." Every single thing she depended on was undependable—except one. Joy knew she could ask Jack for money, and she knew he would provide; he was a generous man, he had the money, and he at least knew her as a friend in need. They were not going to starve on the streets. Besides, hadn't things always worked out for her in England? That was how she chose to remember it; that was what she needed to believe.

In between boarding school tours, Joy returned to the London Circle, which had moved from Fleet Street to the Globe Tavern. When she walked in for the first time, there was the old crowd huddled around their pints. John Christopher's face brightened with delight at the sight of her. What brought her back to England? he asked. Joy told him a very different version of the tale she'd spun for Chad, Eva, Jack, and Warnie. It was her love for Lewis, she confessed, that drew her back—this time permanently. Christopher reeled with discomfort. Was she not married? With children? She told him about Bill's affair, explaining that their marriage had been deteriorating for some time. "[She] decided that a marriage already on the rocks was better abandoned," he later recounted. "She did not deny that her own one-sided involvement with Lewis had contributed . . . I felt, reading between the lines, that she was not too unhappy about this. In fact, I'm sure she wasn't unhappy about it. It made her feel free."

ON DECEMBER 17, Joy, Davy, and Douglas took their first trip to the Kilns. They rode the Tube to Paddington Station, where Joy bought tickets for "one and two halves to Oxford, third class." After the train steamed into its destination, they caught a bus that took them through the center of Oxford to a stop close to Kiln Lane with its silver birches, and finally to the Kilns itself, "what for her must have been a warm shepherd's hearth against the chill moors of loneliness and fear," Douglas recalled years later. It had been almost a year since she had seen Jack, almost a year since, as she wrote in a sonnet, "I brought a load of pain and dumped the lot upon your willing shoulder." This time, Joy decided, she would set a more lighthearted tone from the start: "I shall be wiser, merrier and older." The housekeeper, Mrs. Miller, opened the door and hustled them inside, while a man's voice boomed out a welcome: "Aha! Here they are. Here they are!" And there was Jack, genuinely pleased to see her.

From the start, the boys proved a useful buffer against any lingering awkwardness. When Jack greeted them, Douglas was profoundly, amusingly disappointed. The man who'd created Narnia did not wear a knight's armor. He wore a moth-eaten tweed jacket, sagging gray flannel trousers flecked with cigarette ash, and black leather slippers missing their backs. Jack joked about his own reservations in hosting these American youngsters—"exotic" creatures, he commented. Communicating with children in Narnia came more naturally than doing so in the real world. Determined to discover "the way to a child's heart," he intuited that "what they can't stand (quite rightly) is the common adult assumption that everything they say [should] be twisted into a kind of jocularity." Thereafter he employed a combination of "ordinary civility" and, as Joy put it, "schoolboy tactics." The result was a fast friendship. Jack and Warnie taught Davy chess, while Doug sawed piles of firewood, pleased to please them.

When the five took a four-mile hike through broken hill country, Jack raced ahead alongside the boys, doing his best to keep up, while Joy and Warnie lumbered behind. Her energy was not what it once was; perhaps her thyroid was acting up. Nevertheless, she climbed the steep medieval spiral stairs of Magdalen Tower. From the top they beheld all of Oxford. When they got back to the bottom, the boys asked to climb up again. "The energy of the American small boy is astonishing," Jack exclaimed, recounting the experience with delight to friends. "Whew! Lovely creatures—couldn't meet nicer children—but the pace! I realise I have never respected . . . married people enough and never dreamed of the Sabbath calm [which] descends on the house when the little cyclones have gone to bed and all the grown-ups fling themselves into chairs and the silence of exhaustion." At the end of the visit, Jack would present Davy and Douglas with a typescript of his forthcoming Narnia book, *The Horse and His Boy,* to be published the following September, dedicated to them.

One of only two known surviving letters from Jack to Joy—dated December 22, 1953, the day after she and the boys returned to London—affirms her parting impression that the visit was "very relaxed and friendly." As soon as she and the boys left the Kilns, Jack read Arthur C. Clarke's *Childhood's End* on her recommendation. Clarke, an acquaintance of Joy's from the London Circle, had struck pay dirt with his latest science-fiction novel, selling in the hundreds of thousands. Jack's letter to Joy—long and informal—is part rapturous review, part brilliant criticism studded with casual references to works by Olaf Stapledon, H. G. Wells, Virgil, Richard Wagner, Saint Luke, and Dante. He knew Joy had read them all; she would understand both his meaning and his emotions. Spending time with Jack seemed to weaken Joy's resolve to keep things light. Her sonnets indicate that she had again professed her feelings, and he had again declined her advances—if gently and with regret. She had been through enough heartache the past year. "My love who does not love me but is kind," she recounted, "Lately apologized for lack of love, / Praising the fire and glitter of my mind, / the valour of my heart, and speaking of / Affection, admiration." But no matter how compassionately conveyed, his words were "bitter scraps" flung at "the begging woman at the door." Another sonnet reads:

It is not his fault he does not love me;
It is not his fault he does not know
Any anesthetic word to give me
When the devil makes him tell me so . . .
Whose fault, then? Let the man have his Heaven
He cries for; as for me, I shrug, and pray
Some angel may announce he is forgiven
His good intentions on the judgment day,

While I go down beneath the fatal rod;
For even then I shall not pardon God.

Not surprisingly, given the previous Christmas, Jack did not insist that Joy and the boys spend the holiday at the Kilns, and she didn't push it. Avoca House made for a merry enough celebration, with boughs of holly and a hearty feast. An upstairs neighbor, Mickey, who had lost her only child, showered the boys with affection and books. Joy gave Douglas toys and a tool set. Davy received a chess set and a vivarium to house the family's new pet, a lizard Joy named Bill.

• • •

The new year brought more bad news for Bill Gresham and, by extension, Joy and the boys: he rang in 1954 without a job. After a run of fourteen fairs, his services as press agent for Hamid's grandstand musicals were no longer needed. Hamid decided that either each individual venue should do its own advertising, or the company should hire a high-powered press agent—all of which was fine with Bill. He hated that job anyway. The new plan, he told Joy, was to load up the old car, drive to Florida, and settle in the Hialeah district of Miami. The place was "young and bouncy" and innocent; it gave him a positive "psychic feeling." Hibiscus, palm trees, sunshine—that's what he needed. The New York they had shared with Davy and Douglas was now "just too lonely and desolate," he said. And there was another reason. He and Renee were communicating again, though his letters to Joy—newsy and cordial—claimed it was only friendship. He would rent a small room nearby, he wrote, and save money by eating meals at Renee's place. He would take Rosemary and Bobby, once again living with their mother, to the beach.

Joy suppressed suspicions of a rekindled romance and offered short-term sympathy. She and the boys could make do for now, but by April he would have to supply $350 for school fees. Forbearance, however, soon gave way to frustration. Having depleted her savings on a shopping trip to Selfridges for proper English schoolboy clothes—caps, ties, mackintoshes, and gray flannel suits with short pants—Joy again blamed Bill while exonerating herself, overlooking her spending sprees the previous year. "[Your] trouble has always been improvidence, the principle of 'living in the moment' which kept you from ever building up savings to tide us over times like these. And I went along with you too easily." She simply hadn't had the courage to argue, she said. "I can understand the uncertainties of your position, but I must be able to educate the boys decently," she insisted. "They can't be shifted and dragged around. I've always felt that the one really rock-like and stable part of your personality is your love for the boys, and surely you can see that it's not enough to love them like pets, to amuse and entertain them in the present; we must love them as people, creatures with a future."

Yet at other times Joy seemed more concerned with how the children were disrupting her life than vice versa. She romanticized Bill's lifestyle as freewheeling, and she resented him all the more for it. A letter from Belle mentioned that he had appeared at one of her parties. He looked well, she reported, but missed the boys terribly. "I'm glad you're having such an active grown-up life," Joy wrote to Bill. "Mine, for the most part, is mere routine of shopping and mothering—barring an occasional hour in the near-by pub. Told a woman there it was one of the only *two* places my children couldn't follow me; she said she envied me, *hers* was a girl and the pub was the only *one!*" At least she drank for free, she joked; the men at the pub paid for her beer.

Joy loaded her letters with cruel jabs that heightened Bill's misery over losing the boys. "You should see [them] now," she said, describing how they'd grown rosy-cheeked and chubby. "You'd hardly know them." When Bill's next check amounted to only $35, she contradicted herself by implying that Douglas and Davy were underfed and inadequately clothed. He insisted that he was trying to provide, but work didn't come easy. He proposed a book to Rinehart on daredevils, but they offered him only $1,000—not enough to make the research and writing worth his time. He applied for a public relations job with Pan American World Airways, where Renee was working, but hit a snag with the application. "One of the first questions," he wrote to Joy, "almost before name and date of birth, was 'Are you or have you ever been a member of the Communist Party?'" In the midst of Senator McCarthy's "Commie hysteria," he added, "this question, as worded is about like asking, 'Have you ever had or do you now have smallpox?'" Now he was compiling research for a novel involving "pain-drug-hypnosis," a Hubbard theory, with hopes that it might be lucrative. Joy disapproved. Writing wasn't practical, she reiterated. He should take a lesson from the sci-fi boys at the pub, who held full-time jobs in addition to literary careers for the sake of supporting their families.

Her tone softened when Bill did send money. "For some reason I find myself thinking of you with considerable affection and sympathy—perhaps because you're obviously trying as hard as you can, perhaps because I've had time to get over my fear of you. It was more psychological than physical, anyhow; not so much that I thought you dangerous, but being bewildered about your motives and all tensed up wondering what the hell you were going to spring on me next. At any rate, I seem able to talk to you more freely in letters, in the old way," she wrote to him in early February. But when Bill followed up the next month with a check for a paltry $5, she lashed out again: "I'm pretty near the end of my tether, Bill, and I can't stand much more of this . . . If you really love [the boys] as much as you say, you won't want them to end up in an orphan's home somewhere. But that's the way it's going to go, if this keeps up . . . I'm about ready to call quits."

The tone of Bill's responses remained even-keeled, but a reservoir of resentment was rising. He told Joy that an attorney friend of his, president of the local magicians' club, could usher a divorce through Florida's legal system, settling the matter swiftly without invoking moral turpitude. Joy enthusiastically approved the plan, on two conditions: that Bill agree to the stipulated child support, and that she retain sole custody. She thought nothing of it when he didn't acknowledge her provisos. She assumed he simply wasn't following through—and there was no rush anyhow.

In the second week of January, Joy packed the boys' bags, led them to Waterloo Station, and deposited them with the assistant headmaster, "six feet four of Greek-god-with-brains, who had little boys in school caps swarming all over him . . . [Davy and Douglas] waved merrily and started off with a lot of other perfectly happy schoolboys." School policy barred parents from visiting for several weeks so the children could get settled. After the first few days, the headmaster called to report that the boys were happy, well adjusted, and not homesick in the least.

In reality, they were miserable. "I missed my mother desperately," Douglas later wrote of the experience. "I spent hours in tears day after day, but I soon found that there were worse things than being away from home—having an American accent was one. I learned quickly to speak like an English child, my training at the fists and boots of my school contemporaries, all bigger than I was." For most of six years, he "lived lonely, afraid, frustrated and for much of the time hungry." But he hid his misery from his mother, and Joy sent Bill glowing report after glowing report. "I knew they'd like it," she wrote after her first visit in early February, "but was hardly prepared for the paean of enthusiasm I got . . . Everything pleases them—the food, the work, the games, the walks on the heath, the masters, etc." Davy—the more introverted, bookish of the two—was making loads of friends, memorizing Shakespeare, and studying French and Latin. They swam, played football, studied ornithology and botany. Their accents were changing, too. "You should hear Doug clip his words and broaden his A's!" If only Bill would send more money so she could buy them proper winter coats, visit more often, take them on vacations.

After the boys left for school, Joy spent her days "writing like grim death"—a novella, "Britannia," that would never sell, and dozens of unmarketable short stories that her agent tossed into Brandt & Brandt's "B Files," where lifeless work was laid to rest. "I just can't get my mind round the ladies' magazine gloop," she admitted, "and I haven't too much hope." She thought she might try her hand at science fiction after listening to Arthur C. Clarke speak at a National Book League symposium devoted to the growing genre (it would be "a pity not to cash in" on the trend). And she visited a film agent who suggested there might be a market for scripts set in England with American characters, and whose lovely Park Lane office overlooking Hyde Park persuaded her to reconsider writing for the medium she'd disavowed fifteen years earlier when she walked out on Hollywood.

Other ventures appeared more viable. At the suggestion of Brandt & Brandt's English associate, A. M. Heath, she began stripping *Smoke on the Mountain* of Americanisms for a potential British edition, amused by the agency's insistence that she excise potentially libelous comments about Ingrid Bergman and Ginger Rogers. The project that excited her most was a collaboration Warnie suggested on the life of Madame de Maintenon, morganatic wife of Louis XIV. "She's never been done, and she's fascinating," Joy told Bill, "a noblewoman born in the workhouse, spending a mysterious girlhood in the West Indies, coming back and marrying a paralyzed poet and wit, later becoming the governess of the king's illegitimate children and catching the king! She was interested in education for women, founded a girls' school, and used to pop out of the king's bed at dawn to go and get the little ones up and take a few classes herself. Wow!" Warnie had already done most of the research and created a full working outline, which he sent her, along with a stack of reference books.

LONELINESS SET IN with the worst of winter's chill. Pipes burst; the heat stopped working. Joy developed chilblains on one hand and shivered under thick layers of clothes. "Cold, cold the funeral wind," she wrote in a sonnet called "Fimbulwinter," after the mythological Norse winter—an awesome, awful winter preceding the end of the world. She ached to have Jack by her side. "Love," she whispered through her poem, "let us stand / Against the encroaching dark. Give me your hand."

Joy had little social life apart from Thursday nights. When she was bored, she practiced rolling a coin over the backs of her fingers one-handed. Occasionally she sank pennies into pinball machines at the pub. Finally accepting that she needed to supplement her almost non-existent literary income, she broke down and got a part-time printing job for the European Press, where she earned a pittance operating a varitype machine nearly nine hours a day in a dank basement office. Persistently exhausted, she began using Dexedrine to keep going.

Ironically, one of the European Press's big accounts was Hubbard's new "screwy outfit," Scientology. It wasn't lost on Joy that the London Circle boys never so much as whispered Hubbard's name. He was no longer glanced at with skeptical curiosity; he wasn't glanced at at all. "I'm more and more convinced," Joy wrote to Bill, "that, though [Dianetics] is certainly useful as counter suggestion to psychogenic ailments, it is otherwise nothing but sound and phooey . . . We wuz had. Oh well, it takes a conman to catch a conman!" For decades to come, Hubbard would be widely quoted as saying: "Writing for a penny a word is ridiculous. If a man really wanted to make a million dollars, the best way to do it would be start his own religion."

Suddenly disillusioned with the city, Joy dreamed of a financial break that might allow her to "get out of London altogether and find a country cottage" in the vicinity of Oxford. For warmth and companionship in the meantime, she got a kitten named Sambo and had "at least one brief affair" with a man she met at the Globe Tavern, according to John Christopher: "She spoke of it to me frankly as something pleasant and unimportant." The lover was merely a surrogate for the man she really wanted, but in the bitter freeze of her Fimbulwinter, Joy confessed to Christopher that while her friendship with Jack remained vigorous and her love for him endured, she was "without hope that it could come to anything."

Hopelessness became a muse for the strongest writing Joy did that winter. Almost nightly, Joy "wrenched sonnets out of great pain," primarily employing the first person but sometimes the third, referring to herself as a woman degenerated to an "it." She was a carcass mutilated by the knife of Jack's rejection: He "punctured its eyes to slime / With sharp contempt," hung it by the heels to drain its blood,

> left the tattered ribs to fill with air,
> The shattered brain to light the naked skull
> With a last mockery of life . . .
> And yet the horror is a woman still;
> It grieves because it cannot stroke your hair.

In other poems Joy apologizes to Jack for turning her "bitter tongue" against him, and instead blames God for hoarding his devotion: "If there was wrong it was done by God, not you." But at times, humility gave rise to honesty, and she admitted that her misery was self-inflicted:

No, it was neither you nor God, but I
Whose nature drove the dagger in my side . . .
If I should die
Of loving you, call it a suicide . . .
I can be certain that I would not choose
Any lesser gate of death than you . . .
Only, when I see my children sleeping
I think I have a task to keep alive for;
But they and I must take our chance on God.
Let it be as He wills, and no more weeping.

"Stop complaining," she scolded herself. "He is God's lover not yours . . . / In God's name, leave him / To Christ . . . No, follow. Some day he may need to use / The tatters of your soul to wipe his shoes."

Making life more difficult was Joy's inexplicable "wretched health and weakness." She couldn't have finished any writing that winter without Dexedrine, she believed, though even that boosted her up to only "about half alive." Her teeth troubled her as well. The cheap patch-job dentistry she'd received courtesy of the National Health during her first trip to England was falling apart. On the basis of new X-rays, the National Health Board determined that six teeth needed to be pulled.

Joy wasn't stranded on a plateau of despair for long. March brought a boon of blessings: Heath sold *Smoke* for a small advance. Jack agreed to write a preface for the British edition. And a visit to the Kilns was arranged for mid-April, when the boys would be out of school. If Joy could not have Jack, she could at least be near him. "To look at you [is] / The one necessity that I dare have," she wrote.

The bloom of spring boosted her spirits. The English countryside was magnificent. "The trees are all misted with green already, pink almost and white cherry and flowering rose-colored currant bushes are all in bloom, daffodils and blue primroses and a million flowers I don't know run almost wild; yellow primroses and bluebells *are* wild, so are anemone and violet and kingcup and tiny daisies like innumerable stars in the grass." Joy, Jack, Warnie, and a fellow Inkling, Dr. R. E. "Humphrey" Havard, carried pints of beer into the woods and drank in the company of violets and birds. They took the boys punting on the River Cherwell and to Whipsnade Zoo, overlooking Buckinghamshire's chalk hills. When George Sayer and his wife, Moira, invited Jack and Warnie to dinner during the week of Joy's visit, Jack responded that the timing was regrettable because "our queer, Jewish, ex-Communist, American convert and her two boys will be here all next week." Instead of dinner, Jack suggested meeting at the Eastgate Hotel. Forgetting that George had already met Joy, Jack briefed him: "She's a queer fish and I'm not at all sure that she is either yours or Moira's cup of tea (she is, at any rate, *not* a Bore)."

George and Moira accepted Jack's invitation. Jack was right; they did not get along. Joy drank whiskey instead of tea, an unladylike display in the eyes of her conservative English company. The conversation—about science fiction and fantasy—was polite, but Joy seemed possessive of Jack. "Moira sensed that she was in love with Jack but anxious to disguise the fact. She also thought that he was very fond of her." This affection concerned George, especially given Jack's history with Mrs. Moore. Jack had spoken openly about feeling gloriously unfettered after her death, and his friends preferred him to remain untethered to a woman. "It seemed to be rather sad," George thought after spending more time with Joy, "if he was going to be tied up in another relationship."

But it was Jack's nature to be all the more drawn to Joy because of her circumstances. Even after the difficult years with Mrs. Moore, Jack remained, as his father once put it, "an impetuous, kind-hearted creature who could be cajoled by any woman who had been through the mill." When Joy admitted her concern about her ability to keep Davy and Douglas at Dane Court—blaming Bill's financial negligence and, at least indirectly, fishing for help—Jack offered to pay their tuition for as long as Bill's contributions fell short. He'd had a charitable trust set up for just this sort of predicament; more than half of his royalties were funneled directly into what he called his

"Agapony Fund"—standing for "love" and "money"—out of which he paid educational and medical expenses for the needy.

But Jack didn't see Joy as a standard charity case, and he wasn't merely tolerating her presence. Although he downplayed his respect for Joy to George and Moira, his preface to *Smoke* glinted with admiration, and he engaged her editorial help with the manuscript of his autobiography. The book had been in the works since 1948 and would eventually be titled *Surprised by Joy,* after a William Wordsworth poem, not for the American woman who had entered Lewis's life. The poem, "Surprised by Joy—Impatient as the Wind," evokes a brief, blissful moment when Wordsworth forgets his greatest sorrow, the loss of his daughter. But the moment passes, and the pain comes rushing back. Jack's greatest sorrow, the defining experience of his childhood, was his mother's death. "We lost her gradually," Joy read in the manuscript, "as she was gradually withdrawn from our life into the hands of nurses and delirium and morphia, and as our whole existence changed into something alien and menacing, as the house became full of strange smells and midnight noises and sinister whispered conversations." While the titles certainly alluded to both Wordsworth's sentiment and Lewis's own feelings of loss as he explored the death of his mother in print for the first time, Joy's role in the completion and typing of *Surprised by Joy* certainly lent a happy irony to its title. Jack had perhaps begun to find himself surprised by another Joy as well.

As for his own blissful moments, Jack's memoir accentuated some of the core reasons why Joy was drawn to him. He echoed the foundational moments of her life, those aesthetic experiences and their accompanying sensation, the unquenchable yearning she'd known since her childhood dreams of Fairyland. Jack called that sensation "Joy," referring to "an unsatisfied desire which is itself more desirable than any other satisfaction . . . which is here a technical term and must be sharply distinguished from both Happiness and from Pleasure." He first experienced it one summer day while standing beside a flowering currant bush. "It is difficult to find words strong enough for the sensation which came over me; Milton's 'enormous bliss' of Eden (giving the full, ancient meaning to 'enormous') comes somewhere near it. It was a sensation, of course, of desire; but desire for what?" The answer, he knew, was what Joy had written in "The Longest Way Round," her essay for *These Found the Way:* "proof of the hope of heaven, making itself known."

The manifestations of Jack's goodness—his purity, his clean faith, which contrasted with the dross of her heart—all were attractive to Joy. She wrote in May:

> How I tantalize
> Hunger with praising you, who gleam so far
> Beyond my greedy reach; yet now and then,
> By God's grace, I am given a moment when
> The shadow of pain is lifted from my eyes
> And I rejoice to see how gold you are.

But Joy also detected something perhaps no one else had noticed in Jack: the fact that his spirituality sometimes masked and distracted others from noticing the internal turmoil rendered by the traumas of his childhood and of the war. He protected himself, she thought, behind "monstrous glaciers of [his] innocence."

Joy returned to London feeling lighter than she had in months, but the lightness didn't last long. Despite the spring warmth, she felt chilled all the time, and there were troubling episodes of acute vertigo. At a nearby clinic, eight doctors examined her for the better part of a day and concurred that her problem was hypothyroidism. ("This I didn't know?") When she told them about the radium collar treatment she had received in the mid-1930s, they expressed concern. Radium collars, once thought to be a progressive therapy, were now known to be dangerous. She could have been burned, they said. She could have developed cancer. Joy thought about the lump in her breast; it was still there. She consulted Humphrey Havard, who dismissed it.

Bill's ongoing negligence upset Joy, and she continued to berate him. It didn't help that he and Renee were back together. Was Renee actually willing to put up with him? "Can you really square it with your own conscience," she asked Bill, "to spend your life using up one self-effacing woman after another?" She'd had no spending money in Oxford, she complained to him, and lived for a week "on Jack's kindness." Next term's tuition was due: £150. She couldn't possibly pull the boys out of Dane Court, she said. "It would do them great harm, and it would make any writing at all impossible for me." In the second week of May, Bill finally sent a large enough check to cover most of the school fees. "I thank you," Joy wrote, "Davy thanks you, Doug thanks you; Sambo the cat, who was wondering where his next tin of fishgunk was coming from, thanks you likewise. Also, Jack's charity cases, who will now not have to move over and make room for the boys, thank you!"

But her gratitude was too little, too late. After months of being subjected to verbal beatings from the woman who'd stolen his children, Bill struck back. On June 11, Joy received a notice from the British consul informing her that Bill had initiated divorce proceedings from Florida. She was furious that she had to find out that way. But the worst was yet to come. Shortly thereafter, Joy received a scathing "bill of complaints." Bill accused Joy of "ungovernable displays of temperament," of "liv[ing] in an artistic dream world," and of fixating on life in England as a means of furthering her literary career. "She has neglected, humiliated, embarrassed and berated the Plaintiff no end because of this insatiable appetite," the document alleged. "The Defendant feels that her artistic career is much more important than her domestic career, life and duty to her husband and family, and, although the Plaintiff begged and pleaded with the Defendant to remain with him in the United States, the Defendant left, abandoned and deserted this Plaintiff taking the children with her to the City of London, England, in order to live permanently." The complaint left out anything having to do with Renee, did not mention Bill's alcoholism or mental instability, and claimed that he had been "a kind, affectionate and faithful husband to the Defendant and did everything in his power to make their married life a happy one."

Joy was indignant and "deeply hurt," she told him, by the "lies about my character and my behaviour as a wife and mother . . . If I were a judge I should think twice about awarding the custody of children to the sort of woman you describe." She told the boys, home on holiday, what their father had done and then fired off an angry letter to Bill. ("I'm glad to say that the news of your action doesn't seem to upset them at all.") In response, Bill unleashed his feelings of devastation over losing the boys, claiming that he could barely go through the motions of writing. Renee was helping him with Dianetics treatments again, "using the examiner to run some of that grief off," but he remained heartbroken. "For years the boys were the only things that gave me any apparent reason for being and the only thing I held on to when the going got rough. How you can imagine that I won't do everything I can for them now even though I cannot be with them to watch them grow up—how you can think that is more than I can understand."

Joy struck back with below-the-belt blows, detailing Davy and Douglas's life without a father to accompany them to family days at Dane Court, father-son cricket matches, annual speeches, and prize ceremonies. When they came home on school breaks, she told Bill, they were forced to work with her in the dank basement printing office, folding and collating copy, because he wouldn't send enough money for vacation trips. All their classmates traveled during holidays, she said. "Perhaps you can explain to [the boys] why there is not money to take *them* on trips to anything better than a tenpenny busride and a tea-shop. I'm finding it rather difficult to make them understand." This would become another theme of her letters: "Wish I could take the boys on a trip during the summer holidays, but I don't see how. A pity, with Cornwall and Devon and the Lakes all so near."

ONCE AGAIN, JOY clung to the prospect of her next visit to Oxford, although she would see little of Jack. He and Warnie were going on their annual holiday in Ireland, visiting family and a childhood friend, Arthur Greeves. They offered Joy and the boys use of the Kilns for the entire month of August while they traveled. The boys could swim in the pond out back; she could garden and walk in the woods. Most tempting of all, Jack volunteered his rooms at Magdalen as private writing space. Joy and the boys were to arrive on August 4, planning to overlap briefly with Jack and Warnie, who were scheduled to sail on the sixth. But when the Greshams presented themselves at the Kilns, Jack was downcast and Warnie was missing. After a crippling drinking binge, he had checked into a medical facility, where he was no stranger. The trip would have to be postponed until at least mid-month.

"The usual thing," as Jack phrased it to his friend Arthur, shrouding the matter in euphemisms. "I am full of gloomiest forebodings. Let me have your prayers; I am tired, scared and bewildered." Living with an alcoholic was one of the few points of connection between Joy's and Jack's disparate worlds. Constrained by the inhibitions of era and culture, Jack had few friends with whom he could speak openly about it. If any of his Oxford friends understood the uncertainties of life with a family member who overindulged in drink, custom demanded they remain silent. Not so Joy. With her Jack could speak freely, without shame. She offered empathy and advice for helping Warnie; a strong ginger beverage could alleviate a craving for cordials, for example.

The visit turned out to be timely for both Joy and Jack. Soon after her arrival, Bill informed her that the divorce had been finalized and he and Renee had married. Now it was Joy who needed support, and Jack was there to provide it. She was over Bill, but his marriage to Renee made her ache inside. Jack took her to the Bird and Baby and ordered two pints of house cider. They raised their glasses in a sardonic toast.

"To Bill's happiness," Joy said.

"To the repentance and forgiveness of all sinners," Jack added.

Then they hiked up Shotover Hill with the boys, sun shining bright, wind whipping their hair, and miles of England spread before them. Davy and Douglas flew a kite. It was "all roses and rainbows," Joy thought.

• • •

JACK WAS GLAD for Joy's companionship. He felt lonely when the house was empty and typically invited out-of-town friends for extended visits when Warnie traveled. Joy was more than happy to fill the void. For the first time, she didn't have to share him. They took the boys punting on the Cherwell again, and went to the Eastgate, where Joy met one of Jack's colleagues, Professor J. R. R. Tolkien, whose *Fellowship of the Ring* had recently been published. Joy expressed admiration for the work and interpreted Tolkien's disengaged response as shyness or embarrassment; in reality, something in Joy's words and mannerisms "almost disgusted" him. Jack's friends were "stunned," Havard recounted, "when this tough, brash female erupted into their presence cracking unsuitable jokes and making an obvious pass at Lewis." George Sayer grew increasingly concerned as well. "We thought she had designs on Lewis and we didn't know her well enough to trust her."

Another major topic of conversation was the impending upheaval of Jack's entire life. Magdalene College, Cambridge, had finally granted him the honor that Oxford had long denied him: a professorship that effectively tripled his salary, doubled his prestige, and cut his workload in half. The college had created for him a brand-new position, Chair of Medieval and Renaissance Literature. The announcement, made earlier in the summer, had incited complaints from colleagues and students who wanted Oxford to make it worth Jack's while to stay. But once he established that the job would not require him to live in Cambridge full-time, concerned as he was about looking after Warnie, the opportunity was too great for him to decline. In addition to the prestige, the pay, and the privilege of creating a historic chair, Jack would have more time to write. The transition would be difficult, though. For nearly his entire adult life, Jack had been cradled comfortably in Magdalen's cloisters, within walking distance from home and in arm's reach of his favorite pubs and favorite people. For the first time in three decades, he would soon have a new commute, new colleagues, new rooms and rules and routines. He would live at Magdalene during the week, returning to the Kilns on weekends. The appointment was officially to begin on October 1, but he was given till the first of January to settle his Oxford affairs and move to Cambridge.

Warnie was well enough by mid-August for the brothers to take an abridged trip. When they sailed for Ireland on the seventeenth, Joy set up a writing studio in Jack's cozy rooms at Magdalen, surrounding herself with heaps of research material about Madame de Maintenon. When Joy was in London, Warnie had sent a welcome gift: a copy of *The Splendid Century,* his book about French life under the reign of Louis XIV. Now in Oxford, Joy was delighted. For the first time since her last stay at the MacDowell Colony in 1942, long stretches of unbroken hours aligned with an inspiring environment in which all her material needs were met. The boys stayed busy at the Kilns, playing cricket on the lawn and clearing the orchard under the watchful eye of Paxford, the Kilns' caretaker. Gazing out the windows that overlooked Magdalen's deer park, Joy nearly forgot her troubles. The whinnying of the stags lulled her throughout the day. Even the occasional interruptions added glamour and grandeur. The master of Balliol called one day to inquire about reaching Jack, who hadn't left a forwarding address. "[He] asked ME for it," Joy wrote to Bill. Although anger and resentment lingered between them, the bonds of their shared past were enough to sustain a congenial correspondence that continued for the rest of her life. "Gosh do I feel important." Then there was a knock on the door; Joy opened it to find "two would-be gate-crashing female tourists . . . horrible German yentas . . . no doubt hoping for a glimpse of the great man." The women glanced from Joy to the sign by the door reading "Mr. C. S. Lewis." Joy chastised them for intruding where they didn't belong. "I wish I could have photographed their faces," she said. "Ve chust vanted ve should see . . . ," Joy mocked them as she recounted the anecdote in letters to Bill and others, subtly emphasizing her place within the encircling glow of Jack's prestige.

Privately, though, she agonized about her position in the hierarchy of his relationships. Joy mused on a comment Jack once made about angels bestowing love equally on all men. Did he, too? "You are something short of an angel," she wrote in a new sonnet. "When you wear / One smile for all, you freeze me with despair . . . / Less charity, my angel, might be more." Certainly their friendship had deepened through time and reciprocal moral support; but had his feelings toward her budged beyond the platonic affection he generously dispensed to friends and correspondents? If so, he confessed to no one —not to his brother, not to Arthur, and certainly not to his colleagues or even to himself. It would soon become apparent, though, that a shift *had* occurred. In the months to come, he would begin initiating rendezvous. Jack would come to her.

· 14 ·

Fall 1954–October 1956

Joy regretted returning to London at the end of August 1954, and not just because it meant distance from Jack. August at the Kilns had included the best aspects of the best days in Staatsburg—walking in the woods, cooking leisurely meals, harvesting plums, pears, and apples from the orchard and broad beans from the garden. Now she had nearly three weeks to kill in the city before the next school term began. Doug, now nine, passed the time visiting school friends, while Davy, age eleven, practiced typing and studied botany, and Joy continued exploring ways to bring in money. The battle of divorce lawyers she'd initiated in June saddled both her and Bill with hefty fees. The boys' tuition would soon be due. Bill had recently been keeping up with child support payments—even getting ahead—but Joy was right not to count on that lasting. Her other primary source of income, the European Press, had folded in her absence. *Smoke* wasn't selling well enough to earn back its advance, though she anticipated magazine opportunities accompanying the publication of the British edition. American reviews had been decent, but the scant attention was embarrassing in contrast to Joy's previous successes. *Letter to a Comrade*, *Anya*, and *Weeping Bay* had all earned reviews in reputable national publications, but *Smoke* had barely been mentioned beyond local papers and church magazines. She saw a notice in the *Observer* for a fiction contest—a three-thousand-word short story set in the year 2500, with a prize of £200—and decided to take a crack, but nothing came of it. Jack insisted on paying her for her help, but it wasn't enough. Shortly after her return from Oxford, she went to the bank. Sitting in the manager's office, reaping the consequences of her reckless decisions, Joy broke down and wept—a rare public display of vulnerability.

Help arrived from an unlikely source. Joy's parents, now retired, were passing through London in mid-October for a visit of several weeks, the first stop on a months-long tour of Europe and Israel. "I bet I can get a bicycle for Douglas out of them," Joy wrote to Bill. She was able to get a lot more than that. Joe and Jen paid for lavish lunches, travel, and museum entry fees. Jen, having never completely abandoned hope that Joy would embrace fashion, bought her daughter a few basic items. When they let slip that they had $25,000 in savings, Joy, having assumed that they had only their pensions, was surprised and delighted. She asked for a share. "Bill's not much use," she told friends, "but it turns out that my parents have thousands stashed away in banks and insurance accounts and are willing to hand over some of it." She could quit toiling at commercial short stories and focus solely on the biography, provisionally titled "Queen Cinderella." "[It] smells to me like a money-maker, if I can get it done," she predicted.

Joy joked that her parents' money was "compensation for the wear and tear" of playing host—an exhausting job even if her energy had been at full capacity, which it still wasn't. She made innumerable runs to Woolworth's for assorted necessities. Her mother accompanied her to luxurious Regent Street shops, to the hairdresser, the laundry, the greengrocer's, and to doctors' offices for what Joy guessed to be hypochondriacal symptoms. She took her parents sightseeing to Westminster Abbey and the Tower of London, and brought them to Dane Court, where her father characteristically criticized the condition of the desks, calling them shabby, given the amount of tuition Joy was paying.

Joy had gotten over her anger at Bill and found herself defending him to her parents. A family feud had developed between Joy's parents and Renee's mother. Joy was glad to be on the other side of the Atlantic after hearing their reports of bitter squabbling. "When I can get a word in edgewise," she told Bill, "I insist that at least a third of the responsibility for everything that happened is mine; you may tell anyone I said so." Joy demonstrated her affection for Bill by showing them his recent check. "I've talked myself into a quite admiring frame of mind about you and am glad to have it confirmed," she wrote him. "You're quite the nicest ex-husband I have."

When Joy told Jack that her parents were visiting, he suggested they all have tea on the twenty-seventh, when he would be in London participating in a debate alongside his friend Dorothy Sayers. Joy arranged for the four of them to meet beforehand at the Piccadilly Hotel (and made it clear to her parents that they were to pay). Joy was amused by her mother's outfit: "a fancy black suit with rhinestone buttons, a pearl bracelet, a pearl choker, dingle-dangle pearl earrings, a pink lace blouse and a shocking pink hat." Joe was very proud of her beauty, and so was Jen.

Jack was his typical gracious self, though it was clear to Joy that he was working at projecting a benevolent spirit. "I'm doing my best," he told her under his breath. When Joe sermonized about the righteousness of Prohibition, Joy noticed Jack's gaze "grow slightly fixed." Then Joy chimed in with a story about the private stash of apricot brandy Joe had kept in the late 1920s; Joy sanctimoniously poured it down the drain and got "walloped," she recalled, admitting to youthful priggishness. Joe, agitated, rationalized his possession of alcohol. Jack remarked, "I think there was more than one prig in the family. Of course, our *own* case is always different, isn't it?"

Despite Jack's less than favorable impression of Joy's parents, he invited them to lunch at Magdalen the following week. Spending time with her parents was a sacrifice he made for Joy because he cared about her. Joy gave Jen and Joe a grand tour of Oxford: Christ Church, Magdalen Cloisters, "up the High and down the Broad and round through Turl and by Longwall Street and Holywell Street."

Yet while Jack was drawing closer to Joy, he did not invite her to the celebrations surrounding one of the most momentous public events of his career: his inaugural address at Cambridge, scheduled for November 29. The lecture was open to the public, and Joy had no intention of missing it. After taking the train up from London, she made her way to a hall that was quickly filling to capacity. There was "damn near as much fuss . . . as a Coronation," Joy thought. "There were so many capped and gowned dons in the front rows that they looked like a rookery." Jack was "walled about with caps and gowns and yards of recording apparatus." When all the seats were filled, Jack's friends and former students stormed the stage and sat at his feet. Joy "lurked modestly in the crowd," unable to get close. Yet she was not annihilated with heartache at being excluded from his high-brow sphere. Rather, she was overcome with pride and admiration.

"Instead of talking in the usual professorial way about the continuity of culture," she recounted,

> the value of traditions, etc., he announced that "Old Western Culture," as he called it, was practically dead. Leaving only a few scattered survivors like himself; that the change to the Age of Science was a more profound one than that from Medieval to Renaissance or even Classical to Dark Ages; and that learning about literature from him would be rather like having a Neanderthal man to lecture on the Neanderthal or studying paleontology from a live dinosaur! As I remember, he ended with, "Study your dinosaurs while you may; you won't have us around for long!" How that man loves being in a minority, even a lost-cause minority! Athanasius contra mundum, or Don Quixote against the windmills. He talked blandly of "post-Christian Europe," which I thought rather previous of him. I sometimes wonder what he would do if Christianity really did triumph everywhere; I suppose he would have to invent a new heresy.

As soon as the lecture ended, Joy hopped in a cab to the train station, returned to London, and resumed "living a very quiet life, deep in the seventeenth century." Financially stable—if barely and briefly—and encouraged by Jack's surge of attention, Joy exuded an aura of peace that did not go unnoticed. She had "a calmer manner," Phyl observed, and took better care of her appearance, wearing earrings and cutting her hair short and neat. She stopped writing sonnets, adding no new poems to her COURAGE folder.

Jack's official move to Cambridge was scheduled for New Year's Day, 1955, and he eagerly welcomed Joy's offer to accompany him. The transition made him anxious. Joy arrived in Oxford on December 30 with the boys to help with logistics. She shopped for sheets and other essentials, dusted books, superintended the Oxford end of the move, and, most valuably, provided companionship amid melancholy and doubt. At age fifty-six, Jack was having to restructure the whole of his life. "Oh, what a fool I am!" he whined playfully, turning down his mouth at the corners in a pretend pout. "I had a good home and I left." Joy teased him, affectionately remarking that he was "suffering all the pangs and qualms of a new boy going to a formidable school," but she also comforted him without patronizing. Humorous banter was his defense against "genuine grief, rather like a divorce," she commented when he joked about things like the Cambridge dons being served only one glass of port after dinner instead of Oxford's three. Of all of Jack's friends, Joy alone was able to see beyond every bluff, to wholly set apart the man from the persona, and to challenge Jack by bluntly naming his behavior, moving him into deeper self-awareness.

Joy became Jack's transitional object. When they first met in Oxford, she was trying to insinuate herself into an already established world. In Jack's new life as a Cambridge don, she was part of the foundation. They both created reasons for her to visit: he needed help selecting a hearthrug, or she wanted to hand-deliver proofread chapters of his autobiography. The real purpose of Joy's visits was just to "spend the day, [to] talk, walk, and drink."

He traveled to see her as well. At Avoca House, Joy befriended an Anglican priest, the Reverend Leslie Llewelyn Elliott, who had moved in with his family while on an eight-month leave from his parish in Melbourne, Australia. Elliott had a keen mind and a kind heart, and he had read all of Jack's books. Joy liked him immediately. They struck up a friendship, talking for hours about philosophy, theology, apologetics, and C. S. Lewis. Joy gave him the impression that she was Lewis's "secretary and confidante." She told Jack about the Elliotts, too. "One evening Joy announced that C. S. Lewis was in London and would like to meet us," recalled one member of the Elliott family. Jack soon appeared in the dining room at Avoca House and made their acquaintance. It was a Thursday, and Joy set off with Jack and Leslie for the Globe to meet the sci-fi crowd. John Christopher was thrilled to see them. They talked about writing, science fiction, and religion. The group knew Lewis to be a Christian writer, so it was noted when, on matters of theology, he humbly deferred to the priest. He felt it would be better for an ordained minister of his church to speak on matters of theology, matters in which Lewis was an admitted amateur.

By early February, Jack's period of mourning for Oxford had ended. He glowed with delight over his new home. Cambridge felt like "a country town, with a farming atmosphere about it," compared with Oxford, which had come to feel like "the suburb of a manufacturing town." He described Magdalene as "a tiny college (a perfect cameo architecturally)" and its denizens as "so old fashioned, & pious, & gentle and conservative—unlike this leftist, atheist, cynical, hard-boiled, huge Magdalen." His published books were doing well. Several were out in paperback. *Screwtape* bore what Joy thought to be "a highly flattering" author photo. She wasn't the only one. Jack received "at least one love-letter" praising his handsome looks. He jested about responding, "Dear Madam, the photograph is not at all like me." Joy suggested he "file the letter in the wastebasket instead."

Settled into Cambridge with more time to write, Jack was dismayed to find himself in a creative slump. Joy reassured him that slumps were "inevitable . . . the usual thing in our trade," but he felt "dried up," and it disturbed him. When she visited the Kilns on March 18 for a weekend before the boys returned for midterm holiday, Joy and Jack sat down with a bottle of whiskey between them and "kicked a few ideas around till one came to life." Jack mentioned that the myth of Cupid and Psyche had captured his imagination when he first read it in his late teens. He had tried rewriting the myth in various forms—play, couplet, ballad, prose—and although each attempt had failed to satisfy him, the idea still assailed him from time to time.

Joy was familiar with the story, from Apuleius' *Metamorphoses,* which she herself had read as a teenager. The tale centers on three princesses. The youngest, Psyche, is so exquisitely beautiful that people worship her as their goddess instead of worshipping Venus, the real goddess. Venus becomes enraged with envy, inciting a cascade of consequences that culminate with the king consulting the oracle of Apollo, which instructs him to sacrifice his daughter on a mountain as dragon prey. But when Psyche is abandoned in the wilderness, Cupid whisks her away on the west wind and prepares an opulent palace for her. He visits Psyche only in the dark of night, giving her but one rule: she must never look upon his face. When her sisters visit for a royal feast, they are consumed by jealousy and devise a plan to destroy her happiness, convincing their naïve little sister that her husband is a hideous monster. Why else wouldn't he show his face? They coax her to carry a lantern into the bedchamber, reveal his vile form, and stab him to death. Psyche reluctantly obeys. As Cupid sleeps, she lights a lamp to illuminate her lover. He is beautiful. Her rapture, however, is short-lived. A drop of hot oil falls from the lantern onto Cupid's shoulder. He roars awake, rebukes her, and flies away. Severe punishments befall the sisters. Psyche, devastated, is doomed to wander in the wilderness.

Jack had always believed that Apuleius "got it all wrong." In his atheist days, when he, like Joy, shunned notions of the supernatural, he imagined a version in which Venus was a fable, Psyche's sacrifice a consequence of cultural superstition, and the palace merely her delusion. The sisters, then, were mercifully bringing Psyche into reality. Although Jack was now a believer, he still felt there was a story in the invisible palace, and he had toyed with making the oldest sister a first-person narrator. Joy found the concepts thrilling. She related to his ethos; her own juvenile canon included a short story retelling the myth of Coronis and Apollo. "We had another whiskey each," she later recounted, "and bounced [the ideas] back and forth between us."

By the end of the next day, Jack had written an entire first chapter. He set the story in the barbaric land of Glome and began with the oldest sister—whom he named Orual, and whose face is so ugly that others recoil in disgust—writing an account of how the gods, especially one living on the Grey Mountain, have ruined her. Joy read the chapter earnestly and offered some criticisms. Jack returned to his desk, made the changes she suggested, and started on the next chapter. The epic became more intricate with every sentence Joy read, edited, and critiqued, as she and Jack infused their parallel spiritual journeys into the narrative: the longing he called "Joy," the Fairyland of her dreams, Daylight Street, "the door leading out of time and space into Somewhere Else." Jack could have been speaking for both himself and Joy when he wrote of the story, "[I] could be said to have worked on it most of [my] life."

In the new version, Psyche's mother dies in childbirth, so Orual brings up the girl. They adore each other, but Orual's love is possessive, obsessive. Psyche, however, is more enraptured with the Mountain. She dreams of marrying its king; he will build her a grand gold and amber palace, where she will reign as a great queen. When Psyche is grown, her father is told he must sacrifice his youngest daughter to redeem their plagued kingdom. Psyche, the "Great Offering," must be led up the Grey Mountain, bound to the "Holy Tree," and left as a bride for the "Shadowbrute" (god of the Mountain). Orual goes mad at the news of Psyche's death sentence. When she visits Psyche in the cell where she is being held before the sacrifice, however, she finds her sister at peace. "I have always—at least, ever since I can remember—had a kind of longing for death," Psyche tells Orual. "It was when I was happiest that I longed most. It was on happy days when we were up there on the hills . . . with the wind and the sunshine . . . And because it was so beautiful, it set me longing, always longing. Somewhere else there must be more of it." Her eyes shimmer with bliss.

"The sweetest thing in all my life has been the longing—to reach the Mountain, to find the place where all the beauty came from . . . my country, the place where I ought to have been born." She was speaking of the Island from *Pilgrim's Regress*. Of Joy's Fairyland. Psyche's language closely echoes Joy's door metaphor from her essay "The Longest Way Round": "Death opens a door out of a little, dark room (that's all the life we have known before it) into a great, real place where the true sun shines." There we meet the gods.

After the sacrifice, Orual travels to the Grey Mountain to bury her sister's remains. Moments of Orual's journey to the Mountain echo Joy's dream quest for Fairyland by way of Daylight Street—twists and bends, forest and grass—and her intense "aesthetic experiences." Orual finds Psyche alive and radiant. She moves to take her sister someplace safe at once, but Psyche says that this is her home now, and there is no place safer.

Psyche tells her story. After she was abandoned on the Mountain, attempts to buoy her own spirit with dreams of the gold and amber palace failed. On what she thought was her deathbed, she couldn't comprehend how she had ever believed. Orual, listening, inwardly rejoices that Psyche has rejected that "unnatural and estranging" fantasy. But as Psyche's story progresses, the rejoicing warps into despair. West-wind whisked Psyche from her chains and carried her to the threshold of a house so magnificent that her gold and amber palace seemed simple by comparison. A voice "sweeter than any music" tells her to enter her home, calling her "bride of the god." Dressed in fine clothes, she is led to a bedchamber, where their marriage is consummated. When Psyche talks of her husband, her eyes blaze with rapture.

This can't be true, Orual exclaims. But Psyche says, "It's more likely everything that had happened to me before this was a dream." She claims they are conversing on the threshold of the palace that very moment. Both of them are distraught that the other doesn't understand. Orual briefly wonders if Psyche's palace is real and she simply can't see it, but ultimately she is convinced that her sister is mad. The gulf between them cannot be crossed. The gods have stolen her.

Orual succeeds in destroying Psyche's happiness, and in the process turns her own heart to stone. She begins wearing a veil to cover her face—"the blank wall of the veil"—to hide her ugliness from the world and herself, and to intimidate people. The book is largely about discovering the ugliness in ourselves, the pain that accompanies such an awareness, and the embrace of a God who loves us all the more. It's not clear how forthcoming Joy was—with herself or with Jack—about the foundational theme of corrupted love. Orual's love for Psyche is selfish, possessive, not unlike the early stages of Joy's for Jack.

One of the story's main themes, later echoed in Lewis's book *The Four Loves,* is that love "begins to be a demon the moment he begins to be a god." If ever Joy was confronted with and chastened by the obsessive nature of her love for Jack, it was through Orual. Surely Jack grew through creating the story, too. As George Sayer notes: "Perhaps Jack, through writing [the tale], liberated himself from painful obsessions, confusions, and inhibitions. It was preparation for a complete and successful marriage." After so many years with Mrs. Moore, his heart was walled off from the possibility of true, attainable love. Several years later, when writing *The Four Loves,* he could have been thinking of himself and Joy when he wrote, "When the two people who thus discover that they are on the same secret road are of different sexes, the friendship which arises between them will very easily pass . . . into erotic love." Writing Orual's story with Joy showed Lewis, on a visceral level, what Joy already long knew: they were traveling the same secret road.

The version of Psyche and Cupid conceived with Joy that March night over glasses of whiskey would become *Till We Have Faces: A Myth Retold,* an adult novel that Jack considered his finest literary triumph. "The right form [had] presented itself and the themes suddenly interlocked," Jack wrote to his editor. "I'm v. much 'with book,'" he gleefully told a friend, thrilled by the breakthrough. "*Juno Lucina fer opem.*" Goddess of Childbirth, help me. Joy had helped break Jack's dry spell. The book's dedication reads "To Joy Davidman," but according to Sayer, among others, naming her as co-author would not have been inapt. "Her part in the book, and there is so much that she can almost be called its joint author, put him very much in her debt," declared Sayer. "She stimulated and helped him to such an extent that he began to feel that he could hardly write without her." Jack admitted as much to Joy: her help was "indispensible," he told her. "Whatever my talents as an independent writer," she wrote to Bill, "my *real* gift is a sort of editor-collaborator like Max Perkins, and I'm happiest when I'm doing something like that. Though I can't write one-tenth as well as Jack, I can tell him how to write more like himself." Jack now trusted Joy implicitly with his manuscripts. As *Surprised by Joy* proceeded through production, he directed his editor to discuss the proofs with her directly.

The March visit was distinct for other reasons, too. Joy was no longer a guest. She was an old friend who slipped comfortably into their routine. Jack rose early to tackle mounds of correspondence before writing. Joy got up around eight and toiled at the first chapters of "Queen Cinderella," plus a five-thousand-word outline for the proposal. Warnie worked on a life of the sixteenth-century printer Claude Garamond, Jack on Psyche and Cupid. "The house is practically a book factory," she joked.

Joy's gradual but steady integration into Jack's life established a constancy of contentment he hadn't known since early childhood, before his mother's death stole "all settled happiness, all that was tranquil and reliable," he explained in *Surprised by Joy.* Joy had become his closest companion, emotionally essential throughout Warnie's long absences after alcohol binges. Other than his governess and Mrs. Moore in the early days, Jack hadn't been so doted on since his mother was alive, and while he had intimate friends of both sexes, never had a true confederate offered him such exclusive, steadfast devotion. Neither was he searching for such a figure. He can almost be forgiven for not having recognized her when she first came along, fantastically packaged as an abrasive ex-communist Jewish convert from the Bronx, seventeen years his junior, and married.

• • •

THE FIRST HALF of 1955 saw something of a literary renaissance for Joy, although all her work was derivative or in service of Jack's and Warnie's. The English edition of *Smoke,* published in February, received respectable attention, selling around three thousand copies in its first two months, thanks largely to Jack's preface, Joy thought. She created the index for Warnie's new book. His publisher asked if she would be willing to do freelance indexing. The work paid between £15 and £25 per project. Joy was thrilled by the prospect, though there was no telling if the publisher would follow through. She finished the proposal for "Queen Cinderella," which would sell in August under the title "The King's Governess." Another idea paid off in the meantime: a book she called "Seven Deadly Virtues." She received a $500 advance, with $300 on signing.

The "Seven Deadlies," as Joy called the project, was "an attempt to rehabilitate virtue in the popular vocabulary . . . to free the concept and the very word itself from the associations of drabness, dullness, triteness, harshness and above all sham which they have acquired . . . by distinguishing between the real virtues, which lead to humility, happiness and love, from their Pharisaical or worldly counterfeits, which can only lead to pride, misery, and hate." Joy planned to employ a Lewisian technique, as she described it in her synopsis: "My intention is to do this not by praising true virtue, which has become a dull and trite exercise, but by satirizing the false ones in such a way that the true will appear through contrast." An introductory fable would feature "a modern prig and Pharisee who dies and presents himself confidently at the door of Heaven. He lists all the ways in which he is 'not as other men' . . . the seven virtues he has practiced all his life, Justice, Temperance, Prudence, Fortitude, Faith, Hope, and Charity." Each of seven chapters would begin with an anecdote about "Mr. Pharisee" attempting, self-righteously, to practice each virtue, then continue with analysis of common misinterpretations—"turning justice into inflexibility," for example. "Each chapter will end with a definition, through instances and analysis, of what *real* temperance, or *real* hope are like, and with some practical guides to learning them." Like *Smoke,* Joy's "Seven Deadlies" was a means of connecting with Jack. "I hate writing on theological subjects," she confided to Bill. The drudgery was worth the effort, though, if it meant financial gain and serious discussions with Jack.

BY SPRING 1955, many who knew Joy and Jack suspected that a romance was flourishing. Joy gave herself away when she accompanied Reverend Elliott's wife, June, on a day trip to Oxford. "It turned out to be a prolonged pilgrimage to Magdalen College," recalled Mrs. Elliott's son, "with a running commentary about Lewis: 'That was his room, June, and he used to walk here . . .' She could see that this devoted woman loved the brilliant, but ingenious man, and that she was determined to marry him." When June returned to Belsize, she announced to her husband that Joy would marry C. S. Lewis.

When an author acquaintance of Jack's, Herbert Palmer, asked if Jack would like to meet him and his wife for a meal in early July, Jack responded in the affirmative, suggesting they convene in the bar of the Eastgate Hotel and adding, "I shd. much like to meet Mrs. Hesketh and better still if she is accompanied by you, and to make you both acquainted with Mrs. Gresham (= Joy Davidman, whose *Smoke on the Mountain* I trust you have read)." Jack was increasingly drawing Joy into his circle.

The Walshes visited around that time as well. They paid for Joy's dinners and tickets to plays, and of course they all spent time in Oxford with Jack, who "did the honours in approved tourist guide style: 'On your right Queen's College founded by Boadicea.' They bit, too!" There was a stroll around the deer park, with Jack and Joy quoting Shakespeare to each other. Walking behind them, Chad quietly asked Eva, "Do you think there's anything going on between Joy and [Jack]?" She did. "I smell a marriage in the air." But both agreed that "whether Lewis smelled it [was] more doubtful."

THERE WAS, IN fact, talk of a marriage, but not the type occasioned by mutual love. Joy was "passionately anxious that the two boys grow up English," Warnie recounted years later in a letter to George Sayer, "and was also dreading for herself a compulsory return to America." The British Home Office, Joy told him, was not going to keep renewing her paperwork. She and Jack discussed the idea of a civil union, a legal contract to give Joy English nationality—a marriage on paper only. Neither of them wanted her to leave the country, but he needed time to consider the option of solving the matter through marriage; he would talk it over with Arthur Greeves during his annual late summer visit to Ireland while Joy once again used the Kilns for a holiday.

As it had the previous year, Warnie's alcoholism thwarted plans for the trip. Hiding the illness at this point was futile. "He has never had a year of such long debauches, or so frequent," Jack told Sayer. Dr. Havard used the word "deterioration." Warnie agreed to admit himself to a "hygienic bastille" in Dumfries, Scotland, but refused to entertain Joy's appeals that he begin to attend A.A. meetings. The Ireland trip was postponed till September.

Sad though the circumstances were, Joy and Jack reveled in their time together at the Kilns, shaping their days into family life. Joy did the cooking and grocery shopping on Jack's tab. He tutored Davy in Latin while Doug cavorted outdoors with neighborhood friends, fishing for lunches of perch in the pond, where they all swam on hot days, walking there and back along a slapdash brick path Davy built into the muddy trail through the woods. Both boys, different though they were in talent and temperament, were developing tremendous love and respect for Jack.

Joy and Jack acted out a thin charade about Joy earning her keep by playing secretary. She even took dictation. A "P.S." concluding a letter from Jack to Dorothy Sayers reads, "Joy Gresham, who is in the unhappy position of having borrowed my house and then finding that a change in my plans commits her to having me as a guest, sends her regards. She did all this typing." A "P.P.S. by J.G." follows: "I wouldn't precisely call it an unhappy position."

RETURNING TO LONDON after each visit had become an impractical nuisance. Joy was sick of the city and sick of Avoca House, especially after the benefits afforded to her at the Kilns, not the least of which was Jack's increasingly affectionate company. Her rose-colored glasses had cleared: instead of a nineteenth-century lady's drawing room, she saw a "flophouse" with "half-rate meals." A red brick townhouse in the Headington shopping district a mile from the Kilns caught her eye, and Jack's, too. Number 10 Old High Street was modest but cozy, two-storied with three bedrooms, a sitting room, dining room, and tiny-windowed kitchen overlooking a large shared yard dotted with apple and plum trees. There was a library down the street, and a pub, the White Hart, around the corner. She could walk to the Kilns and look in on Warnie during the week while Jack was at Cambridge. Warnie's present condition required constant attention. According to Sayer, Jack arranged for the lease and began paying rent.

Although the purpose of the move was clearly to be closer to Jack, Joy told the boys that she could no longer afford London; their father was not paying child support. The back-and-forth with Bill continued, he failing to fulfill their agreement, she berating him: "Sometimes I wonder how you can bear to live with yourself at all," Joy wrote. She even threatened to have him put him in jail, saying the boys were very worried about living expenses. Her assertion that "the poor kids don't even have proper winter coats" prompted a sharp defensive response from Renee, saying that Bill was deeply concerned about the boys' not being warm enough and suggesting that her mother, Joy's aunt Rose, could send new clothes. Joy responded caustically, "Well, you are certainly a good wife—it isn't every woman who will make her husband's excuses to a previous wife for him!" Too proud to accept the clothing offer, she told Renee that American outfits would not do in England.

On September 2, Joy returned to London with the boys to pack their few belongings, while Jack took a belated trip to Ireland alone. By mid-month the Greshams were settled into 10 Old High Street, baking apple pies and making plum jam and mint jelly. In the garden behind the White Hart pub—a haven of tamarisks, fuchsias, and aloes—she caught up on correspondence while Davy and Douglas drank ginger beer and read Shakespeare, enjoying the last days of freedom before departing for Dane Court. When Jack returned, he and Joy picked up where they'd left off, walking and drinking, relishing the end of a "marvelous summer," which Jack said was "turning deliciously into still, misty, voluptuous autumn." Joy picked tomatoes from the garden and lined the outside of the house with iris, daffodil, and tulip bulbs. Rosebushes bloomed well into October. And she and Jack began to see each other every day. "It was now obvious what was going to happen," Warnie wrote in his journal.

It was not obvious to Jack. On his trip to Ireland in September, he told Arthur that he was considering civil marriage. From a letter Jack wrote to Arthur in October, it appears that Arthur had taken his friend to task about it. "I don't feel the point about a 'false position,'" Lewis wrote. "Everyone whom it concerned wd. be told. The 'reality' wd. be, from my point of view, adultery and therefore mustn't happen. (An easy resolution when one doesn't in the least want it!)" Joy gave a slightly different account of Jack's position, which she recounted to John Christopher on a visit to the Globe. "She spoke of him then in a different way," he later recalled, "as fondly but with a confidence that was new. It was plain that she knew she had engaged his interest as a woman." With a "smart smile," she relayed remarks that "a mutual acquaintance" had confided to her: "[Lewis] was deeply attracted by her but, having practised Christian celibacy for a quarter-of-a-century, was at a loss how to come to terms again with physical desire." Joy "made it quite clear that she had no doubts in her mind of how he was going to cope with this," Christopher said. "I had no doubt that she felt, and with justification, that she was capable of putting things right in that respect."

Her mission became progressively more straightforward. She slipped into the role of Jack's all-purpose assistant and, with the boys, into Jack's family. She continued helping with his correspondence. When he received a letter from a Dubliner asking his thoughts on Dianetics, it went straight to Joy. "It seems various groups, especially the screwy 'scientology' ones, are still going strong," she recounted to Bill. "I told the lad what little good I could find to say about dianetics—that it was effective with psychogenic illnesses and in some cases with early traumas, but that it could be dangerous in the wrong hands. After this lapse of time I really wonder at our credulousness and our temerity; a technique in which the auditor is so much more active than the traditional psychoanalyst obviously requires something special in the way of balance, intelligence and good will."

Joy's writing life slowed again. The "Seven Deadlies" had become a burden. Joy's heart wasn't in it, but her days were becoming happier and more stable than they had been in years. Putting up the Christmas tree that year, Joy thought back to Staatsburg: Bill affixing eyelets to the mantel, stringing picture wire around the tree to hold it up. Here she bought a tree with roots, set it in a bucket, and packed it with rocks. The boys returned from school on their own. Joy was confident in their ability, but her maternal instincts kicked in when the train she expected them to arrive on yielded no Davy and Douglas. Jack was with her. He soothed her fears, though later he confessed to having been a tad anxious as well. The boys eventually arrived, late but safe.

For two weeks before Christmas the streets were full of carol singers, "quaint and cheery and hallelujish till I could have choked them," Joy joked. Oxford was decked with holly and mistletoe. Jack took the boys to a revival of *The Wizard of Oz* and went book shopping at Blackwell's with David. He paid for food, and Joy did the bulk of the cooking. They feasted on turkey, mince pies, and plum pudding.

Joy suddenly had a social life. "What a change from Staatsburg!" she wrote to Bill.

> I'm beginning to know people and get invited out; last Sunday I had a very swanky lunch (venison and Burgundy) at a country club, in company with Jack and among other people Sir John and Lady Rothenstein, he being the director of the Tate Gallery—this and tuppence'll get me a ride on a bus. So I come home and stretch hamburger for supper! Also Jack is going to give a dinner in Magdalen to introduce me to people; thank God I've still got my nine-year-old Hollywood evening dress. It's out of style and I've had to

> let it out at the seams, but among don's [*sic*] wives is this bad? I feel like a Southern aristocrat after de waw, starving in the grand manner. Not that I'll starve, though, as long as there's more water to put in the soup.

Joy and Jack went on a date of sorts to see *The Bacchae,* performed in the original Greek at the Arts Theatre in Cambridge. Joy had given herself a refresher course in Greek the week before. Undergraduate productions such as this at Oxford and Cambridge were on par with Broadway, she thought. She and Jack were both deeply moved.

She occasionally went to church with Jack, but it didn't agree with her. "The trouble is that while I like Christianity well enough," she confided to Bill, "I hate Churchianity; as far as I can see, every organized church in the world ends either by missing the point and tangling itself in trivialities, or by contradicting the point altogether. And certain of my past experiences have left me suspicious of *all* organization. I got on well enough with the Episcopalians; but the C. of E. is another matter; it's dead on its feet and full of perverts, eunuchs, and Manichees."

JACK TOLD GEORGE Sayer of his plans to marry Joy in a civil ceremony but stressed that it would be nothing more than a formality. "I raised objections," Sayer recalled. "A civil marriage with Joy could not possibly be a formality . . . but would, in fact, make him legally responsible for maintaining the boys if Joy were unable to earn enough to do so." The Sayers' suspicion of Joy had renewed itself after a recent troubling run-in. Moira had been passing time reading in the living room at the Kilns one day while her husband attended a nearby confirmation. Jack was upstairs napping. Joy walked in whistling, arms full of Jack's laundry, and did not immediately recognize the woman sitting on the couch. "Who the hell are you and what the hell are you doing here?" she demanded. Moira, offended by Joy's tone and language, replied indignantly, "We've met before. I'm Mr. Lewis's guest. I have as much right to be here as you." Joy was enraged. She swore, turned on her heel, and stormed out of the house. She was, George thought, "plainly suspicious and jealous . . . at a strange woman being in the house."

When Jack came downstairs, Moira told him of Joy's behavior. He was embarrassed, yet he defended her. In general, he told George, "some of the people he had invited to meet her had failed to appreciate her directness and concern for integrity." She wasn't at her best around strangers. George ultimately accepted Joy's "abrasive New York manner," which masked "her essential kindness and generosity." But he would always be troubled by her "possessiveness . . . and lack of emotional self-control."

ON APRIL 23, 1956, Joy and Jack were married at the local registry office on St. Giles Street, down the road from the Bird and Baby. Humphrey Havard and Austin Farrer, whose wife, Kay, had become a friend of Joy's, acted as witnesses. Kay was a mystery writer whom Joy occasionally typed for, and Austin a close friend of Jack's and a chaplain at Oxford's Trinity College. The marriage "was a pure matter of friendship and expediency," Jack told his friend Roger Lancelyn Green two days later, a formality to allow Joy to stay in England as long as she wished. Joy would continue living at 10 Old High Street as Mrs. Gresham. But others guessed the arrangement wasn't permanent. "I saw the uselessness of disabusing him," Warnie wrote years later in retrospect. "[Joy's] intentions were obvious from the outset."

JOY WAS ASKED to speak at a London church, addressing "The Problem of the Christian Jew." She also gave a lecture at Oxford on Charles Williams, which she felt was a success. "I have never had such a good audience," she wrote Bill.

> Light as Viennese pastry, in contrast to those lumps of soggy dough I used to handle in New York. They got all my jokes, even the hints of jokes, instantly, and roared aloud; instead of sitting back and waiting to be amused or edified, they came all the way to meet me. Jack and the Principal of Pusey House were very compli-

> mentary afterward. I'm all the more pleased as I was taking a bit of a chance—I attacked Manichaeism and prudery in the Church. Nobody liked it better than the parsons! I suspect I wronged the C. of E. in my last letter; it isn't as bad as its bishops.

Life was good. The demands of caring for the boys were more bearable now that they were old enough to roam independently. Doug had a large band of neighborhood friends; Davy had Blackwell's bookshop. In spring, Doug was often outside in the garden, consumed with physical tasks such as covering the pea plants with wire netting to keep out blackbirds and jays. Davy often read the Greek Testament, a gift from Jack, accompanied by grammar references. Joy spent her weekday hours of solitude knitting socks for the boys, mastering a large recorder Bill had given her years earlier, and grinding her teeth over the "Seven Deadlies," "which I don't in the least feel like doing," she told Bill. "How did I get into this theology racket anyway?"

Joy was more settled than she'd been for years, but as her psychological distress ebbed, its place was taken by waves of physical pain. In January she began having "startling" episodes of heart palpitations—"a peculiar hop-skip-and-jump rhythm my heart has been experimenting with"—accompanied by severe nausea. A doctor dismissed the symptoms as "incipient middle age and a touch of strain." Another doctor suggested uremia. On a stroll with Jack in March, as the snowdrops and crocuses bloomed under Oxford's ancient city wall, she felt a sudden searing pain in one leg. The next day she could hardly walk. When she did get back on her feet, the weakness and pain were unrelenting. "I hope it ain't rheumatism!" she joked. Months passed, and new bursts of pain exploded in her chest and back. A doctor diagnosed her with "fibrositis," inflammation of the muscles and joints. "I walk around all crippled and it HURTS," she reported. "I can't so much as open a window without a yelp of pain." It was "the fault of the climate," everyone told her. "It will pass."

Joy managed to plant a small garden of beans, sugar peas, and squash, but the fibrositis tormented her every day—exacerbated, she assumed, by the wet summer. She couldn't sleep without pills. "[It's] not bad enough to stop me working or walking, just bad enough to take all the fun out of both," she wrote to Bill in August. The two corresponded less frequently, but their letters followed the same general pattern as they had since her move to England nearly three years earlier—newsy, friendly, and occasionally spiked with contention over his insufficient payments. Davy's shoes were so small that he could barely walk. Doug mowed neighbors' lawns to help supplement the grocery budget. They lived on baked beans and green beans. Joy threatened to sue. Bill's new excuse for not sending money was that he couldn't see well enough to work; he had cataracts—a side effect, doctors suggested, of Dee Ray (radium) treatment. "Is it certain?" Joy asked, perhaps concerned about the long-term effects of her own radium treatment years earlier. She reminded Bill of the concerned thyroid specialists she'd seen in London. "If so, I'm lucky."

By summer's end, Joy required a cane to hobble about. "I have got something really hellish the matter with my left hip," she told Bill. But despite pain that had her "twisted in knots," she was happy, enjoying autumn at its best. Jack wrote an ethereal description of that fall's inception: "warm, coloured days, but cold nights, and usually misty mornings, every cobweb on the hedge turned into a necklace by heavy dew." He was happy, too.

Jack confided his true feelings for Joy to no one—perhaps not even to himself. Years later, in retrospect, he wrote, "If we had never fallen in love we should have none the less always been together, and created a scandal." Unbeknown to him, a scandal had already erupted. His frequent visits to 10 Old High Street made Jack the subject of whispers among friends and colleagues. "I could never understand why a man of his intelligence couldn't see that that was going to be gossiped about," said Clifford Morris, a driver who often chauffeured Jack to and from the train station at the beginning and end of each week. "He got a terrible name over that . . . They both did." This was Oxford, where unmarried dons were expected to lead an almost monastic life, and it was the 1950s, when the stigma of divorce could render even the most likable woman an outcast; Joy, with her New York brashness and Jewish lineage, was already operating with handicaps. Professor Tolkien was reportedly "concerned for the university." Was the relationship sexual? People speculated, but no one knew for sure.

Joy certainly wasn't one to care about appearances, but this was the perfect opportunity to make her most pivotal move yet. Joy "began to press for her rights," Warnie wrote in his journal, "pointing out with perfect truth that her reputation was suffering from J's being in her house every day, often stopping until eleven at night." For the sake of her honor, she argued to Jack, their marriage should be public knowledge; she should move into the Kilns. Jack agreed. By mid-October "all arrangements had been made for the installation of the family at The Kilns." How Jack planned to explain the arrangement had yet to be determined. Very few of their friends even knew about the civil marriage—or, as Jack called it, "our innocent little secret."

ON THE EVENING of October 18—on the brink of starting the life with Jack she'd spent years yearning and scheming for—Joy had a fall. It was a Thursday. Jack was at Cambridge as usual, and she was home alone. Walking toward the door to let out the cat, Joy fell. As she hit the floor, violent pain ripped through her leg. She could hardly move, but she managed to reach a phone and call Kay and Austin Farrer. They rushed over and helped her to bed.

The next morning she was in too much pain to go to the hospital by any means other than ambulance. In the afternoon a stretcher was wheeled into 10 Old High Street, and Joy was transported to nearby Wingfield Hospital. Urine and blood analysis would take several days. Meanwhile, X-rays were made. The films were devastating. Cancer everywhere. Cancer in her shoulder, cancer in her left breast, cancer in both legs. Doctors described the broken left femur as appearing "moth-eaten." The other test results were, at this point, almost irrelevant.

Joy understood her prospects: "In short, it is fairly probable that I am going to die . . . I've been very tired for a long time."

· 15 ·

Fall 1956–Fall 1957

From her hospital bed, Joy looked out through a wall of windows onto swaths of flowers and the greenest grass. She felt "only moderately afraid"—neither resigned to death nor fixated on the wisp of hope doctors tentatively floated her way as they talked of surgery and radiation. Instead, she busied her mind strategizing solutions to two concerns that superseded the abstract possibility that her life might soon end: she wanted the boys kept in England, away from Bill, and she wanted to live her last days as Jack's wife, openly and sanctioned by the church.

Two days after her fall, Joy informed Bill that she had changed her will, appointing Jack and his lawyer the boys' legal guardians. Jack had promised to see them through school. Although Bill should contribute what he could, said Joy, obviously he was "in no position to look after two *more* children." Besides, the boys disliked Renee. Joy argued finances and education. "*Please, please* don't try to get them back to the States," she implored Bill. It was "essential" that they continue their English education; a move would damage them "irreparably." Bill characteristically restrained himself from pointing out that Joy herself had relocated their boys in a jarring upheaval. Without a definitive prognosis, objections seemed unnecessary; he decided to let Joy's illness play out before pressing for custody. There was no telling how much time she had.

The matter of marriage was more complex, emotionally and ecclesiastically. Jack, by her side immediately, was enormously distressed. "I can hardly describe to you the state of mind I live in at present," he told a friend, "except that all emotion, with me, is periodically drowned in a sheer tiredness, deep lakes of stupor." Joy had spent enough time with *Surprised by Joy* and psychoanalytic theory to know that for Jack, her diagnosis was like a blow from a storm cracking a levee; the reservoir of grief and fear of loss that had been dammed up inside him after his mother died of cancer gushed forth. "It will be a great tragedy for me to lose her," he confided to Arthur Greeves. "I know you will pray for her and for me: and for W., to whom also, the loss if we lose her, will be great."

Joy expressed her wish to marry before God, and Jack agreed. Months later, he was able to admit that he would eventually have married Joy regardless. "You can well understand," he told a friend, "how illness—the fact that she was facing pain and death and anxiety about the future of her children—would be an *extra* reason for marrying her or a reason for marrying her sooner." Of course he was in love with her, he seemed ready only now to admit. Of course their marriage must be consecrated. "They say a rival often turns a friend into a lover," he explained to a friend many months later. "Thanatos," the Greek personification of death, "is a most efficient rival for this purpose. We soon learn to love what we know we must lose." And he loved Joy with a fierceness he had never before known.

Jack rethought his theological position on divorce and remarriage. In Joy's case, there was a loophole. Bill's first wife was still living when he married Joy; thus, in the eyes of the church, his union with Joy was void. Regardless of the laws of the land, because she had not been a wife, she could not be a divorcee.

To convince the bishop of Oxford of the legitimacy of this argument, they needed evidence. Joy hastily wrote to Bill, explaining the circumstances and requesting proof of the existence and dissolution of his previous marriage. Bill responded in detail with the date and location of the ceremony, the date of divorce, the number on the divorce certificate, and the names of the attorneys and judge. Jack began quietly informing friends of the impending marriage: "You may as well know (but don't talk of it, for all is still uncertain) that I may soon be, in rapid succession, a bridegroom and a widower. There may, in fact, be a deathbed marriage."

On the evening of November 17, Jack went to the home of the bishop, Harry Carpenter, and presented his case. Would the church rule Joy's previous marriage invalid so that their union could be blessed? They discussed the matter. Bishop Carpenter "personally felt that it was a harsh rule which could justifiably be relaxed" under certain circumstances. Nevertheless, he decreed, the mandate must stand in Lewis's case. As an internationally best-selling author and high-profile Christian personality in Oxford and Cambridge, he would set a precedent. "If permission were given to such a public figure . . . everyone would demand the right to follow suit." Jack vigorously disagreed with this logic; the church couldn't have it both ways. But his protests were in vain. The civil marriage would have to stand. A notice would run in the paper as soon as he and Joy informed friends.

NOVEMBER PASSED IN a haze of anesthetics and operations: surgery to repair the femur, a lumpectomy, and an oophorectomy, removal of the ovaries—the last of which induced three days of vomiting. The "physical agony was combined with a strange spiritual ecstasy," Joy said when the anesthetics wore off. "I think I know now how martyrs felt. All this has strengthened my faith and brought me very close to God—as if at last I knew all the answers."

She felt comfort, not only from God but from others, too, as she'd never experienced it. Her parents offered any help she needed. Howard reconciled through friendly letters. Jack's family in Ulster sent well wishes, along with an invitation to keep the boys during vacations. Warnie, whose affection had grown steadily in the four years since he'd first met Joy, became a doting brother-in-law. "I never have loved her more than since she was struck down," he recorded in his diary. "Her pluck and cheerfulness are beyond praise, and she talks of her disease and its fluctuations as if she was describing the experiences of a friend of hers. God grant that she may recover." He stayed sober in order to act as interim superintendent during Jack's trips to Cambridge, handling myriad household responsibilities, including the management of domestic staff—now consisting of Paxford, Mrs. Miller, and the nurses—and arranging for a cottage on the property to be outfitted as a place for the boys to play and do schoolwork. Humbled by cancer, moved by expressions of love and compassion, Joy softened.

"I can now tell you that Jack and I are married," Joy wrote ecstatically to Chad and Eva. "Have been for a few months, and are going to publish an announcement soon." She knew they wouldn't "worry unduly about the ecclesiastical difficulty," she wrote, explaining the bishop's dissent. "So Jack and I have been married only civilly; but I don't feel it matters a scrap, though I should like a friendly and independent clergyman to add something."

Jack, though, presented the news quite differently. Not only did he insist that the marriage was motivated by practical considerations around Joy's terminal diagnosis, but also he was curiously unwilling to reveal the fact that a marriage had already taken place. To friends who knew nothing of their "innocent little secret," he continued using the future tense to characterize his soon-to-be status as bridegroom and widower. "If she gets over this bout and emerges from hospital," he wrote to Arthur from the Kilns, "she will no longer be fit to live alone so she must come and live here. That means (in order to avoid scandal) that our marriage must shortly be published." He told Dorothy Sayers, "[Joy] is not likely to live; but if she gets over this go she must be given a home here," adding: "You will not think that anything wrong is going to happen. Certain problems do not arise between a dying woman and an elderly man," suggesting the relationship might never be consummated. "What I am mainly acquiring is two (nice) stepsons." At Jack's request, Warnie reiterated to George and Moira that "the marriage was purely a nominal one."

Had the bishop's unwillingness to bless their marriage induced a guilty conscience? Was Jack concerned about his reputation? None of it mattered to Joy, if she even knew. Jack was by her side every moment he could steal away from Cambridge, and Joy had convinced herself that she was on her way to full recovery. "[I] am now ready for radiation treatment on my affected hip and shall be walking again in a couple of months," she wrote to Chad and Eva. "I've quite a good chance of getting away without further trouble, they say. I'm in fine health aside from the hip . . . and I'm already back to normal in spite of the row of stitches up my tummy." A few days later she was transferred for radiation to Churchill Hospital, "a ramshackle ex–American Army place," and wrote a similar report to Bill. "All my insides are healthy; they're definite about my being able to walk well again—it really looks as if I might get away with this." Doctors "promised me definitely that the X-rays [radiation therapy] would work." That's what she needed to believe.

But Joy was in profound denial—a divine mercy, perhaps, sent to cradle her spirits during painful surgeries and treatments. Doctors had given no such promises, true or false—Jack made certain of that. "No miserable pretense," he insisted. "That means that both can face it side-by-side, instead of becoming something like adversaries in a battle-of-wits." Joy had been fully apprised of her prognosis: "1. A tiny 100th chance of ultimate cure. 2. A reasonable probability of some years more of (tolerable) life. 3. A real danger she may die in a few months."

Surely the long-anticipated marriage announcement had something to do with Joy's fantasy. Jack had arranged for a pithy notice to run in *The Times*, buried on page eight, on Christmas Eve, when most readers were otherwise occupied: "A marriage has taken place between Professor C. S. Lewis of Magdalene College, Cambridge, and Mrs. Joy Gresham, now a patient in the Churchill Hospital, Oxford. It is requested that no letters be sent."

Even if she did "weather it this time," life would proceed under the precarious "sword of Damocles," as Jack put it. He knew. He had watched his mother suffer cancer's "usual course," as he had described it in *Surprised by Joy:* "an operation . . . an apparent convalescence, a return of the disease, increasing pain, and death."

Joy thought she could accept that outcome, as long as the reprieve granted a semblance of normal married life, if only for a year. She anticipated nothing less. "When I come out of here I should go to the Kilns as Mrs. Lewis," she told friends. "All my troubles but one are over!"

Joy was moved back to the Wingfield in late December. Left leg encased in plaster, she lay nearly flat on her back counting down the weeks till the cast would be removed and she could walk. She couldn't wait to be out of the hospital. Despite her having the best care and the best room Jack could arrange, the noise from television sets and wirelesses clamored through the halls, and the nursing was unpredictable. Sometimes she managed a deep sleep, but the night nurse would wake her up at the appointed time to give her sleeping pills. Medical students in mortarboards and gowns gathered around her bed for demonstrations. A hospital chaplain served communion at her bedside once a week.

At the end of January doctors removed Joy's cast, took new X-rays, reviewed the films, and reported the results they had anticipated: the fracture had not healed, and the cancer appeared to be resisting radiation. Joy was shocked. She felt "perfectly well," aside from "mild intermittent" leg pain. That mattered little, they said; how she felt was not an accurate reflection of medical reality. More definitive results would come in six weeks, but Joy should prepare for the worst.

Feelings of anger and sorrow broke through Joy's fortress of denial. She was devastated, angry at God, brokenhearted over the loss of a life with Jack. "I'd pinned all my hopes to having a year or so of happiness with Jack at least," she confided to Chad and Eva, "and instead it seems I shall lie about in hospital with my broken femur waiting for death, and unable to do anything to make my last shreds of life useful or bearable." Faith threatened to slip through her fingers. "There seems such a gratuitous and merciless cruelty in this," she said bitterly. "I hope that all we have believed is true. I dare not hope for anything in *this* world."

When Jack heard the news, he was overcome with grief. "My

world is not bleak or meaningless," he told a friend, "but it is tragic." Watching him suffer only heightened Joy's misery: "How horrible that I, who wanted to bring him only happiness, should have brought him this!" Perhaps, she told him, he would have been better off had they never met. Absolutely not, he insisted. They prayed, together and individually, for grace to bear whatever was to come. They must embrace peace in the absence of hope. They began to accept that they had no other choice but to live moment to moment, hour to hour, day to day, "not adding the past or future to the present." They tried to "remember other sufferers. It's fatal to start thinking 'Why should this happen to *us* when everyone else is so happy.' [We are] of a huge company." Joy began to feel emboldened and, fleetingly, a bit contrite. "I'm not at all sure I didn't deserve it after all," she confessed to Chad and Eva about her fate, "and I'm pretty sure that in some way I needed it."

Eventually she was able to sit up in a wheelchair. Her typewriter was arranged for easy access, and in Jack's weekly absences she kept herself busy with correspondence. Humble hope returned to them both. Joy pressed the doctors for predictions, and they admitted the impossibility of knowing a cancer's course. Jack told her that they had been wrong to accept hopelessness: "Uncertainty is what God has given us for a cross." Determined not to wither helplessly in hospital, Joy pushed herself. "I'll get up, by the aid of will-power and sweat and grace; and if God will let me, I shall walk." In late February she started strengthening her right leg in hopes of graduating to crutches, maybe even a brace; perhaps someday, she dared aspire, a built-up shoe to compensate for the three inches of cancerous femur the doctors had carved out. She vacillated between hope and medical reality: "I shall apparently be a cripple for life, but the life probably won't be long enough to matter, so why worry?"

Jack became increasingly affectionate, both physically and verbally. He brought sherry to drink at Joy's bedside, and they talked and laughed and kissed. "*What* a pity I didn't catch that man younger," she joked. Whatever happened sexually between them behind closed doors had its obvious logistical limitations, but it was passionate enough for Joy to boast that American assumptions about the "intellectual Englishman's supposed coldness" were pure bunk. "The truth about these blokes," she wrote to her ex-husband in a characteristically inappropriate aside, "is that they are like H-bombs; it takes something like an ordinary atom bomb to *start* them off, but when they're started—Whee! See the pretty fireworks! He is mucho hombre, my Jack!"

Jack described this time as "a honeymoon on a sinking ship." He became more open with others about his feelings for Joy. "New beauty and new tragedy have entered my life," he told one friend. "You could hardly believe what happiness, even gaiety, there is between us," he wrote to another. It was "a queer, incredible life," this exquisite happiness shot through with "great misery." Surprisingly, cancer as a concept lost its horror. "The name and the idea of it were in some degree disarmed," Joy told Jack. They discussed the idea that "one never meets just Cancer, or War, or Unhappiness (or Happiness). One only meets each hour or moment that comes. All manner of ups and downs. Many bad spots in our best times, many good ones in our worst. One never gets the total impact of what we call 'the thing itself.' But we call it wrongly. The thing itself is simply all these ups and downs: the rest is a name or an idea."

"ALL I REALLY care about is having a bit of life with Jack and getting adequately on my feet for it," Joy declared. But a new blow struck in mid-March when doctors reevaluated her condition. She had a few months at best, they said. The nurses predicted mere weeks.

Everyone was crushed. Warnie, angry on his brother's behalf, wrote in his journal: "*Why,* one asks, should J have had the life which has been his—the best 32 years of it eaten out by [Mrs. Moore], and then the prospect of 'peace at eventide' so cruelly snatched away. How rapid the whole thing has been too; seven years ago we didn't know that such a person as Joy existed."

Jack would not allow Joy to be "snatched away" without pulling out every stop. Charles Williams had espoused the mystical theology of substitutionary love, a divinely imbued love that allows one person to take on the physical suffering of another, like Christ's substitution on the cross for the pain of the world. Jack prayed for long stretches that God would allow him to take Joy's pain on himself. He also prayed for miraculous healing.

Jack had a priest friend, a former student named Peter Bide, who was said to possess the rare gift of healing. Three years earlier, Bide, a hospital chaplain at the time, had knelt at the bedside of a boy dying from cerebral meningitis, laid his hands on the child, and prayed for healing. The boy fully recovered. Bide did not broadcast the event, but the story spread. Jack wrote a letter asking him to come pray for Joy; the young priest agreed. He traveled to Oxford on March 20 to spend the night at the Kilns before visiting Wingfield the next day. Before the two men said good night, Jack asked Bide if he would perform a bedside ecclesiastical marriage. "Joy desperately wanted to solemnize her marriage before God and to claim the grace of the sacrament before she died," Bide recounted years later. To Jack he responded that he would think about it. "In the end," he said, "there seemed only one Court of Appeal. I asked myself what He would have done and that somehow finished the argument." At 11 A.M. the next day, Jack, Warnie, and Peter Bide gathered around Joy's bed for an abbreviated nuptial mass. They invited the ward sister to join them as another witness. Communion was given, marriage vows exchanged. Bide put his hands on Joy and prayed for healing. "I found it heartrending," Warnie wrote of the woman he now called sister, "and especially Joy's eagerness for the pitiable consolation of dying under the same roof as J; though to feel pity for anyone so magnificently brave as Joy is almost an insult. She is to be moved here next week, and will sleep in the common-room, with a resident hospital nurse installed [in a spare room]. There seems little left to hope but that there may be no pain at the end."

A week after her marriage, Joy was taken home to the Kilns to die. Completely bedridden, she anticipated no more strolls outside with Jack, not even in a wheelchair. She spent hours each day with her leg in traction. Two nurses alternated around-the-clock care—managing medications, changing her bedpan, dressing and bathing her—while Jack performed the duties of a hospital orderly. She couldn't so much as roll on her side without help. Her pain escalated. The cancer riddling her right shoulder rendered that arm nearly useless. "We are entering on a period in [which] we must expect every day to be worse than yesterday and better than tomorrow," Jack informed Chad.

Yet tenacious "wild hopes" persisted despite all the hallmarks of terminal cancer: "bitter nostalgia for lost happiness, mere physical terror turning one sick, agonised pity and self-pity," Jack described it. "In fact, Gethsemane." These days were the closest either of them had ever come to understanding Jesus' purpose when he wept in the garden on the eve of his gruesome death, begging his Father to "let this cup pass." He knew the crucifixion had to happen—it was central to a grand plan. He also knew that people needed a savior who understood their suffering. Yet, having pleaded with God like Jesus in the garden, Jack was able to say, "Thy will be done," and mean it. Among his correspondents were scores of young Narnia fans. Sometimes he shared details of his own life. "My wife is very, very ill," he wrote to one young boy. "I am sure Aslan knows best and whether He leaves her with me or takes her to His own country, He will do what is right. But of course it makes me very sad . . . Pray for us."

Bill was told of the latest turn. He responded with two letters—one to Joy and one to Jack. Given the forecast of imminent death, it was time to inform Joy that he planned to return the boys to America after she died. He would raise them "not in luxury but with plenty to eat and enough to wear which is the main thing, in addition to love. I have plenty of love to give them." He informed Jack of the same, while defending his own competence; he was not the man Joy made him out to be.

"I think that I should tell you my side of the story," Bill wrote to Jack. He began with the months before Joy's first trip to England, when she was working on her *Presbyterian Life* articles, and he held nothing back, recounting her "unsettled state of mind," her reckless spending of money they didn't have, her delusional frenzy to meet Lewis. "She often told me, when she was upset, that she felt she was dying and had to get to England to see you," he wrote, echoing the feelings that Joy herself had infused into her sonnets. "She said many times that she was in love with you and had to get to know you, although at the time she had no hope of ever marrying you." Bill explained his reasoning that a trip to England would help convince Joy that Jack wasn't the marrying type. He added that her indefinite absence, ultimately lasting five months, naturally "alarmed" the boys. "I tried to reassure them that their mother would eventually come back but Christmas came and no Mommy; they were sad little chaps." Bill recounted Joy's fury upon her return, and her disappearance with the children when he came home on weekends from his traveling job. When Joy sailed to England with David and Douglas, he said, he felt he had no recourse. "Little boys needed their mother. I did not know what to do, or what was best to do. I begged her to stay at home and told her that I would do anything she wanted as long as she kept the boys in this country where I could visit them but she refused."

Now Bill wanted his boys back. He pleaded with Jack: "There has never yet been a boarding school that could take the place of a father . . . I believe in helping the boys with whatever hobbies and interests they choose, educating them for self-reliance and self-knowledge and guiding them along their own pathways, in whatever constructive direction they wish to go in life." He thanked Jack for the financial help he had provided toward the boys' tuition: "I appreciate deeply anything good which is done for them more than I can say. But while riding lessons and music and other advantages are fine things for boys to have, I can give them something no one else on earth can give them. They are getting to an age when more than anything else in the world they need their Dad."

Bill's failure to mention his affair with Renee was of little consequence. When Jack showed Joy the letter, she surpassed her ex-husband's sin of omission with a vitriolic story that would become Bill's legacy. "Let's skip the minor reasons why you are unfit to have the boys," she wrote to him.

> Your history of alcoholism, neuroses, sexual and financial irresponsibility, etc.; apparently you don't think they matter. Let's

> not argue about the destruction of the boys' education—you say that doesn't matter either, and apparently you don't mind subjecting a pair of completely Anglicized schoolboys to the utter misery and confusion a shift to the American system would bring them . . .
>
> But there is one thing you won't be able to brush aside; the boys both loathe you. They always disliked and despised you . . . During the years we lived together I tried constantly to defend you to them—"Daddy's not himself today"—and so on. After we separated and I let them speak freely, I was startled myself by the fear and terror they felt . . . It took hard work on my part to keep them civil to you . . . Both of them are horrified at the thought of living with you; they are now old enough to tell the true story in court. You haven't got a chance, my friend.

Joy pointed out what Bill's letter had neglected to mention:

> That you had previously asked me to live with your mistress in a ménage à trois, slapped my face, half-throttled me, and threatened my life. You surely cannot believe the things you now write; and I am at a loss to know why you write them. The grotesque bad taste of your sending such a letter to my present husband hardly qualifies you as a fit guardian for the young; still less when the young concerned are present, articulate and quite ready to testify to their own memories of your customary behaviour. You ought to hear 'em, Bill, you really ought; it would give you a salutary shock. I really haven't the heart to tell you any more.

Joy did not address her decision to leave David and Douglas with this purported monster for five months while she traveled to England to pursue Jack, nor did she acknowledge Bill's general sobriety during the final years of their marriage.

Jack followed up with "the two strongest letters he ever wrote," according to George Sayer, the friend who would become one of Lewis's biographers. "I cannot judge between your account and Joy's account of your married life," he said. That was beside the point; the past needed to be put aside for the sake of the boys' future happiness.

> Why should there not be a real, unconfused, reconciliation between you and them when they are grown up? By forcing them back at a moment when their hearts are breaking you will not facilitate this but render it permanently impossible. The boys remember you as a man who fired rifles thro' ceilings to relieve his temper, broke up chairs, wept in public, and broke a bottle over Douglas's head. David knew, and resented, the fact that you were living with your present wife while still married to his mother . . .
>
> Whose happiness wd. you foster by forcing them back to you now? Not your own. The most patient man on earth wdn't be happy with two resentful boys who regard themselves as prisoners in his house. Not your wife! You bring her two extra mouths to feed, both mouths belonging to boys who do not like her. And certainly not the boys!
>
> Wait, Bill, *wait*. Not now. A bone that breaks in a second takes long to heal. The relation between you and your sons has been broken. Give it time to mend. Forcible surgery (without anesthetics) such as you are proposing is not the way.

In the second letter, written the same day, Jack's language turned stronger.

> Your letter reached Joy after a day of agony. The effect was devastating. She felt that the only earthly hope she now has had been taken away. You have tortured one who was already on the rack; heaped extra weights on one who is being pressed to death. There is nothing she dreads so much as a return of the boys to your charge . . . Their return to the U.S.A. when their education is finished is of course quite a different matter. Now, bitterly against their will, coming on top of the most appalling tragedy that can happen to childhood (I went through it and know), tearing them from all that has already become familiar and shattering all sense of security that remains to them, it would be disastrous . . .

> If you do not relent, I shall of course be obliged to place every legal obstacle in your way.

Jack's admission to Bill—"I cannot judge between your account and Joy's account of your married life"—is astonishing. He loved her despite not knowing if he could fully trust her. After she died he would write to Joy: "We didn't idealize each other. We tried to keep no secrets. You knew most of the rotten places in me already. If you now see anything worse, I can take it. So can you. Rebuke, explain, mock, forgive. For this is one of the miracles of love; it gives—to both, but perhaps especially to the woman—a power of seeing through its own enchantments and yet not being disenchanted."

The matter turned out to be temporarily moot. Joy's condition seemed to reverse itself. The pain eased. One day she asked the nurses to lift her into a wheelchair. When they maneuvered her to a sitting position, she was surprised by how little discomfort she experienced. In late April, doctors performed new tests. The cancer was not discernibly progressing, and they cautiously pronounced her case "arrested." Not cured, but paused, "at least for the time being." It could become active again the next day, or not for three years—no one could say. The femur, everyone agreed, was a lost cause: Joy would never walk again. "I wish . . . they'd arrested the damn thing in time to leave me legs I could use," she joked. "It's so frustrating to have to lie in bed waiting for death when you're full of energy and feel perfectly well."

As her physical strength soared and she regained full use of her right arm, she refused to relinquish hope that the bone might knit back together. By the end of May 1957, nine months after her diagnosis, Joy needed no painkillers—not even aspirin—and the only medication she took was a single pill to help her sleep. If only she could walk fifty feet, "hobble around a little" in a leg brace, she could visit friends, go to the theater, take drives in the countryside with Jack. For now, when he was in Cambridge, she bided her time tucked in bed between Suzie, Jack's shaggy standard poodle, and a cat named Tom, crocheting afghans and knitting socks—"an amazing help with my spiritual difficulties" when her spirits were low, she told a friend of Jack's. "One can work off so many frustrations by stabbing away with a knitting needle! It's better to make pretty things, I find, than just useful ones." And she "superintended" the hired help: "I feel quite the lady of the manor!" The night nurse squabbled with the others until Joy "sacked her . . . amid universal rejoicing." Medical expenses had become exorbitant, and Joy no longer felt she needed her, anyhow. "She *seems* amazingly better," Jack wrote to Dorothy Sayers on June 25.

He, however, was not so well. Around the time Joy's cancer was pronounced arrested, Jack began having leg trouble of his own. At first it was assumed he'd pulled a muscle lifting Joy, but the pain got so bad that he could neither sit nor stand comfortably, and the slightest jolt made him cry out. A doctor diagnosed a slipped disc and prescribed a treatment regime of deep heat, massage, and X-rays. By mid-June, though, he was "completely immobilized." After a full examination by the pathologist Lord Howard Florey, Jack's condition was re-diagnosed as a "quite obscure" case of osteoporosis. The pain, he admitted, brought with it "an odd element of relief," for "it banishes all that wearisome sense of being no use." Meanwhile, he wrote, "poor Joy, after being the sole object of pity & anxiety can now perform the truly wifely function of fussing over me."

Despite their physical condition, they were blissfully happy. The house pulsed with love and laughter. They played Scrabble together—words in any language were fair game—and did crosswords. If Jack couldn't immediately think of the right word, he would make sensational comments about the ineptitude of the puzzle's author. They named Joy's bedpan after Shakespeare's Caliban and the "fish-tailed female invalid urinal" after Miranda. The boys entertained themselves with a family of pet mice. And one of the great blessings of Joy's second marriage was a second brother. The marriage elevated her relationship with Warnie from friendship to kinship, but they hardly needed a formality to augment the affinity that had long existed between them. "What Jack's marriage meant to me," Warnie recounted, "was that our home was enriched and enlivened by the presence of a witty, broad-minded, well-read, tolerant Christian whom I had rarely heard equaled as a conversationalist and whose company was a never ending source of enjoyment."

As for Jack, he began to experience Joy more fully, more deeply than he'd ever known another person. She was "like a garden," he later wrote. "Like a nest of gardens, wall within wall, hedge within hedge, more secret, more full of fragrant and fertile life, the further you entered." Joy opened herself to him fully, guided him into her spirit, taught him the pleasure of being fully known. As Lewis wrote later in *A Grief Observed,* "I once praised her for her 'masculine virtues.' But she soon put a stop to that by asking how I'd like to be praised for my feminine ones. It was a good *riposte,* dear. Yet there was something of the Amazon, something of Penthesileia and Camilla. And you, as well as I, were glad it should be there. You were glad I should recognize it."

They began to welcome visitors. John Christopher stopped by one day when he had a few hours to kill in Oxford, and the Lewises invited him in for tea. A mutual friend had told him that Joy was dying of cancer. He saw her leg, "wired up to the ceiling" in traction, and Jack barely able to raise himself to a standing position. But instead of a somber atmosphere, what he witnessed was astonishing: "I had never been in the presence of two people sharing a gladness so pervasive as to seem almost palpable . . . Although uplifting, the atmosphere was in no way febrile or pious. It was, on the contrary, extremely light and good humoured . . . I was so struck by this almost radiant happiness that bounced between them. I had never encountered two people who were so clearly happy in each other's company. And in love. Quite clearly in love."

Roger Lancelyn Green, an old friend, came for tea in early summer and, with his wife, June, became fast friends of the Lewises. "Lewis the Family Man," Roger noted, "was a role he accepted with kindly amusement." Roger and June's son Scirard would start at Dane Court with Douglas in the fall. They offered to pick up Douglas at the beginning of the term, help that Joy and Jack gladly welcomed. "We'll have Douglas booted and spurred and waiting," Jack said. He was becoming a wonderful father to the boys. "It was amusing to find Jack talking like the most conventional of fathers about school uniforms and pocket money," George Sayer recalled. "The boys' clothes must be entirely correct, that is, just the same as those worn by others. They must have the average amount of pocket money. They must not suffer as he and Warren had done from the shame of not being able to afford things commonly bought by their schoolmates."

Other visitors passed through. Ironically, Joy found herself entertaining a parade of "American lady tourists who seem to regard my poor husband as one of the sights in Oxford which everyone must 'do,' like Magdalen Tower! They usually invite themselves to tea, so my life is unexpectedly lively. One of the most recent was a pathologist—she discussed all the least savoury body processes throughout tea, and lectured us on Higher Indian Thought afterward." Joy described to Bill how "some of them are exactly like the Americans in English novels, a breed I never believed in till now. Pompous, humourless, very slow on the uptake by English standards, ill-educated, full of naïve earnest 'uplift'—I suppose they've all been hiding in the Middle West. I never met them in the States myself!"

But one American visitor came especially for her. Joy had written to Belle to tell her about both the marriage and the cancer. On August 25 her old friend arrived with gifts of French lipstick, perfume, silver earrings, and hankies for Joy, and brandy and a tie for Jack. It broke Belle's heart to see Joy incapacitated, carted off to the hospital on a regular basis for radiation treatments, shot up with testosterone that caused the growth of facial hair. But Joy was so happy. She told Belle, "Now I know that it's true—what the movies and fairy tales tell you." True love really exists. "She was in love for the first time in her life," Belle believed. Yet while Jack clearly adored Joy, Belle sensed that "had she remained healthy, I'm not sure that he would have married her . . . [T]hey would have just enjoyed each other, but I'm not sure he would have gone that far. She wanted it very much."

The palpable intensity of their love astonished everyone who observed them together. Joy was radiant, more settled in spirit than ever before. Jack felt the same, despite his own severe pain. Illness was the norm in their marriage—the occasion for it, even. "My heart is breaking and I was never so happy before: at any rate there is more in life than I knew about," he told Dorothy Sayers. Joy's presence in his life made him think about love in a new way. "I have bad spasms both of body and soul, but they all go on amidst a sort of ballet of agape, storge and eros." To Dom Bede Griffiths he wrote: "It is nice to have arrived at all this by something which began in Agape, proceeded to Philia, then became Pity, and only after that, Eros. As if the highest of these, Agape, had successfully undergone the sweet humiliation of an incarnation."

THEN, A MIRACLE happened. Joy had been flat on her back for over nine months, but in July she found she was able to roll over, push herself up. As summer progressed, she even stood for a few moments. Her face looked less drawn, "far livelier," Jack thought. "She continues (apparently) to mend." Meanwhile, he had to start wearing a surgical belt that he described as "like your grandmother's corsets. It gives me a wonderful schoolboy figure!" he joked. His own pain "didn't matter," he told George Sayer, as long as Joy continued to improve. By September, Joy had made incredible progress. "My wife continues to defeat all the doctors' predictions most gloriously and my own little trouble is much eased." She could stand for longer stretches. "Can it be?—dare one hope? I suppose not." But their lives were full of merriment and delight. "We are at present being accorded all the privileges of shorn lambs!" Moments of discouragement lingered, when they felt the weight of doctors' predictions. "It'll be nice when we all wake up from this life which has indeed something like nightmare about it," Jack wrote to a friend. In October, a year after her fall, Joy got a cane and practiced taking a step, then another. By the end of that month she could hobble about with a nurse by her side. In November she climbed a single step. "The improvement in my wife's condition is, in the proper use of the word, miraculous," Jack told another friend on November 12. "Now not only is there no pain, but she is *walking*. She can now get about the ground floor of the house alone, with of course, a stick and a special shoe for the leg which is permanently shortened; and here of course there is no hope of any improvement; but when I see her state now, and contrast it with that in which she was six months ago, I realize what deep cause for gratitude we both have."

Their love continued to grow through laughter and conversation. In the fall they spent a lot of time talking about a new book Jack was thinking through. He had been experiencing another dry spell. Austin Farrer suggested a treatment of the Psalms, a book people turn to in times of trouble, pain, and desperation. Jack liked the idea and got to work on *Reflections on Psalms*.

Joy kept improving throughout November; she could walk about fifty feet at a stretch, climb as many as three steps, and "use the john like the big folks—no small triumph that! Shall soon be able to ride in a car and get another look at the outside world. I'm extremely lame even with a raised shoe, but it's a damn sight better than lying flat on my back! At present all my strength goes into building myself up and running the household, but I begin to hope I can write again."

Two months later, on the morning of January 14, Jack's driver, Clifford Morris, pulled up to the Kilns, and Joy limped out of the house leaning on a cane. Her left shoe had been fitted with a three-inch lift to compensate for the lost bone. Jack was at her elbow. They settled beside each other in the backseat, and Clifford steered down Kilns Lane onto the main road, driving out of Oxford, leaving Wingfield Hospital behind, coasting through the countryside to Cambridge. Joy and Jack debated some esoteric subject or other, verbally "spar[ring] away like two boxers." When they arrived at their destination, she eased out of the car, lunched with Jack, kissed him good-bye, and was driven home to the Kilns.

It was a successful test run, an outing that could not have been possible even a month earlier, and Joy only continued to improve. In early March her blood count was almost normal; six weeks later, new X-rays showed her femur to be "firm as a rock." Even her doctors used the word "miraculous." Jack said he was tempted to pronounce "a double miracle," that is, "recovery for her, and for me the love that passed me by in youth and middle age." He wondered about Bide's laying on of hands on the day of their marriage, and his own prayers to take on Joy's pain. "The intriguing thing is that while I (for no discoverable reason) was losing the chalcium from my bones, Joy, who needed it much more, was gaining it in hers," Jack remarked to his American friend Sheldon Vanauken, who had recently lost his own wife to cancer, an experience he would recount in his spiritual memoir *A Severe Mercy*. Jack continued: "One dreams of a Charles Williams substitution! Well, never was a gift more gladly given: but one must not be fanciful." In an essay for the *Atlantic Monthly* called "The Efficacy of Prayer," Jack includes Joy's recovery as an example, though admits that he could not with certainty ascribe the miracle to prayer: "The thing we pray for may happen, but how can we ever know it was not going to happen anyway? Even if the thing were indisputably miraculous it would not follow that the miracle had occurred because of our prayers." Either way, he gave credit to God, and they eased into a new reality: Joy had more time to live.

· 16 ·

1958–1960

No one could say whether the miracle was a stay of execution or a complete pardon, but Joy had managed her year with Jack after all—a year and counting—"gift time," he called it, "an uncovenanted mercy" that had her unwrapping each moment like a child at a birthday party. As "lady of the manor," Joy began renovating and redecorating the Kilns "with a vengeance." Significant repairs hadn't been done in some thirty years. Primeval light switches sparked when flipped; the floorboards were suspect, patches of roof bereft of tiles. Joy joked that if the bookcases lining the walls were moved, the house would fall in. She ordered the plumbing updated and the house painted inside and out. Roofers, carpenters, and electricians descended. The tattered carpets were removed, not just worn but filthy with cigarette ashes that Jack and Warnie flicked on the floor as moth deterrent. More than a decade after the end of the war, the army blankets–turned–blackout curtains were taken down from the windows, washed, and subsequently trashed when they disintegrated in the laundry. In their place, Joy installed curtains in a shade of blue just a bit darker than Wedgwood. She bought a modern gas stove, new mattresses, new dishes, and an expensive new tea set; when she told Jack how much it cost, he covered his face with his hands. "But I got it at half price," she added, with a smirk of mischief.

Joy's spending on the house was the only source of marital discord that friends noted. Jack was accustomed to excessive frugality, and his scale of expenditure hadn't changed since before the war. He knew how much money he needed to live comfortably yet without extravagance; most everything else was given away. Mounting home improvement costs, on top of Joy's medical expenses, staff salaries, and the boys' tuition—with university to come—had him worried, if needlessly so. "Tell [Jack] that he won't go broke," Joy grumbled to George Sayer when he popped by one day. Jack "could easily earn far more than he did. He could, for instance, write articles for top American publications, such as the *Saturday Evening Post*. He was a wonderfully quick and fluent writer whose work Americans loved." Though unable to understand Jack's resistance to writing for a quick buck, she abided by his gentle yet firm objection to her proposal that they purchase elegant new furniture to replace the Kilns' shabby yet functional pieces, settling instead for reupholstering the couch to match the curtains and stripping "a horrid yellow finish like congealed egg-yolk" off the bedroom chests and wardrobe to reveal the hidden treasure of simple oak. "Tell me, isn't it less like a tenement in the South Bronx?" she asked Sayer, who couldn't have known the first thing about tenements in the South Bronx. "The Kilns is now a real home," she proclaimed, "with paint on the walls, ceilings properly repaired, clean sheets on the beds." Jack didn't let on that "visitors to the Kilns were often surprised by the lack of taste and quality" of her decorating decisions.

Perhaps such critical assessment stemmed from the fact that some of those visitors would have found fault with anything Joy did. Most of Jack's friends—especially the Inklings—had always viewed Joy with circumspection, even derision. Jack "thrust her forward at them, almost demanding that they should like her. He, who had expected his men friends to leave their own marriages entirely on one side when they came to the Inklings, now assumed that they would all accept her as an equal without a moment's questioning." Instead, they were baffled and disturbed by what Tolkien called a "very strange marriage." He felt she had taken advantage of Jack, just as Mrs. Moore had. According to Sayer, "Tolkien was gloomy about the terrible strains and anxieties Jack was suffering: Warren's drunkenness, two rather difficult boys, and 'a strange marriage' to 'a sick and domineering woman.'" The Gresham boys were not particularly difficult—David, a brooder, read voraciously; Douglas was spirited and gregarious—but children made convenient fodder for Jack's friends' arguments against Joy. "[Jack] did not help matters by overpraising her," the Inklings believed. "He spoke of her almost as if she were an angelic being; whereas in their sight she looked, it had to be admitted, physically unattractive," wrote Humphrey Carpenter, who knew the Inklings and wrote a book about them. "And to those who knew something of her background she seemed to represent everything that Lewis had strenuously opposed . . . She was also, which did not recommend her to the more insular among them, American and Jewish. Had Charles Williams been there to observe, he would undoubtedly have remarked with delight that in choosing a wife for Lewis the Omnipotence had displayed its 'usual neat sardonic touch.'"

Other of Jack's friends embraced Joy, if initially out of allegiance to him. "I liked her—almost automatically," said Sheldon Vanauken, "since if Jack loved her, she must be likeable." He conceded, though, that those who disliked her did so "with reason." Simon Barrington-Ward, chaplain at Magdalene College, encountered Joy when Jack brought her to lunch with the fellows. "She started by being a bit aggressive," he remembered, "but in no time it all seemed to be going very well and she ended up most genially!" Roger and June Lancelyn Green genuinely held Joy in high regard from the start. "She was a marvelous person, absolutely vivacious, full of life, full of interest," Roger recalled. "June loved her even more than I did . . . They got on very well together. She was . . . absolutely the right person for Lewis in those days. Absolutely brought sparks out of each other . . . I never thought of him marrying, but, my goodness, this was the ideal." Even those like George Sayer who would always harbor misgivings about Joy could not deny that the relationship was extraordinary. "What impressed me most about their marriage was its natural quality," Sayer remarked. "There was no striving to be something they were not, to be clever or even good. They just were. They accepted each other simply, naturally, without fret or fuss. They were kind to each other and unusually quick to grasp the nuances of each other's thoughts." No matter what people thought of Joy as a person, her union with Jack was an undeniable success.

JOY TRANSFORMED NOT only the look of the Kilns but also its cuisine. Strong enough to take a taxi to the market with Mrs. Miller, she pointed out exotic ingredients and even helped a bit in the kitchen. "Let's try that on them and see how they like it," she'd say with a mischievous twinkle. Under her direction, Mrs. Miller's repertoire of standard English soups and meats expanded to include schav (sorrel soup), borscht (cold beet soup), and gehackte leber (chopped chicken liver)—all immensely unpopular but received with amusement. Dinner was a convivial affair. Mrs. Miller would bang a gong and then wheel in a trolley of dishes from the kitchen as the family gathered around a table dressed in a lace tablecloth—crocheted by Joy—and cork placemats with pictures of horse-drawn carriages. Warnie said grace, and everyone said "Amen." When the boys were home, dinner table conversation revolved around "Davy botanizing, trotting out Latin names and nuclear chemistry formulae and gruesome medical details and Doug discussing with great expertise different car models, planes, soccer, rugger, cricket, horses and fishing."

In April, Joy and Jack celebrated their marriage with a long-overdue honeymoon at a country inn, their first trip together. Jack felt guilty and laughed at himself for "the absurdity" of it: "I'm such a confirmed old bachelor that I couldn't help feeling I was being rather naughty ('Staying with a woman at a hotel!' Just like people in the newspapers!)." He had at some point consulted Dr. Havard about the advisability of sex for a man of sixty who was somewhat overweight and inclined to high blood pressure. Sex was permissible "if you are careful and sensible," cautioned the doctor. Once the marriage was consummated, one thing is certain: the newlyweds' respective health conditions did not hinder what became a fulfilling sex life. Jack was "a magnificent lover," Joy told Howard, with her characteristic openness verging on the inappropriate, "despite his age" and many years as a celibate bachelor. She was glad she hadn't needed a mastectomy; he loved to caress her breasts.

The April holiday was merely a sweet prelude to an extended "belated honeymoon" to Ireland they began planning for July. Arranging a major event more than a month in advance was risky, but Jack was eager to introduce his bride to his homeland. A nurse still came to help her bathe, but for the most part Joy was self-sufficient. A new hobby—shooting pigeons (or, rather, "shoot[ing] *at*" pigeons, Jack joked)—had her limping around the woods behind the Kilns that summer, nine-millimeter Webley & Scott shotgun in hand, attempting to augment the supper pot. "Though the pot is not noticeably fuller," Jack told a friend, "it is wonderful that she should be able to make such a strenuous attempt to fill it." She also wielded the gun to run off "hooligans" who had been trespassing on the grounds for years, carving graffiti into tree bark, robbing the orchard, and generally making a noisy nuisance. When Joy was bedridden, she once looked up to see them peering through the window at her. Jack, enraged, scared them away. She suggested installing a fence. "It's no use, my love. They'll only cut the wire," he said, voice laden with defeat. "Well," she replied, "if they cut the wire, I'll buy a shotgun." Cradling the gun on a walk in the woods with Jack one day, she glimpsed one of the young troublemakers carrying a longbow and a quiver full of arrows. Jack sharply informed him that he was trespassing on private property and must leave at once. The intruder mockingly nocked an arrow. Jack stepped protectively in front of Joy, who, having raised her shotgun, called out in frustration, "God damn it, Jack, get out of my line of fire!" The neighborhood children believed she would pull the trigger. When the Walsh family visited with their daughters, a boy ran up to the girls in the woods, warning that they'd better leave "or Mrs. Lewis will shoot you."

A trip to Ireland was entirely feasible. On July 4, fifteen months after Joy was taken home to the Kilns to die, she and Jack boarded an airplane for the first time in their lives. Both would have preferred sailing to flying—especially Jack, who was terrified by the concept—but the duration of a sea voyage, combined with the risk of falling on the slippery decks of a pitching steamer, rendered that option moot. Jack prayed as the plane took off into a storybook cloudscape that had them both spellbound. Rifts in the clouds offered glimpses of the Welsh mountains. The sky cleared over the Irish Sea until the sun cast a spotlight on Ireland, and the headlands glinted.

Arthur met them at the airport in his car and drove them to the Old Inn in Crawfordsburn, a partly thatch-roofed seventeenth-century structure where Jack, Arthur, and other friends had convened in years past. Joy met some of Jack's family over dinner, recalled Joan Lewis Murphy, a cousin. To the relatives she seemed a bit standoffish, as private family jokes and stories swirled around her. Her easy use of expletives amused some relatives and shocked others. Joy and Jack went to Belfast, Rathmullan, and Lough Swilly, and took a leisurely drive to Carlingford Mountain and through the Mourne Mountains, which swept to the sea. Although Joy thought the villages themselves were as ugly as towns in upstate New York, she found the rocky hillsides as enchanting as the roughest New England cliffs. They strolled on yellow beaches—Joy could walk almost a mile now—as loud Atlantic breakers crashed beside them and gulls flew above. They saw peat bogs, waterfalls, fields of sheep and braying gray donkeys, hedges of honeysuckle, rolling hills robed in purple heather, rosy wild thyme, and emerald-green grass. "It is the most beautiful place I've ever seen," Joy declared. After a week's stay at the Royal Hotel in Donegal, they returned to Oxford, drunk on natural beauty and love. "[We] feasted on love," Jack wrote of their marriage, "every mode of it—solemn and merry, romantic and realistic, sometimes as dramatic as a thunderstorm, sometimes as comfortable and unemphatic as putting on your soft slippers. No cranny of heart or body remained unsatisfied."

That love—"every mode of it"—inspired one of Jack's greatest works of nonfiction, *The Four Loves,* conceived auspiciously after the April honeymoon when Chad Walsh urged an acquaintance at the Episcopal Radio-TV Foundation of Atlanta to ask Jack if he would record a series of fifteen-minute talks on a subject of his choice, to be broadcast on the *Episcopal Radio Hour.* Jack agreed. "The subject I want to say something about in the near future, in some form or another," he responded, "is the four Loves—Storge, Philia, Eros, and Agape." Affection, friendship, romantic love, and charity—the overlapping yet distinct varieties of love. He well knew and had long practiced three of the four, but not eros in its fullest, purest distillation. In his consecrated marriage with Joy, all four loves converged in purpose and passion.

Jack finished the scripts after returning from Ireland, and the following month went to London to meet a representative from Episcopal Radio-TV, Caroline Rakestraw, and record ten broadcasts, an experience that turned out to be rather trying.

"Today I want to discuss . . ." Jack began.

"Professor Lewis," interrupted Rakestraw, "couldn't you say instead 'Let us think together, you and I about . . . '?"

Jack replied that no, he could not.

"*But* we want you to give the feeling of *embracing* them."

Jack said that "if they wanted an embracer they had the wrong man." At one point she asked him to "sit absolutely silent before the microphone for a minute and a half 'so they could feel his living presence.'" (Joy told him he should charge double for that.)

What he did convey, when he had the chance, was so scandalous that the radio station—conservative and evangelical in 1950s America—declined to air it. Lewis provided a candid exploration of eroticism, going so far as to assert that "the roughness, even fierceness, of some erotic play . . . is harmless and wholesome." He disagreed with society's "ludicrous and portentous solemnization of sex," explaining: "Our advertisements, at their sexiest, paint the whole business in terms of the rapt, the intense, the swoony-devout; seldom a hint of gaiety. And the psychologists have so bedeviled us with the infinite importance of complete sexual adjustment and the all but impossibility of achieving it, that I could believe some young couples now go to it with the complete works of Freud, Kraft-Ebbing, Havelock Ellis and Dr. Stopes spread out on bed-tables all round them . . . We have reached the stage at which nothing is more needed than a roar of old-fashioned laughter." He was advocating not flippancy but fun. "Eating is also serious; theologically, as the vehicle of the Blessed Sacrament; ethically in view of our duty to feed the hungry; socially, because the table is from time immemorial the place for talk; medically, as all dyspeptics know." His point was that we shouldn't behave around the table as we would in church. And Lewis could certainly be talking of his experiences with Joy when he writes of Venus as a "mischievous spirit" who "makes a game of us . . . a game of catch-as-catch-can, and the escapes and tumbles and head-on collisions are to be treated as a romp." Laughter was the right response of all "sensible lovers," he asserted.

ONE OF JOY'S few new friends was a woman named Jean Wakeman, a spunky motoring journalist for *Good Housekeeping*. They had met at Studley Priory, where Joy and Jack made routine stops for beer, tea, a meal, or a romantic weekend getaway. At a pub one day Joy looked up from her seat to see Jean, a woman a bit younger than herself limp with a cane toward the bar. They made each other's acquaintance, bonding over writing and the challenges of their handicaps. Jean had been lame since birth, courtesy of an incompetent obstetrician. Soon she was a fixture at the Kilns, filling a void of companionship during Jack's weekdays in Cambridge, taking Joy on long rides through the English countryside in the name of road-testing new car models, and driving the boys to and from school. A devout Anglican with humor and chutzpah to rival Joy's, Jean became perhaps the closest kindred spirit she'd ever known besides Jack.

In September, Jean took Joy and the boys on holiday to Solva, a quaint Welsh fishing village that smelled of brine and resounded with the cries of gulls. They stayed at a modest hostelry called the Ship Inn, with dark narrow corridors, low ceilings, and a pub where local lobstermen swigged beer and merrily belted patriotic ballads. A pair of boat captains organized a day trip to the picturesque island of Skomer, in St. Brides Bay. Joy and Jean were a pathetic sight when they arrived at the harborside and cautiously began picking their way across the dangerously slick docks. Joy, like her friend, was indifferent to the looks of pity cast their way. Jean had known nothing else, and Joy admired her all the more for it. When they reached the boat, rocking impossibly beside the dock, Joy deferred to experience: "Well, Jean, now what do we do?" Before Jean could think of a solution, a captain bounded off the deck and gallantly carried Jean, and then Joy, aboard the boat. On Skomer, an island of birds and cliffs, they delighted in their sightings of puffins, skuas, and seals, while the boys roamed the shore and climbed hills of bracken.

JOY'S CHRONIC LIMP and surgery scars were the only physical reminders that she had ever been ill. "I feel that resurrection is almost a more accurate word than recovery," Jack told Tolkien as 1958 came to a close. The celebration lasted through the winter, spring, and summer of 1959. Jack and Joy read poetry aloud to each other: A. E. Housman made tears run down their cheeks. Joy took frequent trips to Cambridge to lunch with Jack or attend events—listening to him lecture on Pepys or accompanying him to a staging of *Antigone*. They hosted dinner parties and luncheons. T. S. Eliot, once a literary adversary and now Jack's colleague on the official Commission to Revise the Psalter for the Book of Common Prayer, invited them to dinner with his "statuesque blonde young wife." Joy worked closely with Warnie on *The Scandalous Regent: A Life of Philippe, Duc d'Orléans, 1674–1723, and of His Family,* a book he would dedicate "To My Sister-in-Law Joy Davidman." Jack was finishing editing his radio talks into a book version, *The Four Loves,* his essay "The Efficacy of Prayer," and a piece he would sell to the *Saturday Evening Post* called "Screwtape Proposes a Toast."

Joy and Jack felt bold enough to make plans for the future. When Roger Lancelyn Green visited one night and told them about a recent trip to Greece, Joy spoke of her longing to visit the ancient country. Roger suggested they all go during the next Easter break. Other than during the war and on a boyhood trip to France with his mother and

Warnie, Jack had never traveled outside the British Isles, and he had little desire to do so now. He was especially hesitant about Greece, concerned that seeing the sites of great classical legends and historical events might restrict his pleasure in them. Joy's enthusiasm, however, was infectious. When Roger offered to make all the arrangements, Jack agreed. "It wd. mean a great deal to both of us," he conceded, "to have stood even once on the Acropolis." Plans were worked out in the subsequent months. They would travel from April 3 through 14 with a tour group of about thirty people. Every day would be packed with walks, bus rides, and ruins.

As a cool, wet spring opened the primroses and lined the drive with sunbursts of daffodils, Joy and Jack knelt in the dirt side by side, digging and planting, something they hadn't imagined would ever be possible. Come summer, they anticipated, they would glory in the scent of roses and feast on peas, beans, peppers, eggplant, green tomatoes, turnips, and all kinds of "fancy squashes." Joy was almost completely content: "Woods, garden, books, pets, intelligent company, and lots of love—no wonder I continue to grow stronger." If only, she lamented, she could shake off the "rheumatic aches and pains" that came and went with the weather. In a phenomenon that continued to gratify and astound them, Jack again seemed to take on some of the pain. After a particularly notable spell, he wrote from Cambridge: "Well darling? I hope I shall get a letter tomorrow saying that all those aches have chased themselves off. Mine (as has happened before) arrived a few days later: knees on Monday night, chest, belly, back, and hips yesterday."

The aches did nothing to slow either of them down. Jack's annual excursion to Ireland was now Joy's as well, although they nearly had to cancel after receiving notice that he hadn't paid taxes on a bumper crop of royalties two years earlier. Joy did not relish the thought of pinching pennies while so much of his money was being funneled directly into the Agapony Fund. Although not all of Jack's books were doing well—*Till We Have Faces* was a flop, and the Narnia series just puttered along ("Jack's juveniles have a steady, small sale . . . but we'll never get rich from *those*," Joy speculated)—*Surprised by Joy* and *Screwtape*, in particular, continued to soar. The tax issue turned out to be a false alarm, and in the end they got a refund, but not before Joy made it her mission to hold on to more of Jack's royalties. In another classic contradiction, she, who could not have survived in England without Jack's Agapony Fund, spent months attempting to dismantle it. To her great frustration, she was mostly unsuccessful. "I still have not been able to get Jack's affairs untangled from the lifetime charitable trust he set up, which takes nearly all his royalties," she wrote to Bill that summer, "so we are by no means well off. The money flows in alright, but we don't keep it!" When they did get to Ireland—a three-week trip beginning June 21, largely retracing the previous year's visit—their driver suffered the consequences. Major Frank Henry, brother of a former Kilns housekeeper, lived in Ireland and had served as a chauffer for Jack and Warnie in years past. The Lewises traditionally paid for all expenses: gas, meals, and hotel. But Joy would cover only half the gas, lunches, and drinks along the route. The major, like so many people who met Joy, used the word "abrasive" when describing her.

On October 13, 1959, almost exactly three years after Joy's initial diagnosis, the sword of Damocles fell. Despite months of "rheumatic aches," Joy allowed herself to expect nothing less than another clean bill of health when she met with doctors after a routine exam at Churchill Hospital. Jack was by her side as they explained the damning evidence: the X-rays revealed cancerous spots on numerous bones throughout her body.

It was impossible to reconcile herself to the news, not only because she and Jack didn't want to believe it, but also because, apart from intermittent pain that was by no means debilitating, Joy didn't feel the least bit ill. "We shouldn't know she had cancer if we didn't know," Jack said. "The condemned cell *looks* like an ordinary and comfortable sitting room." Yet doctors discouraged hope, predicting a year or two at best—and that only with extensive radiation or testosterone treatments, which they called "rearguard actions."

The prognosis was no more dire than during the first bout, and Jack and Joy prayed for another miracle. While they knew of no cases in which the same miracle was bestowed twice, they also knew that mysticism is not systematic; the cancer's return was "irrelevant to the question of whether the previous recovery was miraculous," Jack reasoned. "There can be miraculous reprieve as well as miraculous pardon, and Lazarus was raised from the dead to die again." Above all, they prayed that "whatever is [God's] will for the body, the minds of both of us may remain unharmed; that faith unimpaired may strengthen us, contrition soften us and peace make us joyful." Joy and Jack both knew they needed divine help.

Walks, drives to Cambridge, household management—all continued, if dampened by radiation-induced nausea and lethargy. Within weeks, though, walking too much or too fast triggered severe pain, so Joy walked less, and more slowly. Codeine became a prerequisite to daily living. "My skeleton is now such a haywire job that the slightest strain jerks something loose," she wrote to Bill in December. And the cancer showed no mercy: she began to discover "lumps here and there." Some of them "melt[ed] away beautifully" under radiation, but by the new year every examination revealed further metastases. "My wife's condition," Jack solemnly explained to a friend, "is v[ery] like that of a battalion which is almost daily fired on from a new direction. It silences these fires, but new ones always break out till it becomes evident that one is in fact surrounded." Or, as Joy described her situation with characteristic sarcasm, "I've now got so many cancers at work on me that I expect them to start organizing a union."

The defensive levity was more about comforting Jack than soothing herself. The impending loss shattered him. It is not known whether Joy ever showed him her love sonnets, but now he took a turn writing one for her. In a poem called "As the Ruin Falls," Jack admitted to having lived selfishly until only recently; she had changed all that:

> Only that now you have taught me (but how late) my lack.
> I see the chasm. And everything you are was making

> My heart into a bridge by which I might get back
> From exile, and grow man. And now the bridge is breaking.
>
> For this I bless you as the ruin falls. The pains
> You give me are more precious than all other gains.

Joy supported him more than the other way around, Jack told friends. The dawn of his every day was "dreadful," he admitted, "the waking each morning—the moment at which it all flows back." Joy's Daylight Street had merged with his own path, but now the route was splitting. "We were setting out on different roads," he later reflected, and her impending absence terrified him. He already felt isolated from her. But as they lay beside each other one day, Joy said, "Even if we both died at exactly the same moment . . . it would be just as much a separation as the one you're so afraid of." She quoted "Alone into the Alone." That was how she felt; "and how immensely improbable that it should be otherwise," Jack wrote in *A Grief Observed,* a small book that would grow from journals kept after her death. This time around, Joy's miracle was fortitude instead of frenzied desperation, courage imperfect in its humanity but imbued with contentment that defied her condition and love that transcended her self. The growth of her faith through illness, pain, and life with Lewis augmented her virtues. "Courage was her shield," Jean recalled. "She was the bravest person I knew."

There was of course deep sorrow, mourning for the loss of their future, anger, and self-pity. Jack wrote to Peter Bide:

> Joy says (do you agree?) that we needn't be too afraid of questionings and expostulations: it was the impatience of Job not the theodicies of Elihu that were pleasing to God. Does He like us to 'stand up to Him' a bit? Certainly He cannot like mere flattery—resentment masquerading as submission thru' fear. How impossible it wd. be now to face it without rage if God Himself had not shared the horrors of the world He made! I know this is Patripassianism.

> But the other way of putting it, however theologically defensible, lets in (psychologically) perhaps a more serious error.

Jack seemed grateful to his wife for this perspective, which would shape the tone and content of *A Grief Observed.*

ALL ALONG, GREECE hung in the balance. Joy insisted that canceling the vacation was out of the question, and Jack didn't try to convince her otherwise, comparing her wish to a condemned man's selection of a last meal, though he feared "it was madness"; in her state, the trip could kill her. So be it, Joy contended: "I'd rather go out with a bang than a whimper, particularly on the steps of the Parthenon."

On April 3, 1960, Joy and Jack met the Lancelyn Greens at London Airport and boarded a small Viking bound for Athens by way of Lyons, Naples, and Brindisi. From the air, Joy marveled at the Alps rising toward the plane, as if Earth were flexing her muscles in competition with the summits of Joy's imagination—the crest of Fairyland, the Grey Mountain. There would be many heights in Greece, and if she had the strength, she would have liked to climb them all.

June and Roger had been kept abreast of Joy's condition throughout the previous tentative months and were pleased to see the Lewises in a festive mood despite the circumstances. During the Naples layover, Jack merrily kicked off the trip by summoning enough Italian to procure "large quantities" of Chianti. But when they landed in Athens after midnight, a long, wincing walk from the plane to the terminal made Joy's limitations obvious. June and Roger were surprised by the intensity of her pain. Joy smiled through the agony, concerned about making herself "a dreary nuisance," but her suffering was plain to see despite her best efforts to conceal it. They immediately learned the Greek word for "wheelchair"; they would need one at their disposal.

Joy spent part of every day in bed, skipping nearly half the group's activities, but happily hobbling through as much as she could manage. There was a day trip through Eleusis and Megara, with a stop for drinks by the Corinth Canal before pressing onward to Mycenae; they walked between walls of Cyclopean masonry through the Lion Gate, but Joy could go no farther than the Grave Circle. When they flew to Rhodes, Joy felt unable to tour the Old City, but traveled with the group to Kamiros and gazed at Turkey from a hilltop. On a day trip to Lindos, she and Jack wandered around the village while the group climbed to the Citadel. When they visited the Palace of Minos, she had to stop at its entrance. But Joy's limitations only seemed to heighten her pleasure in what she did experience. She adored Rhodes, calling it "pure Garden of Eden." The Greeks were a splendid, hard-working people, she thought, and the country was more vast than she imagined: "incredible mountains, shimmering mists of olive trees, herds of black goats, donkeys and women spinning in the sun and the burning blue sea."

On Easter Sunday the group attended a Greek Orthodox service —all white candles, red eggs, crucifixes, men in hats and robes. Jack found the priests more visually alluring than those of Protestant or Reformed churches. After lunch they flew to Heraklion on Crete and enjoyed a semi-disastrous but uproariously hilarious dinner. The restaurant where they had reservations was inexplicably closed, so they walked to a nearby resort where a lengthy wait was followed by a barely passable meal. A noisy band providing sub-par music was the last straw for Joy. "[She] finally began flicking bread-pellets at the nearest musician," Roger recorded in his diary, "and the four of us whiled away the time by writing alternate lines of the following doggerel":

JACK: A pub-crawl through the glittering isles of Greece,
JOY: I wish it left my ears a moment's peace!
JUNE: If once the crashing Cretans ceased to bore,
ROGER: The drums of England would resist no more.
JACK: No more they *can* resist. For mine are broken!
JOY: He has been hit by a good shot of Joy's!
JACK: What aim! What strength! What purpose and what poise!

When Roger realized that alcohol was the only half-effective remedy for Joy's pain, he worked to make it swiftly available at every stop. He became "adept at diving into the nearest taverna, ordering 'tessera ouzo,' and having them ready at a convenient table by the time June had helped Jack and Joy out of coach or car and brought them in." When Joy hurt herself climbing up and down the steps of the tour bus, Jack hired a car.

On one of their favorite days, their Greek driver took them to Daphne, where they toured a fifteenth-century Byzantine church and saw the ruins of the Temple of Apollo. "I had some ado to prevent Joy (and myself) from relapsing into Paganism," Jack later recounted to Chad. "It was hard not to pray to Apollo the Healer. But somehow one didn't feel it wd. have been very wrong—wd. have only been addressing Christ *sub specie Apollinis* [under the appearance of Apollo]." Then to Thebes road, to the pass over Mount Cithaeron. There they stopped at a tavern for ouzo before proceeding through vineyards, olive groves, and pine forests to the head of the Gulf of Corinth, where they explored more castle ruins and stopped for a meal in a little village called Aigosthena.

There was only one tiny taverna there, right on the shore. The foursome found a table. Cithaeron rose on one side; behind Megara on the other side, the mountains. Ouzo accompanied an appetizer of pickled octopus. The host showed them red mullets, still glinting wet from the sea, then fried them up. There was tender fried squid, ewe's milk cheese, and fresh oranges. Retsina flowed in abundance, "freshly drawn from the great cask in the half-cellar at the back of the taverna." Waves gently kissed the shore; bees hummed and cicadas sang. They sat for hours, enjoying spirited conversation interspersed with stretches of serene silence. "This was the most memorable day on the whole tour," Roger recorded in his diary, "and one which Jack said afterwards was among the supreme days of his life—the last of the great days of perfect happiness." Despite her constant discomfort, Joy was blissful with Jack by her side, June remembered. "I just have memories of them sitting together and enjoying each other in the balmy Greek air. Every night was like a dinner party."

But it was the enterprise of their first day in Greece that seemed to carry the most symbolic weight in Joy's life. When she awoke that morning, at the Hotel Cosmopolis, near Omonia Square, she was not well enough to join the group on a trip to Marathon; instead, she and Jack hung back, reserving energy for the afternoon tour of Athens —including the anticipated Acropolis, which she vowed to climb if it killed her. Recently Joy had been able to walk only about a hundred yards at a time, but she felt strong as she began her uphill climb. The sky turned perfectly blue except for a small tuft of cloud here and there. Joy walked up and up, limping through the Sacred Way, finally hobbling to the very highest point she could reach. "It was as if she was divinely supported," Jack said. As Joy put it, "Athena got me up the Acropolis and all round it!"

Joy sat down with Jack on the steps of the Propylaea, the majestic Pentelic marble entrance to the Acropolis, "drinking in the beauty of the Parthenon and Erechtheum." They gazed at the vacant shell of columns, a broken relic of earthly hopes, the skeletal remains of Athens's golden age, when citizens, politicians, and philosophers believed that together they could create a utopic society. Basking in the bright Aegean sunshine with Jack beside her and three months left to live, Joy could get no closer to heaven on earth. She had climbed one of the world's greatest heights, and all around her were ruins. Beautiful ruins.

Epilogue

Joy returned from Greece in a "*nunc dimittis* [now lettest thou depart] . . . frame of mind," Jack wrote to Chad; the trip was, "beyond hope, her greatest lifelong, this-worldly, desire." But the overexertion had taken a toll, and the cancer was in full command. There were last-ditch efforts and hopes: on May 20, Joy had her right breast removed (she "became an Amazon," she joked), and there followed fleeting fantasies of Ireland in summer; but by mid-June she was unable to make her routine end-of-term trip to Cambridge. Sometimes Warnie pushed her in the wheelchair to the library or up to the pond or greenhouse to inspect the plants, but they all knew the end was near.

On June 19, Jack stayed up all night with Joy while she vomited. "'Nurse,'" she cried out in the morning, "'this is the end, I know now I'm dying.'" Joy asked that Doug be sent for. David was expected home soon. Warnie prayed that death would come swiftly to end her suffering. She pleaded with the doctors: "Finish me off quick, I won't have another operation," and fell into a drug-induced coma. But Joy had one last reprieve, a few weeks of consciousness and conversations. She spent her final night on earth, July 12, reading a play aloud with Jack and playing Scrabble. On the morning of the thirteenth, she woke Warnie at 6:15 with screams of agony. Warnie called out to Jack. Jack summoned the doctor, who arrived within the hour to sedate her. Jack arranged for a bed in a private ward at the Radcliffe Hospital, and Joy was transferred by ambulance. She dozed throughout the day, and used her waking moments to suggest arrangements for her funeral: she wanted to be cremated, and Austin Farrer should preside over the service.

Joy received absolution before her death. To Jack, she said tenderly, "You have made me happy." Among her final words were "I am at peace with God." The eternal Fairyland of her dreams, she knew, lay just ahead.

BILL VISITED OXFORD shortly after Joy's death, and, seeing that his boys, now sixteen and fourteen, were flourishing under Jack's care, did not contest custody. But even as David and Douglas grew into manhood, their lives were riddled with loss. In 1962, after a loving eight-year marriage to Renee, Bill was diagnosed with cancer of the tongue. In September of that year, rather than face disfiguring surgeries and the painful, slow death he had followed in Joy's letters, Bill checked in to the Dixie Hotel in New York City and overdosed on sleeping pills. A year later, on November 22, 1963, Jack died at home at the Kilns of kidney failure.

JOY'S MARRIAGE TO C. S. Lewis surely provides one of the twentieth century's greatest literary love stories. Yet while *Shadowlands* did justice to the ferocity and tragedy of that relationship, Joy's epic narrative, in all its fullness, amounts to far more than a brief romance. If writing and reading biography are attempts to map and study the steps of people who lived meaningful lives in order to better guide our own, then Joy's story teaches us much about love, faith, and embracing ideals that transcend our temporal lives.

Her narrative is one of redemption. The deception of Stalin as savior and of Russia as Fairyland on earth led her to New Testament salvation—Christ as savior, heaven as the only true utopia. Echoes of regeneration played out in her love life, too. Bill brought out the worst in Joy; Jack reclaimed marriage after Joy experienced its brokenness. But although Joy's spiritual journey culminated in Christianity, her human condition continued to be plagued with self-interest, even hypocrisy. Those failings, however, did not nullify her faith; they reinforced the purpose of redemption.

While Joy's times and circumstances were extraordinary, her conflicts and quests are timeless, universally relevant to all who seek value and fight indifference, to all women who struggle to pursue their own visions, and to every heart that yearns for Fairyland.

Acknowledgments

One of the chief pleasures of birthing a book so many years in the making is the opportunity to recognize publicly those who contributed, directly and indirectly, to its long gestation. I want to express my deepest gratitude first to Joy's family, especially her two sons, for their unwavering support of my endeavor to write her biography. David Gresham shared his memories and impressions in many long letters. Douglas Gresham, with his wife Merrie, generously welcomed me into their home and provided me full access to newly discovered caches of his mother's unpublished papers. Susan Davidman Cleveland, Joy's niece, enormously enriched my understanding of her aunt's early life and family history by making available childhood photos, letters, and other documents belonging to Joy's parents. I owe a tremendous debt of gratitude to Susan's mother, the late Ruth Parsons Davidman, whose contributions augment many pages. Thanks to Morton and Joan Davidman for sharing memories. Rosemary and Jack Simmons obligingly left me alone for several days in a room packed with eight boxes of Bill Gresham's papers. I'm grateful to Rosemary for her warmth of spirit, which she inherited from her mother, Renee Gresham. During several phone conversations and meetings in the last year of her life, Renee answered my many questions with humility and gentleness; I am sorry she did not live to see this book.

It has been a profound privilege to be entrusted with so many memories. I'm especially indebted to the following people: Florence Wolfson Howitt, Walter and Susan Doniger, Jackie Jackson, Mary Stevenson, Pete Seeger, Jan Surrage, June Lancelyn Green, Scirard Lancelyn Green, Simon Barrington-Ward, Joan Lewis Murphy, and the late, marvelous Bel Kaufman, who regaled me with her stories for many hours and let me read her diaries, and to the spirited Damaris Walsh McGuire for inviting me to the house on Lake Iroquois.

I am beholden to many libraries and librarians, archives and archivists. I consulted too many to list here, but would like to acknowledge those of particular consequence to this biography: archivist Kathy Kienholz and the American Academy of Arts and Letters; the Margaret Herrick Library, Academy of Motion Picture Arts and Sciences; the University of Arkansas Libraries; the Poetry/Rare Books Collection of the University Libraries, University at Buffalo, State University of New York; the Special Collections Research Center, University of Chicago Library; the Manuscript Division and the Music Division of the Library of Congress; the Special Collections Department, University of Colorado at Boulder Libraries; the Rare Book and Manuscript Library, Columbia University; the University of Delaware, Special Collections; the Archives and Special Collections, Hunter College; the University of Illinois Rare Books and Manuscripts Library; the Special Collections, University of Iowa Libraries; the University of Kentucky Special Collections; the Special Collections Library, University of Michigan; the Milne Special Collections, University of New Hampshire Library; Archives and Special Collections at the City College of New York; archivist David Ment and the New York City Municipal Archives; the Manuscripts and Archives Division and the Berg Collection at the New York Public Library; Tamiment Library and Robert F. Wagner Labor Archives, New York University; Norman MacDonald at the Ossining Historical Society; Rare Books and Special Collections, Princeton University; Harry Ransom Center, University of Texas; American Heritage

Center, University of Wyoming; Beinecke Rare Book and Manuscript Library, Yale University; and Manuscripts and Archives, Sterling Memorial Library, Yale University.

Bob Scott, Digital Humanities Librarian at Columbia University's Butler Library, helped me create an invaluable database to organize and cross-reference my many thousands of pages of research, allowing me to access information easily with a few keystrokes. Ned Comstock, archivist at the University of Southern California Cinematic Arts Library, greeted me with a cartload of material that I could never have known to request, and called me sporadically for months after my visit with new information that he continued to unearth on my behalf. David Smith, retired librarian from the New York Public Library, always seemed to know whom I should ask and where I should look for the most elusive answers. And Robin Rausch, Senior Music Specialist at the Library of Congress and expert on all things MacDowell, assisted on many fronts; her camaraderie added to the delight of this work.

The Marion E. Wade Center at Wheaton College in Wheaton, Illinois, houses the world's leading collection of C. S. Lewis materials, including first editions of his books, scores of oral history interviews with those who knew Lewis, articles by and about him, published reviews and books on Lewis and his writings, family photographs, memorabilia (including what is arguably *the* original wardrobe), letters, manuscripts, and, by association, the papers of Joy Davidman and William Lindsay Gresham. Without the Wade Center's thorough compendium, my job would have been infinitely more complex and not nearly so personally fulfilling. Not only are the resources of the Wade Center readily available to scholars, but also, unlike many special collections, the Wade welcomes visits and inquiries from general readers who are not engaged in a publishable project but are merely interested in Lewis and the six other British authors it collects. This spirit of inclusion contributed to the pleasure of my many research visits, beginning in 2003; by the end of a summer-long stint at the Wade in 2010, the place felt like a second home staffed by extended family. I thank them all, but three people deserve special recognition. Archivist Laura Schmidt promptly and thoroughly responded to my countless emails over the years; without her organization, efficiency, and knowledge of the Wade's collection, this book might still be in the works. Former director Chris Mitchell, who passed away recently and suddenly, was a dependably genial presence, a rock of a man. And finally, my heart is full of gratitude for Marjorie Lamp Mead, the Wade's associate director, a tremendous gift of a friend. Her wisdom, scholarly insights, and spiritual guidance have carried me through, both on the page and in the world. I am also grateful to the Wade Center for the financial support and honor of the 2010 Clyde S. Kilby Research Grant.

The world of C. S. Lewis scholarship, with the Wade Center at its heart, is peopled by a gracious lot. I'm thankful to Lyle Dorsett, whose groundbreaking research on Joy Davidman in the 1980s led to oral histories, interviews, and letters that vastly enriched this book and might never have otherwise become available. When I began investigating Joy's life, Lyle was one of the first people I contacted. Instead of playing the territorial scholar, he asked to pray with me on the phone and urged me to write Joy's biography. Walter Hooper—former secretary to C. S. Lewis and long-standing adviser to the Lewis estate—was an appreciable resource and encouragement, as was Michael Ward. Thanks, too, to Stan Mattson, David Beckmann, and Steven Beebe. My gratitude to Rachel Churchill and the C. S. Lewis Company. And I am hugely indebted to Lewis scholar Andrew Lazo, who donated many hours to vetting the second half of this book. Andrew employed his vast knowledge of Lewis's life and writings to check facts, correct errors, refine the text, and humbly yet incisively challenge my reasoning on new interpretations. We did not agree on every point, but in the spirit of Lewis himself we had great fun debating our differences. I take full responsibility for any mistakes that may remain.

Writing biography requires a unique blend of solitude and solidarity; for these in perfect measure I am indebted to James McGrath Morris, who granted me three glorious weeks in New Mexico through the James and Patty McGrath Morris Fellowship, and who founded the Biographers International Organization, a thriving professional network that has enriched my life with collegiality and a deeper understanding of the craft of biography.

A series of other residencies provided me with much-needed time and space to write. I'm grateful to the Jentel Artist Residency Program, the Ragdale Foundation, and especially the Virginia Center for the Creative Arts (VCCA), a Blue Ridge oasis where I forged lasting friendships and drafted most of this book. Special thanks to Sheila Gulley Pleasants, Dana Jones, and Bea Booker for arranging so many of the details that made my several lengthy VCCA residencies among the more pleasant and productive periods of this journey.

Everything I drafted at the VCCA was conceived or revised in the Frederick Lewis Allen Room at the New York Public Library, where I also completed a great deal of research and fact checking. My heartfelt thanks go to that venerable institution, and to Jay Barksdale for giving me a key.

Many colleagues, friends, and mentors generously contributed their time and expertise in service of this biography. Carl Rollyson and Kate Buford embraced me as a colleague while graciously answering my innumerable novice questions as I navigated the often murky waters of biography for the first time. Maya Petrukhina selflessly sacrificed her last morning at the VCCA in November 2009 to translate portions of Joy's Russian notes. Alan Wald, expert on the twentieth century's literary left, provided a few key details about Joy's days at *New Masses*. Chelsea Carter was my photocopy assistant in Malta. Lisa Paddock's editorial acumen trimmed some two hundred pages of fat off an early draft. Dylan Coughtrey assisted with the endnotes. Tabatha Hoyle transcribed, organized, and continues to be one of the best friends a girl could have. The same goes for Monica Housen, whose close eye to the final manuscript enhanced the integrity of this book. Joyce Maynard and Jessie Chaffee made valuable comments on select chapters. Akiko Busch taught me much about getting there from here. Since the early days of my research, Susan Hertog has sustained me with her friendship, affection, and benevolent mentorship. Her kindness has augmented my life both personally and professionally; her relentless encouragement continues to coax me through challenges. I am immensely grateful.

I might not have begun this book at all without the faith and encouragement of several astounding women. Patricia O'Toole taught me the fundamentals of writing biography and believed in me before I believed in myself. Kathie Donaldson, whose love and prayers have lifted me since birth, seemed to know beyond all doubt that I was meant to tell Joy's story. And Christine Akerman walked alongside me as I mapped my own Daylight Street, illuminating my way with emotional support and powerful prayer; the beauty of her heart, the breadth of her impact, and the depth of my gratitude defy expression.

My literary agent, the wise and indefatigable Sarah Burnes, deftly shepherded me through this long project. I am supremely blessed to have her in my corner. Thanks, too, to the rest of the Gernert Company, especially Chris Paris-Lamb and Logan Garrison.

At Houghton Mifflin Harcourt, thank you to Andrea Schulz for acquiring my book, and to my editor, Jenna Johnson, for persevering beyond a seven-hundred-page monstrosity of a first draft, and calmly but firmly prodding me to suss out the essence. Editorial assistants Nina Barnett and, especially, Pilar Garcia-Brown worked tirelessly on the production side. Amanda Heller's technical expertise as copyeditor lent finesse to every paragraph, and Larry Cooper ably guided me through the final stages.

Finally, I am profoundly grateful to the Santamaria family for their love and forbearance. To my siblings—Brooke, Nathan, Amanda, and David—and my niece and nephew, Anna Perenna and Cassander: I'm sorry for my frequent absences during the long obsession that was this book. To my parents, Jaime and Sharon Santamaria, to whom this book is dedicated: thank you for teaching me the value of perseverance, for your unflagging support, and for standing by me to the finish. To Gloria Santamaria, my Bita: you continue to inspire me. I wish you had lived to see this book and meet your newest great-grandchild. And to my sweet son, Jasper: thank you for waiting until the week after I submitted my final manuscript to be born. I love you with my whole heart. You are my greatest joy.

Notes

Abbreviations

NAMES

CSL: C. S. Lewis
HD: Howard Davidman
JD: Joy Davidman
JID: Joseph Isaac Davidman
KWP: Kenneth W. Porter
WLG: William Lindsay Gresham

FREQUENTLY CITED SOURCES (PUBLISHED, PRIVATE, ARCHIVAL)

And God Came In Collection, Wade Center: And God Came In Collection, A-26 through A-28, Marion E. Wade Center, Wheaton College, Wheaton, Ill.

Benét Correspondence, Beinecke Library: Benét Family Correspondence, Za MSS Benét, Beinecke Rare Book and Manuscript Library, Yale University.

Benét Papers, Beinecke Library: Benét Family Papers, Za Benét family; ZA Benét; Uncat ZA MS; Za MS Benét, Beinecke Rare Books and Manuscripts Library, Yale University.

Chad Walsh Papers, Wade Center: Chad Walsh Papers, A-57, Marion E. Wade Center, Wheaton College, Wheaton, Ill.

Collected Letters, vol. 3: *The Collected Letters of C. S. Lewis*. Edited by Walter Hooper. Vol. 3. *Narnia, Cambridge, and Joy (1950–1963)*. London: HarperCollins, 2004.

FCTC: WLG, "From Communist to Christian." In *These Found the Way: Thirteen Converts to Protestant Christianity*. Edited by David Wesley Soper. 64–82. Philadelphia: Westminster Press, 1951.

GC: Oliver Pilat, "Girl Communist." *New York Post,* October 31, 1949–November 13, 1949.

Jack: A Life of C. S. Lewis: George Sayer, *Jack: A Life of C. S. Lewis.* Wheaton, Ill.: Crossway, 2005.

JD Papers, Wade Center: Joy Davidman Papers, A-109, Marion E. Wade Center, Wheaton College, Wheaton, Ill.

KWP Papers, Schomburg Center: Kenneth Wiggins Porter Papers, Sc MG 222, Schomburg Center for Research in Black Culture, New York Public Library.

LWR: Joy Davidman, "Longest Way Round." In *These Found the Way: Thirteen Converts to Protestant Christianity.* Edited by David Wesley Soper. 11–26. Philadelphia: Westminster Press, 1951.

MacDowell Papers, Library of Congress: Marian MacDowell Papers, Manuscript Division, Library of Congress.

SDC Collection: Susan Davidman Cleveland, private collection of family papers.

Wade Center: Marion E. Wade Center, Wheaton College, Wheaton, Ill.

WHL Diaries, Wade Center: Warren H. Lewis Diaries Collection, A-117 through 121, Marion E. Wade Center, Wheaton College, Wheaton, Ill.

WLG Correspondence, Wade Center: William Lindsay Gresham Correspondence, A-51a–b, Marion E. Wade Center, Wheaton College, Wheaton, Ill.

WLG Papers, Wade Center: William Lindsay Gresham Papers, A-86 through 91, Marion E. Wade Center, Wheaton College, Wheaton, Ill.

Introduction

page

x "Her mind was lithe": CSL, *A Grief Observed* (San Francisco: HarperSanFrancisco, 1994), 4.

"The conclusion I dread": Ibid., 18–19.

xi "[Joy] was a splendid thing": Ibid., 42.

xii "set the record straight": Ruth Parsons Davidman, interview with the author, May 13, 2003.

"myth": Ibid.

"Are you sitting down": Douglas Gresham, conversation with the author, December 4, 2008.

xiv "I am now looking at": Ibid. Douglas Gresham has since donated these papers to the Wade Center, and the sonnets are being published under Joy Davidman, *A Naked Tree: Love Sonnets to C. S. Lewis and Other Poems*, ed. Don W. King (Grand Rapids, Mich.: Eerdmans, 2015).

"Dear Jack, here are some": JD Papers, Wade Center.

"Wingfield Hospital": Personal checkbook, JD Papers, Wade Center.

"COURAGE": JD Papers, Wade Center.

"Sir": Referenced in Sonnets I, X, XII, XIV, JD Papers, Wade Center.

"You have my heart": Sonnet II, JD Papers, Wade Center.

"In a moment of insight": Margin note by JD in the draft of Sonnet II, dated "1948 or 1949," JD Papers, Wade Center.

"Jack": Introductory letter to CSL and Sonnet X, JD Papers, Wade Center.

xv "I have wrenched sonnets out": Sonnet XXVI, JD Papers, Wade Center.

Chapter 1

1 "a strange, golden, immeasurable plane": LWR.
"Hate and heartbreak": JD, "Fairytale," in *War Poems of the United Nations*, ed. Joy Davidman (New York: Dial Press, 1943), 299.
"ghost stories and superscience stories": LWR.
2 "If I remembered the way": LWR.
"Every day, in every way": LWR.
"They showed their affection by": GC.
"well-meaning but strict": JD to Chad Walsh, January 27, 1950. Chad Walsh Papers, Wade Center.
"There is a myth that has": LWR.
3 "By disguising fairyland as heaven": LWR.
4 "Calling or Occupation": "New York Passenger Lists, 1820–1957," database, Ancestry.com, Microfilm Serial M237, roll 594, p. 2, line 41.
"Operator Cloaks": "1900 United States Federal Census," Ancestry.com, census of Manhattan, New York, enumeration district 0369, FHL microfilm 1241098, roll 1098, p. 16B.
"the Jewish disease": Hasia R. Diner, *Lower East Side Memories: A Jewish Place in America* (Princeton: Princeton University Press, 2000), 37.
5 "Now the lowest scum": "Invaded by Filth and Dirt: Changed Conditions in the Old Seventh Ward," *New York Times*, July 20, 1893.
6 "make a proper return to": Joseph Isaac Davidman, "Transitions," commencement address, City College of New York, 1907, SDC Collection.
"Joseph the Dreamer": Joseph Isaac Davidman, "Joseph the Dreamer," SDC Collection.
"interested in the economic and": Joseph Isaac Davidman, "The Educators Division of the People's ORT Federation," *Jewish Teachers Association Bulletin*, January 1935.
7 "Every real educator": Joseph Isaac Davidman, "The Limitations of Education" (Ph.D. diss., New York University, 1917), ProQuest, UMI Dissertations Publishing, http://search.proquest.com.ezproxy.cul.columbia.edu/docview/301761469?accountid=10226.
"He was a pompous ass": Morton Davidman, interview with the author, July 1, 2008.
8 "esteemed chairman": NYC Collegiate Zionist League to Mr. and Mrs. Joseph I. Davidman, June 30, 1909, SDC Collection.
Not every upstate tourist community: Irving Howe, *World of Our Fathers* (New York: Harcourt Brace Jovanovich, 1976), 215.
9 "the melting pot hospital": "St. Mark's Called East Side's Friend," *New York Tribune*, December 12, 1915.
"difficulties . . . sent away": Susan Davidman Cleveland, interview with the author, July 2003.
10 "every row a masterpiece": JD to HD, August 17, 1943, SDC Collection.
11 "the star animals": "World Wide Hunt to Fill Bronx Zoo," *New York Times*, October 22, 1922.
"Friendship for animals": GC.

"discipline without restraint": JID, "Analysis of Recommendations of Board of Examiners," 1931, SDC Collection.

12 "If you left a piece": Helen Margalith, interview with the author, January 20, 2004.

"Tho I confess I had": Bernard Perlmutter to JID, September 18, 1924, SDC Collection.

"In the opinion of the": JID, "Analysis of Recommendations of Board of Examiners," 1931, SDC Collection.

"Absolutely false": Ibid.

13 "America's greatest authority on children": "Angelo Patri, Little Father to Children and Friendly Guide for Their Parents," *Washington Post,* November 10, 1921.

"not in the spirit": Angelo Patri, *A Schoolmaster of the Great City* (New York: Macmillan, 1917), 16.

"work away earnestly and happily": "Angelo Patri, Little Father to Children."

14 "Every child has a potential": Ibid.

"There was never really any": GC.

"precious and dull": Ibid.

"My parents were": JD to Marian MacDowell, April 19, 1950, Edward and Marian MacDowell Collection, Library of Congress.

15 "While perusing a venerable volume": JD, "The Influence of Headgear on the Happiness of Man," unpublished short story, June 1927, JD Papers, Wade Center.

16 "Jen was very meticulous": Renee Gresham, interview with the author, October 21, 2003.

"What spur of gold is": JD, unpublished poem, January 1929. JD Papers, Wade Center.

"We were . . . two oddball": Nina Schneider, "Coming to Terms: A Fact Finding Memoir," Papers of Nina Schneider, Brooklyn College Archives and Special Collections, Brooklyn College Library.

17 "She took an interest in": Julian Zimet to the author, 2008.

"Towers sky-climbing": JD, "Sunset—The Hall of Fame," unpublished poem, JD Papers, Wade Center.

18 "Our schools and newspapers taught": LWR.

a young widow, Mrs. Goldberg: JD, "Dumbwaiter Idylls," unpublished short story, November 1939, JD Papers, Wade Center. All quotations are from this source.

20 "de Profundis melancholies": Schneider, "Coming to Terms."

"I was really": LWR.

21 "great inexperience, immaturity, and every": John Keats, *Endymion: A Poetic Romance* (London: Taylor and Hessey, 1818), xi.

"I had prayed": "Endymion," JD Papers, Wade Center.

22 "clean, cold": LWR.

"fairly often": Ibid.

23 "I suppose the very young": Ibid.

"The world of": JD to Marian MacDowell, April 19, 1950, Edward and Marian MacDowell Collection, Library of Congress.

23 "A Moment of Ecstasy": JD Papers, Wade Center.
"[I] was a girl with": LWR.

Chapter 2

24 "subway student": Jeffery S. Gurock, *Jews in Gotham: New York Jews in a Changing City, 1920–2010*, vol. 3 of *City of Promises: A History of the Jews of New York* (New York: New York University Press, 2012), 63.

25 most freshmen were young: "Freshman Survey," *Hunter Bulletin,* March 2, 1931.
About half had won: "Students List Honors," *New York Times,* October 9, 1930.
"She alone is free to": *Hunter Bulletin,* September 29, 1930.
"I loved Hunter": Bel Kaufman, "A Different World," in *The Echo: Journal of the Hunter College Archives: 125th Anniversary Edition.*

26 One in five freshmen was: "Freshman Survey," *Hunter Bulletin,* March 2, 1931.
"Here on the Atlantic seaboard": "The Wistarion," 1933, 160, Hunter College Archives.

27 "a growing uneasiness": GC.
"I innocently went around": JD to John and Charlie May, John Gould Fletcher Papers, University of Arkansas Libraries.

28 "Of all the problems": Eunice Barnard, "In the Classroom and on the Campus," *New York Times,* March 13, 1932.
"deep in adolescent transition": JD, "Little Girl Lost," unpublished short story, JD Papers, Wade Center.
"My own emotions": JD, "Literary Adventure," unpublished essay, JD Papers, Wade Center.

29 "The poetry of youth": Harriet Monroe, *Echo*, November 1930, 43.
"JUSTIFICATION OF EUROPEAN INDICTMENT": Headlines from *Hunter Bulletin*, 1930–1934.

30 her second-semester grades: JD transcript, Office of the Registrar, Hunter College.
"I envied Angela": JD, "Spoiled Child," unpublished short story, JD Papers, Wade Center.

31 "blind-fury": LWR.
"Joy had a vast": Helen Margalith, interview with the author, January 20, 2004.
"Students were ensorcelled by this": Patricia Edwards Clyne, "Thomas O. Mabbott as Teacher," *Books at Iowa* 34, University of Iowa (April 1981): 29–36.

32 "I never held such things": JD, "Sed Dis Aliter," unpublished short story, JD Papers, Wade Center.
"liaison": Bel Kaufman, interview with the author, February 2003.
Joy recounted the affair: HD, interview by Lyle Dorsett, early 1980s, *And God Came In* Collection, Wade Center.
Joy flung herself: Ibid.

33 "Outside the pavement was black": GC.
"the ugly things": JD, "A Grecian Urn . . . of George Moore," *Echo,* Spring 1933.
"How can you talk": Quoted from GC and LWR.

34 Scholarship eligibility: Adele Bildersee, "State Scholarship Students at Hunter College of the City of New York" (Ph.D. diss., Columbia University, 1932).
"She was a brilliant": Nina Schneider, interview by Lyle Dorsett, *And God Came In* Collection, Wade Center.
"I concern myself": JD, "Literary Adventure," unpublished essay, 1932, JD Papers, Wade Center.
"loves . . . To my thinking": Ibid.
35 "I think that": Ibid.
36 "I am the life": JD, unpublished poem, JD Papers, Wade Center.
"try out" by submitting: "Echo Offers Opportunity to Join Literary Staff," *Hunter Bulletin,* February 20, 1933. Although my description comes from an article in 1933, it can be assumed that the requirements for joining the staff were the same in the previous year.
"I devote a single heart": JD, "Literary Adventure."
37 "I demand a recount!": Florence Howitt Wolfson, interview with the author, July 28, 2006.
"You didn't say": Jackie Jackson, interview with the author, July 12, 2003.
"egoist": JD, "Literary Adventure."
"Ironic, sardonic, but always with": Mildred Kunar, "Joy Davidman Gresham Lewis," in *The Echo: Journal of the Hunter College Archives: 125th Anniversary Edition.*
38 "phrases perfect to eye and ear": JD, "A Grecian Urn . . . of George Moore," *Echo,* Spring 1933.
Moore attempted a career: Ibid.
39 "She has cast off": "Spring Echo Maintains High Standard of Art," *Hunter Bulletin,* June 19, 1933.
"From its secret headquarters": "Echo Asks Students to Send Manuscripts," *Hunter Bulletin,* October 3, 1933.
"Tag Day": *Hunter Bulletin,* October 3, 1933.
"U.S. ANTI-WAR CONGRESS": *Hunter Bulletin,* October 10, 1933.
39–40 "intelligent participation": *Hunter Bulletin,* October 17, 1933.
40 Written endorsements: "Education and Fascism," *Hunter Bulletin,* December 19, 1933.
"I hate you": JD, "Sonnets," *Echo,* December 1933.
41 "ECHO should be an organ": Florence Wolfson, letter to the editor, *Hunter Bulletin,* March 6, 1934.
"Why doesn't Echo try": "Enthusiastic Tones of Echo Editor Presage 'Normal' Surprising Issue," *Hunter Bulletin,* May 14, 1934.
42–43 Dorothy Scheer's suicide: "Hunter Junior Injured," *New York Times,* April 13, 1934; "Girl Dies of Injuries," *New York Times,* April 16, 1934.

Chapter 3

44 "No, I won't": LWR.
45 "improper acts": "City College Foes Scored at Hunter," *New York Times,* June 15, 1933.

46 "The world is in transition": "Woman's New Era Hailed at Hunter," *New York Times,* June 14, 1934.
"This is not": Ibid.

47 "At present . . . general economic conditions": *Columbia University Bulletin of Information, 1934–1935,* Columbiana, Archives of Columbia University.

48 "Only a few years ago": "Stunt Days Are Passing: Dean Hawkes Reports the Student Interests Are Deepening at Columbia," *New York Times,* October 14, 1934.
"No second front": Lily Koppel, *The Red Leather Diary* (New York: HarperCollins, 2008), 233–34.
"[Students] may talk unwisely": "Stunt Days Are Passing."

49 "fiery men with bombs": Ralph L. Woods, "The Communist Formula for Revolution," *Nation's Business,* June 1938, 22.
"Now do not put": JD, "This Woman," in *Letter to a Comrade* (New Haven: Yale University Press, 1938), 54.
"the desperate question": LWR.
"I slashed off three stanzas": JD to Morton Zabel, January 8, 1935, in Poetry: A Magazine of Verse papers, 1895–1961, Special Collections Research Center, University of Chicago Library.

50 "Born in New York City": JD to Editors of *Poetry* magazine, January 18, 1935, Ibid.
"[I] will probably": Ibid.
"I should like to know": Ibid.

51 "picturesque": JD, "My Lord of Orrery" (M.A. thesis, Columbia University, 1935).

52 "Chapayev and his men": Francis Winmar, "The Film and the State," *New York Times,* September 8, 1935.
"the amiable mediocrity": Bella Kashin, *New York Times,* March 31, 1935.
"living truthfulness": Ibid.
"the complete fusion": "The Soviet Cinema," *Manchester Guardian,* November 4, 1935.

53 "represents the spirit": Edward Alden Jewell, "Soviet Art in an Impressive Show," *New York Times,* December 23, 1934.
"nothing but American prosperity": LWR.
"Upstairs, my lady Countess bore": JD, "My Lord of Orrery."

54 "permanent substitute": GC.
"The filthy permanent substitute trick": Ibid.

55 "Ashes and Sparks": JD to Stephen Vincent Benét, August 18, 1936, in Benét Correspondence, Beinecke Library.
"His poetry": JD, "Stephen Vincent Benét," *New Masses,* March 30, 1943, 23–24.

56 "I am twenty-one": JD to Editors of *Poetry* magazine, July 23, 1936, in Poetry: A Magazine of Verse papers, 1895–1961, Special Collections Research Center, University of Chicago Library.

57 "What I keep looking for": SVB to Theodora Roosevelt, January 21, 1940, in *Selected Letters of Stephen Vincent Benét,* ed. Charles Fenton (New Haven: Yale University Press, 1960).

58 "I am very glad": JD to Stephen Vincent Benét, August 18, 1936, in Benét Correspondence, Beinecke Library.
"thing": Ruth Lechlitner, "A New City-Born Poet," *New York Herald Tribune,* December 25, 1938.
"Rich Dine, We Starve": *Seeing Red: Stories of American Communists,* DVD, directed by Jim Klein and Julia Reichert (Heartland Productions, 1983).
59 "read the literature": LWR.
"fight against imperialist war": Henry Hart, ed., *American Writers' Congress* (New York: International Publishers, 1935), 12.
"art for art's sake": "Call for an American Writers' Congress," *New Masses,* January 22, 1935, 20.
Among the leading causes: Franklin Folsom, *Days of Anger, Days of Hope: A Memoir of the League of American Writers, 1937–1942* (Niwot: University Press of Colorado, 1994), 3, 31–32.
60 "was getting a little old": LWR.
"I was conscious": JD to KWP, February 19, 1939, KWP Papers, Schomburg Center.
61 "Anybody who ever tried": GC.
"We knew": *Seeing Red.*
62 "How sweet the scythe": JD, "Japanese Print," in *Letter to a Comrade,* 53.
"live nerve": JD, quoted in Norman V. Donaldson to Grace Vanamee, Discontinued Awards, Loines Award, 1931–1983, box 1, American Academy of Arts and Letters, New York.
"an end to regional peculiarities": JD, "Arcadia, Kentucky," review of Elizabeth Madox Roberts, *Black Is My Truelove's Hair, New Masses,* December 27, 1938, 25.
"is the sentiment": GC.
"Let me have eyes": JD, "Prayer Against Indifference," in *Letter to a Comrade,* 31.
"I believe": LWR.
63 "Any new members": GC.
"It was in this subterranean": David Horowitz, *Radical Son: A Generational Odyssey* (New York: Simon & Schuster, 1998), 36.
64 Sexual promiscuity: GC.
"You were part of something": *Seeing Red.*
65 "Communism Is 20th-Century Americanism": Joseph R. Starobin, *American Communism in Crisis, 1943–1957* (Berkeley: University of California Press, 1975), 45.
66 "I never really lived": John Meldon, "Fla. Delegates Bring Proof of C.P. Growth," *Daily Worker,* May 27, 1938.
"One could totally live": *Seeing Red.*
"Jobs": Fraser M. Ottanelli, *The Communist Party of the United States: From the Depression to World War II* (New Brunswick: Rutgers University Press, 1991), 126.
"The people are beginning": Earl Browder, "Address for the 10th Communist Party Convention" (May 26, 1938), *Daily Worker,* May 27, 1938.
"I and twenty thousand": LWR.

Chapter 4

68 "an arrogant and uncertain creature": JD to Marian MacDowell, April 19, 1950, MacDowell Papers, Library of Congress.

69 "I have to thank you": JD to Stephen Vincent Benét, April 2, 1938, Benét Papers, Beinecke Library.

"Dear Sir": Ibid.

70 "When any man is gnawed": JD, "Strength Through Joy," *New Masses*, April 5, 1938, 5.

"the surest way": "If They Only Understood," *New Masses,* April 5, 1938.

71 "I tried very hard": JD to Marian MacDowell, April 19, 1950, MacDowell Papers, Library of Congress.

"superintend correspondence": Marian MacDowell to Mr. Langs, May 12, 1938, MacDowell Papers, Library of Congress.

She thanked Bénet: Marian MacDowell to Stephen Vincent Benét, April 4, 1938, Benét Papers, Beinecke Library.

"Nobody is expected": "Writing About the Colony by Colonists," box 67, folder 7, Edward and Marian MacDowell Collection, Performing Arts Reading Room, Library of Congress.

72 Joy was assigned: Ethel Glenn Hier, "A Day in the Peterborough Woods," scrapbook, The MacDowell Colony Papers, Manuscript Division, Library of Congress.

"fairy godmother": Ibid.

73 "a rather exquisite binding": Marian MacDowell to Miss Eliza L. Willets, fall 1938, The MacDowell Colony Papers, Manuscript Division, Library of Congress.

Sixty-two poets: "The MacDowell Colony News Bulletin for Members—Close of Season 1938," The MacDowell Colony Papers, Manuscript Division, Library of Congress.

"Here": Stephen Vincent Benét, foreword to JD, *Letter to a Comrade.*

74 "I am glad": JD to Stephen Vincent Benét, July 26, 1938, Benét Papers, Beinecke Library.

"I am sending you": Ibid.

"By all means": JD to Stephen Vincent Benét, July 25, 1938, Benét Papers, Beinecke Library.

"I am sorry": JD to Stephen Vincent Benét, July 21, 1938, Benét Papers, Beinecke Library.

"It will be obvious enough": Stephen Vincent Benét, foreword to *Letter to a Comrade,* 7–9.

75 "Thank you very much": JD to Stephen Vincent Benét, July 26, 1938, Benét Papers, Beinecke Library.

"a very considerable command": Stephen Vincent Benét, foreword to *Letter to a Comrade*, 7–9.

"The critical introductions": JD, "Stephen Vincent Benét," *New Masses*, March 30, 1943, 23–24.

"I'm apt to splash colors": JD to James Still, September 1, 1938, James Still Papers, University of Kentucky Special Collections.

76 "She is ostentatious": JD, "Rough Sonnets II," JD Papers, Wade Center.

"I hate the thought": JD, "November 15, 1938," JD Papers, Wade Center.
"I had a high time": JD to James Still, September 1, 1938, James Still Papers, University of Kentucky Special Collections.
"I'd never been allowed": JD to Marian MacDowell, April 19, 1950, Edward and Marian MacDowell Collection, Performing Arts Reading Room, Library of Congress.

77 "I praise my youth": JD, "Through Transitory," Poetry/Rare Books Collection of the University Libraries, University at Buffalo, State University of New York.
"New York": JD to James Still, September 1, 1938, James Still Papers, University of Kentucky Special Collections.
"Stephen Vincent Benét": *New York Times,* September 4, 1938.
"Words must now be used": Langston Hughes, "Writers and the World," *Bulletin of the League of American Writers* 5, no. 1 (Fall 1938): 1, Tamiment Library and Robert F. Wagner Labor Archives, New York University.

78 on a volunteer basis: Exactly when Joy started working at *New Masses* is unclear; it's possible that she began as an unpaid reader in the spring of 1938, but more evidence points to her beginning in September of that year. The 1949 "Girl Communist" *New York Post* profile says, "After a few of her poems saw print, Joy Davidman came around to the New Masses office at 27th Street and Lexington Avenue, met the editors and was given the unpaid job of reader." Norman Rosten refers to Joy as his assistant in a letter to John Malcolm Brinnin on September 17, 1938 (John Malcolm Brinnin Papers, University of Delaware, Special Collections). *New Masses* had published only one of her poems before she went to the MacDowell Colony in the summer of 1938, although several others were under contract.
"with acute 'social' material": Ibid.
"As the political": JD to H. H. Lewis, June 7, 1943.

79 "I think that we": Interview with Annette Rubinstein, Oral History of the American Left, Radical Histories Collection OH.002, series 1, Tamiment Library/Wagner Archives.
"poet's poet": Norman Rosten to John Malcolm Brinnin, September 17, 1938, John Malcolm Brinnin Papers, University of Delaware, Special Collections.
"*She's a great poet*": Norman Rosten to John Malcolm Brinnin, undated letter, John Malcolm Brinnin Papers, University of Delaware, Special Collections.
"I can no longer read": JD to John and Charlie May Fletcher, November 13, 1938, John Gould Fletcher Papers, University of Arkansas Libraries, Special Collections.
"I should have done worse": JD to KWP, February 19, 1939, KWP Papers, Schomburg Center.
("They would do me in red!"): JD to John and Charlie May Fletcher, November 13, 1938, John Gould Fletcher Papers, University of Arkansas Libraries, Special Collections.

80 "masculine diction": Ruth Lechlitner, "A New City-Born Poet," *New York Herald Tribune,* December 25, 1938.
"She has respect": R. P. Blackmur, "Nine Poets," *Partisan Review* (Winter 1939): 112.

80 "integration of spirit and sensibility": C. A. Millspaugh, "Among the New Books of Verse," *Kenyon Review* (1940): 2.
"[I] prepared myself heroically": JD to KWP, March 31, 1939, KWP Papers, Schomburg Center.
"prosaic": Oscar Williams, *Poetry* (April 1939): 54.

81 "It is surprising": Dorothy Ulrich, review of *Letter to a Comrade, New York Times Book Review,* August 6, 1939.
"The only thing": JD to KWP, March 31, 1939, KWP Papers, Schomburg Center.
"I've had another monosyllabic letter": JD to John and Charlie May Fletcher, January 2, 1939, John Gould Fletcher Papers, University of Arkansas Libraries, Special Collections.

82 "everyman's fair": Federal Writers' Project, *New York City Guide,* rev. ed., American Guide Series (New York: Random House, 1939), 630.
"The Devil Will Come": JD, "The Devil Will Come," *New Masses*, June 27, 1939, 6.

83 "the decisive factors": Alan M. Wald, *Exiles from a Future Time: The Forging of the Mid-Twentieth-Century Literary Left* (Chapel Hill: University of North Carolina Press, 2002), 120.
"Poetry Czarina": Alan M. Wald to the author, February 12, 2012.
"a sort of": JD to Willard Maas, January 16, 1939, Harry Ransom Center, University of Texas.
"[Writers] must seize the media": JD, unpublished manuscript, Poetry/Rare Books Collection of the University Libraries, University at Buffalo, State University of New York.

84 She told Rodman: JD to Selden Rodman, January 7, 1939, Selden Rodman Papers, American Heritage Center, University of Wyoming.
"Capitalism divorced [poetry]": JD, unpublished lecture notes, Poetry/Rare Books Collection of the University Libraries, University at Buffalo, State University of New York.

85 "the impending degradation": John Updike, ed., *A Century of Arts & Letters: The History of the National Institute of Arts & Letters and the American Academy of Arts & Letters as Told, Decade by Decade, by Eleven Members* (New York: Columbia University Press, 1998), 97.
"to become safe": Sinclair Lewis to the Pulitzer Prize Committee, 1930.
"cuts itself off": Sinclair Lewis, "The American Fear of Literature," Nobel lecture, Stockholm, December 12, 1930, Nobelprize.org, http://www.nobelprize.org/nobel_prizes/literature/laureates/1930/lewis-lecture.html.
"exhale[d] a smell as ancient": JD, unpublished lecture notes, Poetry/Rare Books Collection of the University Libraries, University at Buffalo, State University of New York.
"Was it a Jew": Arthur Schlesinger Jr., "1928–1937: The Infiltration of Modernity," in Updike, *A Century of Arts & Letters,* 91.
The next day's: "Robert Frost Gets Medal of National Arts Institute," *New York Herald Tribune,* January 19, 1939.
"that you may know": Grace Vanamee to JD, Discontinued Awards, Loines Award, 1931–1983, American Academy of Arts and Letters, New York.

86 "The award was": E. Loines to John H. Finley, December 14, 1931, Discontin-

ued Awards, Loines Award, 1931–1983, American Academy of Arts and Letters, New York.

"There is an odor": Harrison Morris to Grace Vanamee, Harrison Morris Papers, American Academy of Arts and Letters, New York.

"Miss Davidman is certainly": Grace Vanamee to Harrison Morris, Harrison Morris Papers, American Academy of Arts and Letters, New York.

"I am extremely grateful": JD to Grace Vanamee, January 29, 1939, Discontinued Awards, Loines Award, 1931–1983, American Academy of Arts and Letters, New York.

"I was so drunk": JD to Willard Maas, January 23, 1939, Willard Maas Collection, Harry Ransom Center, University of Texas.

87 "It's the logical organization": JD to KWP, March 31, 1939, KWP Papers, Schomburg Center.

"Good God, what an assemblage": Ibid.

"pathetic old ladies": JD to Selden Rodman, August 7, 1939, Selden Rodman Papers, American Heritage Center, University of Wyoming.

88 "Modern Trends in English Poetry": "Notes British Authors Speak on Modern Trends in English Writing," *Daily Worker,* April 5, 1939.

"on behalf of": Franklin Folsom, *Days of Anger, Days of Hope: A Memoir of the League of American Writers, 1937–1942* (Boulder: University Press of Colorado, 1994).

More than three hundred people: *League of American Writers Bulletin,* June 1939, 2.

"There was much speaking": Millen Brand, unpublished journals, Millen Brand Papers, Rare Book and Manuscripts Library, Columbia University.

"Joy Davidman and Genevieve Taggard": Selden Rodman, unpublished journals, Yale University Manuscripts and Archives.

89 "Everyone expected 'fighting words'": JD to Selden Rodman, August 7, 1939, Selden Rodman Papers, American Heritage Center, University of Wyoming.

"My mother claims": JD to Stephen Vincent Benét, March 1, 1939, Benét Papers, Beinecke Library.

"A great poet": JD, unpublished lecture notes, Poetry/Rare Books Collection of the University Libraries, University at Buffalo, State University of New York.

"For the present": JD, "Nazi Classroom," *New Masses*, March 14, 1939, 24–25.

90 "If the World's Fair": JD, "The Power-House," *New Masses*, May 16, 1939, 23–24.

"in an age when": JD, "Kansas Poet," Ibid., 26–27.

"I was rather hasty": JD to KWP, February 19, 1939, KWP Papers, Schomburg Center.

91 "I live in the": JD, unpublished notes, Poetry/Rare Books Collection of the University Libraries, University at Buffalo, State University of New York.

"God help me": JD to John Gould Fletcher, May 12, 1939, John Gould Fletcher Papers, University of Arkansas.

"Dosvedanye tovarishch": JD to KWP, March 31, 1939, KWP Papers, Schomburg Center.

92 "Practically everyone": Interviews with Annette Rubinstein and Herbert Ap-

theker, Oral History of the American Left, Radical Histories Collection OH.002, series 1, Tamiment Library/Wagner Archives.

Chapter 5

93 "Leaving New York": JD, "Letter to a Comrade," in *Letter to a Comrade,* 13.
"It pays for my food": JD to James Still, July 18, 1939, James Still Papers, University of Kentucky Special Collections.
94 "The cinema": Francis Winmar, "The Film and the State," *New York Times,* September 8, 1935.
"If it weren't": JD to Selden Rodman, August 7, 1939, Selden Rodman Papers, American Heritage Center, University of Wyoming.
"the question of how": "Writers Congress: League of American Writers Issues Call to Its Third Congress," *New Masses,* May 16, 1939, 17.
"million holes": *Minneapolis Evening Tribune,* June 7, 1939.
"There was tremendous rejoicing": Interview with Annette Rubinstein, Oral History of the American Left, Radical Histories Collection OH.002, series 1, Tamiment Library/Wagner Archives.
approximately two thirds: Gerald Clarke, "Show Business: 1939: Twelve Months of Magic," *Time,* March 13, 1989; at over fifteen thousand: Otto Friedrich, *City of Nets: A Portrait of Hollywood in the 1940s* (University of California Press, 1986), 14.
"When the spirit": Friedrich, *City of Nets,* 13.
95 The writing staff at MGM: Oral History with Richard Goldstone, vol. 1, American Academy of Motion Picture Arts and Sciences, 188–89.
97 "too many sex angles": "Lack of Yarns Sending Studios to Remakes; Few Books, Plays as Writers Turn Political," *Hollywood Reporter,* June 9, 1939.
Drafts of these screenplays and treatments may be found in the Margaret Herrick Library, Academy of Motion Picture Arts and Sciences, and the University of Southern California Cinematic Arts Library.
"We brought you here": Andrew Turnbull, *Scott Fitzgerald* (New York: Scribner, 1962), 294.
"The Hollywood writer": Leo Rosten, *Hollywood: The Movie Colony, the Movie Makers* (New York: Harcourt, Brace and Co., 1941), 308.
"the world's great bullshit center": Virginia Spencer Carr, *Dos Passos: A Life* (Evanston: Northwestern University Press, 2004), 329.
98 "We discovered that": Lee Server, *Screenwriter: Words Become Pictures* (Pittstown, N.J.: Main Street Press, 1987), 115.
"The trouble is": Budd Schulberg, quoted in Robert Van Gelder, *Writers and Writing* (New York: Charles Scribner's Sons, 1946), 199.
"The work here": JD to Selden Rodman, July 13, 1939, Selden Rodman Papers, American Heritage Center, University of Wyoming.
99 "dear": Rosten, *Hollywood,* 48.
Myrna Loy: Ibid., 12.
"a hideous town": Fitzgerald to Alice Robertson, July 29, 1940, in *The Let-*

ters of F. Scott Fitzgerald, ed. Andrew Turnbull (New York: Scribner's, 1963), 603.
"Have you seen a tortoise": JD to Selden Rodman, July 13, 1939, Selden Rodman Papers, American Heritage Center, University of Wyoming.
"I'm a New Yorker": JD to James Still, July 18, 1939, James Still Papers, University of Kentucky Special Collections.
"Murder Prefers Blondes": JD to Selden Rodman, June 27, 1939, Selden Rodman Papers, American Heritage Center, University of Wyoming.
those "who were once Marxists": JD to Selden Rodman, June 27, 1939, Selden Rodman Papers, American Heritage Center, University of Wyoming.

100 "There is a story": JD, "Monopoly Takes a Screen Test," *New Masses*, June 24, 1941, 28–30.
"GARBO LAUGHS": "Ninotchka," promotional insert, *Hollywood Reporter,* September 6, 1939.

101 "very nice boy": GC.
"a girl scientist": Ibid.
"I am homesick": JD to James Still, July 18, 1939, James Still Papers, University of Kentucky Special Collections.
"In six months": JD to Dorothy, July 19, 1939, Wade Center.

102 "The boss": JD to Selden Rodman, July 13, 1939, Selden Rodman Papers, American Heritage Center, University of Wyoming.
"I gloated over": JD to James Still, February 15, 1940, James Still Papers, University of Kentucky Special Collections.
"bossy bossy bossy": Walter Doniger, interview with the author, October 25, 2009.

102–3 "A lion is like": GC.

103 "for protection": JD to James Still, February 15, 1940 James Still Papers, University of Kentucky Special Collections.
"The film business fired me": Ibid.

104 Rodman enjoyed: JD to Selden Rodman, August 7, 1939, Selden Rodman Papers, American Heritage Center, University of Wyoming.

105 "He writes because": Selden Rodman to JD, August 16, 1939, Selden Rodman Papers, American Heritage Center, University of Wyoming.
"there is as much chance": Earl Browder, quoted in Friedrich, *City of Nets,* 24.

106 "As the mob of us": GC.

Chapter 6

107 "I rushed home": JD to James Still, February 15, 1940, James Still Papers, University of Kentucky Special Collections.

108 ("I was serving"): JD to Charles Abbott, January 10, 1940, Poetry/Rare Books Collection of the University Libraries, University at Buffalo, State University of New York.
"I seem to be emerging": JD to Selden Rodman, May 6, 1940, Selden Rodman Papers, American Heritage Center, University of Wyoming.
"Red Primer": JD to James Still, July 18, 1939; and "Rise and Shine": JD to

James Still, February 15, 1940, James Still Papers, University of Kentucky Special Collections.
"I looked forward": JD, "Stephen Vincent Benét," *New Masses*, March 30, 1943, 23–24.
109 "Here is my new book": JD to Stephen Vincent Benét, May 20, 1940, Benét Papers, Beinecke Library.
"We're going on record": Ibid.
110 "The American League": Guenter Lewy, *The Cause That Failed: Communism in American Political Life* (New York: Oxford University Press, 1990), 62, 25–26.
"1.) the need for": Folsom, *Days of Anger, Days of Hope,* 165.
111 "We insist, therefore": "In Defense of Peace," 1940, Folsom-Elting Collection, Special Collections Department, University of Colorado at Boulder Libraries.
"She was ardent": Schneider, "Coming to Terms."
112 "Our quarrel was final": Ibid.
"I don't feel as cordial": William Rose Benét to JD, November 19, 1940, JD Papers, Wade Center.
113 There was certainly: Oral history interview excerpt with HD, October 14, 1983, OH/SR-79 and CSL-Z/SR-5, Wade Center.
"Scandal!": Bel Kaufman, unpublished journals, November 23, 1940, private collection of Bel Kaufman.
"The tragedy of today": Alfred Kazin, Journal, Holograph and Typescript, May 14, 1933–December 31, 1980, Berg Collection, New York Public Library.
"They were *screaming!*": Bel Kaufman, interview with the author, February 7, 2003.
"Men, I said": LWR.
114 "Middle-class philistinism is bad": Alfred Kazin, personal diary, December 27, 1940, Journal, Holograph and Typescript, May 14, 1933–December 31, 1980, Berg Collection, New York Public Library.
"At night, when we dreamed": JD, "Fairytale," in *War Poems of the United Nations,* 299.
115 "The League had nothing": Folsom, *Days of Anger,* 182.
"Theory and Technique of Poetry": Franklin Folsom, quoted in League of American Writers, *Bulletin of the League of American Writers,* Spring 1942, Tamiment Collection.
116 "Truth and falsehood": JD, "The Equivocal Bell," *New Masses*, July 27, 1943, 30–31.
"No one should ever": JD, "St. George Pets the Dragon," *New Masses,* June 3, 1941.
"Far out": JD, "Neptune's Pets," reviews of *Washington Murderdrama, Power Dive,* and *Border Vigilantes, New Masses*, June 10, 1941, 28–29.
"Red propaganda": "2 Russian Films Are Barred as Red Propaganda," *Chicago Daily Tribune,* July 29, 1941.
117 "My life!"; JD, "Soviet Love Story," *New Masses*, April [illegible], 1941, [illegible]–29.
"Do the Soviets": JD, "Volga-Volga," *New Masses*, May 27, 1941, 25.
"reviewers on the commercial press": Ibid.

118 "If Miss Veronica Lake": JD, "Rover Boys on Wings," *New Masses*, April 8, 1941, 28-29.
"The most irritating thing": JD, "Pepe le Moko," *New Masses*, March 25, 1941, 29.
"offensive": JD, "Tripe and Taylor," *New Masses*, July 1, 1941, 30–31.
"talked of her": Bel Kaufman, private journal, July 20, 1940, private collection of Bel Kaufman.
"quiet silky sinister voice": JD to Chad and Eva Walsh, February 13, 1957, Chad Walsh Papers, Wade Center.
"She always pursued": Lyle Dorsett, notes from interview with HD, early 1980s, *And God Came In* Collection, Wade Center.
119 "flotsam of the Old South": FCTC.
"accepted lower-middle-class life": Ibid.
120 "man is not meant": WLG to Osborn Andreas, October 11, 1959, WLG Papers, Wade Center.
"Perhaps": WLG, "Suggested Lecture Outline," WLG Papers, Wade Center.
121 "where the jazz blew hot": Alan Prendergast, "One Man's Nightmare: The Noir Journey of William Lindsay Gresham," *The Writer's Chronicle*, Summer 2006.
"[I] asked no definite": FCTC.
"for a legal party": Ibid.
"We drew strength": Ibid.
122 "I came home": Ibid.
"pleurisy of tubercular origin": WLG to Local Board No. 16, February 10, 1944, WLG Papers, Wade Center.
"anxiety and paranoic symptoms": Dr. Walter Briehl, WLG medical history report, February 22, 1944, WLG Papers, Wade Center.
"two years of disintegration": FCTC.
"He had a nice bass": Pete Seeger, interview with the author, November 16, 2008.
"I snatched at love": FCTC.
"the big dragon": WLG to Major Walter Briehl, February 16, 1944, WLG Papers, Wade Center.
"Finally, since my mind": FCTC.
123 "The Outstanding Intellectual Event": *New Masses,* June 3, 1941.
The conference opened: Unless otherwise noted, all descriptions of the conference are drawn from Panel and Lecture Notes, League of American Writers Fourth Annual Congress, Folsom-Elting Collection, Special Collections Department, University of Colorado at Boulder Libraries.
124 "[he] was never": JD, foreword to Alexander F. Bergman, *They Look Like Men* (New York: B. Ackerman, 1944), 8–9.
126 "She was aggressive": Jerome Hoffman to Lyle Dorsett, February 14, 1982, *And God Came In* Collection, Wade Center.
"[Joy] had a system": Ibid.
127 "I see what she is": Christina Stead to William J. Blake, June 3, 1942, in *Dearest Munx: The Letters of Christina Stead and William J. Blake,* ed. Margaret Harris (Carlton, Victoria: Miegunyah Press, 2005), 164.

127 "You cannot escape": Craig Shirley, *December 1941: 31 Days That Changed America and Saved the World* (Nashville: Thomas Nelson,2011), 177–78.
128 "Joy Davidman has a guy": Christina Stead to William J. Blake, June 3, 1942, in *Dearest Munx,* 199.

Chapter 7

129 "Love is not": JD, "Women: Hollywood Style," *New Masses*, July 14, 1942, 28–31.
131 "couldn't feel quite right": Marian MacDowell, unpublished typescript, Edward and Marian MacDowell Collection, Performing Arts Reading Room, Library of Congress.
"There was always": Ibid.
132 "his own little": Ibid.
"Marrying off": Marian MacDowell to JD, JD Papers, Wade Center.
"a human filing cabinet": Helen Myers, "The Greshams Live in Pleasant Plains," *Poughkeepsie Sunday New Yorker,* June 6, 1948.
"swell guy": Bel Kaufman, unpublished journal, September 20, 1942, private collection of Bel Kaufman.
133 "For a time": FCTC.
"I seem": JD to Jean Starr Untermeyer, July 2, 1943, Jean Starr Untermeyer Collection, State University of New York at Buffalo.
134 "to be not less": JD, book contract with Dial Press, JD Papers, Wade Center.
"The sooner this volume appears": JD to Ruth Lechlitner, October 28, 1942, Papers of Ruth Lechlitner, Special Collections, University of Iowa Libraries.
135 "young poets": JD, *War Poems of the United Nations*, 267.
"purified": Ibid., dust jacket flap copy.
"flitting butterfly stuff": LWR.
"There are 11 of us": GC.
"appalling shortage": Joy Davidman to Edwin Rolfe, December 29, 1942, University of Illinois Rare Books and Manuscripts Library.
"a driving person": Franklin Folsom, interview by Lyle Dorsett, May 30, 1982, *And God Came In* Collection, Wade Center.
136 "British poetry": JD, *War Poems of the United Nations,* 23.
"Hayden Weir": Ibid., 50.
"supplement": GC.
"The funny thing was": Ibid.
137 "*That* was a rush job": JD to KWP, May 29, 1951, KWP Papers, Schomburg Center.
"superficial patriotism": H. R. Hays, "Poems with Mars for a Muse," *New York Times Book Review,* November 28, 1943.
"the weakest sections": Ibid.
138 "Service Man's Book Committee": "Books—Authors," *New York Times*, May 10, 1943.
"This is job enough": JD to Jean Starr Untermeyer, July 2, 1943, Jean Starr Untermeyer Collection, State University of New York at Buffalo.

"So I've plenty of reasons": Ibid.

139 "When I asked": Myers, "The Greshams Live in Pleasant Plains."

140 "Smart, these CLICK folks!": Tom Slater, "Click Clicks," *Click Magazine,* November 1943.

"By and large": WLG to Major Walter Briehl, February 16, 1944, WLG Papers, Wade Center.

141 "When Mr. Gresham": Walter Briehl to Local Board No. 16, February 28, 1944, WLG Papers, Wade Center.

"Both of them": Ruth Parsons Davidman, interview with the author, May 20, 2003.

142 "He was a mess": Ibid.

"terribly impressed": Ibid.

"the element of surprise": JD to HD, August 17, 1945, SDC Collection.

"We are both very happy": WLG to Major Walter Briehl, February 16, 1944, WLG Papers, Wade Center.

143 "Young David or Miriam": Ibid.

"seven leading American poets": Thomas Yoseloff, ed., *Seven Poets in Search of an Answer* (New York: B. Ackerman, 1944), dust jacket copy.

"While you rave": JD, "For the Nazis," ibid., 34.

"They killed him": Ibid., 34–35.

"Flaming words smoke": Review of *Seven Poets in Search of an Answer, San Francisco Chronicle.*

"In one of": Franklin Delano Roosevelt, "Address to the Nation," March 24, 1944, quoted in Michael Beschloss, *The Conquerors: Roosevelt, Truman, and the Destruction of Hitler's Germany, 1941–1945* (New York: Simon & Schuster, 2002), 59.

144 "Go easy with the Nazis": JD to Ruth and Howard Davidman, May 10, 1944, SDC Collection.

"Will take seven ounces": Ibid.

145 "certainly not": Ibid.

"I guggle over [Davy]": Ibid.

146 "working like a demon": Ibid.

"I've got her in the habit": Ibid.

"sweet-voiced . . . well-dressed": JD, "Life with Mother," *New Masses*, July 10, 1945, 26–27.

"Now I've got her rationed": JD to Ruth and Howard Davidman, May 10, 1944, SDC Collection.

147 "Everything is very serene": Ibid.

Chapter 8

149 "The Japanese": JD to HD, June 25, 1945, SDC Collection.

"Life up here": JD to Alice and Jerry [Jerome], January 19, 1945, Victor Jeemy Jerome Papers, Manuscripts and Archives, Sterling Memorial Library, Yale University.

149 "Time brings a sad sobriety": JD, unpublished sonnet, August 4, 1944, JD Papers, Wade Center.
150 "I will be very glad": JD to HD, June 25, 1945, SDC Collection.
"Why, why, why": JD to Alice and Jerry [Jerome], January 19, 1945, Victor Jeremy Jerome Papers, Manuscripts and Archives, Sterling Memorial Library, Yale University.
151 "I myself wouldn't dream": Ibid.
152 "a forty year old": Ibid.
153 "A dying class": Ibid.
"patients": CSL, *The Screwtape Letters* (New York: Simon & Schuster, 1996), 40, 2, 26, 3–4, 16.
154 "These books stirred": LWR.
"early, uneasy stage": JD to Charles D. Abbott, March 31, 1945, Poetry/Rare Books Collection of the University Libraries, University at Buffalo, State University of New York.
"my next offspring": JD to HD, May 25, 1945, SDC Collection.
"Suggested idea": Ibid.
155 "Her erudition was overwhelming": Ruth Parsons Davidman, interview with the author, May 20, 2003.
"grinding stories": Ruth Parsons Davidman to HD, June 11, 1945, SDC Collection.
"finished at last": JD to HD, June 25, 1945, SDC Collection.
"all ready for": JD to HD, May 25, 1945, SDC Collection.
156 "Hell, I shoulda": Ibid.
157 "I let Mother": JD to HD, June 25, 1945, SDC Collection.
"very tense": Ruth Parsons Davidman to HD, July 30, 1945, SDC Collection.
"seeing them through": JD to HD, August 17, 1945, SDC Collection.
"saw through every": Ruth Parsons Davidman to HD, July 30, 1945, SDC Collection.
"a confounded *bore*": Ibid.
158 "adequate": JD to HD, June 25, 1945, SDC Collection.
"She was beginning": Ruth Parsons, interview with the author, May 20, 2003.
159 "the old bitch": JD to HD, August 17, 1945, SDC Collection.
"The food shortage": JD to HD, June 25, 1945, SDC Collection.
160 "It would seem": Ibid.
"new words, new teeth": JD to HD, August 17, 1945, SDC Collection.
161 "like a steer": Ibid.
"the nullity of Truman": Ibid.
"relative to it": "The Bomb," *Time,* August 20, 1945.
162 "The last years": JD to HD, August 17, 1945, SDC Collection.
"that civilization may be destroyed": JD to V. J. and Alice Jerome, January 21, 1948, Victor Jeremy Jerome Papers, Manuscripts and Archives, Sterling Memorial Library, Yale University.
"in order to avoid": Oral history interview excerpt with HD, October 14, 1983, OH/SR-79 and CSL-Z/SR-5, Wade Center.
"I wanted to": LWR.
"Poor poet": JD, "Tragic Muse," JD Papers, Wade Center.
163 "ashes that were babies": JD, "When They Grow Up," JD Papers, Wade Center.

"In a week he's changed": JD to HD, September 10, 1945, SDC Collection.
164 "good enough": Ibid.
"our first income": Ibid.
"had a way of going": Ruth Parsons, interview with the author, May 20, 2003.
165 "Any other time": JD to HD, September 10, 1945, SDC Collection.
"a trifle uneasy": JD to HD, October 18, 1945, SDC Collection.
166 "Over all of this": Ibid.
"like a runaway": Ibid.
"rather unnecessarily drastic": JD to HD, November 21, 1945, SDC Collection.
167 "overwork, starve, and underpay": Ibid.
"These dames": Ibid.
168 "was a killer": WLG to HD, note attached to JD's letter to HD, November 21, 1945, SDC Collection.
"x-ray treatments": Ibid.
"My god how": JD to HD, November 21, 1945, SDC Collection.
169 "All the world": LWR.
"eloquent talk": Bel Kaufman, unpublished journal, February 8, 1946, private collection of Bel Kaufman.
"I have two sons": JD, "This Year of the Atom," JD Papers, Wade Center.
170 "in a large": Helen Puner to Lyle Dorsett, November 29, 1981, *And God Came In* Collection, Wade Center.
"My days were filled": FCTC.
"weeks have gone": JD to Ruth Parsons Davidman, April 3, 1946, SDC Collection.
"There's violets and appil blossoms": Ibid.
"escaped from prison": JD to HD and Ruth Parsons Davidman, April 15, 1946, SDC Collection.
170–71 "a more open kind of poetry": Interview with Thomas McGrath, Oral History of the American Left, Radical Histories Collection OH.002, Tamiment Library/Wagner Archives.
171 "They didn't know": JD to William Rose Benét, February 1, 1949, Benét Correspondence, Beinecke Library.
"less chained down": JD to HD and Ruth Parsons Davidman, April 25, 1946, SDC Collection.
"Davy has sworn": JD to HD and Ruth Parsons Davidman, April 15, 1946, SDC Collection.
"Po' Bill": JD to Ruth Parsons Davidman, April 3, 1946, SDC Collection.
172 "[I'm] having a nervous breakdown": Accounts of Bill's breakdown and Joy's spiritual awakening can be found in GC, FCTC, and LWR.
"She wasn't sure": Oral history interview excerpt with HD, October 14, 1983, OH/SR-79 and CSL-Z/SR-5, Wade Center.
173 "slogged along": Ibid.
"By nightfall": LWR.
"There is only": JD, "The Language Men Speak," *New Masses*, November 30, 1943, 26–27.
"there was nothing": LWR.
174 "When my husband": Ibid.

Chapter 9

175 "I assumed that science": LWR.
"just another of man's": JD to William Rose Benét, October 31, 1948, Benét Papers, Beinecke Library.
"It suddenly seemed": WLG, *Grapevine* typescript, WLG Papers, Wade Center.
"Revelation: Once experienced": JD, unpublished notes for "Bright Reason Will Mock Thee," JD Papers, Wade Center.
"aesthetic experiences": LWR.
176 "an unsystematic but intense course": FCTC.
"What do you want": GC.
"What we comrades": JD to Chad Walsh, January 27, 1950, Chad Walsh Papers, Wade Center.
"Logical enough": LWR.
177 "Hmm": GC.
"Fellow of Magdalen College": Chad Walsh, "C. S. Lewis: Apostle to the Skeptics," *Atlantic Monthly,* September 1946, 115–19.
"the fact that Lewis": Ibid.
178 "The Jew who enters": JD, unpublished notes, "Seven Deadly Virtues," JD Papers, Wade Center.
"constant reference points": FCTC.
"sinister and compelling": Clip Boutell, review of *Nightmare Alley, Washington Post,* July 7, 1946.
179 "We looked around": WLG to "Jeanne," July 14, 1948.
"had to have a woodlot": Myers, "The Greshams Live in Pleasant Plains."
180 "[My] southern plantation": Renee Gresham, interview with Lyle Dorsett, May 28, 1981, *And God Came In* Collection.
"They were very": Mary Stevenson, interview with the author, February 19, 2009.
"Upper-level Salvation Army": Ibid.
"Everything [is] coming to life": JD to Aaron Kramer, February 7, 1948, Aaron Kramer Papers, Special Collections Library, University of Michigan.
181 "We are crying out": JD, *Smoke on the Mountain: An Interpretation of the Ten Commandments* (Philadelphia: Westminster Press, 1954), 14.
"one of the most": "Don v. Devil," *Time,* September 8, 1947, 67.
"With erudition": Ibid.
182 "1) That the material": GC.
"lunatic, liar, or Lord": CSL, *Mere Christianity* (New York: HarperCollins Publishers, 2001), 52.
"History is full": JD to Chad Walsh, January 27, 1950, Chad Walsh Papers, Wade Center.
183 "What convinced us": Ibid.
"Some [religions] had wisdom": LWR.
184 "a forum for": "Mainstream: A New Literary Quarterly," advertisement in *New York Times,* December 22, 1946.
"I reminded myself": LWR.
"A sum can": CSL, *The Great Divorce* (New York: Macmillan, 1946).

"It was a difficult": LWR.
"The book is pathetic": JD to V. J. and Alice Jerome, January 21, 1948, Victor Jeremy Jerome Papers, Manuscripts and Archives, Sterling Memorial Library, Yale University.

185 "Why *this* is *bull*shit": This anecdote appears in a handwritten note in the margin of a copy of C. S. Lewis's obituary that belonged to Renee Gresham, now available in the *And God Came In* Collection, Wade Center.
"the *real* ground": JD to William Rose Benét, October 31, 1948, Benét Correspondence, Beinecke Library.
"I don't mind": Ibid.

187 "supper club": Mary Stevenson to the author, February 19, 2009.
"Bill had social skills": Ibid.
"impatient when people": Ibid.

188 "self-centered, arrogant": HD, interview with Lyle Dorsett, *And God Came In* Collection, Wade Center.
"My sister got converted": Oral history interview excerpts with HD, October 14, 1983, OH/SR-79 and CSL-Z/SR-5, Wade Center.
"'We're broke'": Myers, "The Greshams Live in Pleasant Plains."
"Don't forget the": Ibid.

189 "One of the most": WLG, *Houdini: The Man Who Walked Through Walls* (New York: Holt, 1959), 288.
"Drinking was no longer fun": FCTC.
"phoney rhetoric": LWR.

190 "I said": WLG, "From the Land of the Head Shrinkers," *Grapevine: The International Journal of Alcoholics Anonymous.*
"first attempts": *Newsweek,* February 20, 1950, 70.
"I no longer doubted": FCTC.
"When *Nightmare Alley*": WLG to Jeanne Ziering, July 14, 1948.

191 "A free-lance has": WLG to Rose, Walter, and Dorothy, published as "More Ghosts from 'Shadowlands' Past: An Old Friend Shares a Letter from Joy Davidman Gresham's Husband," *Taconic Newspapers,* March 3, 1994.
"The house Joy": Franklin Folsom to Lyle Dorsett, May 30, 1982, *And God Came In* Collection, Wade Center.

192 "[She] told me": Father Victor White, quoted in George Sayer, *Jack: A Life of C. S. Lewis* (Wheaton, Ill.: Crossway, 2005), 351.
"I *felt* I knew him": Chad Walsh, afterword to CSL, *A Grief Observed* (New York: Bantam Books, 1976).

193 "The books had wit": Chad Walsh, *C. S. Lewis: Apostle to the Skeptics* (New York: Macmillan, 1949), 11–13.
"no matter how asinine": Ibid., 14, 18.

194 "By the way": JD to Chad Walsh, June 21, 1949, Chad Walsh Collection, Wade Center.
"We more than share": Ibid.
"idyllic": Oral history interview excerpts with Chad and Eva Walsh, October 12, 1983, OH/SR-47, October 12, 1983, Wade Center.
("I'm afraid my inspiration"): JD to Chad Walsh, June 21, 1949, Chad Walsh Collection, Wade Center.

194 "Having loved my love": JD, Sonnet II, JD Papers, Wade Center.

195 "I'm feeling rather shaken": JD to William Rose Benét, August 19, 1949, Benét Correspondence, Beinecke Library.

196 "As your brother": HD, interview with Lyle Dorsett, *And God Came In* Collection, Wade Center.

"My conscience wouldn't": JD to unknown person, undated letter fragment, JD Papers, Wade Center.

"I tell my memories": JD, unpublished poem, JD Papers, Wade Center.

197 "You would not think": JD, unpublished poem, JD Papers, Wade Center.

198 "With Miss Davidman's cooperation": Joseph Starobin, "The N.Y. Post's Girl Communist," *Daily Worker,* November 8, 1949.

"Helen Joy Davidman": JD FBI file, memo, May 5, 1953, acquired under Freedom of Information Act (FOIA).

"no information of real value": JD FBI File, H. B. Fletcher, memo to D. M. Ladd, Assistant Director of the FBI, December 13, 1949, acquired under FOIA.

"It is noted": JD FBI file, memo, May 5, 1953.

199 "Until 10th January 1950": Warren H. Lewis, November 5, 1956, WHL Diaries, Wade Center.

"I think I told you": JD to Chad Walsh, January 27, 1950, Chad Walsh Collection, Wade Center.

200 "You've not only": JD to Lotte Jacobi, February 12, 1950, Lotte Jacobi Papers, Milne Special Collections, University of New Hampshire Library.

"Which should we use": JD to Lotte Jacobi, March 10, 1950, Lotte Jacobi Papers, Milne Special Collections, University of New Hampshire Library.

"insight": Joseph Henry Jackson, "A Bookman's Notebook: Novel of the Gaspe," *Los Angeles Times,* March 8, 1950.

201 "How Gresham freed himself": *Newsweek,* February 20, 1950, 70.

"Looking at his face": Chad Walsh, introduction to FCTC, *Presbyterian Life,* February 18, 1950.

"No story of": FCTC.

"some visceral or glandular": LWR.

202 "Most of his struggles": Alan Jacobs, *The Narnian: The Life and Imagination of C. S. Lewis,* 1st ed. (New York: HarperSanFrancisco, 2005), 159.

"It's strange": LWR.

203 "My present hope": Ibid.

Chapter 10

204 "almost unbelievable": John Campbell, quoted in Janet Reitman, *Inside Scientology: The Story of America's Most Secretive Religion* (Boston: Houghton Mifflin Harcourt, 2011), 23.

"intelligent layman": Hubbard, *Dianetics: The Modern Science of Mental Health, a Handbook of Dianetic Therapy,* 1st ed. (New York: Hermitage House, 1950), l.

205 "without whose speculations": Hubbard, quoted in Reitman, *Inside Scientology,* 26.

"from all indications": Walter Winchell, quoted ibid., 23.

"computing machine": Hubbard, *Dianetics,* 56, 74.
"corrosive douche": Elaine C. Stewart, *Liberty,* Summer 1952.
Assessing another case: "Of Two Minds," *Time,* July 24, 1950.

206 "achieve at least": Hubbard, quoted in Rollo May, "How to Backtrack and Get Ahead," *New York Times,* July 2, 1950.
"bursts of irrational rage": WLG to Al, undated letter, WLG Papers, Wade Center.
"I was cutting back": WLG to Al, January 27, 1959, WLG Papers, Wade Center.

207 "technology": WLG to JD, December 3, 1956, WLG Correspondence, Wade Center.
"no attempt": WLG to Al, undated letter, WLG Papers, Wade Center.

208 "Words, Terms and Phrases": Hubbard, *Dianetics,* 539.
"I've given her three runs": JD to WLG, October 24, 1952, JD Papers, Wade Center.
"pseudo-psychiatric cult": Oral history interview excerpts with HD, October 14, 1983, OH/SR-79 and CSL-Z/SR-5, Wade Center.
"the encouragement": Stewart, *Liberty.*

209 "had a long": WLG to Phylis Haring, May 9, 1960, WLG Papers, Wade Center.
"You see, chances": Stewart, *Liberty.*

210 "She accused my": Oral history interview excerpts with HD, October 14, 1983, OH/SR-79 and CSL-Z/SR-5, Wade Center.
"dragon": WLG to Phylis Haring, May 9, 1960, WLG Papers, Wade Center.
"One of the things": Oral history interview excerpts with Chad and Eva Walsh, October 12, 1983, OH/SR-47, Wade Center.
"cussed her out proper": WLG to Phyllis Haring, May 9, 1960, WLG Papers, Wade Center.

211 "My love for him": JD to Chad Walsh, February 27, 1953, Chad Walsh Collection, Wade Center.
"It's been an unpleasant winter": JD to Mr. and Mrs. Reiss, March 21, 1951, Lotte Jacobi Papers, Milne Special Collections, University of New Hampshire Library.
"Bill and I": JD to KWP, May 29, 1951, KWP Papers, Schomburg Center.
"all they were": HD to Susan Davidman Cleveland, October 22, 1983, SDC Collection.
"crying and hollering": Mary Stevenson to the author, February 19, 2009.

212 "big and warm": Douglas H. Gresham, *Lenten Lands* (New York: Macmillan, 1988), 32.
"began to have": WLG to Al, January 15, 1960, WLG Papers, Wade Center.
"Do you know": WLG to Chad Walsh, postscript attached to letter from JD to Chad Walsh, January 27, 1950, Chad Walsh Collection, Wade Center.
"my teacher": JD to KWP, August 16, 1951, KWP Papers, Schomburg Center.
"If fundamentalism means": CSL to Janet Wise, May 10, 1955, in *Collected Letters* vol. 3 (London: HarperCollins, 2004).

213 "I don't believe": JD to KWP, August 16, 1951, KWP Papers, Schomburg Center.

213 "I am shocked": CSL to Mary Margaret McCaslin, August 2, 1954, in *Collected Letters,* vol. 3.
"the substance of things": Hebrews 11:1.
"running argument": JD to KWP, August 16, 1951, KWP Papers, Schomburg Center.
"hungry for": CSL, *The Quotable Lewis,* ed. Wayne Martindale and Jerry Root (Carol Stream, Ill.: Tyndale House Publishers, 1989), 462.

214 "one of the most powerful": Norman Parkinson, "Oxford Personalities," *Vogue,* November 1951, 98–103.
"the handsomest thunderstorms": JD to KWP, August 16, 1951, KWP Papers, Schomburg Center.
"in literary terms": Oral history interview excerpts with Chad and Eva Walsh, October 12, 1983, OH/SR-47, Wade Center.

215 "lord": JD, "First Meeting," Sonnet VI, December 19, 1952, JD Papers, Wade Center.
"distinctly sexual undertones": John Christopher, "Notes on Joy," in *Encounter,* April 1987, 41–43.
(From my great pain): JD, "Courage" folder, JD Papers, Wade Center.

216 "Begin again": JD, "First Meeting," Sonnet I, December 19, 1952, JD Papers, Wade Center.
"terrible third": JD, margin note in draft of Sonnet II, JD Papers, Wade Center.
"America, 1951": JD, sonnets, JD Papers, Wade Center.
"It was her ambition": CSL, *Collected Letters*, vol. 3, 508.
"quite sensible": Paul Sargent, "Marry? I'll Be Miles Away, Says the Professor," *Daily Mail,* October 26, 1956.
"When he stopped replying": Ibid.

217 "Let me not lie": JD, Sonnet IV, JD Papers, Wade Center.

218 "the greatest discovery": JD, "Into the Full Light," *Presbyterian Life,* April 4, 1953; JD, "God Comes First," *Presbyterian Life,* May 2, 1953.

219 "an excuse for": JD, "Into the Full Light"; JD, "God Comes First."
"What should": CSL, foreword to *Smoke on the Mountain,* 9.
"The beast in the heart": JD, "God Comes First."
"I have loved you": JD, Sonnet X, February 14, 1953, JD Papers, Wade Center.
"What if the medium": JD, margin notes in her copy of CSL, *The Problem of Pain* (New York: Macmillan, 1943), Wade Center.

220 "It has been said": WLG to Carl, May 5, 1955, WLG Papers, Wade Center.
Joy now believed: Joy recounts several ESPER incidents in her letters to Bill from England in the fall of 1952.

221 "[Joy] was an opportunist": Mary Stevenson to the author, February 19, 2009.
"proper breakfast": Renee Gresham to the author, October 21, 2003.
"We'd sit at": Ibid.

222 "Every evening practically": Ibid.
"I must ask myself": Gresham, *Lenten Lands,* 16.
"My sister always knew": Oral history interview excerpts with HD, October 14, 1983, OH/SR-79 and CSL-Z/SR-5, Wade Center.
"Joy was in": WLG to CSL, April 2, 1957, WLG Correspondence, Wade Center.

$925: Attorney Charles A. Butts to WLG, February 26, 1954, WLG Correspondence, Wade Center.

223 "As the time": WLG to CSL, April 2, 1957, WLG Correspondence, Wade Center.

"not the marrying sort": Ibid.

Chapter 11

225 "So": JD to WLG, August 20, 1952, JD Papers, Wade Center.

"enormous stone jewel": JD to WLG, August 16, 1952, JD Papers, Wade Center.

"an incredible law-abiding people": JD to WLG, August 29, 1952, JD Papers, Wade Center.

"practically mother you": JD to WLG, August 20, 1952, JD Papers, Wade Center.

226 "and they showered me": JD to WLG, September 1, 1952, JD Papers, Wade Center.

"London sunlight is never": JD to WLG, August 29, 1952, JD Papers, Wade Center.

"Londoners basking": JD to WLG, August 20, 1952, JD Papers, Wade Center.

"God help my figure": JD to Renee Pierce, August 16, 1952, JD Papers, Wade Center.

"Got a luscious Jaeger": JD to WLG, August 20, 1952, JD Papers, Wade Center.

227 "You know what": JD to Renee Pierce, August 16, 1952, JD Papers, Wade Center.

"Sorry . . . you're still busted": JD to WLG, September 1, 1952, JD Papers, Wade Center.

"I shocked 'em": JD to WLG, August 20, 1952, JD Papers, Wade Center.

"Hubbard has now gone": Ibid.

228 "with deep dark distrust": JD to WLG, August 29, 1952, JD Papers, Wade Center.

"callow": Christopher, "Notes on Joy," 41–43.

229 "Mrs. Williams suggested": JD to WLG, September 1, 1952, JD Papers, Wade Center.

"Joy Gresham is an old": CSL to Michal Williams, September 12, 1952, in *Collected Letters,* vol. 3.

The chronology of those first: Details about Joy's initial meetings with C. S. Lewis remain cloudy, at points almost byzantine. Both George Sayer and Warnie Lewis, and even some comments by Jack himself, offer accounts that are at points inconsistent, even outright contradictory. Neither Sayer nor Warnie nor Joy, in her copious, candid letters to Bill Gresham, mentions her having visited the Kilns in September 1952, but in a letter to Roger Lancelyn Green on the twenty-sixth of that month, Jack refers to "the American writer Joy Davidman (who has been staying with us)." This note seems to imply that Joy visited the Lewis brothers at the Kilns; whether Lewis meant that Joy was staying with them at the Kilns or staying with them in England is uncertain. After thorough research and analysis of all available evidence, I have ordered the events as closely as I can given the varying accounts, published and unpublished. In the course of my investigation, C. S. Lewis scholar Andrew Lazo generously afforded me access to his forthcoming work on Joy's role in the composition of *Till We Have Faces*. Lazo discovered the September 17 date and agrees in principle to my assessment; his valuable book promises to explore this seminal meeting further.

229 "I call this civilized": Sayer, *Jack: A Life of C. S. Lewis,* 353–54.
"laughed uproariously": George Sayer, interview with Lyle Dorsett, August 7, 1981, *And God Came In* Collection, Wade Center.
"Everything she saw in England": Sayer, *Jack: A Life of C. S. Lewis,* 352, 353.

230 "What's that place": Ibid., 353.
"When I first loved you": JD, "The Sacred Chest Gone," Sonnet XXIV, February 6, 1954, JD Papers, Wade Center.
"Jack asked me to stay": Sayer, *Jack: A Life of C. S. Lewis,* 353.
Should he and his brother: George Sayer, interview with Lyle Dorsett, August 7, 1981, *And God Came In* Collection, Wade Center.
While the Kilns had: CSL to Vera Gebbert, September 20, 1952, in *Collected Letters,* vol. 3.
"Live your normal life": George Sayer, interview with Lyle Dorsett, August 7, 1981, *And God Came In* Collection, Wade Center.

231 Sayer was shocked: Ibid.
"I confess": Albert Lewis, May 20, 1919, quoted in CSL, *All My Road Before Me* (Boston: Houghton Mifflin Harcourt, 1992), 8.

232 "I don't think": Warren H. Lewis, January 17, 1951, WHL Diaries, Wade Center.
"as good as": Warren H. Lewis, "Memoir of C. S. Lewis," in *The Letters of C. S. Lewis* (London: Geoffrey Bles, 1966), 16.
"the rape of J's life": Warren H. Lewis, January 17, 1951, WHL Diaries, Wade Center.
"For most men": CSL to Sarah Neylan, March 4, 1949, in *Collected Letters,* vol. 3.
"One evening with him": JD to WLG, October 4, 1952, JD Papers, Wade Center.
"I notice Jack's principles": JD to WLG, October 15, 1952, JD Papers, Wade Center.
"either the ultra masculine": CSL to Dorothy Sayers, August 5, 1955, in *Collected Letters,* vol. 3.

233 "I'm enjoying myself": JD to WLG, September 30, 1952, JD Papers, Wade Center.
"and, above all, sliced bacon": JD to Renee Pierce, August 16, 1952, JD Papers, Wade Center.
"run it off": JD to WLG, October 4, 1952, JD Papers, Wade Center.

234 "Lawsy, what a tale": Ibid.
"Ah, well": Ibid.
In his next dispatch: This letter has never come to light, but Joy's response on October 6 suggests the contents.
"Golly, I had no idea": JD to WLG, October 6, 1952, JD Papers, Wade Center.

235 "Glad of the one": Ibid.

"panic-stricken . . . feeling guilty": JD to WLG, October 13, 1952, JD Papers, Wade Center.

"I was some little time": Warren H. Lewis, November 5, 1956, WHL Diaries, Wade Center.

236 "A rapid friendship developed": Ibid.

"treated her": Warren H. Lewis to George Sayer, quoted in *Jack: A Life of C. S. Lewis*, 353.

"[Lewis] had not met anyone": Ibid., 354.

"She had high spiritual": Oral history interview excerpt with George Sayer, October 10–12, 1989, OH/SR-35 and OH/VR-19, Wade Center.

"[I] returned Jack": JD to WLG, October 13, 1952, JD Papers, Wade Center.

237 "a poor loony": JD to WLG, October 18, 1952, JD Papers, Wade Center.

"rage": JD to WLG, October 24, 1952, JD Papers, Wade Center.

"Hubbard is now": JD to WLG, October 29, 1952, JD Papers, Wade Center.

238 "Chillun crying for bread": JD to WLG, October 24, 1952, JD Papers, Wade Center.

"I scanned off": JD to WLG, October 29, 1952, JD Papers, Wade Center.

"demanding and bossy": JD to WLG, November 3, 1952, JD Papers, Wade Center.

239 "I felt I was": Ibid.

"The inhabitants": Michal Williams to Chad Walsh, November 14, 1952, Chad Walsh Papers, Wade Center.

240 "I think you'll find": JD to WLG, November 4, 1952, JD Papers, Wade Center.

"had a brain wave": JD to WLG, November 8, 1952, JD Papers, Wade Center.

"I've been having": JD to WLG, November 14, 1952, JD Papers, Wade Center.

"Such a relief": JD to WLG, November 8, 1952, JD Papers, Wade Center.

241 "very lovely": WLG to JD, October 31, 1952, WLG Correspondence, Wade Center.

"spellbound": JD to Douglas H. Gresham, November 10, 1952, JD Papers, Wade Center.

"I wonder why": JD to WLG, November 17, 1952, JD Papers, Wade Center.

242 "Lingering vestiges of sin": JD to WLG, November 23, 1952, JD Papers, Wade Center.

"Hooker's Laws of Ecclesiastical Polity": Ibid.

243 "I find that": Ibid.

"You have written": WLG to JD, undated letter, WLG Correspondence, Wade Center.

244 "Joy wept": In her letter to Bill dated December 1, 1952, Joy refers to her "weepiest letter," evidently in response to his undated letter declaring his love for Renee. The "weepiest letter" has not survived, but the reference suggests that Bill's undated letter was received in late November.

245 "Gothic forest": JD to WLG, December 1, 1952, JD Papers, Wade Center.

"My lord and love": JD, "First Meeting," Sonnet VI, December 19, 1952, JD Papers, Wade Center.

246 "Talking of Americans": CSL to Bel Allen, December 9, 1952, in *Collected Letters*, vol. 3.

246 "There are three images": CSL, inscription to Joy Davidman in her copy of *The Great Divorce*, December 29, 1952, private collection of Steven Beebe.

247 "O Hell!": CSL, quoted in a footnote in *Collected Letters,* vol. 3, 45.
"In a sense": CSL, foreword to JD, *Smoke on the Mountain,* 7–8.
"I am completely": CSL to Laurence Harwood, December 19, 1952, in *Collected Letters,* vol. 3.
248 "The whole vac.": CSL to George and Moira Sayer, December 23, 1952, ibid.
"What is offered as Friendship": CSL, *The Four Loves* (New York: Harcourt, Brace, 1960), 72–73.
"I brought my love obedience": JD, "Sonnet of Misunderstanding," Sonnet VIII, January 1953, JD Papers, Wade Center.

Chapter 12

249 "project": WLG to Joe and Kay Mullin, October 26, 1959, WLG Papers, Wade Center.
"gnawed [his] knuckles": WLG to Al, February 8, 1960, WLG Papers, Wade Center.
"Clever spiderwebs I weave": JD, Sonnet XIV, February 22, 1953, JD Papers, Wade Center.
250 "He earned almost no money": JD to Chad Walsh, February 27, 1953, Chad Walsh Papers, Wade Center.
"[He] has always insisted": JD to Chad Walsh, August 3, 1953, Chad Walsh Papers, Wade Center.
"Bill greeted me": JD to Chad Walsh, February 27, 1953, Chad Walsh Papers, Wade Center.
"The worst part": Douglas Gresham, email to the author, November 22, 2014.
"drunken wastrel of a husband": WHL Diary, November 5, 1956, WHL Diaries, Wade Center.
"a propaganda campaign": David Lindsay Gresham, letter to the author, January 7, 2007.
"It is also": David Lindsay Gresham, email to the author, March 21, 2006.
251 "My conscience wouldn't": JD to Chad Walsh, February 27, 1953, Chad Walsh Papers, Wade Center.
"very upset": Bel Kaufman, unpublished journal, January 30, 1953, private collection of Bel Kaufman.
"Look, it's up to you": Renee Gresham to the author, October 21, 2003.
252 "there is actually nothing": Chad Walsh to JD, March 6, 1953, Chad Walsh Papers, Wade Center.
"I keep at it": JD to Renee Pierce, March 19, 1953, WLG Correspondence, Wade Center.
"I hope to take": JD to Chad Walsh, February 27, 1953, Chad Walsh Papers, Wade Center.
"I feel as if": JD to Renee Pierce, April 16, 1953, WLG Correspondence, Wade Center.
253 "I have forgot": JD, "Sonnet of Memories," Sonnet VIII, Christmas 1952, JD Papers, Wade Center.

"I said it did not hurt": JD, "Non Dolet," Sonnet XIII, March 20, 1950.
"Don't worry, cookie": JD to Renee Pierce, April 16, 1953, WLG Correspondence, Wade Center.
"most of the time": Ibid.
"Living in the same house": WLG to Al, January 22, 1959, WLG Papers, Wade Center.

254 "I begged her to stay": WLG to CSL, April 2, 1957, WLG Correspondence, Wade Center.
"It is not": JD to WLG, July 28, 1953, WLG Correspondence, Wade Center.
"I cannot bear": JD to Renee Pierce, July 9, 1953, WLG Correspondence, Wade Center.
"One of the things": Ibid.

255 "fellow victims": JD to Renee Pierce, July 20, 1953, WLG Correspondence, Wade Center.
"saying what I thought": JD to Chad and Eva Walsh, August 3, 1953, Chad Walsh Papers, Wade Center.

256 "[He] continues to build": JD to Renee Pierce, July 20, 1953, WLG Correspondence, Wade Center.
"I shall come lightly": JD, "Hopeful Sonnet," Sonnet IX, August 21, 1953, JD Papers, Wade Center.
"Stumbling among the tussocky": Gresham, *Lenten Lands,* 33.

257 "You were so sweet": JD to WLG, November 14, 1953, WLG Correspondence, Wade Center.

Chapter 13

258 "O may the rooks": JD, "Hopeful Sonnet," Sonnet IX, August 21, 1953, JD Papers, Wade Center.
"I do not like": Lyle Dorsett, *And God Came In* (New York: Macmillan, 1983), 95.
"dressed in a knight's armor": Gresham, *Lenten Lands,* 105.

259 "You know I can't": JD to WLG, November 14, 1953, WLG Correspondence, Wade Center.

260 "The boys are clamoring": JD to WLG, November 19, 1953, WLG Correspondence, Wade Center.
"even *better* proportioned": Ibid.

261 "What I want most": JD to WLG, December 22, 1953, WLG Correspondence, Wade Center.
"vague dreamy": JD to WLG, December 10, 1953, WLG Correspondence, Wade Center.

262 "You and I had": JD to WLG, December 22, 1953, WLG Correspondence, Wade Center.
"the roller-coaster ride": JD to WLG, January 4, 1954, WLG Correspondence, Wade Center.

263 "[She] decided that a marriage": Christopher, "Notes on Joy," 41–43.
"one and two halves": Gresham, *Lenten Lands,* 29, 39, 55.

264 "exotic": CSL to Vera Gebbert, December 23, 1953, in *Collected Letters,* vol. 3.

264 "the way to": JD to WLG, December 22, 1953, WLG Correspondence, Wade Center.

"The energy of the American": CSL to Vera Gebbert, December 23, 1953, in *Collected Letters,* vol. 3.

"Whew! Lovely creatures": CSL to Nell Berners-Price, December 26, 1953, ibid.

"very relaxed": JD to WLG, December 22, 1953, WLG Correspondence, Wade Center.

265 "My love who does": JD, "Gentlemen Prefer," Sonnet XX, January 22, 1954, JD Papers, Wade Center.

"It is not his fault": JD, "The Problem of Pain," Sonnet XXII, JD Papers, Wade Center.

266 "young and bouncy": Edna Dwelley, "Old Carnival Addict Finds 'Nightmare Alley' Author Living, Working in Hialeah," *Home News,* June 24, 1955, 15.

"just too lonely": WLG to JD, December 1953, WLG Correspondence, Wade Center.

"[Your] trouble has always been": JD to WLG, April 2, 1954, WLG Correspondence, Wade Center.

"I can understand": JD to WLG, January 25, 1954, WLG Correspondence, Wade Center.

267 "I'm glad you're having": JD to WLG, December 22, 1953, WLG Correspondence, Wade Center.

"You should see [them] now": JD to WLG, January 4, 1954, WLG Correspondence, Wade Center.

"One of the first questions": WLG to JD, January 1954, WLG Correspondence, Wade Center.

"For some reason": JD to WLG, February 8, 1954, WLG Correspondence, Wade Center.

268 "I'm pretty near": JD to WLG, March 25, 1954, WLG Correspondence, Wade Center.

"six feet four": JD to WLG, January 25, 1954, WLG Correspondence, Wade Center.

"I missed my mother": Gresham, *Lenten Lands,* 59–61.

269 "I knew they'd like it": JD to WLG, February 8, 1954, WLG Correspondence, Wade Center.

"writing like grim death": JD to WLG, February 19, 1954, WLG Correspondence, Wade Center.

270 "She's never been done": Ibid.

"Cold, cold the funeral wind": JD, "Fimbulwinter," Sonnet XVII, JD Papers, Wade Center.

"screwy outfit": JD to WLG, July 30, 1954, WLG Correspondence, Wade Center.

"I'm more and more convinced": JD to WLG, December 22, 1953, WLG Correspondence, Wade Center.

271 "Writing for a penny": L. Ron Hubbard, quoted in Eugene H. Methvin, "Scientology: Anatomy of a Frightening Cult," *Reader's Digest,* May 1980.

"get out of London": JD to WLG, February 26, 1954, WLG Correspondence, Wade Center.

"at least one brief affair": Christopher, "Notes on Joy," 41–43.
"punctured its eyes": JD, Sonnet XXI, JD Papers, Wade Center.
"If there was wrong": JD, Sonnet XXXIII, JD Papers, Wade Center.
272 "No, it was neither": JD, Sonnet XXXIV, March 10, 1954, JD Papers, Wade Center.
"Stop complaining": JD, Sonnet XXV, JD Papers, Wade Center.
"wretched health": JD to WLG, April 2, 1954, WLG Correspondence, Wade Center.
"To look at you": JD, "Whine from a Beggar," January 31, 1954, JD Papers, Wade Center.
"The trees are all misted": JD to WLG, April 15, 1954, WLG Correspondence, Wade Center.
273 "our queer, Jewish": CSL to George and Moira Sayer, April 2, 1954, in *Collected Letters,* vol. 3.
"Moira sensed that she": Sayer, *Jack: A Life of C. S. Lewis,* 361.
"It seemed to be": Oral history interview excerpt with George Sayer, October 10–12, 1989, OH/SR-35 and OH/VR-19, Wade Center.
"an impetuous": Albert Lewis to Warren H. Lewis, May 20, 1919, in CSL, *All My Road Before Me,* 8.
274 "We lost her gradually": CSL, *Surprised by Joy* (Boston: Houghton Mifflin Harcourt, 1966), 19.
"an unsatisfied desire": Ibid., 16–18.
275 "proof of the hope": LWR.
"How I tantalize": JD, Sonnet XLII, May 1954, JD Papers, Wade Center.
"monstrous glaciers": JD, Sonnet XXXVI, JD Papers, Wade Center.
("This I didn't know?"): JD to WLG, May 19, 1954, WLG Correspondence, Wade Center.
276 "Can you really": JD to WLG, April 15, 1954, WLG Correspondence, Wade Center.
"I thank you": JD to WLG, May 10, 1954, WLG Correspondence, Wade Center.
"ungovernable displays of temperament": "bill of complaints," July 2, 1954, JD Papers, Wade Center.
"deeply hurt": JD to WLG, June 18, 1954, WLG Correspondence, Wade Center.
277 ("I'm glad to say"): JD to WLG, June 11, 1954, WLG Correspondence, Wade Center.
"using the examiner": WLG to JD, 1954, WLG Correspondence, Wade Center.
"Perhaps you can explain": JD to WLG, March 8, 1954, WLG Correspondence, Wade Center.
"Wish I could take": JD to WLG, June 17, 1954, WLG Correspondence, Wade Center.
278 "The usual thing": CSL to Arthur Greeves, August 6, 1954, in *Collected Letters,* vol. 3.
"I am full": CSL to Arthur Greeves, August 15, 1954, ibid.
"To Bill's happiness": JD to WLG, August 10, 1954, WLG Correspondence, Wade Center.
279 "almost disgusted": George Sayer, review of A. N. Wilson, *C. S. Lewis: A Biography, Canadian C. S. Lewis Journal*, Spring 1991, 15.

279 "stunned": Humphrey Carpenter, "Of More Than Academic Interest," *Sunday Times,* February 27, 1994.
"We thought she had": Oral history interview excerpt with George Sayer, October 10–12, 1989, OH/SR-35 and OH/VR-19, Wade Center.
280 "[He] asked ME for it": JD to WLG, August 27, 1954, WLG Correspondence, Wade Center.
"You are something": JD, Sonnet XVIII, August 28, 1954.

Chapter 14

283 "I bet I can get": JD to WLG, September 23, 1954, WLG Correspondence, Wade Center.
"Bill's not much use": JD to Robert and Jackie Jackson, January 19, 1955, in *And God Came In* Collection, Wade Center.
"[It] smells to me": JD to WLG, November 4, 1954, WLG Correspondence, Wade Center.
284 "When I can get": JD to WLG, October 22, 1954, WLG Correspondence, Wade Center.
"a fancy black suit": JD to WLG, October 29, 1954, WLG Correspondence, Wade Center.
"I'm doing my best": Ibid.
"up the High": JD to WLG, November 4, 1954, WLG Correspondence, Wade Center.
285 "damn near": JD to WLG, November 30, 1954, WLG Correspondence, Wade Center.
"There were so many": JD to Chad Walsh, December 13, 1954, Chad Walsh Papers, Wade Center.
"Instead of talking": JD to WLG, November 30, 1954, WLG Correspondence, Wade Center.
"living a very quiet": JD to Chad Walsh, December 13, 1954, Chad Walsh Papers, Wade Center.
286 "a calmer manner": Phyllis Haring to WLG, March 28, 1955, WLG Papers, Wade Center.
"Oh, what a fool": JD to Robert and Jackie Jackson, January 19, 1955, in *And God Came In* Collection, Wade Center.
"spend the day": JD to WLG, February 8, 1955, WLG Correspondence, Wade Center.
287 "secretary and confidante": Msgr. Peter J. Elliott, "A Child's Memories of C. S. Lewis," *In Review: Living Books Past and Present* 1, no. 3 (Summer 1994).
"a country town": CSL to Bel Allen, January 17, 1955; and "the suburb": CSL to John Gilfedder, February 5, 1955, in *Collected Letters,* vol. 3.
"a tiny college": CSL to Mary Willis Shelburne, November 1, 1955, Ibid.
"a highly flattering": JD to WLG, March 16, 1955, WLG Correspondence, Wade Center.
"inevitable . . . the usual": JD to WLG, March 16, 1955, WLG Correspondence, Wade Center.

288 "kicked a few ideas": JD to WLG, March 23, 1955, WLG Correspondence, Wade Center.
"got it all wrong": CSL to Christian Hardie, July 31, 1955, in *Collected Letters,* vol. 3.
289 "We had another": JD to WLG, March 23, 1955, WLG Correspondence, Wade Center.
"[I] could be said": CSL to Jocelyn Gibb, February 29, 1956, in *Collected Letters,* vol. 3.
"I have always": CSL, *Till We Have Faces: A Myth Retold* (New York: Harcourt, 1984), 74–76.
291 "Perhaps Jack, through writing": Sayer, *Jack: A Life of C. S. Lewis,* 386.
"When the two people": CSL, *The Four Loves,* 67.
"The right form": CSL to Jocelyn Gibb, February 29, 1956, in *Collected Letters,* vol. 3.
"I'm v. much": CSL to Katherine Farrer, April 2, 1955, ibid.
292 "Her part": Sayer, *Jack: A Life of C. S. Lewis,* 361.
"indispensible": JD to WLG, April 29, 1955, WLG Correspondence, Wade Center.
"The house is": JD to WLG, March 23, 1955, WLG Correspondence, Wade Center.
"all settled happiness": CSL, *Surprised by Joy,* 21.
293 "an attempt to rehabilitate": JD, "Seven Deadly Virtues," unpublished ms., JD Papers, Wade Center.
294 "I hate writing": JD to WLG, October 10, 1955, WLG Correspondence, Wade Center.
"It turned out": Elliot, "A Child's Memories of C. S. Lewis."
"I shd. much like": CSL to Herbert Palmer, June 20, 1955, in *Collected Letters,* vol. 3.
"did the honours": Oral history transcript with Chad and Eva Walsh, October 12, 1983, OH/SR-47, Wade Center.
"whether Lewis smelled it": Chad Walsh, afterword, in CSL, *A Grief Observed,* 140.
"passionately anxious": Warren H. Lewis, quoted in Sayer, *Jack: A Life of C. S. Lewis,* 366.
295 "hygienic bastille": CSL to Cecil Harwood, June 14, 1955, in *Collected Letters,* vol. 3.
"Joy Gresham, who is in": CSL to Dorothy Sayers, August 9, 1955, ibid.
296 "flophouse": JD to WLG, September 17, 1955, WLG Correspondence, Wade Center.
"Sometimes I wonder": JD to WLG, August 19, 1955, WLG Correspondence, Wade Center.
"the poor kids": JD to WLG, October 29, 1955, WLG Correspondence, Wade Center.
"Well, you are certainly": JD to Renee Gresham, December 13, 1955, WLG Correspondence, Wade Center.
297 "marvelous summer": CSL to Mary Willis Shelburne, October 5, 1955, in *Collected Letters,* vol. 3.
"It was now obvious": Warren H. Lewis, November 5, 1956, WHL Diaries, Wade Center.

297 "I don't feel": CSL to Arthur Greeves, October 30, 1955, in *Collected Letters,* vol. 3.

"She spoke of him": Christopher, "Notes on Joy," 41–43; oral history excerpt with John Christopher, September 26, 1990, OH/SR-52, Wade Center.

"It seems various groups": JD to WLG, January 8, 1956, WLG Correspondence, Wade Center.

298 "quaint and cheery": JD to WLG, December 31, 1955, WLG Correspondence, Wade Center.

"What a change": JD to WLG, December 13, 1955, WLG Correspondence, Wade Center.

299 "The trouble is": JD to WLG, February 14, 1956, WLG Correspondence, Wade Center.

"I raised objections": Sayer, *Jack: A Life of C. S. Lewis,* 363.

"Who the hell": George Sayer recounted this story many times, with slight variations. See ibid., 362; oral history excerpt with George Sayer, October 10–12, 1989, OH/SR-35, OH/VR-19, Wade Center; George Sayer, interview with Lyle Dorsett, August 7, 1981, *And God Came In* Collection, Wade Center.

300 "some of the people": Sayer, *Jack: A Life of C. S. Lewis,* 357.

"possessiveness": Ibid., 362.

"was a pure matter": Roger Lancelyn Green and Walter Hooper, *C. S. Lewis: A Biography,* 1st American ed. (New York: Harcourt, Brace, Jovanovich, 1974).

"I saw the uselessness": Warren H. Lewis, November 5, 1957, WHL Diaries, Wade Center.

"I have never had": JD to WLG, February 29, 1956, WLG Correspondence, Wade Center.

301 "which I don't": JD to WLG, February 14, 1956, WLG Correspondence, Wade Center.

"startling": JD to WLG, January 22, 1956, WLG Correspondence, Wade Center.

"I hope it": JD to WLG, April 13, 1956, WLG Correspondence, Wade Center.

"fibrositis": JD to WLG, June 15, 1956, WLG Correspondence, Wade Center.

302 "[It's] not bad enough": JD to WLG, August 1, 1956, WLG Correspondence, Wade Center.

"Is it certain?": JD to WLG, September 13, 1956, WLG Correspondence, Wade Center.

"I have got": JD to WLG, October 19, 1956, WLG Correspondence, Wade Center.

"twisted in knots": JD to WLG, September 13, 1956, WLG Correspondence, Wade Center.

"warm, coloured days": CSL to Vera Gebbert, October 18, 1956, in *Collected Letters*, vol. 3.

"If we had never": CSL, *A Grief Observed*, 48.

"I could never understand": Oral history with Clifford Morris, May 27, 1986, CSL/JRRT, Wade Center.

303 "began to press": Warren H. Lewis, November 5, 1956, WHL Diaries, Wade Center.

"our innocent little secret": CSL to Kay Farrer, October 25, 1956, in *Collected Letters*, vol. 3.
"moth-eaten": JD to WLG, October 20, 1956, WLG Correspondence, Wade Center.
"In short": Ibid.

Chapter 15

304 "in no position": JD to WLG, October 20, 1956, WLG Correspondence, Wade Center.
"*Please, please* don't": JD to WLG, October 19, 1956, WLG Correspondence, Wade Center.
305 "I can hardly describe": CSL to Mary Willis Shelburne, November 16, 1956, in *Collected Letters*, vol. 3.
"It will be": CSL to Arthur Greeves, November 25, 1956, ibid.
"You can well understand": CSL to Mary Willis Shelburne, February 17, 1957, ibid.
"They say a rival": CSL to Dorothy Sayers, June 25, 1957, ibid.
306 "You may as well": CSL to Mary Willis Shelburne, November 16, 1956, ibid.
"personally felt that": Carpenter, "Of More Than Academic Interest," 2.
"physical agony was combined": JD to Chad and Eva Walsh, December 3, 1956, Chad Walsh Papers, Wade Center.
"I never have loved": Warren H. Lewis, November 5, 1956, WHL Diaries, Wade Center.
307 "I can now tell you": JD to Chad and Eva Walsh, December 3, 1956, Chad Walsh Papers, Wade Center.
"If she gets over this": CSL to Arthur Greeves, November 25, 1956, in *Collected Letters,* vol. 3.
"What I am mainly": CSL to Dorothy Sayers, December 24, 1956, ibid.
"the marriage was": Sayer, *Jack: A Life of C. S. Lewis*, 368.
308 "[I] am now ready": JD to Chad and Eva Walsh, December 3, 1956, Chad Walsh Papers, Wade Center.
"a ramshackle ex-American": JD to WLG, December 7, 1956, WLG Correspondence, Wade Center.
"promised me": JD to Chad and Eva Walsh, February 5, 1957, Chad Walsh Papers, Wade Center.
"No miserable pretense": CSL to Mary Van Deusen, April 10, 1959, in *Collected Letters*, vol. 3.
"1. A tiny 100th chance": CSL to Arthur Greeves, November 25, 1956, ibid.
"A marriage has taken place": CSL, marriage announcement in *The Times,* December 24, 1956.
"weather it this time": CSL to Mary Willis Shelburne, January 17, 1957, in *Collected Letters*, vol. 3.
"usual course": CSL, *Surprised by Joy,* 18.
309 "When I come out": JD to Chad and Eva Walsh, December 3, 1956, Chad Walsh Papers, Wade Center.

309 "perfectly well": JD to Chad and Eva Walsh, February 5, 1957, Chad Walsh Papers, Wade Center.
"I'd pinned all my hopes": Ibid.

309–10 "My world is not": CSL to Mrs. D. Jessup, January 29, 1957, in *Collected Letters*, vol. 3.

310 "How horrible that I": JD to Chad and Eva Walsh, February 5, 1957, Chad Walsh Papers, Wade Center.
"not adding the past": CSL to Mary Willis Shelburne, October 20, 1957, in *Collected Letters*, vol. 3.
"remember other sufferers": CSL to Mary Van Deusen, April 10, 1959, ibid.
"I'm not at all": JD to Chad and Eva Walsh, February 13, 1957, Chad Walsh Papers, Wade Center.
"Uncertainty is what God": Ibid.
"I shall apparently": JD to WLG, February 28, 1957, WLG Correspondence, Wade Center.
"*What* a pity": JD to Chad and Eva Walsh, February 13, 1957, Chad Walsh Papers, Wade Center.

310–11 "intellectual Englishman's": JD to WLG, February 28, 1957, WLG Correspondence, Wade Center.

311 "a honeymoon": CSL to Chad Walsh, February 13, 1957, in *Collected Letters*, vol. 3.
"New beauty": CSL to Sister Penelope CSMV, March 6, 1957, ibid.
"You could hardly believe": CSL to Mrs. Jessup, February 19, 1957, ibid.
"a queer, incredible life": CSL to Mary Van Deusen, March 7, 1957, ibid.
"The name and the idea": CSL, *A Grief Observed*, 12.
"All I really care about": JD to WLG, February 28, 1957, WLG Correspondence, Wade Center.
"*Why*, one asks": Warren H. Lewis, March 21, 1957, WHL Diaries, Wade Center.

312 "Joy desperately wanted": Reverend Peter Bide to Lyle Dorsett, September 17, 1981, *And God Came In* Collection, Wade Center.
"In the end": Peter Bide, quoted in *Collected Letters*, vol. 3, 1651.
"I found it heartrending": Warren H. Lewis, March 21, 1957, WHL Diaries, Wade Center.

313 "We are entering": CSL to Chad Walsh, April 5, 1957, in *Collected Letters*, vol. 3.
"wild hopes": CSL to Mary Van Deusen, April 10, 1959, ibid.
"let this cup pass": Matt. 26:39.
"My wife is very": CSL to Laurence Krieg, April 21, 1957, in *Collected Letters*, vol. 3.
"not in luxury": WLG to JD, April 2, 1957, WLG Correspondence, Wade Center.
"I think that I should": WLG to CSL, April 2, 1957, WLG Correspondence, Wade Center.

314 "There has never yet": Ibid.
"Let's skip the minor reasons": JD to WLG, April 7, 1957, WLG Correspondence, Wade Center.

315 "the two strongest letters": Sayer, *Jack: A Life of C. S. Lewis*, 370.

"I cannot judge": CSL to WLG, April 6, 1957, in *Collected Letters,* vol. 3.

316 "Your letter reached Joy": CSL to WLG, April 6, 1957, in *Collected Letters,* vol. 3.

317 "We didn't idealize": CSL, *A Grief Observed* (San Francisco: HarperSanFrancisco, 1994).

"arrested": JD to WLG, April 26, 1957, WLG Correspondence, Wade Center.

"It's so frustrating": JD to Mrs. D. Jessup, May 27, 1957, in *Out of My Bone.*

"hobble around a little": JD to Chad and Eva Walsh, June 6, 1957, Chad Walsh Papers, Wade Center.

"an amazing help": JD to Mary Shelburne, June 6, 1958 in *Collected Letters,* vol. 3.

318 "superintended": JD to Chad and Eva Walsh, June 6, 1957, Chad Walsh Papers, Wade Center.

"She *seems* amazingly better": CSL to Dorothy Sayers, June 25, 1957, in *Collected Letters,* vol. 3.

"completely immobilized": CSL to Clyde S. Kilby, June 12, 1957, ibid.

"quite obscure": CSL to Mrs. Johnson, July 9, 1957, ibid.

"fish-tailed female": CSL to Dorothy Sayers, July 1, 1957, ibid.

"What Jack's marriage meant": Warren H. Lewis, "Memoir of C. S. Lewis," 24.

319 "like a garden": CSL, *A Grief Observed,* 63.

"wired up to the ceiling": Oral history excerpt with John Christopher, Oxford, September 26, 1990; Christopher, "Notes on Joy."

"Lewis the Family Man": Roger Lancelyn Green and Walter Hooper, *C. S. Lewis: A Biography,* rev. & expanded ed. (London: HarperCollins, 2002), 270.

"We'll have Douglas": CSL to Roger Lancelyn Green, September 18, 1957, in *Collected Letters*, vol. 3.

320 "It was amusing": Sayer, *Jack: A Life of C. S. Lewis,* 375–76.

"American lady tourists": JD to Mrs. D. Jessup, July 17, 1957, in *Out of My Bone.*

"some of them": JD to WLG, August 22, 1957, WLG Correspondence, Wade Center.

"Now I know": Bel Kaufman, interview with the author, February 7, 2003.

321 "My heart is breaking": CSL to Dorothy Sayers, June 25, 1958, in *Collected Letters,* vol. 3.

"I have bad spasms": CSL to Dom Bede Griffiths, September 24, 1957, ibid.

"far livelier": CSL to Mary Willis Shelburne, August 12, 1957, ibid.

"like your grandmother's corsets": CSL to Anne and Martin Kilmer, August 7, 1957, ibid.

"didn't matter": CSL to George Sayer, September 29, 1957, ibid.

"Can it be": CSL to Cecil Harwood, September 21, 1957, ibid.

"It'll be nice": CSL to Mary Willis Shelburne, October 20, 1957, ibid.

"The improvement in": CSL to Vera Gebbert, November 12, 1957, ibid.

322 "use the john": JD to WLG, November 29, 1957, JD Papers, Wade Center.

"spar[ring] away": Oral history with Clifford Morris, May 27, 1986, CSL/JRRT, Wade Center.

"firm as a rock": CSL to Sheldon Vanauken, April 26, 1958, in *Collected Letters,* vol. 3.

"a double miracle": Sayer, *Jack: A Life of C. S. Lewis,* 371.

323 "The intriguing thing": CSL to Sheldon Vanauken, November 27, 1959, in *Collected Letters*, vol. 3.
"The thing we pray for": CSL, "The Efficacy of Prayer," *Atlantic Monthly*, January 1959, 59–60.

Chapter 16

324 "gift time": CSL to Reverend Canon Harold A. Blair, November 2, 1959, in *Collected Letters*, vol. 3.
"lady of the manor": JD to Kay Farrer, January 30, 1958.
325 "But I got it": Oral history excerpt with Jean Wakeman, August 6, 1981, OH/SR-46 and OH/VR-21, Wade Center.
Jack was accustomed: Sayer, *Jack: A Life of C. S. Lewis*, 372.
He knew how much: George Sayer, interview with Lyle Dorsett, August 7, 1981, D1–5, 1a–r, Wade Center.
"Tell [Jack] that he": Sayer, *Jack: A Life of C. S. Lewis*, 374.
"a horrid yellow finish": JD to Kay Farrer, January 30, 1958.
"Tell me, isn't it less": Sayer, *Jack: A Life of C. S. Lewis*, 374.
"The Kilns is now": JD to Roger Lancelyn Green, May 23, 1958
"visitors to the Kilns": Sayer, *Jack: A Life of C. S. Lewis*, 374.
"thrust her forward": Carpenter, *The Inklings*, 242.
326 "very strange marriage": J. R. R. Tolkien to Christopher Bretherton, July 16, 1964, in *The Letters of J. R. R. Tolkien*, ed. Humphrey Carpenter (Boston: Houghton Mifflin, 2000), 349.
"Tolkien was gloomy": Sayer, *Jack: A Life of C. S. Lewis*, 375.
"[Jack] did not help": Carpenter, *The Inklings*, 242.
"I liked her": Sheldon Vanauken to Lyle Dorsett, June 10, 1981, *And God Came In* Collection, Wade Center.
"She started by": Simon Barrington-Ward, email to the author, November 1, 2010.
"She was a marvelous person": Oral history excerpt with Roger Lancelyn Green, June 12, 1986, OH/SR-10, Wade Center.
327 "What impressed me": Sayer, *Jack: A Life of C. S. Lewis*, 375.
"Let's try that on": Oral history excerpt with Jean Wakeman, August 6, 1981, OH/SR-46 and OH/VR-21, Wade Center.
"Davy botanizing": JD to WLG, August 8, 1958, WLG Correspondence, Wade Center.
"the absurdity": CSL to Mary Willis Shelburne, April 15, 1958, in *Collected Letters*, vol. 3.
"if you are careful": Sayer, *Jack: A Life of C. S. Lewis*, 372; A. N. Wilson, *C. S. Lewis: A Biography* (London: Collins, 1990), 260.
328 "a magnificent lover": Oral history excerpt with HD, October 4, 1983, OH/SR-79 and CSL-Z/SR-5, Wade Center.
"belated honeymoon": CSL to Jessie M. Watt, August 28, 1958, in *Collected Letters*, vol. 3.
"shoot[ing] *at*": CSL to Barbara Reynolds, March 11, 1959, ibid.

"hooligans": CSL, "Delinquents in the Snow," *Time and Tide,* December 7, 1957, 38.
"It's no use": Gresham, *Lenten Lands,* 84.
"or Mrs. Lewis": Chad Walsh, afterword to CSL, *A Grief Observed,* 142.
329 "It is the most beautiful": JD to WLG, August 8, 1958, WLG Correspondence, Wade Center.
"[We] feasted on love": CSL, *A Grief Observed,* 7.
"every mode of it": CSL to Bishop Henry I. Louittit, May 1, 1958, in *Collected Letters,* vol. 3.
330 "Today I want to discuss": JD to Chad and Eva Walsh, December 29, 1959, Chad Walsh Papers, Wade Center.
"the roughness, even fierceness": CSL, *The Four Loves.*
331 "mischievous spirit": Ibid.
332 "Well, Jean, now what": Gresham, *Lenten Lands.*
"I feel that resurrection": CSL to J. R. R. Tolkien, November 10, 1958, in *Collected Letters,* vol. 3.
"statuesque blonde young wife": JD to WLG, July 14, 1959, WLG Correspondence, Wade Center.
"To My Sister-in-Law": Warren H. Lewis, *The Scandalous Regent: A Life of Philippe, Duc d'Orléans, 1674–1723, and of His Family* (New York: Harcourt, Brace, 1961).
333 "It wd. mean": CSL to Mary Willis Shelburne, February 13, 1960, in *Collected Letters,* vol. 3.
"fancy squashes": JD to WLG, August 20, 1959, WLG Correspondence, Wade Center.
"Woods, garden, books": JD to WLG, March 2, 1959, WLG Correspondence, Wade Center.
"rheumatic aches and pains": JD to Chad Walsh, January 29, 1959, Chad Walsh Papers, Wade Center.
"Well darling? I hope": CSL to JD, March 11, 1959, in *Collected Letters,* vol. 3.
"Jack's juveniles have a steady": JD to WLG, September 26, 1959, WLG Correspondence, Wade Center.
334 "I still have not": JD to WLG, July 14, 1959, WLG Correspondence, Wade Center.
"abrasive": Oral history excerpt with Major Frank Henry, December 12, 1984, OH/SR-16, Wade Center.
"We shouldn't know": CSL to Mary Van Deusen, December 8, 1959, in *Collected Letters,* vol. 3.
"rearguard actions": CSL to Mary Willis Shelburne, October 18, 1959, ibid.
335 "irrelevant to the question": CSL to Sheldon Vanauken, April 16, 1960, ibid.
"whatever is [God's] will": CSL to Don Luigi Pedrollo, December 15, 1959, ibid.
"My skeleton is now": JD to WLG, December 15, 1959, WLG Correspondence, Wade Center.
"melt[ed] away beautifully": CSL to Bernard Acworth, March 5, 1960, in *Collected Letters,* vol. 3.
"I've now got": JD to WLG, March 30, 1960, WLG Correspondence, Wade Center.

335 "Only that now": CSL, *The Collected Poems of C. S. Lewis,* ed. Walter Hooper (London: Fount Paperbacks, 1996), 123.
336 "dreadful": CSL to Mary Willis Shelburne, October 18, 1959, in *Collected Letters*, vol. 3.
"We were setting out": CSL, *A Grief Observed*, 14.
"Courage was her shield": Oral history excerpt with Jean Wakeman, August 6, 1981, OH/SR-46 and OH/VR-21, Wade Center.
"Joy says": CSL to Peter Bide, June 14, 1960, in *Collected Letters*, vol. 3.
337 "it was madness": CSL to Chad Walsh, May 23, 1960, ibid.
"I'd rather go": JD to WLG, March 30, 1960, WLG Correspondence, Wade Center.
"large quantities": Roger Lancelyn Green, personal journals, Roger Lancelyn Green estate.
"a dreary nuisance": JD to WLG, May 2, 1960, WLG Correspondence, Wade Center.
338 "pure Garden of Eden": JD to WLG, April 10, 1960, WLG Correspondence, Wade Center.
"incredible mountains, shimmering mists": JD to WLG, May 2, 1960, WLG Correspondence, Wade Center.
"[She] finally began": Roger Lancelyn Green, personal journals, Roger Lancelyn Green estate.
339 "adept at diving": Ibid.
"I had some ado": CSL to Chad Walsh, May 23, 1960, in *Collected Letters*, vol. 3.
"freshly drawn": Roger Lancelyn Green, personal journals, Roger Lancelyn Green estate.
"I just have": June Lancelyn Green, interview with the author, November 1, 2010.
340 "It was as if": CSL to Chad Walsh, May 23, 1960, in *Collected Letters*, vol. 3.
"Athena got me up": JD to WLG, April 10, 1960, WLG Correspondence, Wade Center.

Epilogue

341 "*nunc dimittis*": CSL to Chad Walsh, May 23, 1960, in *Collected Letters*, vol. 3.
"became an Amazon": CSL to Peter Bide, June 14, 1950, ibid.
"Nurse": Warren H. Lewis, June 21, 1960, WHL Diaries, Wade Center.
342 "You have made me": CSL to Arthur Greeves, August 30, 1960, in *Collected Letters*, vol. 3.

Selected Bibliography

Aaron, Daniel. *Writers on the Left*. New York: Oxford University Press, 1977.

Allego, Donna M. "The Construction and Role of Community in Political Long Poems by Twentieth-Century American Women Poets: Lola Ridge, Genevieve Taggard, Joy Davidman, Margaret Walker, and Muriel Rukeyser." Ph.D. diss., Southern Illinois University at Carbondale, 1997. http://search.proquest.com.ezproxy.cul.columbia.edu/pqdtft/docview/304370805/abstract/2D6252B061D84F83PQ/2?accountid=10226.

Bender, Daniel E., and Richard A. Greenwald, eds. *Sweatshop USA: The American Sweatshop in Historical and Global Perspective*. New York: Routledge, 2003.

Benét, Stephen Vincent. *America*. London: W. Heinemann, 1945.

———. *John Brown's Body*. New York: Holt, Rinehart and Winston, 1961.

Bergman, Alexander F. *They Look Like Men*. New York: B. Ackerman, 1944.

Buhle, Mari Jo, Paul Buhle, and Dan Georgakas, eds. *Encyclopedia of the American Left*. 2nd ed. New York: Oxford University Press, 1998.

Carpenter, Humphrey. *The Inklings: C. S. Lewis, J. R. R. Tolkien, Charles Williams, and Their Friends*. 1st American ed. Boston: Houghton Mifflin, 1979.

Cohen, Rose. *Out of the Shadow*. The American Immigration Library. New York: J. S. Ozer, 1971.

Como, James T., ed. *C. S. Lewis at the Breakfast Table and Other Reminiscences*. New York: Macmillan, 1979.

Como, James T., ed. *Remembering C. S. Lewis: Recollections of Those Who Knew Him*. San Francisco: Ignatius Press, 2005.

Davidman, Joseph Isaac. "The Limitations of Education." Ph.D. diss., New York University, 1917. http://search.proquest.com.ezproxy.cul.columbia.edu/pqdtft/docview/301761469/citation/E21398559A44503PQ/1?accountid=10226.

Davidman, Joy. *Anya*. New York: Macmillan, 1940.

———. *Letter to a Comrade*. The Yale Series of Younger Poets. Vol. 37. Edited by S. V. Benét. New Haven: Yale University Press, 1938.

———. "My Lord of Orrery." M.A. thesis. Columbia University, 1935.

———. *Out of My Bone: The Letters of Joy Davidman*. Edited by Don W. King. Grand Rapids, Mich.: William B. Eerdmans, 2009.

———. *Smoke on the Mountain: An Interpretation of the Ten Commandments*. Philadelphia: Westminster Press, 1954.

———, ed. *War Poems of the United Nations: Three Hundred Poems, One Hundred and Fifty Poets from Twenty Countries*. New York: Dial Press, 1943.

———. *Weeping Bay*. New York: Macmillan, 1950.

Diner, Hasia R. *Lower East Side Memories: A Jewish Place in America*. Princeton: Princeton University Press, 2000.

Dorsett, Lyle W. *And God Came In*. New York: Macmillan, 1983.

Epstein, Lawrence J. *At the Edge of a Dream: The Story of Jewish Immigrants on New York's Lower East Side, 1880–1920*. 1st ed. San Francisco: Jossey-Bass, 2007.

Federal Writers' Project. *New York Panorama: A Companion to the WPA Guide to New York City: A Comprehensive View of the Metropolis, Presented in a Series of Articles*. 1st Pantheon ed. New York: Pantheon Books, 1984.

Federal Writers' Project (N.Y.). *New York City Guide*. American Guide Series. Rev. ed. New York: Random House, 1939.

Fenton, Charles A. *Stephen Vincent Benét: The Life and Times of an American Man of Letters, 1898–1943*. New Haven: Yale University Press, 1958.

Figes, Orlando. *The Whisperers: Private Life in Stalin's Russia*. 1st ed. New York: Metropolitan Books, 2007.

Folsom, Franklin. *Days of Anger, Days of Hope: A Memoir of the League of American Writers, 1937–1942*. Niwot: University Press of Colorado, 1994.

Friedrich, Otto. *City of Nets: A Portrait of Hollywood in the 1940s*. Berkeley: University of California Press, 1997.

Gibb, Jocelyn. *Light on C. S. Lewis*. 1st American ed. New York: Harcourt, Brace & World, 1966.

Goldman, Eric Frederick. *Rendezvous with Destiny: A History of Modern American Reform*. New York: Knopf, 1970.

Gresham, Douglas H. *Lenten Lands: My Childhood with Joy Davidman and C. S. Lewis*. New York: Macmillan, 1988.

Gresham, William Lindsay. *Houdini: The Man Who Walked Through Walls*. 1st ed. New York: Holt, 1959.

———. *Limbo Tower*. New York: Rinehart, 1949.

———. *Monster Midway: An Uninhibited Look at the Glittering World of the Carny*. New York: Rinehart, 1953.

———. *Nightmare Alley*. New York: Rinehart and Co., 1946.

Grugel, Jean. *Franco's Spain*. Contemporary History Series. London: Arnold, 1997.

Gurock, Jeffrey S., Daniel Soyer, Annie Polland, Howard B. Rock, and Deborah Dash Moore, eds. *City of Promises: A History of the Jews of New York*. New York: New York University Press, 2012.

Hamilton, Ian. *The Writers in Hollywood, 1915–1951*. London: Heinemann, 1990.

Hertzberg, Arthur. *The Jews in America: Four Centuries of an Uneasy Encounter; A History*. New York: Simon and Schuster, 1989.

Holmes, T. Michael. *The Specter of Communism in Hawaii.* Honolulu: University of Hawaii Press, 1994.

Hooper, Walter. *C. S. Lewis: A Companion and Guide.* San Francisco: HarperSanFrancisco, 1996.

Howe, Irving. *World of Our Fathers.* New York: Harcourt Brace Jovanovich, 1976.

Howe, Irving, and Kenneth Libo, eds. *How We Lived: A Documentary History of Immigrant Jews in America, 1880–1930.* New York: R. Marek, 1979.

Hubbard, L. Ron. *Dianetics, the Modern Science of Mental Health: A Handbook of Dianetic Therapy.* 1st ed. New York: Hermitage House, 1950.

Jacobs, Alan. *The Narnian: The Life and Imagination of C. S. Lewis.* 1st ed. New York: HarperSanFrancisco, 2005.

Jewish Museum (New York, N.Y.). *Getting Comfortable in New York: The American Jewish Home, 1880–1950.* Edited by Jenna Weissman Joselit, Barbara Kirshenblatt-Gimblett, Irving Howe, and Susan L. Braunstein. New York: The Jewish Museum, 1990.

King, Patricia Grace. "The Autobiographical Witness: American Women Writers and the Spanish Civil War." Ph.D. diss., Emory University, 2000. http://search.proquest.com.ezproxy.cul.columbia.edu/pqdtft/docview/304657996/abstract/2D6252B061D84F83PQ/1?accountid=10226.

Koch, Stephen. *Double Lives: Espionage and the War of Ideas.* New York: Free Press, 1994.

Koppel, Lily. *The Red Leather Diary: Reclaiming a Life Through the Pages of a Lost Journal.* 1st ed. New York: Harper, 2008.

Lancelyn Green, Roger, and Walter Hooper. *C. S. Lewis: A Biography.* 1st American ed. New York: Harcourt Brace Jovanovich, 1974.

———. *C. S. Lewis: A Biography.* Rev. and expanded ed. London: HarperCollins, 2002.

Leffler, Melvyn P. *The Specter of Communism: The United States and the Origins of the Cold War, 1917–1953.* 1st ed. New York: Hill and Wang, 1994.

Lewis, C. S. *The Abolition of Man; Or, Reflections on Education with Special Reference to the Teaching of English in the Upper Forms of Schools.* New York: Macmillan, 1968.

———. *The Allegory of Love: A Study in Medieval Tradition.* Oxford: Oxford University Press, 1938.

———. *All My Road Before Me: The Diary of C. S. Lewis, 1922–27.* Edited by Walter Hooper. London: Collins Fount (HarperCollins), 1991.

———. *The Collected Letters of C. S. Lewis.* Edited by Walter Hooper. 3 vols. London: HarperCollins, 2000–2004.

———. *The Four Loves.* New York: Harcourt, Brace, 1960.

———. *The Great Divorce.* New York: Macmillan, 1946.

———. *A Grief Observed.* San Francisco: HarperSanFrancisco, 1994.

———. *Letters to Children.* Edited by Lyle W. Dorsett and Marjorie Lamp Mead. New York: Macmillan, 1985.

———. *Letters to Malcolm: Chiefly on Prayer.* 1st American ed. New York: Harcourt, Brace & World, 1964.

———. *Mere Christianity: A Revised and Amplified Edition, with a New Introduction, of the Three Books, Broadcast Talks, Christian Behaviour, and Beyond Personality.* 1st HarperCollins ed. San Francisco: HarperSanFrancisco, 2001.

———. *Out of the Silent Planet.* New York: Macmillan, 1944.

———. *Perelandra: A Novel.* New York: Macmillan, 1968.

———. *The Pilgrim's Regress: An Allegorical Apology for Christianity, Reason, and Romanticism.* 3rd ed. Grand Rapids, Mich.: Eerdmans, 1982.

———. *The Problem of Pain.* New York: Macmillan, 1943.

———. *The Quotable Lewis.* Edited by Wayne Martindale and Jerry Root. Carol Stream, Ill.: Tyndale House Publishers, 1989.

———. *The Screwtape Letters.* New York: Macmillan, 1944.

———. *Surprised by Joy: The Shape of My Early Life.* New York: Harcourt, Brace & World, 1955.

———. *That Hideous Strength: A Modern Fairy-Tale for Grown-Ups.* New York: Macmillan, 1946.

———. *They Stand Together: The Letters of C. S. Lewis to Arthur Greeves (1914–1963).* Edited by Walter Hooper. 1st American ed. New York: Macmillan, 1979.

———. *Till We Have Faces: A Myth Retold.* New York: Harcourt, 1980.

———. *The World's Last Night and Other Essays.* New York: Harcourt Brace Jovanovich, 1973.

Lewis, R. W. B., and John Updike, eds. *A Century of Arts & Letters: The History of the National Institute of Arts & Letters and the American Academy of Arts & Letters as Told, Decade by Decade, by Eleven Members.* New York: Columbia University Press, 1998.

Lewy, Guenter. *The Cause That Failed: Communism in American Political Life.* New York: Oxford University Press, 1990.

MacDonald, George. *The Light Princess.* New York: Farrar, Straus and Giroux, 1969.

———. *Phantastes: A Faerie Romance.* Grand Rapids, Mich.: Eerdmans, 1981.

———. *The Princess and the Goblin and The Princess and Curdie.* London: Collins, 1970.

MacSwain, Robert, and Michael Ward, eds. *The Cambridge Companion to C. S. Lewis.* Cambridge Companions to Religion. Cambridge: Cambridge University Press, 2010.

Markowitz, Ruth Jacknow. *My Daughter, the Teacher: Jewish Teachers in the New York City Schools.* New Brunswick: Rutgers University Press, 1993.

McGrath, Alister E. *C. S. Lewis: A Life; Eccentric Genius, Reluctant Prophet.* London: Hodder & Stoughton, 2013.

Michels, Tony. *A Fire in Their Hearts: Yiddish Socialists in New York.* Cambridge: Harvard University Press, 2005.

Miller, Alexander. *The Christian Significance of Karl Marx.* New York: Macmillan, 1952.

Moore, Deborah Dash. *At Home in America: Second Generation New York Jews.* Columbia History of Urban Life. New York: Columbia University Press, 1981.

Nissenson, Marilyn. *The Lady Upstairs: Dorothy Schiff and the New York Post.* 1st ed. New York: St. Martin's Press, 2007.

North, Joseph. *New Masses: An Anthology of the Rebel Thirties.* 1st ed. New York: International Publishers, 1969.

Ossining Historical Society. *Ossining Remembered.* Images of America. Charleston, S.C.: Arcadia, 1999.

Patri, Angelo. *A Schoolmaster of the Great City.* New York: Macmillan, 1917.

Radmacher, Rebecca Sue. "Nothing Said Clearly Can Be Said Truly: Modernism in

C. S. Lewis's 'Till We Have Faces.'" Ph.D. diss., Arizona State University, 1997. http://search.proquest.com.ezproxy.cul.columbia.edu/pqdtft/docview/304329702/abstract/2D6252B061D84F83PQ/3?accountid=10226.

Ranzato, Gabriele. *The Spanish Civil War: A Century in Focus. Windrush History of the Twentieth Century.* Gloucestershire: Windrush Press, 1999.

Reitman, Janet, and OverDrive, Inc. *Inside Scientology: The Story of America's Most Secretive Religion.* Boston: Houghton Mifflin Harcourt, 2011.

Rose, Lisle Abbott. *The Cold War Comes to Main Street: America in 1950.* Lawrence: University Press of Kansas, 1999.

Rosten, Leo. *Hollywood: The Movie Colony, the Movie Makers.* New York: Harcourt, Brace, 1941.

Sayer, George. *Jack: A Life of C. S. Lewis.* Wheaton, Ill.: Crossway, 2005.

Schakel, Peter J. *Reason and Imagination in C. S. Lewis: A Study of Till We Have Faces.* Grand Rapids, Mich.: W. B. Eerdmans, 1984.

Schulberg, Budd. *Moving Pictures: Memories of a Hollywood Prince.* New York: Stein and Day, 1981.

Schwartz, Nancy Lynn. *The Hollywood Writers' Wars.* 1st ed. New York: Knopf, 1982.

Shirley, Craig. *December 1941: 31 Days That Changed America and Saved the World.* Nashville: Thomas Nelson, 2011.

Shlaes, Amity. *The Forgotten Man: A New History of the Great Depression.* 1st ed. New York: HarperCollins, 2007.

Soper, David Wesley, ed. *These Found the Way: Thirteen Converts to Protestant Christianity.* Philadelphia: Westminster Press, 1951.

Sowell, Thomas. *Marxism: Philosophy and Economics.* 1st ed. New York: Morrow, 1985.

Stead, Christina. *Dearest Munx: The Letters of Christina Stead and William J. Blake.* Carlton, Victoria: Miegunyah Press, 2005.

Vanauken, Sheldon. *A Severe Mercy.* San Francisco: Harper & Row, 1977.

Wald, Alan M. *Exiles from a Future Time: The Forging of the Mid-Twentieth-Century Literary Left.* Chapel Hill: University of North Carolina Press, 2002.

———. *The New York Intellectuals: The Rise and Decline of the Anti-Stalinist Left from the 1930s to the 1980s.* Chapel Hill: University of North Carolina Press, 1987.

Walsh, Chad. *C. S. Lewis: Apostle to the Skeptics.* New York: Macmillan, 1949.

———. *The Literary Legacy of C. S. Lewis.* 1st ed. New York: Harcourt Brace Jovanovich, 1979.

Wenger, Beth S. *New York Jews and the Great Depression: Uncertain Promise.* New Haven: Yale University Press, 1996.

Williams, Charles, and Dorothy L. Sayers, eds. *Essays Presented to Charles Williams.* London: Oxford University Press, 1947.

Wilson, A. N. *C. S. Lewis: A Biography.* London: Collins, 1990.

Yoseloff, Thomas. *Seven Poets in Search of an Answer: Maxwell Bodenheim, Joy Davidman, Langston Hughes, Aaron Kramer, Alfred Kreymborg, Martha Millet, Norman Rosten.* New York: B. Ackerman, 1944.

Photo Credits

Courtesy of Susan Davidman Cleveland: Joy with bow in her hair, Joy with her parents, Joy with her mother and a boy, Joy with her father and Howard, Joy's father at desk, Joy in bathing suit, Joy and Howard at Devoe Park, Joy in hat, Joy and Bill wedding photo, Howard in uniform, Ruth Davidman.

Archives and Special Collections, Hunter College Libraties, Hunter College of The City University of New York: Yearbook photos: Joy with *Echo* staff, Belle Kaufman, Joy Davidman.

Edward and Marian MacDowell Collection, Music Division, Library of Congress: Joy at MacDowell Colony.

Marion E. Wade Center, Wheaton College, Wheaton Illinois: Staatsburg house, Gresham family outside church, The Kilns, C. S. Lewis and Warnie in Ireland, Joy's certificate of registration, Jack and boys, Joy and Jack in Kilns garden (1958).

Courtesy of Douglas Gresham: Bill smoking on porch, David and Douglas with dog, Joy with David and Douglas passport photo, Joy (reclining) and Jack in Kilns garden (1957), Joy with afghan.

Use of the New York Post *courtesy of NYP Holdings, Inc.*

Courtesy of The University of New Hampshire, Lotte Jacobi Collection: Book jacket photo of Joy.

Courtesy of Rosemary Simmons: Renee Pierce, Renee with Bill and children.

Hans Wild/The LIFE Picture Collection/Getty Images: C. S. Lewis at Oxford.

Courtesy of the C. S. Lewis Foundation: Joy with shotgun.

Courtesy of the Roger Lancelyn Green Estate: Joy and Jack in Greece.

Index